Rethinking the Law of Private Property

Rethinking the Law of Private Property

Edited by

Jan G. Laitos

Joe T. Juhan Endowed Professorship in Property Rights and Policy and Professor of Law, Sturm College of Law, University of Denver, USA

EE Edward Elgar
PUBLISHING

Cheltenham, UK · Northampton, MA, USA

Published by

Edward Elgar Publishing Limited
The Lypiatts
15 Lansdown Road
Cheltenham
Glos GL50 2JA
UK

Edward Elgar Publishing, Inc.
William Pratt House
9 Dewey Court
Northampton
Massachusetts 01060
USA

Authorised representative in the EU for GPSR queries only: Easy Access System Europe – Mustamäe tee 50, 10621 Tallinn, Estonia, gpsr.requests@easproject.com

A catalogue record for this book is available from the British Library

Library of Congress Control Number: 2025937347

This book is available electronically in the **Elgar**online
Law subject collection
https://doi.org/10.4337/9781035311361

FSC
www.fsc.org
MIX
Paper | Supporting
responsible forestry
FSC® C014540

ISBN 978 1 0353 1135 4 (cased)
ISBN 978 1 0353 1136 1 (eBook)
ISBN 978 1 0353 6996 6 (ePub)

Printed and bound in the UK by Short Run Press Ltd, Exeter EX2 7LW

Contents

v

Contributors

Vicki Been is the Judge Edward Weinfeld Professor of Law at NYU School of Law, an Affiliated Professor of Public Policy at the NYU Wagner Graduate School of Public Service, and a Faculty Director of NYU's Furman Center for Real Estate and Urban Policy. Her scholarship focuses on the interplay of land use, urban policy, and housing, and has included such topics as inclusionary zoning, historic preservation, tenant protections, environmental justice, constitutional protection of property rights, and racial and economic neighborhood integration. She served as New York City's deputy mayor for housing and economic development from May 2019 until the end of 2021 and as commissioner of housing from 2014 to 2017, where she was charged with designing and implementing many of the land use and housing policy reforms that her scholarship explores, so she brings an unusual combination of practical experience and theoretical grounding to debates about housing and land use policy.

Daniel Cole is the Robert H. McKinney Emeritus Professor of Law and Professor Emeritus of Public & Environmental Affairs at Indiana University, Bloomington. He also serves as a Senior Research Fellow in the Ostrom Workshop, where he continues to teach the graduate Seminar in Institutional Analysis and Development. Professor Cole's research is predominantly at the intersection of Property Law, Institutional Analysis, Natural Resources Management, and Pollution Control. He has published 12 books and 70 journal articles, essays, and book chapters. His writings have been published in England, Italy, and France, as well as in the United States. His 2002 book, *Pollution and Property: Comparing Ownership Institutions for Environmental Protection* (Cambridge University Press, 2002), was translated into Chinese in 2010. In 2012 he co-edited a volume with Elinor Ostrom titled *Property in Land and Other Resources* for the Lincoln Institute of Land Policy. Professor Cole has served on several Editorial Boards and on review panels for the National Science Foundation. He is currently a member of the governing Council of the World Interdisciplinary Network for Institutional Research and serves on the Scientific Advisory Board for its publication, *Journal of Institutional Economics*. Professor Cole is a Life Member of Clare Hall (College for Advanced Study), Cambridge, and has served as a Visiting Scholar in the Faculties of Law and Land Economy at the University of Cambridge. He teaches a section of a Law & Economics course in Land Economy each year on polycentric governance and institutional analysis. In Fall 2001, Professor Cole was the John S. Lehmann Distinguished Visiting Professor of Law at Washington University in St. Louis. Professor Cole received his JD, *cum laude*, with a Certificate in Environmental and Natural Resources Law, from the Northwestern School of Law of Lewis & Clark College. He holds JSM (1991) and JSD (1996) degrees from Stanford University.

Robin Craig is the Robert A. Schroeder Distinguished Professor at the University of Kansas School of Law, where she teaches Environmental Law, Water Law, Ocean and Coastal Law, Toxic Torts, and Civil Procedure. She was formerly the Robert C. Packard Trustee Chair at the University of Southern California Law School. Craig specializes in all things water, including climate change adaptation in the water sector and the oceans; the food–water–energy nexus; water quality and water allocation law; marine protected areas and marine spatial planning; and the intersection of freshwater and ocean and coastal law. She is the author, co-author, or editor of 13 books, including *Re-Envisioning the Anthropocene Ocean* (2024), *The End of Sustainability* (2017), *Contemporary Issues in Climate Change Law and Policy* (2016), *Comparative Ocean Governance: Place-Based Protections in an Era of Climate Change* (2012), *The Clean Water Act and the Constitution* (2nd ed. 2009), and textbooks on Environmental Law, Water Law, and Toxic Torts. She has also written or co-written over 100 law or science journal articles and book chapters. Craig is an elected member of the American Law Institute and the American College of Environmental Lawyers and a member of the IUCN's World Commission on Environmental Law. Her comments on contemporary water, marine, and climate change issues have been quoted in *National Geographic, The Atlantic, The New York Times, Popular Science*, and many other news outlets. Craig received her BA from Pomona College, Claremont, CA; her MA in Writing About Science from Johns Hopkins University; her PhD in English Literature, specializing in how the English Romantic poets used contemporary science to explain social change, from the University of California, Santa Barbara; and her JD *summa cum laude* with a Certificate in Environmental Law from the Lewis & Clark School of Law.

Richard Epstein is the Inaugural Laurence A. Tisch Professor of Law at NYU Law School; a senior research fellow at the Civitas Institute at the University of Texas Austin; and the James Parker Hall Distinguished Professor of Law Emeritus and Senior Lecturer at the University of Chicago. He received a BA degree *summa cum laude* from Columbia College in 1964; a BA in Jurisprudence, first-class honors at Oxford University; and an LL.B. *cum laude* from Yale Law School. Professor Epstein teaches and writes in a wide range of areas, and among his many books are *Takings* (1985); *Simple Rules for a Complex World* (1995); and *The Classical Liberal Constitution* (2014). Epstein does extensive work in the print and broadcast media, writing for such publications as the *Wall Street Journal*, and is a regular guest on *CBS Eye on the World* with John Batchelor. He has also been an active lawyer in major cases, as principal counsel, an author of amicus briefs, and an expert witness.

Jan G. Laitos holds the Joe T. Juhan Endowed Professorship in Property Rights and Policy at the University of Denver Sturm College of Law. He earned his Bachelor of Arts degree from Yale University, his Juris Doctorate from the University of Colorado, and his Doctorate of Juridical Science from the University of Wisconsin. Previously, he held the John A. Carver, Jr. Chair in Natural Resources and Environmental Law. He is the author of the leading treatise, *Law of Property Rights Protection* (4th ed.), published by Wolters Kluwer. He is a regional board member of the Rocky Mountain Land Use Institute; and from 1982 to 2022 was a Trustee of the Foundation for Natural Resources and Energy Law. He was Vice Chair of the Colorado Water Quality Control Commission. He was also the Director of the nationally ranked Environmental and Natural Resources Law Program at the University of Denver Law School from 1981 until 2004. In 1996, he was given the University of Denver's Distinguished Teaching Award, and in 2005, he was selected as a "DU Law Star." Prior to joining the faculty at the law school, he was the law clerk to the Chief Justice of the Colorado Supreme Court, and then an attorney with the Office of Legal Counsel within the United States Department of Justice, where he worked under Assistant Attorney General Antonin Scalia during the Watergate Era.

He is the author of several textbooks, treatises, and casebooks published by Oxford University Press, Cambridge University Press, West Academic, Foundation Press, Aspen Publishing, Wolters Kluwer, Duke University Press, and Edward Elgar Publishing. He is also the author of over 56 published law review articles. He has worked as a consultant on several cases decided by the 9th Circuit Court of Federal Appeals, the Montana Supreme Court, the Nevada Supreme Court, the Idaho Supreme Court, and the Colorado Supreme Court, and on several cert. petitions before the United States Supreme Court. He has lectured or taught classes at Austral University Law School in Buenos Aires, Argentina, the European Network for Housing Research Institute in Istanbul, Turkey, the Central European University, Budapest, Hungary, the National University of Ireland at Galway, Ireland, the University of Oslo, Norway, the University of Tarragona, Spain, the University of Edinburgh, Scotland, and the University of Western Sydney, Australia.

Roger Pilon is a senior fellow in the Cato Institute's Robert Levy Center for Constitutional Studies, which he founded in 1989 and directed until 2019; the inaugural holder emeritus of Cato's B. Kenneth Simon Chair in Constitutional Studies, Cato's first endowed chair, established in 1998; and the publisher emeritus of the *Cato Supreme Court Review*, which he founded in 2001. He also served as Cato's vice president for legal affairs, a position to which he was appointed in 1999. Prior to joining Cato, Pilon held five senior posts in the Reagan administration, including at the Office of Personnel Management, the Department of State, and the Department of Justice, and was a national fellow at Stanford's Hoover Institution. In 1989, the Bicentennial Commission presented him with its Benjamin Franklin Award for excellence in writing on the US Constitution. In 2001, Columbia University's School of General Studies awarded him its Alumni Medal of Distinction. Pilon lectures and debates at universities and law schools across the country and abroad, and testifies often before Congress.

His writings have appeared in the *Wall Street Journal*, the *Washington Post*, *The New York Times*, the *Los Angeles Times*, *Legal Times*, *National Law Journal*, *Harvard Journal of Law and Public Policy*, *Stanford Law and Policy Review*, *Notre Dame Law Review*, and elsewhere. He has appeared on ABC's *Nightline*, CBS's *60 Minutes II*, Fox News, NPR, CNN, MSNBC, CNBC, C-SPAN, and other media. Pilon holds a BA from Columbia University, an MA and a PhD from the University of Chicago, and a JD from the George Washington University School of Law.

J.B. Ruhl is the David Daniels Allen Distinguished Chair of Law at Vanderbilt University Law School, where he also serves as Director of the Program on Law & Innovation and Co-director of the Energy, Environment, and Land Use Program. His research focuses on environmental and natural resources law and climate change adaptation, with special attention to endangered species protection, ecosystem services, adaptive management, and complex social-ecological-technological systems. His work in these fields has appeared in leading law journals and peer-reviewed scientific journals, including *Science* and *PNAS*. J.B.'s doctoral dissertation in geography studied the effects of wetland mitigation banking on the spatial distribution of ecosystem services, which led to his 2007 publication, *The Law and Policy of Ecosystem Services*, the first book-length interdisciplinary study of ecosystem services policy across geographic, economic, and legal domains. He has authored or co-authored over 15 articles on ecosystem services in legal and science journals. Before joining the Vanderbilt faculty in 2011, J.B. taught at Florida State University and Southern Illinois University, and he has been a Visiting Professor at Harvard and George Washington Universities. Prior to entering academia, he was a partner with Fulbright & Jaworski (now Norton Rose Fulbright), practicing environmental and land use law in Austin, Texas. He received his JD from the University of Virginia, an LL.M. in Environmental Law from George Washington University, and a PhD in Geography from Southern Illinois University. He is an elected member of the American Law Institute and the American College of Environmental Lawyers.

James Salzman is the Donald Bren Distinguished Professor of Environmental Law with joint appointments at the UCLA School of Law and at the Bren School of Environmental Science & Management at UC Santa Barbara. In 12 books and more than 100 articles and book chapters, his broad-ranging scholarship has addressed topics spanning drinking water, policy instrument design, and creating markets for ecosystem services. His co-authored book, *Mine*, was reviewed by *The New York Times* and was on its best-sellers list. One of the most-read environmental law professors in the world, his work has been translated into six languages with over 115,000 article downloads.

Ilya Somin is Professor of Law at George Mason University and B. Kenneth Simon Chair in Constitutional Studies at the Cato Institute. He is the author of *Free to Move: Foot Voting, Migration, and Political Freedom* (Oxford University Press, rev. ed., 2022), *Democracy and Political Ignorance: Why Smaller Government is Smarter* (Stanford University Press, revised ed., 2016), and *The Grasping Hand:* Kelo v. City of New London *and the Limits of Eminent Domain* (University of Chicago Press, 2015). Somin has also published articles in a variety of popular press outlets, including *The New York Times, Washington Post, Wall Street Journal, Los Angeles Times*, CNN, *The Atlantic*, and *USA Today*. He is a regular contributor to the popular Volokh Conspiracy law and politics blog, affiliated with *Reason* magazine.

Preface

This is a book that considers the topic of private property. A property interest is a legally acknowledged "thing" or "object" or "good" that typically has value and is capable of ownership – i.e., it can belong to someone or something. Anglo-American common law property conceives of the property interest as something that may be acquired and possessed, owned to the exclusion of others, used and developed, and perhaps also transferred to another by some contractual transaction. It is also a *relational* concept, permitting property items and objects and lands to have some status with respect to *others* who do not possess or own them. A private property interest, which is owned by some private party, also has a relationship with the relevant government in which that property exists. That government usually has the power, sometimes called the police power, to regulate, affect, limit, and sometimes prohibit the property's use.

Most law students learn about private property when they take the required first-year course in "Property Law." In that first-year law school course, students typically learn about how the original "common law" of property sorts out the various interests and conflicts that can arise when one seeks to own, or does own, a property interest. Those interests can be in land, natural resources, living things (for example, timberlands), buildings and houses, or even intangible concepts such as intellectual property. That judge-made common law is usually superseded by state statutes based on common law doctrines. Those courses also introduce students to how governments at all levels can, and do, regulate private property interests, such as by zoning laws or rent control laws and public nuisance laws.

This traditional conception of property and private property law has been a mainstay of Anglo-American law for many centuries. The concept of privately-owned property, and the "law" of property rights for owners, has been a necessary precondition of the neoclassical economic "market." For an economic market to arise, as it has in America and England, there must be legally acknowledged and protected goods that are privately owned and in demand by others. Such property interests have a perceived utility value to others, who are willing to pay a certain price for the interest in order to maximize the utility of the buyers. That demand for the property, in conjunction with the supply of that product, creates the relevant market. Those economic markets, in theory, incentivize an efficient allocation of property interests among buyers and sellers. Countries that rely on markets and capitalism to produce and distribute properties have tended to be the most economically successful countries on the planet. Indeed, the Nobel Prize for Economics in 2024 was awarded to three economists who helped explain why some countries become rich while others remain poor: Countries that uphold the rule of law and *private property rights* have, over time become more prosperous. By contrast, countries that "squeeze" resources from the wider population to benefit elites have experienced persistently low economic growth.

This book takes a fresh look at private property as a valuable market asset for owners that simultaneously benefits the larger community, despite being buffeted by relentless government regulation. The book also considers property as a distinct and malleable legal interest, capable of transforming traditional perceptions of two critical markets – housing and natural resources. By the twenty-first century, property and private property rights have been experiencing unprecedented pressures and conflicting demands from owners, governments, and courts. In this book, scholars are proposing creative new ways to use the idea of property to better reflect the reality of how property rights function in organized societies, how property plays a determinative role in housing policy, and how valuable natural resources might be better allocated. Legal institutions are responding to these dynamic market-and-government conditions and innovative suggestions about new roles for property. The result is that historic conceptions of property and property law now seem ripe for reevaluation and rethinking.

Part I reexamines a traditional tension that has long characterized property use by owners and regulation by government. Historically, owners have wanted the freedom and "liberty" to use their property as an essential component of the economic market. Government, in turn, has a countervailing obligation to regulate and condition and sometimes even prohibit owner uses of property, if lawmakers and their regulators believe that property uses are contrary to some larger public interest. These diametrically opposed forces were in the past refereed in reviewing courts, which would determine when the government's exercise of police power had gone too far, and had violated an owner's property right, protected by common law and the Constitution. The chapters in Part I are authored by four thoughtful and knowledgeable scholars who have studied this growing tension between private property and police power – Roger Pilon, Ilya Somin, Jan Laitos, and Dan Cole. Part I summarizes their arguments and conclusions about how best to maintain, modify, and manage the ongoing dynamic that exists between owners, regulators, and reviewing courts.

Part II considers how the concept of legally protected rights in goods, assets, and resources may be extended to encompass (1) the unique relationship between owners of property for *housing*, and (2) property in scarce but valuable, and shared, *natural resources*, such as water and ecosystem services.

Private property dedicated to *housing* is highly regulated by local governments, with those regulations become exceptionally contentious in urban areas needing affordable housing and wherever rentals are common. Richard Epstein and Vicki Been examine the dynamic that exists between government limits and conditions imposed on owners' autonomy regarding developing property for other property owners to purchase and for transforming residential property into rental housing. Because the property being regulated involves housing, these regulations affect a critical legal and personal entanglement that arises between owner and property. Epstein and Been offer insight into how constitutional law, police power dynamics, private property rights, and court review should play out when the property interests affected by these laws involve housing.

Property law might also need to be rethought so that the concept of private property might apply to a special kind of interest – unique *natural resources*. For some natural resources, the standard model of private ownership of an asset may not work, especially when it is a shared resource. The book considers two models of hybrid "ownership" for two important natural resources: water and ecosystem services. For these resources, a joint private-public model should be explored.

Robin Craig proposes a creative way for property law to be overlaid on water, water bodies, and water rights. Water is a unique natural resource that is in high demand, but often there is not enough of it, or it is in the wrong place. And unlike other natural resources, water is both renewable and capable of being used and reused sequentially by different private parties who have a right to that water. Craig advances a proposal, based on the concept of "panarchy," that requires us to rethink how a more holistic concept of property might be deployed to better allocate scarce sources of water. J.B. Ruhl and James Salzman suggest yet another creative proposal for reshaping conceptions of property so that there is a better way of sorting out interests in "ecosystem services" – natural resources like rangelands, forests, wetlands, and other natural services that support and sustain human livelihoods without cost to us. Ruhl and Salzman argue for a rethinking of property that permits property law concepts to be applied to shared ecosystem services and their benefits bestowed on us.

Jan G. Laitos

Acknowledgements

This book is a publication of the scholarly papers addressing new demands on the concept of "private property rights." The book has two purposes. One is to examine and critique the contentious dynamic that has arisen between multiple actors in the private property market – property owners wishing to use their property; government policymakers and regulators seeking to limit that use, and courts which decide whether constitutional protections can be raised to resist these regulations. The other purpose is to explore whether property law concepts can be reimagined and applied successfully (1) to better allocate property for housing, and (2) to create new property rights status for certain natural resources that are in high demand.

The authors of the chapters in this book are among the "best and the brightest and most preeminent" scholars who have addressed the topic of private property. Their essays in this book are meant to literally "rethink" many of the features of private property law, applying them to ongoing societal conflicts and tensions. These notable authors are -

- Roger Pilon, CATO Institute
- Ilya Somin – George Mason Law School
- Jan Laitos – University of Denver Sturm College of Law
- Dan Cole – University of Indiana Maurer School of Law
- Richard Epstein – New York University Law School
- Vicki Been – New York University Law School
- Robin Craig – formerly University of Southern California Law School, presently University of Kansas Law School
- J.B. Ruhl – Vanderbilt Law School
- James Salzman – UCLA Law School

Acknowledgement is extended also to Neil and Susan Ray, who supported the ideas and goals of the book, Dean Bruce Smith of the University of Denver College of Law, who encouraged the scholarship in the book, as well as Makayla Shoults, who helped copy-edit the book. And thank you to Edward Elgar Publishing, particularly Stephen Gutierrez, who made possible the publication of these papers in this important book.

PART I

Rethinking the Fundamental Tension Between
Private Property and the Police Power

PART A

Are the courts wrong about private property and the police power?

Errata Slip

The following text should replace pp. 3 and 4 of Pilon, Roger (2025), 'Restoring the right to property as fundamental to a free society', in Jan Laitos (ed.), *Rethinking the Law of Private Property*, Cheltenham, UK and Northampton, MA, USA: Edward Elgar Publishing. Please note that footnotes 11 onwards in this chapter should be read as one number lower than shown (e.g. 11 should be read as 10).

1. Restoring the right to property as fundamental to a free society

Roger Pilon

INTRODUCTION[*]

When the French Revolution shifted its focus from the right to liberty to the right to bread, it sowed the seeds for a division between human rights and property rights that socialists and American Progressives would later exploit, denigrating property rights in ways that plague us to this day. Classical liberals, emerging from the Enlightenment, had earlier understood that human rights and property rights are one and the same: property rights are simply the rights of people to justly acquire, use, and dispose of their property, toward which we all strive. That vision inspired America's Founders and the Framers of the United States Constitution. They saw the protection of property—broadly understood as "lives, liberties, and estates"[1]—as the principal business of government.[2]

---

[*] This chapter expands on remarks I gave at the opening of a conference on "Private Property and the Police Power" at the Sturm College of Law, University of Denver, Denver, Colorado, 4–5 April 2024. It draws from an unpublished speech I delivered at an international colloquium, "Property and Human Rights", held at the Catholic University of Leuven, Leuven, Belgium, 23–25 August 2006, and, as slightly revised, for the 24th Economic Conference of the Progress Foundation in Zurich, Switzerland, 13 June 2007. In footnotes below, I have taken note of several decisions the U.S. Supreme Court has handed down more recently. At those earlier forums and at this one, the audiences ranged from laymen to law professors. Accordingly, in this chapter I have not assumed a greater knowledge of the issues than many in those audiences may have had.

[1] The phrase is from John Locke, *The Second Treatise of Government*, in TWO TREATISES OF GOV'T para. 123 (Peter Laslett ed., rev. ed. 1965); see also *id.* at para. 87.

[2] James Madison, the principal author of the U.S. Constitution, wrote, "Government is instituted to protect property of every sort; as well that which lies

Toward the end of the nineteenth century, however, with the rise of Progressivism in America and the growth of government that followed, the division between human rights and property rights began slowly to seep into American law.[3] In 1938, in a famous footnote, the United States Supreme Court finally constitutionalized it.[4] As a result, we have a body of property law today—at least as it relates to the relationship between private property and public law—that is often little more than ad hoc, leaving owners seriously disadvantaged when up against the claims of the state.[5] In its 2004–2005 term, for example, the Supreme Court decided three property rights cases that pitted individual owners against the government, and in all three the owners lost, despite having legitimate claims from a consideration of first principles.[6]

Thus, in 1922 Justice Oliver Wendell Holmes observed "that while property may be regulated to a certain extent, if regulation goes too far it will be recognized as a taking."[7] Citing that "bright line" some seven decades later, Justice Antonin Scalia noted that for 70-odd years the Court had generally engaged in an "essentially ad hoc" regulatory takings jurisprudence, even as he was adding another year to the string.[8] Two years later, in 1994, Chief Justice William Rehnquist likened the status of the Fifth Amendment's Takings Clause in the Bill of Rights to that of a "poor relation."[9] When even the Supreme Court's leading lights acknowledge the Court's failings in this fundamental area of our law, a symposium like this is surely in order.

---

in the various rights of individuals, as that which the term particularly expresses. This being the end of government, that alone is a just government, which *impartially* secures to every man, whatever is his own." James Madison, *Property, The Nat'l Gazette*, Mar. 27, 1792, in 14 THE PAPERS OF JAMES MADISON (R. Rutland ed., 1983) (original emphasis).

[3] See Richard A. Epstein, How Progressives Rewrote the Constitution (2006).

[4] United States v. Carolene Products Co., 304 U.S. 144, 153 n.4 (1938).

[5] "[T]his Court, quite simply, has been unable to develop any 'set formula' for determining when 'justice and fairness' require that economic injuries caused by public action be compensated by the government, rather than remain disproportionately concentrated on a few persons," and instead has engaged in "these essentially *ad hoc*, factual inquiries." Penn Cent. Transp. Co. v. New York City, 438 U.S. 104, 124 (1978) (quoting Goldblatt v. Hempstead, 369 U.S. 590, 594 (1962)).

[6] For a critical discussion of those cases, see James W. Ely Jr., *"Poor Relation" Once More: The Supreme Court and the Vanishing Rights of Property Owners*, 2004–2005 CATO SUP. CT. REV. 39.

[7] Penn. Coal Co. v. Mahon, 260 U.S. 393 (1922).

[8] Lucas v. S.C. Coastal Council, 505 U.S. 1003 (1992).

[9] Dolan v. City of Tigard, 512 U.S. 374, 392 (1994).

1. Restoring the right to property as fundamental to a free society

Roger Pilon

INTRODUCTION

When the French Revolution shifted its focus from the right to liberty to the right to bread, it sowed the seeds for a division between human rights and property rights that socialists and American Progressives would later exploit, denigrating property rights in ways that plague us to this day. Classical liberals, emerging from the Enlightenment, had earlier understood that human rights and property rights are one and the same: property rights are simply the rights of people to justly acquire, use, and dispose of their property, toward which we all strive. That vision inspired America's Founders and the Framers of the United States Constitution. They saw the protection of property—broadly understood as "lives, liberties, and estates"[1]—as the principal business of government.[2][3]

---

[1]   The phrase is from John Locke, *The Second Treatise of Government*, in Two Treatises of Gov't para. 123 (Peter Laslett ed., rev. ed. 1965); see also *id.* at para. 87.

[2]   James Madison, the principal author of the U.S. Constitution, wrote, "Government is instituted to protect property of every sort; as well that which lies in the various rights of individuals, as that which the term particularly expresses. This being the end of government, that alone is a *just* government, which *impartially* secures to every man, whatever is his *own.*" James Madison, *Property, The Nat'l Gazette*, Mar. 27, 1792, in 14 The Papers of James Madison (R. Rutland ed., 1983) (original emphasis).

[3]   This chapter expands on remarks I gave at the opening of a conference on "Private Property and the Police Power" at the Sturm College of Law, University of Denver, Denver, Colorado, 4–5 April 2024. It draws from an unpublished speech I delivered at an international colloquium, "Property and Human Rights", held at the Catholic University of Leuven, Leuven, Belgium, 23–25 August 2006, and, as slightly revised, for the 24th Economic Conference of the Progress Foundation in

Toward the end of the nineteenth century, however, with the rise of Progressivism in America and the growth of government that followed, the division between human rights and property rights began slowly to seep into American law.[4] In 1938, in a famous footnote, the United States Supreme Court finally constitutionalized it.[5] As a result, we have a body of property law today—at least as it relates to the relationship between private property and public law—that is often little more than ad hoc, leaving owners seriously disadvantaged when up against the claims of the state.[6] In its 2004–2005 term, for example, the Supreme Court decided three property rights cases that pitted individual owners against the government, and in all three the owners lost, despite having legitimate claims from a consideration of first principles.[7]

Thus, in 1922 Justice Oliver Wendell Holmes observed "that while property may be regulated to a certain extent, if regulation goes too far it will be recognized as a taking."[8] Citing that "bright line" some seven decades later, Justice Antonin Scalia noted that for 70-odd years the Court had generally engaged in an "essentially ad hoc" regulatory takings jurisprudence, even as he was adding another year to the string.[9] Two years later, in 1994, Chief Justice William Rehnquist likened the status of the Fifth Amendment's Takings Clause in the Bill of Rights to that of a "poor relation."[10] When even the Supreme Court's leading lights acknowledge the Court's failings in this fundamental area of our law, a symposium like this is surely in order.

Zurich, Switzerland, 13 June 2007. In footnotes below, I have taken note of several decisions the U.S. Supreme Court has handed down more recently. At those earlier forums and at this one, the audiences ranged from laymen to law professors. Accordingly, in this chapter I have not assumed a greater knowledge of the issues than many in those audiences may have had.

4   See Richard A. Epstein, How Progressives Rewrote the Constitution (2006).

5   United States v. Carolene Products Co., 304 U.S. 144, 153 n.4 (1938).

6   "[T]his Court, quite simply, has been unable to develop any 'set formula' for determining when 'justice and fairness' require that economic injuries caused by public action be compensated by the government, rather than remain disproportionately concentrated on a few persons," and instead has engaged in "these essentially *ad hoc*, factual inquiries." Penn Cent. Transp. Co. v. New York City, 438 U.S. 104, 124 (1978) (quoting Goldblatt v. Hempstead, 369 U.S. 590, 594 (1962)).

7   For a critical discussion of those cases, see James W. Ely Jr., *"Poor Relation" Once More: The Supreme Court and the Vanishing Rights of Property Owners*, 2004–2005 CATO SUP. CT. REV. 39.

8   Penn. Coal Co. v. Mahon, 260 U.S. 393 (1922).

9   Lucas v. S.C. Coastal Council, 505 U.S. 1003 (1992).

10   Dolan v. City of Tigard, 512 U.S. 374, 392 (1994).

Given the Court's uneven property-rights jurisprudence over the years, therefore, the aim of this symposium is to shed a better light on the rights of people to acquire and use primarily real property. Toward that end, I have been asked by the symposium's director, Prof Jan Laitos, to address the first principles of the matter, the moral, political, and constitutional foundations and framework for the articles that follow that will drill down on specific areas of our subject. For that, I will draw on America's founding documents, first, to develop the theory of rights, including property rights, that underpins the Declaration of Independence, a vision the Constitution largely institutionalizes, especially after the Civil War Amendments were ratified. I will then show how the ideas of the Progressive Era undercut that vision by effectively turning the Constitution on its head through the New Deal constitutional revolution, giving us the modern redistributive, regulatory, administrative state where much of our law is created by executive branch agencies. Finally, I will focus more particularly on the implications for property rights.

More specifically, to show how American property law has gone astray, I will begin with an outline, drawn from the Declaration of Independence, of the theory of legitimacy that underpins our law, at least in principle. I will then show how property rights arise and operate within that natural rights context, drawing from the English common law in the process. With that "pure theory" in view, as a touchstone of legitimacy, I will turn to the positive law of the Constitution to show, first, how it is largely consistent with the pure theory of the Declaration; then, second, how "constitutional law" departed from that theory following the Progressive Era. Finally, with that positive law as background, I will examine how the Supreme Court has treated property rights over the twentieth century and beyond, increasingly deferring to "public policy" to give us a body of law that is often far removed from America's organic principles.

I.   THE AMERICAN THEORY OF LEGITIMACY

Although positive law in America today is often little connected to natural law, that was not so in the beginning, and for good reason.[11] Those who wrote our founding documents understood that positive law alone, even when the product of democratic will, is only contingently legitimate: its legitimacy, that is, is a function for the most part not of its democratic pedigree but of its conformity to deeper principles of right and wrong, grounded in reason, with their origins in antiquity. Given that many today have lost touch with those understandings,

---

[11]   See generally Edward S. Corwin, The "Higher Law" Background of American Constitutional Law (1955).

it may be useful to begin with a brief review of why it was that classical liberals thought it necessary to ground positive law in natural law.

A.   Natural Rights and the Limits of Political Consent

Recall that in challenging the legitimacy of monarchical rule, classical liberals began with a simple question: By what right does one man have power over another? The difficulty in answering that question led them to a simple premise that had emerged slowly from early modernity—the right of every individual to rule himself. But the transition from individual self-rule, in a theoretical state of nature, to collective self-government, once government is established, encounters well-known problems.

To begin, only unanimity will answer the question satisfactorily; anything short of that leaves some fraction of the whole ruling the rest. For that reason, social contract theorists distinguished two levels of consent. In the original position, the argument runs, we agree unanimously to be bound thereafter by some fraction of the whole—most often the majority. But that solves the problem, when it does, only for those in the original position or for immigrants who come later and expressly agree to be bound by such arrangements, not for domestic generations that follow either group. Given that difficulty, democratic theorists fall back finally on "tacit" consent: those who stay, they argue, tacitly agree to be bound by the will of the majority.[12]

But that "love-it-or-leave-it" argument is circular: it has majorities putting minorities to a choice between two of their entitlements—their right to stay where they are, and their right to rule themselves, the very premise of the argument. In the end, therefore, will theories of legitimacy, grounded in consent, leave us exactly where we were with rule by the king, except that now the majority stands where the king once stood. And political majorities, often believing themselves imbued with an air of legitimacy the king rarely assumed, can be even more tyrannical than the king.

B.   Individual Liberty, Limited Government

America's Founders had a fair grasp of those points. As George Washington is said to have put it, "government is not reason, it is not eloquence, it is force."[13] Recognizing government's inherent nature as a forced association, the Founders sought to limit it as much as possible so that individuals,

---

[12]   An early version of the argument can be found in Plato's *Crito*.
[13]   Attributed to George Washington. Frank J. Wilstach, A DICTIONARY OF SIMILIES 526 (2d ed. 1924).

families, and associations would be free to pursue happiness as they saw fit, but mainly—and here is the crucial point—in their *private* capacities, where it could be done freely, rather than through government, where coercion was inherent. Thus, government was created first to secure those private rights, second to pursue various but limited public ends.

That vision of individual liberty, secured by limited government, was captured in 1776 in a few simple phrases in America's founding document, the Declaration of Independence. We Americans are fortunate to have such a document, for not only does it mark our beginning as a politically independent nation; more importantly, it serves as a touchstone of moral, political, and legal legitimacy. Addressed to "a candid World," the Declaration draws on a long tradition of "higher law" that holds that there are "self-evident truths" of right and wrong, rooted not in will but in reason, from which to derive the positive law and against which to judge that law at any point in time. Stated elegantly by the document's principal author, Thomas Jefferson, those truths are:

> that all Men are created equal, that they are endowed by their Creator with certain unalienable Rights, that among these are Life, Liberty, and the Pursuit of Happiness—That to secure these Rights, Governments are instituted among Men, deriving their just Powers from the Consent of the Governed.[14]

Notice that by outlining first the moral order, then the political and legal order that follows, the Founders placed us squarely in the tradition of state-of-nature theory, reflecting the influence especially of John Locke's *Second Treatise of Government*. For if the aim is to show how government and its powers might be legitimate, we assume their existence only on pain of circularity. Thus, we begin in a world without government; and using pure reason alone we determine what our rights and obligations are vis-à-vis *each other*. Only then can we determine how government might arise through the exercise of those pre-existing rights.[15] Stated otherwise, government does not give people their rights; rather, the people give government its powers, drawing from the powers they have to give. To know what powers we have to give, however, we need first to know what rights we have to give. Thus are political and legal legitimacy derived from moral legitimacy.

---

[14]   U.S. Declaration of Independence para. 2 (U.S. 1776). I have discussed the points that follow more fully in Roger Pilon, *The Purpose and Limits of Government*, in LIMITING LEVIATHAN ch. 2 (Donald P. Racheter and Richard E. Wagner eds., 1999); *reprinted as* Cato's Letter No. 13, CATO INST.

[15]   For an elegant argument along those lines, see Robert Nozick, ANARCHY, STATE, AND UTOPIA, Part I (1974).

Toward determining our rights, then, we begin with the Declaration's premise of equality. Here again, to reduce circularity we assume as little as possible, invoke a rule of parsimony, and establish the simplest premise: that all men are created equal, as defined by rights to life, liberty, and the pursuit of happiness. Thus, anyone wishing to challenge that premise—say, a king, dictator, or democratic majority—has the burden of showing why his more complex premise of unequal rights should prevail. Assuming no such challenge succeeds, we now have a starting point—the equal liberty of all.

Individuals are thus born free: either to live in splendid isolation, if they wish, enjoying their natural rights, with others obligated essentially to leave them alone; or, most likely, to associate with others. At bottom, there are two morally relevant ways to associate: voluntarily, or by force or fraud—through promise or contract, on one hand, or tort, crime, or contractual breach, on the other hand. And in both cases, by our actions we change the pre-existing world of equal natural rights and obligations: we alienate certain of our *general* rights and obligations, good against the world, and bring into being new *special* rights and obligations, good only against the parties to the transaction.[16] Finally, torts, crimes, and contractual breaches bring enforcement rights into being—the second-order rights that arise when our first-order rights are threatened or violated, enabling us to secure those rights. Such rights, as powers, constitute what Locke called the "Executive Power" that each of us enjoys in the state of nature: the power to protect against and to punish and seek restitution for wrongs.[17] When we leave the state of nature, that is the main power we yield up to government to exercise on our behalf—the "police power," the power to protect our first-order rights.[18]

C.   Political and Legal Legitimacy

With that bare sketch of our rights and obligations in the state of nature, about which more below, we are now in a position to inquire about political and legal legitimacy—and to see further the problems that surround the inquiry. As Locke showed, there are certain "inconveniences" in the state of nature, pertaining mainly to securing our rights; and those impel us toward creating government to serve that end.[19] Thus, just as individuals have a right to associate voluntarily, so also, to address the inconveniences of life in the state of

---

[16]   See H.L.A. Hart, *Are There Any Natural Rights?*, 64 PHIL. REV. 175 (1955).

[17]   Locke, *supra* note 1, para. 13.

[18]   I have discussed the theory of rights more fully in Roger Pilon, A THEORY OF RIGHTS: TOWARD LIMITED GOVERNMENT (1979) (unpublished PhD dissertation, University of Chicago).

[19]   Locke, *supra* note 1, at para. 13.

nature, may they associate as a *political* group—so defined because that association purports to sweep *everyone* in a given geographical area into its maw, and it claims a near monopoly on the powers of enforcement within that area. Note how the Declaration treats that move from the moral to the political and, eventually, legal order: "that to secure these Rights [the rights we have just outlined], Governments are instituted among Men, deriving their just Powers from the Consent of the Governed." Thus, the government's purported legitimacy is a function, first, of our exercising our rights to create it; second, of its serving all and only the ends we charge it to serve; and, third, of its doing so through means we have authorized. Government is thus twice limited: by its ends, mainly to secure our rights; and by its means, through our consent. And in both cases we can give government only those powers we first have to give it.

But as seen above, that theory of political and legal legitimacy must immediately be qualified, for "the people," collectively, rarely create and empower government through a constitution or change it through constitutional amendment, meaning that most of the people who compose that constantly changing body called "the people" take no part in the organic processes that serve ultimately to legitimate positive law. To be sure, the people may vote to fill offices provided for in a constitution, but rarely do most vote to affirm or deny the powers those officers exercise, or vote for or against the offices themselves. As a practical matter, that is, short of frequent constitutional conventions, themselves impractical, there are inherent and intractable limits on consent as a foundation for political and legal legitimacy.[20] The argument from consent—for democracy, that is—may be the best we have—it is better, certainly, than the argument from divine right, or from might-makes-right. But it still leaves government, unlike private entities, with an air of illegitimacy about it. For that reason, one wants to limit government's scope and powers, as noted above; and one hopes that the powers that have been given to a government—ideally through a constitution reflecting the consent of a large fraction of the population, however rarely that happens—conform closely to the powers natural law would authorize.

II.   PROPERTY IN THE STATE OF NATURE

A.   Human Rights as Property Rights

We move now toward a fuller account of the rights and obligations we have in the state of nature. As should be clear already, the human rights thus far

---

[20]   See Randy E. Barnett, RESTORING THE LOST CONSTITUTION ch. 1 (2014).

mentioned are in reality *property* rights. On one hand they are *claims* to things that *belong* to the claimant—his life, liberty, or property. On the other hand they entail further claims upon the actions or omissions of others—obligations correlative to those rights. They are claims to be *entitled* to those things and those actions—to hold "title" to them.[21] It may sound odd to speak of holding title to the actions of another, yet what do contracts ordinarily entail if not a "title" to some future performance? And our rights to life and liberty entail, as correlative obligations, simply the omissions of others: we are entitled to their not *taking* the property that belongs *naturally* to us, our lives or liberties. Even modern welfare "rights," so called, are claims to be entitled to the goods or services claimed, except that here the titles to the things thus claimed are held by others, which is why we are not really entitled to such things and why welfare "rights" are spurious—not really rights at all.[22]

The basic point, however, is that it is impossible, in the end, even to talk about rights, real or spurious, without using the language of possession or property.[23] Locke put it well: "Lives, Liberties, and Estates, which I call by the general Name, *Property*."[24] He understood that all rights, at bottom, are reducible to property.[25] And that insight helps us, in turn, to distinguish legitimate from spurious rights claims, as just noted: to have a right is to hold title, free and clear, to the object claimed—one's life, one's liberty, one's property in the ordinary signification. One may need, or want, or have an "interest" in other things, but that is not the same as having a *right* to such things, to hold a *title*, free and clear, in those things, whether held "by nature," as life and liberty, by original acquisition of unowned things, or by creation through contract or tort, crime, or contractual breach.

---

[21]   See Roger Pilon, *Ordering Rights Consistently: Or What We Do and Do Not Have Rights To*, 13 GA. L. REV. 1171 (1979).

[22]   See Maurice Cranston, *Human Rights, Real and Supposed*, in POL. THEORY AND THE RTS. OF MAN ch. 4 (D.D. Raphael ed., 1967).

[23]   Pilon, *supra* note 20.

[24]   Locke, *supra* note 1, at para. 123 (original emphasis).

[25]   Madison put it well: "In a word, as a man is said to have a right to his property, he may be equally said to have a property in his rights." Among a man's "property" he included his land, merchandise, money, opinions and the free communication of them, religious opinions and the profession and practice dictated by them, safety and liberty of his person, and free use of his faculties and free choice of the objects on which to employ them." Madison, *supra* note 2.

B.   Original Acquisition

What, then, do we hold title to, free and clear, in the state of nature. Setting aside the complex issues of moral epistemology that demonstrate that we have natural rights, which are beyond our scope here,[26] pure reason will get us only so far in answering that question. After that, to more fully flesh out our rights we will have to introduce contested values, about which reasonable people can have reasonable differences. But pure reason will at least give us a strategy for going forward, as suggested above in the case of equality. Thus, while it may not be possible to justify all of our rights apodictically, by getting the presumptions and burdens of proof right it should be possible to construct an argument that is good enough, and certainly better than any alternative based on mere will.

Following Locke again,[27] therefore, it seems plain that each of us holds title to his life and liberty (or actions) by a certain "natural necessity," as it were. Surely, other things being equal, no one else has a *better* title to the life or liberty that "belongs" to each of us than we ourselves do. The presumption, that is, must be that each of us alone owns himself—each of us has "a property" in himself, as Locke put it—and anyone who would argue otherwise has the burden of showing how it is that he has a right not only over himself but over what "belongs," after all, to others, "their" lives and liberties.

The virtue of that strategy becomes evident as we move farther afield and ask the more difficult question of how we acquire title in tangible and intangible things: land and land uses, chattels, intellectual property, privacy, reputation, and the like. Drawing by implication on the English common law that had evolved since the twelfth century, itself rooted in "right reason,"[28] Locke laid out the basic theory of the matter, especially as it took root in America, devoid as we were of any feudal legacy. In a nutshell, by mixing the labor we own with unowned things—by picking an apple from an unowned tree, catching a fish from the sea, claiming and working an unowned parcel of land—we acquire title in those things. Thus, consistent with the common law principle that title arises, *prima facie*, from possession,[29] Locke outlines his labor theory of original acquisition.

---

[26]   See Alan Gewirth, REASON AND MORALITY (1978); *cf.* Pilon, *supra* note 17, on issues of casuistry.

[27]   Locke, *supra* note 1, at para. 25–51.

[28]   "[T]he notion that the common law embodied right reason furnished from the fourteenth century its chief claim to be regarded as higher law." Corwin, *supra* note 10, at 26.

[29]   See Richard A. Epstein, *Possession as the Root of Title*, 13 GA. L. REV. 1221 (1979).

We need to pause here, however, because in the Lockean account, things are not unowned in the beginning. Rather, Locke posits as his premise that God gave the Earth "to Mankind in common."[30] Thus, he needs to show how *private* property can arise, but without the consent of all, which of course would be impossible to obtain. Toward that end he offers both deontological and consequentialist arguments of varying merit. Clearly, however, he might better have started with a more parsimonious premise: not with the world held in common—by generations past, present, and future—but with it unowned.[31] Not only would that have rendered moot even the seeming need for the consent of all; more importantly, it would have been more consistent with the entire enterprise. After all, it is *ownership*—individual *or* common—that must be justified, not its absence; for ownership is an *affirmative* claim, absent which we must presume things to be unowned. Indeed, it is doubtless more important still to justify the more complex idea of holding things *in common* than the simpler idea of individual ownership. Thus, again, a rule of parsimony.

Had Locke proceeded in that fashion, he would have had a cleaner argument. And he would not have had to resort to a pair of devices of dubious merit: the famous Lockean proviso, which prohibits one from taking something out of the common if there is not "enough and as good left in common for others;" and the argument from spoilage, which prohibits taking more than can be used without waste. Starting with things held in common, however, Locke is driven to such devices in a world of scarcity because others may complain when we take "too much" or "waste" what we have taken. Yet the proviso undercuts *all* private ownership, for there will always be a "last" parcel where the person claiming it leaves none for others; and if that is so, the next-to-last person then becomes the "last person," and so on back down the line.[32] And the argument from spoilage is problematic as well since it undercuts the traditional common law right to use our property as we wish, including destroying it.

To return to the main line of argument, however, if we begin not with things held in common but with the more parsimonious and justifiable premise of unowned things, no one can be heard to complain that his rights are violated when someone else acquires something by a rule of first possession, for such a complainant, to begin with, had no prior right to the thing thus acquired. This is truly a case of first come, first served. And if ownership based on a rule of first possession is challenged by latecomers, the owner can always respond—like the little red hen in the children's fable—by saying that he, at least, *did* something to establish his claim, which is more than the challenger

---

[30]   Locke, *supra* note 1, at para. 25.

[31]   For a fuller discussion, see Roger Pilon, *Corporations and Rights: On Treating Corporate People Justly*, 13 GA. L. REV. 1245, 1277–84 (1979).

[32]   See Nozick, *supra* note 14, at 178–82.

can say. That may not be an apodictic argument, but it is better than anything those who have done nothing can offer. (In our world where "squatters" have returned, these first principles matter!)

C.   Positive Law

That summary of the natural rights argument for private property—which captures fairly well how titles in land arose as America's "manifest destiny" unfolded[33]—gives rise to any number of related matters, only a few of which can be addressed here. Before touching on them, however, we should note that the initial act of acquisition, the "mixing of labor with unowned things," can take many forms—from easy cases like picking the unowned apple to more complex cases like "staking out" unowned land, to cases arising in contexts like auctions or securities markets where a mere nod of the head can switch titles. Yet in all of that, the generic act is essentially one of *claiming*: it is the first step in transforming unowned into owned things, whatever form the claiming takes.

To "perfect" a claim, of course, more than a mere act of claiming will often be required. That raises additional matters that must be considered in a full account of original acquisition, such as how one identifies what one has claimed, how boundaries and limits on acquisition are established, and how one gives notice of and defends a claim. As seen above, Locke tried to address questions like those in a kind of ad hoc way. In truth, they all point to the need ultimately for positive law of some sort as the power of pure reason starts to wane. It is one thing, for example, to stake out Blackacre, quite another to put one's toe on the shore of today's Florida and claim the New World for Queen Isabella. Yet there is no bright line between those two claims. State of nature theory helps us understand how property rights have their origins in natural rights, but it is not sufficient if we are to have a full and useful account of those rights. And that is especially so when we turn to intellectual property, privacy, reputation, and the like, where consequentialist considerations bear so directly on the very conceptions of the property.[34]

---

[33]   I do not mean to discount the claims that Native Americans may have had as European settlers arrived and moved west in America. For several perspectives on this complex subject, see *Special Issue: American Indians and Property Rights*, 24 PROP. AND ENV'T RSCH. CTR. REPS. (June 2006) and Terry L. Anderson and Peter J. Hill, THE NOT SO WILD, WILD WEST: PROPERTY RIGHTS ON THE FRONTIER (2004).

[34]   In granting Congress the power "[t]o promote the Progress of Science and useful Arts, *by securing for limited Times* to Authors and Inventors the exclusive Right to their respective Writings and Discoveries," the U.S. Constitution

Finally, the objection may be made that this approach to original acquisition would be fine if we were working with a clean slate; but even if, as Locke said, "in the beginning all the World was America,"[35] so much has happened since then, so many pristine titles have wrongly changed hands, that this approach, if legitimacy is our concern, is futile today. True, with wars, conquests, fraud, and much else, few titles today are immaculate—as would be so if we picked up the apparently abandoned coin on the ground. But once again, what is the alternative? Much as with the rule of adverse possession, the passage of time tends to settle titles, even as it closes the book on earlier injustices as new generations come along. In an imperfect world, the cost of righting every wrong may be too great. In this context, possession as the root of title takes on a different hue, for on balance it works less injustice than a rule by which all titles are lifted, in the name of justice, and then redistributed through some central planning agency. Witness how such a scheme worked in Zimbabwe.[36] No thoughtful person wants that. Considerations such as those argue for a strong presumption in favor of reasonably settled titles and against redistribution.

D.   Rights of Use

But the right of acquisition, even with settled boundaries, limits, and so forth, is only the initial element in the theory of private property. The rights of use and disposal are the other two basic elements. And as with acquisition, here too liberty is the starting point—the presumption—bounded only by the rights of others. Thus, people are free to use and dispose of their property as they wish, provided only that they respect the equal rights of others to do the same. But because others' rights limit that liberty, it is crucial to be clear about the initial distribution of rights—the rights we have at the start, so to speak. And for that, it is useful to begin with relatively simple examples and contexts, the better to develop the principles and rules systematically. The old common law judges did not have that luxury, of course; they decided cases as they

---

recognizes the practical considerations that come into play in recognizing many forms of property. U.S. CONST. art. I, § 8, cl. 8 (emphasis added). Nevertheless, natural rights principles should still underpin those considerations. Thus, even complex forms of property like radio broadcast frequencies arose in America originally by a rule of first possession. See Turner Broad. Sys., Inc. v. FCC, 819 F. Supp. 32, 65–66 (D.D.C. 1993), *vacated and remanded*, 114 S. Ct. 2445 (1994) and Thomas H. Hazlett, *The Rationality of U.S. Regulation of the Broadcast Spectrum*, 33 J.L. & ECON. 133, 147–52, 163 (1990).

[35]   Locke, *supra* note 1, at para. 49.
[36]   See Craig J. Richardson, *The Loss of Property Rights and the Collapse of Zimbabwe*, 25 CATO J. 541 (Fall 2005).

came before them. Nevertheless, using reason and custom, they did the casuistry fairly well, adjudicating disputes that neighbors brought before them, all
of which established the precedents that constituted, essentially, a theory of
rights. Here, a few illustrations will suffice.[37]

After acquisition is established, the easiest rights of use to justify are what
might be called passive or quiet uses, because all such rights, by definition, can
be exercised simultaneously, without conflict. They are thus universalizable.
At the other extreme, active uses like trespass to person or property, including
tort, crime, and trespass on the case, are prohibited because they intrude on
rights of both quiet and active enjoyment, denying those who have such rights
the exclusive use of their property; and the right to exclude others, the right to
sole dominion over what one owns, is the very mark of private property. Thus,
the right of quiet enjoyment is essentially the right to be left alone, just as the
exercise of that right leaves others alone.

When owners use their property more actively, two sorts of complaints may
arise. The first involves actions that turn out to be perfectly legitimate, even
though others may be "harmed" by them. Thus, if *A* builds an addition on his
home, thereby blocking neighbor *B*'s lovely view, *B* may be thus harmed—
he may even lose some of the market value in his home. But *A* has violated
no *right* of *B*, for he has taken nothing that belongs free and clear to *B*. No
one "owns" the market value of something, of course, since that is a function
simply of what others are willing to pay, and that can change for any number
of reasons. As for the view, the loss of which caused the market value of *B*'s
home to drop, that was never *B*'s, free and clear, to begin with since it ran over
A's property. *B* could not have enjoined *A* from building the addition, for that
would have taken a right belonging to *A*, the same right to build that *B* himself
has. Of course, there *is* a way *B* might have preserved "his" view and made it
truly *his*: he might have offered to purchase an easement to run with *A*'s title.
That would have been the legitimate way to preserve the view, to make it his.
Alternatively, once out of the state of nature, he could have taken the illegiti-
mate route of petitioning the local government to redistribute use rights in his
favor, about which more below.

What we have here is a simple application of the ancient *ad coelum* rule,
which says that within the bounds of one's property one owns from the nadir to
the zenith, from the center of the earth to the heavens, which permits all uses
that take nothing belonging free and clear to others. Notice first the simplic-
ity of the rule and the ease of application. Courts need not make subjective
value judgments about which uses are and are not more important than others; they work simply with straight lines, from the nadir to the zenith. Thus,

---

[37]   For a fuller discussion see generally Corwin, *supra* note 10.

if *A* may build to his property line, so may *B*, even if his doing so blocks *A*'s "ancient lights."[38] Notice also that the rule need not be absolute: obviously, the advent of the airplane—and, more recently, drones—gave rise to public law limits on an owner's control of his airspace; yet the basic right, albeit qualified, remains. Notice finally the importance of being clear about the initial distribution of rights, which a do-no-harm rule easily obfuscates. One wants to ask not whether a use is "harmful," a term fairly inviting subjective value judgments, but whether it takes what belongs *free and clear* to another, a more objective standard. Market offers, for example, can "harm" competitors, even drive them out of business; but those competitors never owned that trade in the first place, which was perfectly free to go elsewhere. We have here *damnum absque injuria*.

E.   Nuisance, Risk, Remedies, and Enforcement

Unlike complaints where reason alone can often sort matters out, a second sort of complaint arising from active uses may turn out to be credible. There is no bright line, of course, between passive and active uses; yet clearly, as uses become more active they may conflict with both the passive and active uses of others, giving rise to the need for adjudication or legislation to draw such lines, for reasonable people can have reasonable differences about just where to draw the lines. And there are four main areas where this will arise: nuisance, risk, remedies, and enforcement. How much in the way of noise, odors, vibrations, etc. or risk may you impose on your neighbor or on the public? What are the remedies if you exceed those limits? And what procedural rights do the parties have in adjudicating such questions?

By our actions we create "externalities," as economists say. We are faced thus with the possibility of incompatible uses and, if that is so, with a need to draw a line beyond which active uses intrude on the rights of others.[39] Here again we will need public law of some sort. We can "reason" about such matters, but there is no principle of reason that tells us where precisely to draw such lines. Reason does tell us, however, that unlike with ordinary torts, where tortfeasors take their victims as they find them, in these cases extra-sensitive plaintiffs get no relief; for if they were to set the standard for permissible conduct concerning nuisance and risk, they could shut down the world. Instead, the "reasonable man" standard prevails.[40] Those who want more relief than

---

[38]   See Fontainebleau Hotel Corp. v. Forty-Five Twenty-Five, Inc., 114 So. 2d 357 (Fla. App. 1959).

[39]   I discuss these issues more fully in Roger Pilon, *Property Rights, Takings, and a Free Society*, 6 HARV. J.L. & PUB. POL'Y 165, 189–94 (1983).

[40]   See, for example, Rodgers v. Elliott, 146 Mass. 349, 15 N.E. 768 (1888).

the standard allows may insulate themselves through various self-help remedies, of course, or purchase greater relief from those who are acting within the standard. By the same token, those who want to create greater nuisances or risks than permitted by that standard may offer to purchase the right to do so.

To flesh out our rights, therefore, to complete that part of morality that properly serves, for a free society, as a model for positive law, we must turn to often contested values and invoke consequentialist considerations. Similarly, in two other areas—remedies and enforcement—we must also introduce values if the world of rights is to be completed. Reason can tell us that, if *A* injures *B*, he must make *B* whole again, but it often cannot tell us what will do that, what a life or a limb may be worth, for example. Nor can it tell us precisely what *B* may do when he alleges that his rights have been violated, including whether that is so. The process that is due both alleged plaintiff/victims and potential suspect/defendants involves many close and disputed questions that can be answered only by positive law reflecting some public consensus about such procedural matters as probable cause, rules of evidence, standards of proof, and more.

Still, despite the need for positive law to complete the picture that natural law begins, that beginning is crucial; for it sets the fundamental principles—broad principles that serve in turn, ideally, to limit the positive law as it unfolds. And here we should note especially, as just outlined, that our property rights—and rights of use, in particular—are limited only by the property rights of others, not by their "interests," nor, initially, by anything like the "public interest," a notion we will take up shortly. Nor should the public interest be equated or otherwise confused with the positive law that is needed to flesh out the theory of rights. The positive law thus far discussed is simply that law that we might all agree to, if asked, when reason has come to its limit, yet issues remain to be resolved if we are to be clear about what rights we have.

F.   Rights, Values, and the Pursuit of Happiness

Those fundamental principles are nowhere better distilled, perhaps, than in the uniquely American phrase "the pursuit of happiness." It is often asked why Jefferson used "Life, Liberty, and the Pursuit of Happiness" to illustrate our unalienable rights rather than the more common "life, liberty, and property." There are several possible answers. For one, and without getting into the complex question of whether this applies to life and liberty as well, the right to property is of course alienable.[41] Another answer is that Jefferson did not

---

[41]   For that answer see Douglas W. Kmiec, *The Coherence of the Natural Law of Property*, 26 VAL. U.L. REV. 367, 369 (1991) (citing Jean Yarbrough, *Jefferson*

want to broach the difficult contemporaneous issue of slaves as property. Yet again, property is already subsumed under "the pursuit of happiness"—people pursue happiness, in large part, by acquiring and enjoying the property that sustains them.

But an answer that may be closer to the mark goes to a fundamental distinction that is implicit in the phrase. That distinction, between rights and values, was at the core of the classical liberal vision and was pivotal in the evolution of natural rights theory from the older natural law. As the late H.L.A. Hart has argued, rights and values are very different moral notions: they come from "different segments of morality."[42] What makes us happy is a subjective matter, varying from person to person according to his values. Rights, by contrast, are objective claims against others, derived from reason. Thus, the basic principle is that each of us has an objective right to pursue happiness according to his own subjective values, provided he respects the equal right of others to do the same.

Once the distinction between rights and values is grasped, we need not succumb to moral skepticism, on one hand, or moral dogmatism, on the other. Skepticism leaves us with no moral compass. Dogmatism leaves us with no liberty. Natural rights theory threads its way between those two poles, yet it does so not by striking a compromise but by discerning the principle of the matter. It gives us a moral compass, setting forth objective standards of right and wrong, derived from reason and grounded in property, broadly understood, that limit what we may do to each other. But those rights also leave us free to pursue happiness by our own subjective values, however wise or foolish. They draw public lines that serve as the moral foundation of a free society.

III.   FROM NATURAL TO CONSTITUTIONAL LAW

As should be clear from that brief outline of the moral foundations of political and legal legitimacy plus the theory of rights implicit in the Declaration of Independence, if we are to bring about a free society, given the enforcement uncertainties that arise even among people of good will, we will need more than natural law. For, in a state of nature, absent government, "judges" may adjudicate disputes by discovering, declaring, and applying "law," making it "positive" to that extent; but their authority and the effect of their doing so will be little different from that of a priest or rabbi having done so in civil society. Some people may agree with those decisions and agree to be bound by that

---

and Property Rights, in LIBERTY, PROP., AND THE FOUNDS. OF THE AM. CONST. 66 (Ellen Frankel Paul and Howard Dickman eds., 1989)).

[42]   Hart, *supra* note 15, at 179 n.1.

"law." Others may not. Such are among the "inconveniences" in the state of nature of which Locke spoke.

A.   Public Goods and Private Goods

Prudence suggests, therefore, the need to standardize matters and bring everyone under a common and known rule, thereby securing and enhancing the authority of judges, giving them a greater measure of legitimacy. At their best, constitutions aim at least for that: to bring about a recognized, common legal order, to make positive what otherwise is only natural law, and to authorize judges both to make that law positive and to enforce any statutory law that is necessary to complete that process, as discussed above. One hopes that one's constitution does that and does it accurately—that is, that the framers and subsequent judges and legislators "get it right."

But constitutions are usually written and ratified with more in mind. Beyond that first and most basic purpose of securing our rights, they often authorize and empower the governments thus created to pursue *other* ends, "public" ends of various kinds, reflecting the will and wishes of citizens—or at least those of that portion of the current population that votes to ratify them. Therein lies a moral problem, of course, for if government as such has an air of illegitimacy about it by virtue of its being a forced association, as discussed above, then the more ends we pursue through government, the more we resort to force to get what "we" want. Thus, on a continuum running from limited government to leviathan, the presumption must be for the former, with the burden on those who would pursue ever more ends through government to show why those ends should not be left to individuals to pursue in their private capacities, where they can be pursued without resort to force. It is one thing to pursue collectively what economists call "public goods" like justice, national defense, clean air and water, and certain basic infrastructure, available to all, quite another to pursue collectively the many goods and services governments today are providing, many of which projects many citizens may want no part of.[43]

---

[43]   "Public goods," as economists define them narrowly, are goods enjoyed roughly equally by all but that are not likely to be provided privately in a state of nature due to the "free-rider" problem. Genuine public goods are characterized by "non-excludability" and "non-rivalrous consumption," meaning that once they are provided or paid for by some, others cannot be excluded from enjoying them (non-excludability), and the marginal cost of another person's consuming them, once they have been produced, is zero (non-rivalrous consumption). In the state of nature, even if we could overcome the coordination problems, private parties would be disinclined to provide such goods if there are substantial numbers of free riders—people willing to enjoy but unwilling to bear their share of the

In that connection, diplomacy and national defense, like police protection and adjudication services, may be seen as public goods, as facilitating the basic function of government—to secure our rights. Likewise, agencies that facilitate free commerce or standardize intellectual property may be necessary to flesh out our rights in uncertain contexts, at least when they limit themselves to that end. And certain environmental measures may be thought of as clarifying the uncertain lines of nuisance law and risk, especially in large number contexts, such as automobile pollution. When we move farther afield, however, to such goods as health care, education, retirement security, housing, business subsidies, environmental and cultural amenities, and the like—the stuff of modern government that could be and often is provided more efficiently by the private sector—we are no longer talking about *public* goods, as properly defined, or about government's core function of securing rights. On the contrary, such goods and services are provided in violation of the rights of those whose property, through redistribution, affords their existence, and no democratic voting rationale can change that brute moral fact.

B.   A Constitution for Liberty

Fortunately, the United States Constitution was drafted by men who had a good grasp of such basic issues. Having recently fought a long war to unburden themselves of overweening government, yet knowing that they still lived in a dangerous world, the Framers in 1787 crafted a document that carefully balanced powers and limits, reflecting on one hand the natural law the Declaration had outlined 11 years earlier, and on the other their experience in self-government in the states gained since independence.

The Constitution's Preamble, reflecting state-of-nature theory, makes it clear from the start that all power comes from the people. Thus, government does not give people their rights—an idea arising from declarations of rights. To the contrary, the people give government its powers—but they can give government only those powers that they first already have *before* they establish government. That alone limits the government's powers. And we discover the powers the people have given simply by looking at the document.

---

costs of such goods—so they generally will not be produced. It is crucial, therefore, to distinguish these goods from *private* goods like education, housing, health care, childcare, retirement security, and so on, which may be goods for all but which individuals can and will provide for themselves through private markets to whatever extent they wish and can. In fact, a useful test for whether a good is public or private is whether the market is already providing it; education and housing, for example, are likely goods for all, but they are readily available in the private market.

Structurally, in our Constitution, powers are divided between the federal and state governments and separated among the three branches of the federal government, with each branch defined functionally. Congress's legislative powers are limited to those "herein granted," as the first sentence of Article I states. Article I, Section 8 lists Congress's 18 such powers. Articles II and III vest the "executive Power" and the "judicial Power," respectively, in the president and the Supreme Court and such inferior courts as Congress may establish. And throughout the document we find various checks and balances: a bicameral legislature, each chamber differently constituted; an executive veto and legislative override; judicial review, implicit in a written constitution; periodic elections to fill offices set forth in the document; amendment of the document, and so forth.

The main restraint on overweening government, however, was meant to be the doctrine of enumerated powers, not the Bill of Rights, which was an afterthought, added four years later. That doctrine says that the federal government has only those powers that have been delegated to it by the people, as enumerated in the Constitution. And most power was *not* delegated but rather was left with the states or the people. As the Tenth Amendment, the last documentary evidence from the founding period, makes clear, "The powers not delegated to the United States by the Constitution, nor prohibited by it to the States, are reserved to the States respectively, or to the people." In short, the Constitution creates a government of delegated, enumerated, and thus limited powers.

The Bill of Rights, which many today think of first when they think of the Constitution, was made necessary when several states, as a condition of ratification, insisted on such a bill. But others objected that a bill of rights was both unnecessary and dangerous: unnecessary because the doctrine of enumerated powers would be sufficient to limit power; dangerous because no such bill could enumerate all of our rights, yet the failure to do so would be read, by ordinary principles of legal construction, as implying that those rights not enumerated were not meant to be protected. To address that problem, once it became clear that a bill of rights would be needed to ensure ratification, the Ninth Amendment was written: "The enumeration in the Constitution of certain rights shall not be construed to deny or disparage others retained by the people." Thus, the Constitution protects both enumerated and unenumerated *rights*; but it grants the federal government only enumerated *powers*.

The Constitution's vision was thus essentially the same as the Declaration's. Individuals were free to plan and live their lives as they wished, pursuing happiness by their own lights, provided only that they respect the rights of others to do the same. And government's main business was to ensure that liberty. Again, most government took place at the state level. In Federalist 45, the principal author of the Constitution, James Madison, put it simply: the powers of the new government, he said, would be "few and defined," directed largely against foreign threats and at ensuring free trade at home. It fell mainly to the states to conduct the rest of government's limited affairs.

The Constitution was not perfect, of course. Its cardinal flaw was its oblique recognition of slavery, made necessary to ensure ratification by all 13 states. It could hardly be denied that slavery was inconsistent with the grand principles the Founders and Framers had articulated. They hoped simply that it would wither away over time. It did not. It took a civil war to end slavery, and the passage of the Civil War Amendments to end it as a matter of constitutional law. The Thirteenth Amendment did that in 1865. In 1870 the Fifteenth Amendment prohibited states from denying the franchise on the basis of race, color, or previous condition of servitude. And in 1868 the Fourteenth Amendment defined federal and state citizenship and provided for federal remedies against state violations of rights. Prior to that time, the Bill of Rights had been held to apply only against the federal government, only against the government that was created by the document it amended.[44] Thus, the Civil War Amendments, plus the later Nineteenth Amendment extending the franchise to women, are properly read as "completing" the Constitution by bringing into the document at last the principles and promise of the Declaration.[45]

C.   The Constitution and Property Rights

With that outline of the Constitution as completed by the Civil War Amendments, we can turn at last to the question of how it protects property rights. It is noteworthy that nowhere in the document do we find explicit mention of a right to acquire, use, or dispose of property. Yet given that the Constitution arises ultimately from state-of-nature theory, albeit through the people in their states, that should come as no surprise. We start with a world of rights and no government; we create government and give it certain powers; by implication, where no power is given that might interfere with a right, there is a right. Thus, the failure to mention a right implies nothing about its existence. In fact the Framers simply assumed the existence of such rights, defined and protected mainly by state law, because the common law, grounded in property, was the background for all they did. The Constitution made no basic change in that law. It simply authorized a stronger federal government than had been afforded by the Articles of Confederation it replaced, and for two main reasons. First, to enable the nation to better address foreign affairs—both war and commerce. And second, to enable the federal government to ensure the free

---

[44]   Barron v. City of Baltimore, 32 U.S. 243, 250 (1833).

[45]   See Robert J. Reinstein, *Completing the Constitution: The Declaration of Independence, Bill of Rights, and Fourteenth Amendment*, 66 TEMP. L. REV. 361 (1993).

flow of commerce among the states by checking state efforts, arising under the Articles of Confederation, to erect tariffs and other protectionist measures that were frustrating that interstate commerce.

Like the state law that recognized and protected them, therefore, property rights were a fundamental part of the legal background the Framers assumed when they drafted the Constitution.[46] That explains the document's *indirect* protection of property rights, mainly through the Fifth and Fourteenth Amendments. Both contain Due Process Clauses that prohibit government from depriving a person of life, liberty, or property without due process of law. The Fifth Amendment protects against the federal government; the Fourteenth Amendment against the states. The Fifth Amendment also contains the Takings Clause, which is good against the federal government and has been held by the Supreme Court to be "incorporated" by the Fourteenth Amendment against the states.[47] The Takings Clause reads, "nor shall private property be taken for public use without just compensation." Most state constitutions contain such clauses. Thus, actions can be brought in state courts under either state or federal law or in federal courts under federal law.[48]

Read narrowly, the Due Process Clauses guarantee only that if government takes a person's life, liberty, or property, it must do so through regular procedures, with notice of the reason, an opportunity to challenge the reason, and so forth. Strictly speaking, of course, the clauses say nothing about the reasons that would justify depriving a person of life, liberty, or property. That has led to a heated debate between narrow "textualists," who would allow deprivations for any reason a legislative majority wishes, within constitutional constraints of its authority, and others advocating "substantive due process," who point to the historical understanding of "due process of law" as limiting the lawful reasons that a judge or a legislature may invoke. The first group tends toward legal positivism and legislative supremacy, the second toward natural rights and judicial supremacy.

---

[46] As Professor Steven J. Eagle writes, "in *Gardner v. Trustees of Village of Newburgh* [2 Johns. Ch. 162 (N.Y. 1816)], probably the leading early decision, Chancellor Kent required compensation on natural principles at a time when there was no eminent domain clause in the New York Constitution. Indeed, many American decisions, mostly up to about the Civil War era, explained eminent domain principles in natural law terms." REGULATORY TAKINGS (3d ed. 2005). See also J.A.C. Grant, *The "Higher Law" Background of the Law of Eminent Domain*, 6 WIS. L. REV. 67 (1931).

[47] Chicago, Burlington and Qunicy R.R. Co. v. City of Chicago, 166 U.S. 226 (1897).

[48] But see *infra* Part V.B.3 for the difficulties of bringing suits in federal court.

By contrast, the Takings Clause is clearly a substantive guarantee, but it too has problems. To begin, like the Due Process Clauses, which are aimed at protecting rights, the Takings Clause has a similar aim, but it is couched within an implicit grant of power, the power of government to take private property for public use, provided the owner is paid just compensation—the power of eminent domain. The problem, however, is that no one had such a power in the state of nature. No one has a right to condemn his neighbor's property, however worthy his purpose, not even if he does give the owner just compensation. Where then does government, which gets its power from the people, get such a power? It is patently circular, of course, to say that eminent domain is an "inherent" power of sovereignty. The most we can say, it seems, is that in the original position we "all" consented to government having this power, and its exercise is Pareto Superior, as economists say, meaning that at least one person is made better off by its exercise (the public, as evidenced by its willingness to pay), and no one is made worse off (the person who receives just compensation is presumed to be indifferent to its exercise).

It was not for nothing, then, that eminent domain was known in the seventeenth and eighteenth centuries as "the despotic power."[49] In the case of unwilling "sellers," after all, it amounts to a forced association. Indeed, if there is a presumption against government because, from its inception at the initial collective level, it is a forced association, as we saw above, then *a fortiori* there is a presumption against using eminent domain at the individual level because it is a forced association yet again. And that is especially so when the compensation is "market value," as it usually is, for if the "seller" does not have his property on the market, it is obviously more valuable to him than market value.

But two more problems have plagued eminent domain in actual practice. First, in many cases courts have narrowly defined "private property" to exclude the use rights that are inherent in the very idea of property. That has led to the "regulatory takings" problem that will be discussed below. Second, courts have also expanded the meaning of "public use" such that eminent domain is used today to transfer private property from one private party to another as long as there is arguably some "public benefit" to the transfer. That problem will also be discussed below. For the moment, however, it is enough to note that, far from there being a presumption against the use of eminent domain, its use in America today is promiscuous.

---

[49]   Vanhorne's Lessee v. Dorrance, 2 U.S. 304, 311 (1795).

D.   From Limited Government to Leviathan

To place those problems in context it will be useful to outline the larger constitutional history within which they have developed, the better to appreciate the several forces that have weakened property rights in America over the twentieth century.[50] That history is one of constitutional demise and government growth. As discussed above, the Constitution, especially after it was completed by the Civil War Amendments, stood for individual liberty secured by limited government. Yet today, government in America is anything but limited. Because property rights especially have fallen victim to that growth in government, an account of how the growth came about will help explain the Supreme Court's more particular treatment of property rights over the period.

In practice, of course, the Constitution's principles have never been fully respected, even after the document was completed following the Civil War, and nowhere has that been more troubling than with racial policy. Official "Jim Crow" segregation in the South would last for nearly a century, until the Supreme Court and Congress brought it to an end in the 1950s and 1960s. One of the main reasons it took so long to do that was that courts, despite their counter-majoritarian character, were reluctant to act against the dominant political will, especially in the area of race relations. That reluctance was illustrated early on in the notorious *Slaughterhouse Cases* of 1873, when a bitterly divided Supreme Court effectively eviscerated the Privileges or Immunities Clause of the Fourteenth Amendment barely five years after the amendment was ratified, upholding in the process a state-created New Orleans monopoly. That left the Court trying thereafter to restrain the states, where most power rested, under the less substantive Due Process Clause. For the next 65 years the Court would do that unevenly, in large part because it never did grasp deeply or comprehensively the theory of rights that underpins the Constitution.[51]

Toward the end of the nineteenth century, however, with the rise of Progressivism in America, the courts also found themselves swimming upstream against changing intellectual currents that were flowing toward ever-more government. Coming from the elite universities of the Northeast and drawing from German schools of "good government," from British utilitarianism as an attack on natural rights, and from home-grown democratic

---

[50]   I have discussed these issues more fully in Roger Pilon, *Freedom, Responsibility, and the Constitution: On Recovering Our Founding Principles*, 68 Notre Dame L. Rev. 507 (1993); Roger Pilon, *On the Folly and Illegitimacy of Industrial Policy*, 5 Stan. L. & Pol'y Rev. 103 (1993).

[51]   See Kimberly C. Shankman and Roger Pilon, *Reviving the Privileges or Immunities Clause to Redress the Balance Among States, Individuals, and the Federal Government*, 3 Tex. Rev. L. & Pol. 1 (1998).

theory, Progressives were looking to the new social sciences to solve, through government programs, the social and economic problems that had accompanied industrialization and urbanization after the Civil War. Whereas previous generations had seen government as a necessary evil, Progressives viewed it as an engine of good. It was to be better living through bigger government, with "social engineers" leading the way.[52]

Standing athwart that political activism, however, was a Constitution authorizing only limited government, and courts willing to enforce it—as courts were, in large part. Things came to a head, however, during the Great Depression, following the election of Franklin Roosevelt, when activists shifted their focus from the states to the federal government. During Roosevelt's first term, as the Supreme Court was finding one New Deal program after another to be unconstitutional, there was a great debate within the administration about whether to try to amend the Constitution, as had been done after the Civil War when that generation wanted fundamental change, or instead to pack the Court with six new members who would see things Roosevelt's way. Shortly after the landslide election of 1936, Roosevelt chose the latter course. The reaction in the country was immediate: not even Congress would go along with his Court-packing scheme. But the Court got the message. There followed the famous "switch in time that saved nine," and the Court began rewriting the Constitution without benefit of constitutional amendment.[53]

The Court did so in three main steps. First, in 1937 it eviscerated the very centerpiece of the Constitution, the doctrine of enumerated powers. It read the Commerce Clause, which was meant mainly to enable Congress to ensure free interstate commerce, as authorizing Congress, far more broadly, to regulate anything that "affected" interstate commerce, which of course is everything at some level.[54] And it read the power of Congress to tax to provide for "the General Welfare of the United States" as authorizing Congress to tax and spend for the "general welfare," which in practice meant that Congress could spend on virtually anything.[55] The floodgates were thus opened for federal regulatory and redistributive schemes, respectively—for the modern welfare state.

Second, because federal power, now all but plenary, and state power could still be checked by individuals claiming that federal and state programs were

---

[52]   See Epstein, *supra* note 3.

[53]   See William E. Leuchtenburg, THE SUPREME COURT REBORN: THE CONSTITUTIONAL REVOLUTION IN THE AGE OF ROOSEVELT (1995).

[54]   See Randy E. Barnett, *The Original Meaning of the Commerce Clause*, 68 U. CHI. L. REV. 101 (2000); *cf.* Richard A. Epstein, *The Proper Scope of the Commerce Power*, 73.

[55]   See *Spending Clause Symposium*, 4 CHAP. L. REV. 1 (2001).

violating their rights, that impediment to expansive government was addressed in 1938 in the infamous *Carolene Products* case.[56] In famous footnote four of the opinion the Court distinguished two kinds of rights, in effect, fundamental and nonfundamental, and two levels of judicial review, strict and rational basis review. If a measure implicated "fundamental" rights like speech, voting, or, later, certain personal rights, courts would apply "strict scrutiny," meaning the burden would be on the government to show that the measure served a "compelling state interest" and the means it employed were "narrowly tailored" to serve that interest, which meant that in most cases the measure would be unconstitutional. By contrast, if a measure implicated "nonfundamental" rights like property, contract, or the rights exercised in "ordinary commercial relations," courts would apply the "rational basis test," meaning they would defer to the political branches and ask simply whether the legislature had some rational or conceivable basis for the measure, which in effect meant the measure would sail right through. With that, the die was cast: judges would give speech, voting, and, later, certain "personal rights" special attention; property rights and economic liberty would become like "poor relations" in the Bill of Rights.

Finally, in 1943 the Court jettisoned the non-delegation doctrine,[57] which arises from the very first word of the Constitution: "*All* legislative Powers herein granted shall be vested in a Congress ...." Not some; all. As government grew, especially during the New Deal era, Congress began delegating ever more of its legislative powers to the executive branch agencies it had been creating to carry out its programs. Some 450 such agencies, boards, commissions, and more exist in Washington today. Nobody knows the exact number.

That is where most of the law Americans live under today is written, in the form of regulations, rules, guidance, and more, all issued to implement the broad statutes Congress passes. Not only is this "law" written, executed, and adjudicated by unelected, non-responsible agency bureaucrats—raising serious separation-of-powers questions—but the Court has developed doctrines under which it defers to *agencies'* interpretations of statutes, thus largely abandoning its duty to oversee the political branches. Governed largely today under administrative law promulgated by the modern executive state, we

---

[56] United States v. Carolene Products Co., 304 U.S. 144, 153 n.4 (1938). For a devastating critique of the politics behind the *Carolene Products* case, see Geoffrey P. Miller, *The True Story of Carolene Products,* 1987 SUP. CT. REV. 397 (1987).

[57] National Broad. Co. v. United States, 319 U.S. 190 (1943).

are far removed from the limited, accountable government envisioned by the Founders and Framers.[58]

E.   Judicial "Activism" and "Restraint"

That judicial methodology was nowhere to be found in the Constitution, of course. It was invented from whole cloth to enable New Deal programs to pass constitutional muster.[59] Not surprisingly, there has followed a massive growth of government in America—federal, state, and local—for the Constitution now served more to facilitate than to limit power. And it was only a matter of time until those measures found their way back to a Court now being asked not to check power and find rights but to find powers nowhere granted and ignore rights plainly retained—judicial "activism" often mistaken, due to the Court's deference, for judicial "restraint"—and to do the interstitial lawmaking needed to save often inconsistent and incoherent legislation—itself a form of judicial activism.

In the late 1950s, however, the Warren Court—"liberal" in the modern American sense—got its second wind with activism that continued, more or less, until roughly the mid-1990s. Much of that "activism" has amounted to nothing more, nor less, than a properly engaged court, finding and protecting rights too long ignored, like civil rights. But modern liberals on the Court were also finding "rights" nowhere to be found even among our unenumerated rights,[60] while ignoring rights plainly enumerated, like property and contract rights, even as they continued to ignore the doctrine of enumerated powers.

---

[58]   See Philip Hamburger, Is ADMINISTRATIVE LAW UNLAWFUL? (2014); Philip Hamburger, THE ADMINISTRATIVE THREAT (2017). That is expected to change, for in its October 2023 term, in Loper Bright Enterprises v. Raimondo, 603 U.S. 369 (2024), the Supreme Court overruled Chevron U.S.A., Inc. v. Natural Resources Defense Council, Inc., 467 U.S. 837 (1984) and its *Chevron* Deference doctrine.

[59]   Don't take my word for that. Here is Rexford Tugwell, a member of Roosevelt's "Brain Trust" and one of the principal architects of the New Deal, reflecting on his handiwork some 30 years later: "To the extent that these [New Deal policies] developed, they were tortured interpretations of a document intended to prevent them." Rexford G. Tugwell, *A Center Report: Rewriting the Constitution*, CTR. MAGAZINE, March 1968, at 20. They knew exactly what they were doing. They were turning the Constitution on its head.

[60]   The most contentious example, of course, was the Court's 1973 abortion decision, Roe v. Wade, 410 U.S. 113 (1973), which the Court finally overturned in Dobbs v. Jackson, 597 U.S. 215 (2022). I discussed *Roe* briefly in Roger Pilon, *Alito and Abortion*, WALL ST. J., Nov. 28, 2005, at A16.

As that patently political jurisprudence grew, it led to a conservative backlash, beginning in the 1960s, and a call for judicial "restraint."[61] But most conservatives directed their fire only against liberal *rights* activism. Ignoring the New Deal Court's evisceration of the doctrine of enumerated *powers*— a lost cause, they believed—they called for judicial deference to the political branches, including the states, and for protecting only those rights that were enumerated in the Constitution, thus ignoring the Ninth Amendment, the Privileges or Immunities Clause of the Fourteenth Amendment, and the substantive implications of the Due Process Clauses of the Fifth and Fourteenth Amendments.

In often confused, confusing, and uneven practice, however, both camps tended toward deference to power. Liberal jurists tended to protect "personal" rights, variously understood, leaving property rights and economic liberties to the tender mercies of the political branches. Conservative jurists, by contrast, tended to protect property rights and, to a far lesser extent, economic liberties, while leaving unenumerated rights, including many personal liberties, exposed to majoritarian tyranny.

As those two camps warred, a third, classical liberal or libertarian school of thought (re)emerged in the late 1970s.[62] Reflected in this chapter, it criticized both liberal "activism" and conservative "restraint"—both stemming from the mistaken jurisprudence of the New Deal. Judges, it argued, should be concerned less with whether they were active or restrained than with whether they were discerning and applying the law, including the background law, correctly—recognizing only those powers that have been authorized,[63] protecting all and only those rights we have, enumerated and unenumerated alike. That, of course, is what judges are supposed to do. To do it well, however, requires

---

[61] The most influential exposition of that view is in ROBERT H. BORK, THE TEMPTING OF AMERICA: THE POLITICAL SEDUCTION OF THE LAW (1990), which I discuss in Roger Pilon, *Online Alexander Bickel Symposium: Bickel and Bork Beyond the Academy*, SCOTUSBLOG, at https://www.scotusblog.com/2012/08/online-alexander-bickel-symposium-bickel-and-bork-beyond-the-academy/.

[62] See, *for example*, Bernard H. Siegan, ECONOMIC LIBERTIES AND THE CONSTITUTION (1980); Roger Pilon, *On the Foundations of Justice*, 17 INTERCOLLEGIATE REV. 3 (Fall/Winter 1981); and Roger Pilon, *On the Origins of the Modern Libertarian Legal Movement*, 16 CHAP. L. REV. 255 (2013).

[63] Over several years the Rehnquist Court made modest efforts toward reinvigorating the doctrine of enumerated powers: see, for example, United States v. Lopez, 514 U.S. 549 (1995) and United States v. Morrison, 529 U.S. 598 (2000). But with Gonzales v. Raich, 545 U.S. 1 (2005), that effort stalled. See Douglas W. Kmiec, Gonzales v. Raich: Wickard v. Filburn *Displaced*, 2004–2005 CATO SUP. CT. REV. 71. *But cf.* NFIB v. Sebelius, 567 U.S. 519 (2012) (placing limits on Congress's power to regulate interstate commerce).

grasping the basic theory of the matter, the Constitution's first principles—an understanding too little found today, steeped as we now are in legal positivism and statutory law aimed at providing manifold public goods and services, far removed from our natural rights origins.

IV.   THE SUPREME COURT'S TREATMENT OF PROPERTY RIGHTS

As that brief history shows, to a great extent in America today, politics has trumped law. Ignoring and often disparaging our Constitution of limited government, Progressives promoted instead the virtues of expansive "democratic" government.[64] And under political pressure, the New Deal Court "constitutionalized" that agenda by wrongly and radically rereading the Constitution. Today, government intrudes into virtually every aspect of life, politicizing nearly everything in its wake. The result is massive redistribution through either taxation or regulation—coercing some for the benefit of others. In a word, public policy today is far less concerned with protecting rights than with providing all manner of goods and services by redistributing *property*, including our property in our liberty.

Lest there be any doubt about the modern Supreme Court's view of regulatory redistribution, here is the Court in 1985 speaking directly to the issue:

> In the course of regulating commercial and other human affairs, Congress routinely creates burdens for some that directly benefit others. For example, Congress may set minimum wages, control prices, or create causes of action that did not previously exist. Given the propriety of the governmental power to regulate, it cannot be said that the Takings Clause is violated whenever legislation requires one person to use his or her assets for the benefit of another.[65]

---

[64]   In fact, as early as 1900 we could find *The Nation*, before it became an instrument of the modern left, lamenting the demise of classical liberalism. In an editorial entitled *The Eclipse of Liberalism*, the magazine's editors surveyed the European scene, then wrote that in America, too, "recent events show how much ground has been lost. The Declaration of Independence no longer arouses enthusiasm; it is an embarrassing instrument which requires to be explained away. The Constitution is said to be 'outgrown.'" THE NATION, Aug. 9, 1900, at 105.

[65]   Connolly v. Pension Benefit Guar. Corp., 475 U.S. 211, 223 (1985). Contrast that with the 1936 Court's view of direct redistribution through taxation: "A tax, in the general understanding of the term, and as used in the Constitution, signifies an exaction for the support of the government. The word has never been thought to connote the expropriation of money from one group for the benefit of another." United States v. Butler, 297 U.S. 1, 61 (1936).

To illustrate, systematically, how modern Supreme Court decisions have under-mined property rights, limiting "property" here to its ordinary signification, I will first sketch four basic scenarios involving government actions that affect property, distinguishing those actions that do not and those that do violate rights. I will then take the last of those scenarios and distinguish four versions of that, again distinguishing those actions that do not and those that do violate rights. Finally, I will raise a few procedural issues surrounding the Court's property rights jurisprudence. An outline of this kind, drawing on points made earlier, gives us a theory of the matter that is grounded in first principles, as mentioned above, something that is often not evident in the cases.[66] I will then turn to cases evidencing the scenarios that involve violations.

A.   Government Actions Affecting Property: In Summary

In scenario one, government acts in a way that causes private property values to drop, but it violates no rights. It closes a local public school, for example, or a military base, and local property values drop accordingly; or it builds a new public highway some distance from the old one, reducing the flow of trade to businesses located on the old highway. In those kinds of cases, owners some-times believe the government owes them compensation under the Takings Clause because its action has "taken" the value in their property. But as dis-cussed earlier, the government has taken nothing they own free and clear— they do not own the value in their property. Absent some contractual right against the government on which they might rely, there is no property right the government has violated; thus, it owes them no compensation.

In scenario two, government regulates, through its basic police power, to prohibit private or public nuisances or excessive risk to others, and here too property values decline accordingly. But once again, no rights are violated. As discussed earlier, no compensation is due the owners thus restricted, even if their property values are reduced by the regulations, because they had no right to engage in those uses to begin with. Thus, the government takes nothing that belongs to them. In fact, it is protecting the property rights of others—their right to the quiet enjoyment of *their* property. We have to be careful here, of course, to ensure that the regulated activity *is* noxious or risky to others and so is properly subject to regulation under the police power. But if it is, absent reliance based on a recent drawing of such lines, government owes the owners no compensation for their losses.

---

[66]   For a detailed treatment along these lines, see Richard A. Epstein, TAKINGS: PRIVATE PROPERTY AND THE POWER OF EMINENT DOMAIN (1985).

Scenario three is the classic regulatory taking: when regulations designed to give the public various goods take otherwise legitimate uses an owner has in his property, thereby reducing its value, with no offsetting equivalent benefit, the Takings Clause, properly understood and applied, requires just compensation for the loss.[67] Here, government regulates not to prohibit wrongful but rather rightful uses, not to protect the rights of others, as under scenario two, but to provide the public with various goods—lovely views, historic preservation, agricultural reserves, wildlife habitat—goods that are afforded by restricting or compelling the owner. Regulations prohibit the owner from using his property as he otherwise might—thus taking those uses—and the value of the property drops. If the government is authorized to provide such goods to the public, it may do so, of course. But if doing so requires restricting an owner from doing what he otherwise could do, and the value of the property drops accordingly, the Takings Clause should apply and the government should pay for what it takes. Were it not so, as is the case so often today, government could simply provide the public with those goods "off budget," with the costs falling entirely on the owner and the public enjoying them cost free. No wonder there is public demand for such "free" goods. It was precisely to prevent that kind of expropriation that the Takings Clause was included in the Constitution in the first place.[68]

That, unfortunately, is not how American law works so often today when owners bring actions against governments for the great variety of regulatory takings that happen every day. In so many of these cases, owners face an uphill battle, struggling against a body of law that is largely ad hoc, as we will see below. Those who defend the government's not having to pay owners for regulatory takings often claim, among other things, that "the property" has not been taken. But that objection rests on a definition of "property" found nowhere else in our law. Property can be divided into many estates, after all, the underlying fee being only one. Take any of the uses that convey with the title and you have taken something that belongs to the owner. In many cases, however, the regulations are so extensive that the owner is left holding an empty title. Apart from *de minimis* losses, and losses that arise when regulations restrict everyone equally in order to provide roughly equal benefits for everyone, the public should pay for the goods it acquires through restricting the rights of an owner,

---

[67]   For a detailed treatment of the American law of regulatory takings, see Eagle, *supra* note 45.

[68]   In 1960 the Court stated the principle well: "The Fifth Amendment's guarantee that private property shall not be taken for a public use without just compensation was designed to bar Government from forcing some people alone to bear public burdens which, in all fairness and justice, should be borne by the public as a whole." Armstrong v. United States, 364 U.S. 40, 49 (1960).

just like any private party would have to do. It is quite enough that the public can simply take those uses through the "despotic power" of eminent domain. That it should not pay for them besides adds insult to injury, amounting to plain theft. Yet that is happening all across America today.

It is a mistake, then, to think of regulatory takings as "mere" regulation: they are *takings*—through regulation rather than through condemnation of the whole estate. In fact, they are usually litigated, when they are, through an "inverse condemnation" action whereby the regulated owner sues either to have his property condemned outright so that he can be compensated for it, or to retain title and be compensated for the losses caused by the regulatory restrictions. Thus, condemnation and the power of eminent domain, parading as regulation, are plainly at issue in either case. Even though the government does not condemn the property outright, it condemns the uses taken by the regulation.

That brings us to scenario four, condemnation in the full sense, with government taking the whole estate. These are usually called "eminent domain" cases, as if to imply that regulatory takings do not also involve eminent domain, as just noted. In these cases, however, government is ordinarily the moving party as it seeks to take title and oust the owner from his property, offering him compensation in the process. Unlike with regulatory takings, therefore, the obligation of government to compensate the owner is not at issue—although whether the compensation is just often is. Rather, the "public use" restraint comes to the fore.

The Takings Clause authorizes government to take private property, but only for a "public use" and with just compensation. Here again we see the Progressives' agenda facilitated by courts willing to expand the definition of "public use" so that government may grow. Either directly or by delegating its eminent domain power to private entities, government takes property for projects that are said to "benefit" the public. And the courts have accommodated that expansion by reading "public use" as "public benefit." Clearly, those terms are not synonymous: one restricts government, the other facilitates it, since virtually any public project can be rationalized as benefiting the public at some level.

There are four basic contexts or rationales for such full condemnations. In the first context, property is taken from a private person and title is transferred to the government for a clear public use—to build a military base, a public road or school, or some other public facility. Assuming just compensation is paid, those takings are constitutionally sound because the public use restraint is clearly satisfied.

The second context, involving network industries, is more complicated but no less justified. It arises when eminent domain is needed to complete a road, railroad, telephone, gas, electric, cable, water, sewer, or other network industry

line. Otherwise, the classic "holdout" problem can easily arise, with the owners of the last parcels needed to complete a line demanding extortionate compensation. Here, the power is sometimes delegated to a private entity, but the
public use restraint is satisfied once the subsequent use is open to the public
on a nondiscriminatory basis and often at regulated rates. Although collusion
must be guarded against in these cases, the virtue of this reading of "public
use" is that it avoids many of the problems of public ownership, enabling the
public to take advantage of the economic efficiencies that ordinarily accom-
pany private ownership.

By contrast, the third and fourth rationales for using eminent domain are
deeply problematic. Over the years in America, many cities, often spurred on
by federal money, have engaged in "urban renewal," bulldozing whole neighborhoods and then rebuilding them, taking title from one private party and
giving it to another, all in the name of "blight reduction." If there is a genuine
nuisance, labeled "blight," the uses that create the blight can often be enjoined
through a state's general police power; title does not have to be transferred.

But if blight reduction stretches the definition of "public use," the closely
related fourth rationale for using eminent domain, "economic development,"
stretches it even farther. Here again title is transferred from private parties
to other private parties—often to a quasi-governmental entity, a developer,
or a corporation—and "downscale" housing and commercial properties are
replaced by "upscale" properties, including industries. Providing jobs, increasing the tax base, promoting tourism, and other "public benefits" are invariably
claimed for such projects, although the actual benefits rarely materialize as
promised. Neither here nor with blight reduction are holdouts a real problem,
nor are the subsequent uses ordinarily open to the public on a nondiscriminatory basis and at regulated rates like the public utility condemnations discussed in the second context. Far from satisfying a public use standard, these
economic development condemnations are naked transfers of property, usually from poorer, less politically connected populations to wealthier, better-
connected people who are often looking to get the property "on the cheap"
rather than at the prices the owners are willing to accept. Moreover, it is not
uncommon to find special-interest corruption accompanying these economic
development takings.

Finally, if this deterioration of property rights were not enough, the procedural rights needed to vindicate the substantive rights that remain have deterio-
rated as well. Prior to the rise of the modern regulatory state and the reduction
of property rights to a second-class status, one simply exercised one's property
rights, by and large. If neighbors or the government objected, an action for an
injunction and/or damages might be brought; but the presumption was on the
side of free use, the burden on the complainant to show that the use objected to
was in some way wrongful—essentially, because it violated the complainant's

rights. With zoning and many other forms of land-use planning in place in most of America today, however, that presumption has been reversed. Rights are exercised only "by permit," with permits often needed from several levels of government. This is just one more example of how "human rights" and property rights have parted ways: we would never tolerate making people get official permission before they exercised their right to speak or to practice their religion; but before they can make often the most trivial changes to their property, they have to get government permission to do so.

That is only the beginning of the problem, however, because obtaining the permits needed before an owner can develop his property or change its use is often just the start of a procedural nightmare that can go on for years. Until very recently, as noted below, the Supreme Court's "ripeness" test has kept cases out of federal court until all administrative remedies have been exhausted. But exhausting those remedies often means clearing vague and ever-changing administrative hurdles erected by local regulators opposed to any change. And under the Court's test, until an agency issues a final denial, it cannot be sued. Once the owner does obtain a final denial, however, if he is not exhausted financially and emotionally by then he must go to state court to seek compensation for the taking of his property, albeit under a regulatory takings regime that is anything but favorable. But if wrongly denied compensation by the state court, he will find that he is denied federal court review on the merits by the federal Full Faith and Credit Act.[69] That is just a summary of procedural problems discussed more fully below.

B.   The Court Stumbles Through the Cases

We now turn to a number of cases, both those that do not and those that do protect property rights, the latter to show how the reasoning even there so often misses the mark. We will start with the regulatory takings cases (scenario three above), then look at cases involving the full use of eminent domain (scenario four, focusing on the third and fourth rationales), before finally considering the procedural cases. As noted at the outset, and as will soon be apparent, rather than having developed a sound and systematic jurisprudence based on a natural reading of the Takings Clause, as outlined above, the Court admits that it, "quite simply, has been unable to develop any set formula" and instead has engaged in "essentially ad hoc, factual inquiries."[70]

---

[69] 28 U.S.C. § 1738 (2006) (providing that "judicial proceedings ... shall have the same full faith and credit in every court within the United States and its Territories and Possessions as they have by law or usage in the courts of such State").

[70] Penn Cent. Transp. Co. v. New York City, 438 U.S. 104, 124 (1978).

1. Regulatory Takings. Given the ad hoc character of this jurisprudence, any taxonomy of the cases must of course be inexact. Nevertheless, the regulatory takings decisions with which we begin, despite their great variety, can be roughly divided into four categories: government acts or authorizations that constitute physical invasion or occupancy; diminution of value without occupancy; unreasonable regulatory exactions; and temporary takings. That is only one possible taxonomy, to be sure, doubtless suggesting more order than the cases admit; but it will serve our purpose, which is to try to discern where and how the Court has gone wrong. Naturally, we will consider only a small sampling of cases.

a. Physical Invasion Cases. The physical invasion cases are perhaps the easiest to get right, and the Court has generally done so, because exclusive dominion—the right to exclude—is the very mark of private property, and physical invasion usually leaves little room for ambiguity. Thus, early on the 1871 Court found an owner's property taken after it was flooded by a state-authorized dam.[71] In 1903 the Court found a taking when river dredging flooded a rice plantation,[72] and in 1917 when a government dam and lock system flooded land.[73] The military's repeated firing of guns over an owner's property was declared a taking in 1922,[74] as were military overflights that interfered with business operations on the ground in 1946[75] and regular and continuous daily flights at low altitudes that interfered with the owner's quiet enjoyment of his property in 1962.[76]

The modern case that established a nearly categorical rule that physical invasions constitute takings is *Loretto v. Teleprompter Manhattan CATV Corp.*[77] There a New York State statute required residential landlords to permit cable TV companies to install wiring and small cable boxes on their apartment buildings, upon payment of a nominal fee of one dollar, so that tenants could enjoy the cable TV services. Writing for the majority, Justice Thurgood Marshall said:

> we have long considered a physical intrusion by government to be a property restriction of an unusually serious character for purposes of the Takings Clause. Our cases further establish that when the physical intrusion reaches the extreme form of a permanent physical occupation, a taking has occurred. In such a case, the

71   Pumpelly v. Green Bay Co., 80 U.S. 166 (1871).
72   United States v. Lynah, 188 U.S. 445 (1903).
73   United States v. Cress, 243 U.S. 316 (1917).
74   Portsmouth Harbor Land & Hotel Co. v. United States, 260 U.S. 327 (1922).
75   United States v. Causby, 328 U.S. 256 (1946).
76   Griggs v. Allegheny County, 369 U.S. 84 (1962).
77   Loretto v. Teleprompter Manhattan CATV Corp., 458 U.S. 419 (1982).

"character of the government action" not only is an important factor in resolving whether the action works a taking but also is determinative.[78]

Still, in a complex fact case the Court was unable to discern a physical invasion when the court below said, correctly, that there was one.[79] And even in the relatively easier overflight cases, state courts today are split over whether building height restrictions constitute a physical taking, even as the Supreme Court recently declined to hear a case directly on point.[80] For the most part, however, the Court has decided the physical invasion cases correctly.

b. Diminution-of-Value Cases. By contrast, the cases involving diminution of value without occupancy—the stock "regulatory takings" cases—are far more numerous and have proven far more difficult for courts and owners alike. Recall that these do not include cases involving mere diminution of value, cases in which regulations protect the rights of others by prohibiting noxious or risky uses, or cases with offsetting benefits. Rather, the uses or, sometimes, omissions prohibited, so that goods may be provided to others, including the public, are otherwise perfectly legitimate. In principle, owners who suffer more than *de minimis* losses under such regulations should be compensated for their losses, whatever they may be. In practice, they are compensated today in most cases only if their property is rendered all but useless—if their losses, that is, are near total.

Not surprisingly, the problem of regulatory takings came to the fore with the birth of the modern regulatory state. An early example, arising in 1921 when Progressivism was in full flower, involved landlord challenges to wartime rent control measures enacted by Washington, DC, and New York City.[81] The Court upheld the statutes in 5–4 rulings, one of which, *Block v. Hirsh*, reversed a decision below that had found the Washington measure "void, root and branch."[82] Writing in dissent, Justice Joseph McKenna nicely summarized the facts in the Washington case, succinctly criticizing the statute in the process:

---

[78]   *Id.* at 426.
[79]   See, for example, Yee v. City of Escondido 503 U.S. 519 (1992).
[80]   Hsu v. Clark County, 544 U.S. 1056 (May 23, 2005). But see Ark. Game & Fish Comm'n v. United States, 568 U.S. 23 (2012), a more recent physical invasion and temporary takings case where the owner prevailed, discussed in Ilya Somin, *Two Steps Forward for the "Poor Relation" of Constitutional Law:* Koontz, Arkansas Game & Fish, *and the Future of the Takings Clause*, 2012–2013 CATO SUP. CT. REV. 215; and DeVillier v. Texas, 601 U.S. 285 (2024).
[81]   Block v. Hirsh, 256 U.S. 135 (1921); Marcus Brown Holding Co. v. Feldman, 256 U.S. 170 (1921).
[82]   Block, 256 U.S. at 158.

The statute in the present case is denominated "the Rent Law" and its purpose is to permit a lessee to continue in possession of leased premises after the expiration of his term, against the demand of his landlord, and in direct opposition to the covenants of the lease, so long as he pays the rent and performs the conditions as fixed by the lease or as modified by a commission created by the statute. This is contrary to every conception of leases that the world has ever entertained, and of the reciprocal rights and obligations of lessor and lessee.[83]

As grounds for dissent, McKenna cited "the explicit provisions of the Constitution" and "the irresistible deductions from those provisions."[84] Writing for the majority, Justice Oliver Wendell Holmes, the quintessential Progressive, cited exigent circumstances.

The confusion in the Holmes opinion begins with his invocation of the police power as the rationale for rent controls: he appears to appreciate neither the rationale for nor the limits on that power. Instead, all is policy. Thus, "the general proposition to be maintained is that circumstances have clothed the letting of buildings in the District of Columbia with a public interest so great as to justify regulation by law."[85] Note the ambiguity of "law:" public policy, reflected in a statute that itself reflected the will of a legislative majority, trumps the law established by the Constitution and the contract between the parties. In the same vein, and equally vague: "a public exigency will justify the legislature in restricting property rights in land to a certain extent without compensation."[86] And finally:

All the elements of a public interest justifying some degree of public control are present. The only matter that seems to us open to debate is whether the statute goes too far. For just as there comes a point at which the police power ceases and leaves only that of eminent domain, it may be conceded that regulations of the present sort pressed to a certain height might amount to a taking without due process of law.[87]

The idea that there is a point at which the police power "ceases" and the eminent domain power begins is utterly confused. Recall that Locke spoke of the Executive Power that each of us enjoys in the state of nature, which we yield up to government as the police power: its function is not to *create* rights but to secure the rights we *already* have, which limits its scope to the rights there are to be secured. Yet here the tenant's "right" to renew the lease at a controlled rent is *created* by statute *pursuant* to the police power, Holmes tells us. But we need not rely on natural law alone to find the error in that view, for the

---

[83] *Id.* at 159 (McKenna, J., dissenting).
[84] *Id.* (McKenna, J., dissenting).
[85] *Id.* at 155.
[86] *Id.* at 156.
[87] *Id.*

parties themselves had settled the matter: the lease they had agreed to left the risk of subsequent rent increases with the tenant. What the statute did was undo that agreement: to benefit the tenant, it extinguished the right of the landlord to charge market rents upon renewal, thus taking from him the difference between the market rent he could otherwise have charged and the rent permitted by the statute. In effect, the landlord alone is made to serve the "public interest" that purports to justify this statute. Unfortunately, all of that escaped Holmes. His opinion exhibits no understanding of the theory of the matter; not remotely does it go to first principles. It is essentially a policy ruling.

A year later, however, Holmes faced a statute that did go "too far," so he went the other way, finding it unconstitutional. In a case that has come to stand for the beginning of regulatory takings jurisprudence in America, *Pennsylvania Coal Co. v. Mahon*,[88] the Court ruled against Pennsylvania's Kohler Act because it worked a taking of private property. The facts, in a nutshell, are these. Beginning in the late nineteenth century, landowners in Pennsylvania entered into contracts with coal companies to mine the coal beneath their property. They retained ownership of the surface estates; the companies bought the subsurface estates, where the coal was; and the risk of subsidence and cave-ins, a not uncommon occurrence as mining proceeded, was borne by the surface owners, for which they were paid at the time of the contract. As subsidence began occurring over time, however, the surface owners sought legislative relief in the form of the Kohler Act, which the state legislature was only too happy to provide, the votes of surface owners being far more numerous than those of coal company owners.

Clearly, the statute here is on all fours with the rent control statutes just discussed: the parties had settled their relationships by contract, including the distribution of risk; the challenged statute upset that agreement. The rent control statutes took the landlords' rent differential. The Kohler Act took the coal companies' right to mine coal in their subsurface support estates. Yet here, unlike in the cases a year earlier, Holmes found a taking.

Once again the police power played prominently in his opinion—"[t]he question is whether the police power can be stretched so far"[89]—but again, one finds no theory of the matter. And here too Holmes treats the police power and the eminent domain power as if they were opposite ends of some continuum:

> Government hardly could go on if, to some extent, values incident to property could not be diminished without paying for every such change in the general law. As long

---

[88]   Penn. Coal Co. v. Mahon, 260 U.S. 393 (1922). For a trenchant discussion of the case, see Richard A. Epstein, *Takings: Descent and Resurrection*, 1987 SUP. CT. REV. 1.

[89]   *Id.* at 413.

recognized, some values are enjoyed under an implied limitation and must yield to
the police power. But obviously the implied limitation must have its limits, or the
contract and due process clauses are gone. One fact for consideration in determining such limits is the extent of the diminution. When it reaches a certain magnitude,
in most if not in all cases, there must be an exercise of eminent domain and compensation to sustain the act.[90]

Or, as Holmes famously put it, "[t]he general rule at least is that while property
may be regulated to a certain extent, if regulation goes *too far* it will be recognized as a taking."[91]

Here again we see Holmes trying to define a taking by examining "the
extent of the diminution" of "values incident to property." Yet that has nothing
to do with the definition: restrict rights and you have a taking, even if the loss is
minimal; restrict wrongful uses and you have no taking, even if the losses are
great. Holmes understands the function of the Takings Clause, of course: "We
are in danger of forgetting that a strong public desire to improve the public
condition is not enough to warrant achieving the desire by a shorter cut than
the constitutional way of paying for the change."[92] But when he adds immediately that "this is a question of degree—and therefore cannot be disposed of by
general propositions,"[93] we are left with no principle of the matter, no way to
distinguish this case from the earlier rent control cases. Why may government
take property in one case but not in the other?

And so we see the beginnings of regulatory takings jurisprudence in America
mired in confusion. Holmes showed little grasp of the foundation, function, or
scope of the basic power of government, the police power, which is intimately
connected, as we saw earlier, to the theory of natural rights that underpins the
Constitution. Indeed, detached from that theory, the police power is simply a
function of political will, restrained only by such positive law as may restrain
it. And if restraint should come from something like the Takings Clause, that
is hardly a restraint if the "property" protected by the clause is itself a function
merely of positive law and hence of political will.

The confusion in Holmes, an inveterate legal positivist, is no doubt best
explained by his reluctance to come to grips with the nation's first principles.
And it is evidenced here in easy cases, cases in which the parties themselves
had spelled out their respective property rights by contract. Is it any wonder,
therefore, that a Court under the sway of ideas like those that informed his
thinking should have gone astray when more difficult cases came its way, cases

---

[90]   *Id.*

[91]   *Id.* at 415 (emphasis added).

[92]   *Id.* at 416.

[93]   *Id.*

in which government was alleged to be taking property defined not by contract but by natural or common law? In fact, it was just such a case that would next come before the Court, and it proved a further, massive undoing of property rights by opening the door to government land-use planning.

That case, *Village of Euclid v. Ambler Realty Co.*,[94] decided in 1926, upheld a local zoning scheme, reversing the decision below 6–3. In 1922 the village council of Euclid, Ohio, a suburb adjoining the city of Cleveland, adopted a comprehensive zoning plan for regulating the location and character of housing of all sorts, businesses, trades, industries, municipal services, charities, churches, signage, the size of lots, the heights of buildings, and on and on. The detail was exquisite—stables for fewer than five horses, for more than five, dance halls, dry cleaners, institutions for the insane, crematories—it was the very model of Progressive planning. Amber Realty owned 68 acres of land, part vacant, held for years with the idea of selling it "for industrial uses, for which it [was] especially adapted, being immediately in the path of progressive industrial development."[95] Zoned residential, as the plan required, its value dropped by 75 percent.

Here again the scope of the police power was at issue, but unlike in the cases just discussed, the regulation did not seek to rearrange rights the parties had already declared and arranged themselves through contract; rather, it was directed against rights that owners held under common law, to be discerned by judges, as discussed earlier. In fact, Justice George Sutherland, writing for the majority, seemed to recognize as much when he mentioned the plaintiff's pleadings: "It is specifically averred that the ordinance attempts to restrict and control the *lawful uses* of appellee's land, so as to confiscate and destroy a great part of its value"[96]—uses lawful because running with the land, presumably, rather that because authorized by statute, which was just the issue at stake.

Rather than try to discern and declare those "lawful uses," however, Sutherland focused instead on the character and scope of the police power. "The ordinance now under review, and all similar laws and regulations," he said, "must find their justification in some aspect of the police power, asserted for the public welfare."[97] Notice the door that is opened wide by that understanding of the police power: it serves "the public welfare." To be sure, Sutherland begins his analysis, rightly, by saying that the power must be determined in context, pointing to the law of nuisance as a "helpful aid." Thus, he notes

---

[94]   Village of Euclid v. Ambler Realty Co., 272 U.S. 365 (1926).
[95]   *Id.* at 384.
[96]   *Id.* at 384 (emphasis added).
[97]   *Id.* at 387.

colorfully, "a pig in the parlor instead of the barnyard" is a nuisance.[98] But he never homes in on the specifics of the complaint that gave rise to the suit.

Instead, he latches on to the fact that "the exclusion is in general terms of all industrial establishments, and it may thereby happen that not only offensive or dangerous industries will be excluded, but those which are neither offensive nor dangerous will share the same fate."[99] Reflecting the utilitarianism of the times, he dismisses any concern for individual cases: "we are not prepared to say that the end in view was not sufficient to justify the general rule of the ordinance, although some industries of an innocent character might fall within the proscribed class."[100] The question, rather, is whether, "as a whole, the statute is invalid."[101]

There, precisely, we find policy trumping principle, politics trumping law. What can it mean, after all, to assess the scheme "as a whole" except to engage in some sort of utilitarian calculus—to ask, for example, whether it provides the greatest good for the greatest number, a policy question? The effect of the plan, Sutherland says, is to divert this "natural" industrial development elsewhere, in accordance, he adds, with the will of the majority. That would be unobjectionable had it come about voluntarily, of course: we see all manner of private communities today with far-reaching covenants running with the land. But here, recalling the earlier discussion of political legitimacy, we have a *political* majority imposing its will on the minority, with no limiting principle—which makes it all the more curious for Sutherland to be adding that he does not mean "to exclude the possibility of cases where the general public interest would so far outweigh the interest of the municipality that the municipality would not be allowed to stand in the way."[102] How would we ever know whether "the general public interest" outweighed the interest of the community? Are they not the same?

But we get a more precise understanding of the problem before us from this contention:

> If it be a proper exercise of the police power to relegate industrial establishments to localities separated from residential sections, it is not easy to find a sufficient reason for denying the power because the effect of its exercise is to divert an industrial flow from the course which it would follow to the injury of the residential public if left alone, to another course where such injury will be obviated.[103]

---

98   *Id.* at 388.
99   *Id.*
100 *Id.* at 389.
101 *Id.* at 396.
102 *Id.* at 390.
103 *Id.* at 389–90.

That inference does indeed follow, but the problem is with Sutherland's premise. In this context, it is *not* a proper exercise of government's police power to "relegate" industrial establishments to nonresidential locations. Nor is it the Court's proper business to do more, in this context, than discern and secure the relevant rights, which is precisely what Sutherland failed to do.[104] Had he done so, and done it properly, he would have discerned that the property the zoning scheme took from Amber Realty was the ancient use of holding for speculation, which Sutherland dismissed as "speculative." To a certain extent it is, because it is difficult to know *ex ante* what offers will be made for the land once the natural "industrial flow" gets there. But uncertainty in determining precisely what that use is worth is no reason for taking it from the owner and giving him nothing in return. Rather, it is one more reason for letting nature take its course and allowing the economic forces to play out, which would enable the land to be put to its highest valued use. No zoning board can determine what that use is. Only markets can.

Once a court authorizes government to "relegate" industries to different locations, however, it is but a short step to authorizing it to divert the industrial flow itself from its "natural" course. But in either case, government is now in the planning business. As a corollary, and more importantly, the presumptions and burdens of proof have switched: property is no longer used *by right* but only *by permit*. That places vast powers and discretion in the hands of government bureaucrats, often only indirectly answerable to the people being regulated—power and discretion that are invitations to corruption, as history amply demonstrates. And it has government planners doing what only markets can do efficiently and rightly—and courts saying, as this Court did, that "the exclusion of buildings devoted to business, trade, etc., from residential districts, bears a rational relation to the health and safety of the community."[105] For reasons of economy, that kind of segregation often happens in any event, and happens far more efficiently when done by the market.[106] But who are

---

[104]   Of course, were Amber Realty engaged in an offensive use, as discussed earlier, the Court might have enjoined that use. It would then fall to the firm to (a) cease or change its operation so that it no longer constituted a nuisance, (b) offer to buy enough surrounding property from neighbors to be able to continue operating, without offense, since the operation would be sufficiently insulated, or (c) move. But no planning board, much less court, should be making those sorts of economic decisions.

[105]   *Euclid*, 272 U.S. at 391.

[106]   Houston, Texas, the fourth largest city in America with a population of more than two million, has managed quite well without zoning, proposals for which have been voted down by the citizens several times over the years. See Bernard H. Siegan, LAND USE WITHOUT ZONING (1972); Robert C. Ellickson, *Alternatives to*

judges to make that value judgment? What is the Court to say to the person who wants to remain living next to the factory, having accepted and been paid for an easement running with his property? That he cannot do that because the planning board says otherwise?

Sutherland saw neither the ethics nor the economics of the matter. He found "no difficulty in sustaining [industrial] restrictions."[107] "The serious question," he said, "arises over the provisions of the ordinance excluding from residential districts apartment houses, business houses, retail stores and shops, and other like establishments."[108] To him, one imagines, those uses seemed less "intrusive" and hence more acceptable. "Nuisance," for this Court, was a function not of uses that intruded on *rights*, as discussed earlier, but of *aesthetics*. As with Holmes—who voted, not surprisingly, with the *Euclid* majority—it was all a matter of degree, with aesthetics determining the issue here.

Thus, while *Mahon* secured the principle that regulations can take property if they go "too far," its flawed analysis of the issue—in particular, its open-ended reading of the police power—led directly to *Euclid* and to the Court's authorization of massive land use planning by state and local governments. Eleven years later the Court would unleash federal power by eviscerating the Constitution's doctrine of enumerated powers, as discussed earlier, and a year after that, in *Carolene Products*, the Court would reduce property rights to a second-class status. Not surprisingly, regulation burgeoned over the ensuing years: some of it was long overdue, if sometimes overdone, as with the protection of air and water; but much of it was at the expense of individual owners, as with the provision, "free" to the public, of such environmental amenities as viewsheds, wildlife habitat, and the like. The result has been an uneven[109] yet steadily growing assault on property rights. In fact, 65 years after *Mahon* was decided, the Court faced a statute identical in all relevant respects to the one it faced in *Mahon*, yet its decision went the other way, finding against the

---

Zoning: Covenants, Nuisance Rules, and Fines as Land Use Controls, 40 U. Chi. L. Rev. 681 (1973).

[107]   *Euclid*, 272 U.S. at 390.

[108]   *Id.*

[109]   *Compare, for example*, Claridge v. N.H. Wetlands Bd., 125 N.H. 745, 752, 485 A.2d 287, 292 (1984) (owner may, without compensation, be barred from filling wetlands because landfilling would deprive adjacent coastal habitats and marine fisheries of ecological support), *with, for example*, Bartlett v. Zoning Comm'n of Old Lyme, 161 Conn. 24, 30, 282 A.2d 907, 910 (1971) (owner barred from filling tidal marshland must be compensated, despite municipality's "laudable" goal of "preserv[ing] marshlands from encroachment or destruction").

coal companies.[110] That is but one of countless examples of owners having no recourse because they retained the title to their devalued property and it still had some uses available to them.

Finally, in 1992, now 70 years past *Mahon*, a case came before the Court that was so simple on its facts and so egregious that it could not be ignored: *Lucas v. South Carolina Coastal Council*.[111] In 1986 David Lucas, a local real estate developer, paid nearly one million dollars for two oceanfront parcels near Charleston, South Carolina, with the idea of building a home for himself on one and a home to sell on the other. Nothing was extraordinary about his plans: the land was zoned residential; homes stood adjacent to and between his two lots. Before he began building, however, the state passed a Beachfront Management Act. Aimed at promoting tourism, preserving various flora and fauna, and other such public benefits, its effect was to deny Lucas all but the most trivial uses of his property: he could picnic or pitch a tent on it, but that was about all. In essence, to provide the public with the goods listed in the Act, Lucas was wiped out. He retained title, and the obligation to pay property taxes, but the title was now all but worthless.

Shocking as those facts were, Lucas lost 3–2 in the South Carolina Supreme Court. Fortunately, the U.S. Supreme Court agreed to hear his case.[112] In the end, the Court remanded the case so that it could be decided below under the law its opinion articulated; in effect, however, the Court decided that Lucas was entitled to compensation under the Takings Clause because the regulation had all but wiped out his investment. Justice Antonin Scalia wrote for himself and four other justices. Justice Anthony Kennedy concurred in the judgment. Here again, however, we were left with an opinion that was less than clear, in part because Scalia was drawing on what he openly granted was the Court's "70-odd years" of ad hoc regulatory takings jurisprudence.[113]

At bottom, the case is known for its categorical rule that "the Fifth Amendment is violated when land use regulation does not substantially advance legitimate state interests *or denies an owner economically viable use*

---

[110] Keystone Bituminous Coal Ass'n v. DeBenedictis, 480 U.S. 470 (1987). See Epstein, *supra* note 87, for a critical contrast of the two cases.
[111] Lucas v. S.C. Coastal Council 505 U.S. 1003 (1992).
[112] The Supreme Court grants only 75 or 80 of the more than 9,000 cert. petitions (petitions for writ of certiorari) it now receives each year.
[113] *Id.* at 1015. There is little justification for the Court's continuing efforts to square new decisions with old error-filled ones. Given that stare decisis is far less important in constitutional law than in, say, commercial law, the Court would be better advised to start with a clean slate in deciding these regulatory takings cases.

of his land."[114] But the Court had never set forth a justification for that rule, Scalia noted. Thus, he began doing so, first, by entertaining the idea that such a wipe-out is tantamount to a physical invasion; and second, by observing that when the loss is total, the usual rationales for allowing uncompensated takings do not seem to apply. That takes him in no time to the heart of the matter, for him, the police power. The court below had found against Lucas—who was asking merely to be compensated for his total loss—on the ground that he had failed to challenge the police power rationale for the regulation; instead, he had simply accepted the state's argument that prohibiting him from building was designed to protect valuable public resources. "In the [lower] court's view," Scalia wrote, "these concessions brought petitioner's challenge within a long line of this Court's cases sustaining against Due Process and Takings Clause challenges the State's use of its 'police powers' to enjoin a property owner from activities akin to public nuisances."[115] In other words, the Court below likened the building of a house, similar to others in the neighborhood, to creating a nuisance that the state could stop through its police power.

But the lower court concluded too quickly that the noxious use principle decided this case, Scalia added. True, the Supreme Court's early cases had held that noxious uses could be prohibited without compensation—"a reality we nowadays acknowledge explicitly with respect to the full scope of the State's police power."[116] But while the Court had not elaborated on the standards for determining what constituted a "legitimate state interest," it had made it clear, Scalia continued, "that a broad range of governmental purposes and regulations satisfy these requirements."[117] Indeed, nuisance analysis was "simply the progenitor of [the Court's] more contemporary statements that land-use regulation does not effect a taking if it 'substantially advance[s] legitimate state interests.'"[118]

Notice the move there from nuisance analysis, which focuses on the actions of the plaintiff that are enjoined under the police power, to "legitimate state interests," which may reach well beyond the prevention of noxious activities to include the state's pursuit of all manner of public benefits—yet under the "police power," no less. Plainly, that power has greatly expanded. It has been transformed into the "policy power," as it were; and the implications for exercising it free from the Fifth Amendment's compensation requirement are

---

[114]   *Id.* at 1016 n.6 (quoting Agins v. City of Tiburon, 447 U. S. 255, 260 (1980)) (emphasis added).
[115]   *Id.* at 1022.
[116]   *Id.* at 1023.
[117]   *Id.*
[118]   *Id.* at 1023–24 (quoting Nollan v. Cal. Coastal Comm'n, 483 U.S. 825, 834 (1987)).

palpable. If government acting under the police power to prohibit nuisances need not compensate individuals thus restricted—and it need not—why not the same when it acts under the police power in pursuit of a wide range of "legitimate state interests"?

Surprisingly, Scalia rationalizes that expansion—and the attendant contraction of the compensation requirement. "The transition from our early focus on control of 'noxious' uses to our contemporary understanding of the broad realm within which government may regulate without compensation was an easy one, since the distinction between 'harm-preventing' and 'benefit-conferring' regulation is often in the eye of the beholder."[119] It is all a matter of perspective and, indeed, values, Scalia says. "A given restraint will be seen as mitigating 'harm' to the adjacent parcels or securing a 'benefit' for them, depending upon the observer's evaluation of the relative importance of the use that the restraint favors."[120] Scalia then draws the following conclusion:

> When it is understood that "prevention of harmful use" was merely our early formulation of the police power justification necessary to sustain (without compensation) any regulatory diminution in value; and that the distinction between regulation that "prevents harmful use" and that which "confers benefits" is difficult, if not impossible, to discern on an objective, value-free basis; it becomes self-evident that noxious-use logic cannot serve as a touchstone to distinguish regulatory "takings"—which require compensation—from regulatory deprivations that do not require compensation. A fortiori, the legislature's recitation of a noxious-use justification cannot be the basis for departing from our categorical rule that total regulatory takings must be compensated. If it were, departure would virtually always be allowed. The South Carolina Supreme Court's approach would essentially nullify *Mahon*'s affirmation of limits to the noncompensable exercise of the police power.[121]

Thus, Scalia comes full circle at the end, turning the allegedly impossible-to-discern distinction between preventing harms and conferring benefits *against the state*. If the individual cannot use the distinction to block the state's pursuit of legitimate state interests under the expanded police power, neither can the state use it to depart from the Court's categorical rule regarding total takings.

Notwithstanding that come-around at the end, Scalia has seriously overstated the difficulty of drawing the distinction at issue here. To be sure, it is easy to become confused if you have no baseline. That is why the distinction between passive and active uses was drawn earlier, with a focus on uses that intrude, in context, on the rights of others. Thus, to take a famous example, the doctor's injunction against the next-door confectioner's noise can be said

---

[119]   *Id.* at 1024.
[120]   *Id.* at 1025.
[121]   *Id.* at 1026.

to harm the confectioner and benefit the doctor rather than simply prevent harm to the doctor; but the doctor sought that injunction only because he was *first* harmed by the confectioner's noise, *while giving no harm in turn to the confectioner.* Without a baseline of rights, however, one is reduced to a morally neutral theory of "reciprocal causation,"[122] with nothing other than a value criterion for deciding between incompatible uses.

It is hard to know exactly why Scalia went down that harm/benefit road, because in the end he does offer a baseline, albeit one grounded in positive law rather than the background theory of that law—and limited, apparently, to wipe-out cases like *Lucas*. "Where the State seeks to sustain regulation that deprives land of all economically beneficial use," he writes, "we think it may resist compensation only if the logically antecedent inquiry into the nature of the owner's estate shows that the proscribed use interests were not part of his title to begin with."[123] Again, "[a]ny limitation so severe cannot be newly legislated or decreed (without compensation), but must inhere in the title itself, in the restrictions that background principles of the State's law of property and nuisance already place upon land ownership."[124] And he concludes finally that "[i]t seems unlikely that common-law principles would have prevented the erection of *any* habitable or productive improvements on petitioner's land; they rarely support prohibition of the 'essential use' of land. The question, however, is one of state law to be dealt with on remand."[125]

At least four closely connected problems leap out from that analysis. First, the Court's ruling is limited to cases, as here, in which regulations deprive the

---

[122]   Scalia is plainly drawing here from Ronald Coase, *The Problem of Social Cost*, 3 J.L. & Econ. 1 (1960):

> The traditional approach has tended to obscure the nature of the choice that has to be made. The question is commonly thought of as one in which A inflicts harm on B and what has to be decided is: how should we restrain A? But this is wrong. We are dealing with a problem of a reciprocal nature. To avoid the harm to B would inflict harm on A. The real question that has to be decided is: should A be allowed to harm B or should B be allowed to harm A? The problem is to avoid the more serious harm.

In a world free of political constraints, with low or no transaction costs, rights will be distributed efficiently, of course, but it is important to know about the initial distribution before any voluntary redistribution through market offers takes place. See Pilon, *supra* note 38, at 191–94.

[123]   *Lucas*, 505 U.S. at 1027.

[124]   *Id.* at 1029.

[125]   *Id.* at 1031 (emphasis added).

owner of *all* beneficial use. Yet few regulatory takings fall into that category.[126] Recall that the plaintiff in *Euclid* alleged "only" a 75 percent reduction in the value of his land, not a complete loss. Thus, it is the rare victim of a regulatory taking who will be able to avail himself of the Court's categorical rule. Scalia addressed that problem, unsatisfactorily, in a footnote responding to Justice John Paul Stevens in dissent:

> Justice Stevens criticizes the "deprivation of all economically beneficial use" rule as "wholly arbitrary," in that "[the] landowner whose property is diminished in value 95% recovers nothing," while the landowner who suffers a complete elimination of value "recovers the land's full value ... . It is true that in at least some cases, the landowner with 95% loss will get nothing, while the landowner with total loss will recover in full. But that occasional result is no more strange than the gross disparity between the landowner whose premises are taken for a highway (who recovers in full) and the landowner whose property is reduced to 5% of its former value by the highway (who recovers nothing). Takings law is full of these "all-or-nothing" situations.[127]

That is cold comfort, of course, for owners who have been *mostly* wiped out, but who have some uses remaining, almost all of whom, unlike David Lucas, will never have their cases heard by the Supreme Court. Yet those cases are everywhere today, none more common than the "downzoning" cases that result from anti-growth measures.

That leads to the second problem. Because we now have a categorical rule, we have what has come to be called the "takings fraction" or "relevant parcel" problem. If a regulation prohibits the owner of 50 acres of land from developing all but one acre, while leaving the rest fallow—say, to preserve "open space" or a "viewshed" for the public—is the denominator of the fraction the 49 acres from which all economically beneficial use has been taken, or the whole parcel, on which some use remains? Because of the categorical rule, owners argue that all use has been taken from the regulated portion; government officials, uncharacteristically concerned about taxpayer well-being, argue that use remains for the parcel taken as a whole. Although the

---

[126] In fact, even here, Justice David Souter, who did not join the majority, wrote a separate "statement" questioning both the extent of Lucas's loss and, more deeply, the very idea of a categorically compensable taking. *Id.* at 1076.

[127] *Id.* at 1019–20 n.8. The second example in Scalia's penultimate sentence would presumably fall into our scenario one above and hence not constitute a taking.

issue predated *Lucas*,[128] that decision brought it to the fore in stark relief. And courts have gone both ways.[129]

Third, Scalia has given us no real answer to the takings problem—to the problem of the boundless and thus ever-expanding police power—because he misapplies the background theory of property rights that should confine that power. If we think of the right to property as comprising a "bundle of sticks," as the common metaphor has it, the Court's categorical rule tells us we have a taking when every stick, except the one for title, is taken by the police power. But on one hand, and once again, that should not be so in the rare case in which the taking is to stop a wrongful use and no other use of the land is possible—no other "stick" remains save that of title. On the other hand, when the taking stops an otherwise rightful use (in context), that "stick"—that property—is taken. In other words, a taking occurs not simply when the *next to last* stick is taken; it occurs from the moment the *first* stick is taken. (After all, we would hardly say that a thief had taken someone's money *only* if he took all of it.) Thus, the scope of the police power is a function of the background theory of rights. Apart from that theory, it is boundless, save for the Court's arbitrary wipe-out rule, which has nothing to do with that theory.

That leads directly to the final problem: it is hard to know what to make of the promising turn Scalia takes toward the end of his opinion when he speaks of a baseline of "background" "common law principles" that inhere in the owner's title, because he undermines the importance of the turn by applying it only to wipe-out cases ("[i]t seems unlikely that common law principles would have prevented the erection of *any* habitable or productive improvements on petitioner's land"[130]), and his expansive reading of the police power only buttresses that limitation (short of a wipe out, presumably, the police power can take "economically beneficial uses" without having to compensate the owner). One would have hoped for more. Instead, Scalia says, "[i]t seems to us that the property owner necessarily expects the uses of his property to be restricted, from time to time, by various measures newly enacted by the State in legiti-

---

128 See, for example, Frank Michelman, *Property, Utility, and Fairness: Comments on the Ethical Foundations of "Just Compensation" Law*, 80 HARV. L. REV. 1165 (1967).

129 Thus, in Florida Rock Industries, Inc. v. United States, 18 F.3d 1560, 1567 (Fed. Cir. 1994), the U.S. Court of Appeals for the Federal Circuit allowed for a categorical taking where there was a 95 percent loss of economic value, while in Palazzolo v. Rhode Island, 533 U.S. 606 (2001), the U.S. Supreme Court found that regulations that allowed the owner to build only one home on his 18 acres, thereby reducing the value of the land from an asserted $3,150,000 to $200,000, did not constitute a taking because it did not leave the property "economically idle."

130 *Lucas*, 505 U.S. at 1031 (emphasis added) (citation omitted).

mate exercise of its police powers."[131] True, but we still do not know which exercises *are* legitimate? The categorical rule tells us only that the state may take right up to the last stick, and only then do the background principles seem to kick in.

Yet, if the background common law tells us what rights are in the bundle, there is no reason why those principles should not kick in from the start—no reason why the state should be able to take *any* rights free from the obligation to pay for them. That does not mean, however, that those rights cannot be "lost" from time to time, without compensation, as *circumstances* change. A case that illustrates something like that is *Spur Industries v. Del Webb*.[132] As Del Webb, a developer, was building homes closer and closer to Spur Industries' cattle feedlot, the feedlot's operations, legal at one time, became a nuisance at a later time, and were rightly enjoined; for if rights (of quiet enjoyment) run with the (homeowners') land, then the feedlot owner's "coming-to-the-nuisance" defense in response to the developer's suit to enjoin the nuisance will not avail. He has to change his operations, buy out his neighbors, or move.[133] But none of that analysis would be possible without a theory of how the background principles play out over time. And that theory must begin from the beginning, not simply kick in at the end. Once again, from a consideration of first principles, the police power is a function of the theory of rights, not the other way around.

Despite those problems in the *Lucas* opinion, the growing property rights movement in America[134] was buoyed after the decision came down, first, because an owner had won for a change, and, second, because only five years earlier owners had won in two other cases before the Supreme Court.[135] The hope was short-lived, however, because in time the Court reverted to its all but inscrutable three-factor "balancing" test for diminution-of-value cases that

---

[131]   *Id.* at 1027.
[132]   Spur Indus. v. Del E. Webb Dev. Co., 108 Ariz. 178, 494 P.2d 700 (Ariz. 1972); see also Hadacheck v. Sebastian, 239 U.S. 394 (1915) (Los Angeles brick-yard, pre-dating residential development, ordered shut down despite reduction in value of the land from $800,000 to $60,000).
[133]   Actually, this was not a "clean" case because (a) Spur Industries never did have a right to spill his noxious activities over on the plaintiff's unimproved lots; and (b) the case ended with an injunction purchased by the developer on behalf of the homeowners who eventually bought homes from him, perhaps in recognition of his having sat on his rights while the feedlot owner was despoiling his lots.
[134]   See Stephen J. Eagle, *The Birth of the Property Rights Movement*, CATO INST. (Dec. 15, 2005), https://www.cato.org/policy-analysis/birth-property-rights-movement-0.
[135]   First Eng. Evangelical Lutheran Church of Glendale v. County of Los Angeles, 482 U.S. 304 (1987); Nollan v. Cal. Coastal Comm'n, 483 U.S. 825 (1987).

it had announced in 1978 in *Penn Central Transportation Co. v. City of New York*.[136] Today, the *Penn Central* test, despite its incoherence, dominates the analysis of diminution-of-value cases.

Very briefly, that case arose when the Penn Central Corporation sought to build a 55-story office building above its famous Beaux-Arts Grand Central Terminal in New York City, which the city's Landmarks Preservation Commission had designated a landmark. After the commission rejected Penn Central's application to build, despite the plan's meeting all other building and zoning requirements, the company brought suit in the state trial court and won. With that, the case became a cause célèbre, eventually ending up in the U.S. Supreme Court, which upheld the commission, 6–3. Writing for the majority, Justice William Brennan lamented the Court's inability to find any "set formula" for such cases, then wrote most famously, or infamously, as follows:

> In engaging in these essentially ad hoc, factual inquiries, the Court's decisions have identified several factors that have particular significance. The economic impact of the regulation on the claimant and, particularly, the extent to which the regulation has interfered with distinct investment-backed expectations are, of course, relevant considerations. So, too, is the character of the governmental action. A "taking" may more readily be found when the interference with property can be characterized as a physical invasion by government than when interference arises from some public program adjusting the benefits and burdens of economic life to promote the common good.[137]

If there is any connection between that language and the language of the Constitution's Takings Clause, it has yet to be discovered. No one knows with any confidence, least of all the Court, how to apply the elements of *Penn Central*'s three-factor test: "economic impact," "investment-backed expectations," and "the character of the government action." The test does serve, however, to keep owners seeking compensation under the Takings Clause at bay. It is the main reason today why diminution-of-value claimants rarely find relief.

Yet the issue, at bottom, is strikingly simple. If "the people," acting democratically, want some good afforded only by restricting the property rights of one or a few among them, and their constitution authorizes it, they may take those rights through eminent domain, but only if they pay the owners for their losses.[138] But if they fail to pay and obtain those goods not by taxing themselves but "off-budget," by regulations restricting those owners, the demand

---

[136]   Penn Cent. Transp. Co. v. City of New York, 438 U.S. 104 (1978). The first major reversion was in Tahoe-Sierra Preservation Council v. Tahoe Regional Planning Agency, 535 U.S. 302 (2002).
[137]   *Penn Central*, 438 U.S. at 124 (citations omitted).
[138]   See Armstrong v. United States, 364 U.S. 40, 49 (1960).

for such "free" goods will increase exponentially—hence the explosion today of regulatory takings. If that is what the people do, their actions will be no different in principle than those of a common thief. That's what we've come to.[139]

c. Regulatory Exaction Cases. Beyond the direct expropriations of uses by government lie the indirect expropriations, which the modern permit regimes have facilitated. To obtain a permit to do what one would otherwise have a perfect right to do, owners are sometimes coerced by planning or regulatory agencies to give up other rights as a condition for receiving the permit. Two modern Supreme Court cases, one decided in 1987, the other in 1994, addressed this form of regulatory taking, and both were decided for the owner. But the story, unfortunately, does not end there.

In *Nollan v. California Coastal Commission*,[140] the Nollans had sought permission from the commission to tear down their old bungalow on their oceanfront lot, situated between two public beaches, and then to build a new house much like others along the coast. But the commission conditioned the permit on the Nollans granting a public easement along their beach that would connect the two public beaches on either side. The issue for the Court was whether there was a connection between the relevant statutory purpose of the permit regime—to protect public access to the ocean—and the condition imposed on the Nollans. Justice Scalia, writing for a 5–4 Court, held that there was no "essential nexus" between the two.[141]

The commission's "power to forbid construction of the house in order to protect the public's view of the beach," Scalia wrote, "must surely include the power to condition construction upon some concession by the owner, even a concession of property rights, *that serves the same end.*"[142] But the absence of such a connection was the problem here:

> the lack of nexus between the condition and the original purpose of the building restriction converts that purpose to something other than what it was. The purpose then becomes, quite simply, the obtaining of an easement to serve some valid governmental purpose, but without payment of compensation. Whatever may be the outer limits of "legitimate state interests" in the takings and land-use context, this is not one of them. In short, unless the permit condition serves the same governmental

---

[139] For recent developments in our regulatory takings law, see Sam Spiegelman and Gregory C. Sisk, *Cedar Point: Lockean Property and the Search for a Lost Liberalism*, 2020–2021 Cato Sup. Ct. Rev. 165.

[140] *Nollan*, 483 U.S. at 825.

[141] *Id.* at 837.

[142] *Id.* at 836 (emphasis added).

purpose as the development ban, the building restriction is not a valid regulation of land use but "an out-and-out plan of extortion."[143]

In the years following *Nollan*, lower courts gave an uneven application of the "essential nexus" test, so in 1994, in *Dolan v. City of Tigard*,[144] the Court refined the test to one of "rough proportionality." Here again a conditioned permit was at issue. The Dolans had sought a permit from the Tigard City Planning Commission to expand their hardware store and pave their adjacent parking lot. As a condition for granting the permit, however, the commission required the Dolans to dedicate approximately 10 percent of their 1.67 acre lot to a public greenway along an adjacent creek, to minimize flooding that was said to be exacerbated by the proposed expansion, and for a pedestrian/bicycle pathway intended to relieve downtown traffic congestion.

Writing for a 5–4 majority, Chief Justice William Rehnquist first determined that here, unlike in *Nollan*, there was a nexus between the interests of the city in controlling floods and traffic and the conditions imposed by the commission. The next question, however, was whether the findings of the commission relative to that connection were sufficient to justify imposing the conditions on the Dolans. After looking at various state standards for answering that question, Rehnquist determined that the appropriate test was one of "rough proportionality."[145] "No precise mathematical calculation is required," he said, "but the city must make some sort of individualized determination that the required dedication is related both in nature and extent to the impact of the proposed development."[146] Here, however, the city had failed to provide such an individualized determination. Moreover, it had not shown why a private greenway, rather than a public dedication, would not serve just as well for flood control. Finally, the city had not shown, apart from a conclusory statement, how a pedestrian/bicycle pathway would ease any additional traffic occasioned by the Dolans' expansion.

Three things stand out in *Dolan*. First, Rehnquist's "rough proportionality" test, opaque as it may be, is an effort to elevate the standard of review in exaction cases, especially as Rehnquist went out of his way in the opinion to distinguish that standard from the minimal "rational basis" review that emerged in 1938 from *Carolene Products*, as discussed earlier. Second, requiring "individualized determinations" shifts the burden to the government to justify its exactions, which is also consistent with a heightened standard of review.

---

[143]   *Id.* at 837 (quoting J.E.D. Assocs., Inc. v. Atkinson, 121 N.H. 581, 584, 432 A.2d 12, 14–15 (1981)).
[144]   Dolan v. City of Tigard, 512 U.S. 374, 391 (1994).
[145]   *Id.*
[146]   *Id.*

Finally, the doctrine of "unconstitutional conditions" came into play in *Dolan*. That doctrine holds that government may not condition the receipt of a discretionary benefit on the recipient's giving up a constitutional right, like the right to receive just compensation when property is taken for a public use, where the right has little relation to the benefit. Yet that is just what the city was attempting here—to obtain the land, without compensation, in exchange for the permit. When Rehnquist cited two free speech cases in support of that point[147]—two "fundamental rights" cases—Justice John Paul Stevens objected in dissent,[148] implying that property rights and "human rights" were to be treated differently. Taken together, those points underscore Rehnquist's aside: "We see no reason why the Takings Clause of the Fifth Amendment, as much a part of the Bill of Rights as the First Amendment or Fourth Amendment, should be relegated to the status of a poor relation in these comparable circumstances."[149]

Unfortunately, the Court's moves in *Nollan* and *Dolan* to better protect property rights in exaction cases seem to have stalled in the years since. One reason is that, on remand, *Dolan* settled: the city agreed to pay the Dolan family $1.5 million as compensation for imposing its restrictions. As Professor Steven J. Eagle notes: "This settlement truncated the legal proceedings, thus leaving us with *Dolan* ... as it was decided in 1994. Since then, the Court has said that Dolan was 'inapposite' in *City of Monterey v. Del Monte Dunes at Monterey, Ltd.*,[150] a case in which it also displayed great reticence to revisit fundamental takings precepts."[151] And a number of more recent cases have held that *Del Monte Dunes* "limits the *Dolan* 'rough proportionality' test to cases involving excessive exactions of real property interests."[152]

d. Temporary Takings. From physical invasion, to diminution-of-value, to exaction cases, the Court has shown a decreasing ability to apply the Takings Clause in anything like a consistent or even coherent manner. Given the twentieth century's switch in presumptions from owners to government, that should not surprise. Nor should it surprise that owners have found even less

---

[147] Perry v. Sindermann, 408 U.S. 593 (1972) (state college instructor allegedly stripped of de facto tenure because of his views) and Pickering v. Bd. of Educ. of Township High School District, 391 U.S. 563 (1968) (teacher allegedly dismissed because of letter to newspaper critical of district's financial practices). See Eagle, REGULATORY TAKINGS, *supra* note 45, at 871–72.

[148] *Dolan*, 512 U.S. at 407 (Stevens, J., dissenting).

[149] *Id.* at 392.

[150] City of Monterey v. Del Monte Dunes at Monterey, Ltd., 526 U.S. 687 (1999).

[151] Eagle, REGULATORY TAKINGS, *supra* note 45, at 879.

[152] *Id.* at 905. But for a more recent decision where the owner prevailed on *Nollan* and *Dolan* grounds, see Koontz v. St. Johns River Water Mgmt. Dist., 570 U.S. 595 (2013), discussed in Somin, *supra* note 79.

relief when they have been subject to temporary takings. After all, in a world of planning, in which owners can exercise their rights only after they have received a government permit allowing them to do so, the distinction between a normal planning delay and a temporary taking will be difficult to draw. One court described it as the difference between a "prospectively temporary" moratorium and a "retrospectively temporary" moratorium.[153] The planning delay, in other words, is intended to be temporary, whereas the temporary taking is not obviously intended to be temporary but turns out to be such only when it is invalidated, repealed, or amended. Unfortunately, in the real world of planning the distinction is often blurred.

The Court tackled the issue of temporary takings in 1987 in *First English Evangelical Lutheran Church of Glendale v. County of Los Angeles*.[154] In 1979 the county passed an interim ordinance that prohibited the church from rebuilding on land a flood had devastated the year before. Shortly thereafter the church filed an inverse condemnation action claiming the ordinance denied it all use of its property, leading to complex litigation below in which the church ultimately failed. Finally, years later, the case reached the U.S. Supreme Court, which agreed to consider whether compensation is required for takings that operate only for a period of time.

Writing for a 6–3 majority, Chief Justice Rehnquist did not reach the merits of the case but focused instead on the question at hand concerning compensation for temporary takings. Looking at a number of World War II cases in which the government needed property temporarily, he noted that they "reflect the fact that 'temporary' takings which, as here, deny a landowner all use of his property, are not different in kind from permanent takings, for which the Constitution clearly requires compensation."[155] But simply invalidating the ordinance, as the court below had done, will not satisfy the Takings Clause, he continued. "Once a court determines that a taking has occurred, the government retains the whole range of options already available—amendment of the regulation, withdrawal of the invalidated regulation, or exercise of eminent domain."[156] Whichever option it chooses, however, "where the government's activities have *already* worked a taking of all use of property, no subsequent action by the government can relieve it of the duty to provide compensation for the period during which the taking was effective."[157]

---

[153] Woodbury Place Partners v. City of Woodbury, 492 N.W.2d 258, 262 (Minn. Ct. App. 1992).

[154] First Eng. Evangelical Lutheran Church of Glendale v. County of Los Angeles, 482 U.S. 304 (1987).

[155] *Id*. at 318.

[156] *Id*. at 321.

[157] *Id*. (emphasis added).

Unfortunately, that victory, after a decade of litigation, was short-lived: on remand the California appellate court found that there was no taking since the interim ordinance constituted a "reasonable moratorium for a reasonable period of time" while the city conducted a study to determine what uses, if any, were compatible with public safety.[158] Thus, we are back with the problem of distinguishing normal planning delays from temporary takings, which is exacerbated by the Court's difficulty in distinguishing partial takings, which temporary takings seem to be, from full takings—the "denominator" problem. Yet planning delays, even if they turn out not to be temporary takings, can work great hardship on those whose lives are put on hold to accommodate them. *Tahoe-Sierra Preservation Council v. Tahoe Regional Planning Agency*[159] is a case in point.

Beginning in the 1970s, the Tahoe Regional Planning Agency, created by the states of California and Nevada to plan land use around Lake Tahoe, began instituting a series of temporary moratoria on new construction to give it time to develop a comprehensive land-use plan. Aimed in large part at protecting the quality of the lake, the effect of the rolling moratoria was to deny development of their property to those who had not yet begun building. Starting in the early 1980s some 700 such owners sought relief. By the time the Supreme Court decided their case in 2002, 55 of the plaintiffs had died and many others had dropped out from sheer exhaustion, financial and emotional, their land still undeveloped.

Notwithstanding deprivations of use running for more than two decades, Justice Stevens, writing for a 6–3 Court, focused on only two moratoria running for 32 consecutive months during the 1980s. The plaintiffs argued, not surprisingly, that whenever government deprives them of all economically viable use of their property (*Lucas*), even temporarily (*First English*), it has taken that property. But Stevens dismissed that "categorical approach" in favor of the ever-malleable *Penn Central* balancing test. Pointing to "the 'denominator' question," he said that separating out the 32-month segment and then asking whether it had been taken in its entirety would ignore *Penn Central*'s admonition to focus on "the parcel as a whole."[160] Instead, "we are persuaded that the better approach to claims that a regulation has effected a temporary taking 'requires careful examination and weighing of all the relevant

---

[158]   First Eng. Evangelical Lutheran Church of Glendale v. County of Los Angeles, 210 Cal. App. 3d 1353, 1356 Cal. Rptr. 893, 894 (1989).
[159]   Tahoe-Sierra Pres. Council, Inc. v. Tahoe Reg'l Plan. Agency, 535 U.S. 302 (2002).
[160]   *Id.* at 331 (quoting Penn Cent. Transp. Co. v. New York City, 438 U.S. 104, 130–31).

circumstances.'"[161] And chief among those circumstances, it seems from the rest of Stevens's opinion, is the impact a compensation requirement would have on "prevailing practices:" it would impose "serious financial constraints on the planning process,"[162] he said. In fact, "the consensus in the planning community appears to be that moratoria, or 'interim development controls' as they are often called, are an essential tool of successful development."[163]

Tahoe was a complex case that required balancing the environmental interests of the community with the rights of landowners in the Tahoe basin. Unfortunately, the Court took it as an opportunity to cement the return of *Penn Central*'s incoherent balancing test, after a period during which it looked like the Court might be moving in a more principled direction. The result was to leave in place the allegedly deleterious uses of residents who had already developed their lots, while imposing the entire cost of protecting the environment on those who had not yet built their homes, rendering their investments nearly worthless. That distribution of benefits and burdens escaped the Court's majority, whose approach was essentially that of the planner.[164]

2. Eminent Domain and the Public Use Restraint. We turn now from government actions that take part of a person's property to actions that take the whole property, including title, through eminent domain, focusing on the third and fourth rationales outlined above: to reduce blight and to promote economic development. Recall that two problems arise here. First, the compensation owners normally receive is "market value"—sometimes not even that—whereas their losses are usually far greater. Ideally, "just compensation" should mean, given that the transaction is not voluntary for the owners, an amount that leaves them indifferent as to whether they receive the compensation or keep their property—in other words, what a private party would have to pay to induce owners to surrender their property. Short of that, they should receive compensation that reflects the full extent of their losses, including relocation expenses, business losses, sentimental value, and so forth.

Second, property is taken by government today not simply for "public use," the authorization found in the Takings Clause, but for "public benefit," a much

---

[161]   *Id.* at 335 (quoting Palazzolo v. Rhode Island, 533 U.S. 606, 636 (2001)).

[162]   *Id.* at 337.

[163]   *Id.* at 338.

[164]   For a critical analysis of the case from that perspective, see Richard A. Epstein, *The Ebbs and Flows in Takings Law: Reflections on the Lake Tahoe Case*, 2001–2002 CATO SUP. CT. REV 5. For a more recent temporary taking and physical invasion case where the owner prevailed, see Ark. Game & Fish Comm'n v. United States, 568 U.S. 23 (2012).

broader standard that opens the door for expansive use of eminent domain.[165] Indeed, given that there is virtually no public undertaking that cannot be said in some way to benefit the public, it is no standard at all. Courts have focused mainly on that issue, and so will we.

    a. Blight Reduction Cases. It was a 1954 case, *Berman v. Parker,*[166] that opened the door to an expansive reading of "public use." Before the Court was a classic "urban renewal" project, funded like so many others by massive infusions of federal money. Not only do such projects often destroy whole neighborhoods but, as Professor Ilya Somin has written, "[s]o many poor African Americans were dispossessed by urban renewal condemnations in the 1950s and 1960s that '[i]n cities across the country urban renewal came to be known as "Negro removal."'"[167] Under consideration in *Berman* was a comprehensive scheme Congress had enacted for clearing an area of the District of Columbia said to be "blighted." The plan authorized the acquisition of parcels by eminent domain for later sale to private parties. Yet the department store owned by the plaintiff could not be described as "blighted," which is one reason he fought to keep it.

    Writing for a unanimous Court, Justice William O. Douglas would have nothing of the owner's complaint. In fact, his opinion so perfectly captures the mind-set of the New Deal Court—except for new Chief Justice Earl Warren, every member had been appointed by either Franklin Roosevelt or Harry Truman—that it bears quoting at length:

> We deal, in other words, with what traditionally has been known as the police power. An attempt to define its reach or trace its outer limits is fruitless, for each case must turn on its own facts. The definition is essentially the product of legislative determinations addressed to the purposes of government, purposes neither abstractly nor historically capable of complete definition. Subject to specific constitutional limitations, when the legislature has spoken, the public interest has been declared in terms well-nigh conclusive. In such cases, the legislature, not the judiciary, is the main guardian of the public needs to be served by social legislation, whether it be Congress legislating concerning the District of Columbia or the States legislating concerning local affairs. This principle admits of no exception merely because the power of eminent domain is involved. The role of the judiciary

---

[165] See, for example, Nicole Stelle Garnett, *The Public-Use Question as a Takings Problem*, 71 Geo. Wash. L. Rev. 934 (2003).

[166] Berman v. Parker, 348 U.S. 26 (1954).

[167] Ilya Somin, *Robin Hood in Reverse: The Case against Taking Private Property for Economic Development*, Cato Inst. (Feb. 21, 2005) (citing Wendell E. Pritchett, *The "Public Menace" of Blight: Urban Renewal and the Private Uses of Eminent Domain*, 21 Yale L. & Pol'y Rev. 1 (2003)), https://www.cato.org/policy-analysis/robin-hood-reverse-case-against-taking-private-property-economic-development.

in determining whether that power is being exercised for a public purpose is an extremely narrow one.

Public safety, public health, morality, peace and quiet, law and order—these are some of the more conspicuous examples of the traditional application of the police power to municipal affairs. Yet they merely illustrate the scope of the power, and do not delimit it. Miserable and disreputable housing conditions may do more than spread disease and crime and immorality. They may also suffocate the spirit by reducing the people who live there to the status of cattle. They may indeed make living an almost insufferable burden. They may also be an ugly sore, a blight on the community which robs it of charm, which makes it a place from which men turn. The misery of housing may despoil a community as an open sewer may ruin a river.

We do not sit to determine whether a particular housing project is or is not desirable. The concept of the public welfare is broad and inclusive. The values it represents are spiritual as well as physical, aesthetic as well as monetary. It is within the power of the legislature to determine that the community should be beautiful as well as healthy, spacious as well as clean, well balanced as well as carefully patrolled. In the present case, the Congress and its authorized agencies have made determinations that take into account a wide variety of values. It is not for us to reappraise them. If those who govern the District of Columbia decide that the Nation's Capital should be beautiful as well as sanitary, there is nothing in the Fifth Amendment that stands in the way.

Once the object is within the authority of Congress, the right to realize it through the exercise of eminent domain is clear. For the power of eminent domain is merely the means to the end. Once the object is within the authority of Congress, the means by which it will be attained is also for Congress to determine. Here, one of the means chosen is the use of private enterprise for redevelopment of the area. Appellants argue that this makes the project a taking from one businessman for the benefit of another businessman. But the means of executing the project are for Congress, and Congress alone, to determine once the public purpose has been established.[168]

With the Court's deference to the political branches so complete—amounting virtually to judicial abdication—it is no wonder that "public use" ceased to be a serious restraint on eminent domain. In fact, 30 years after *Berman* was decided the Court would find "public use" satisfied by a Hawaii land reform plan that authorized the state to condemn private land and transfer title to tenants who had built or bought homes on the land under long-term ground leases.[169] Much like Douglas above, Justice Sandra Day O'Connor, writing again for a unanimous Court (Justice Thurgood Marshall took no part in the decision), said that "[t] he 'public use' requirement is thus coterminous with the scope of a sovereign's police powers,"[170] and those, as we've seen, have been found to be all but boundless. If that is so, then plainly the cover of "blight reduction" was no longer needed.

---

[168] Berman, 348 U.S. at 32–33 (citations omitted).
[169] Haw. Hous. Auth. v. Midkiff, 467 U.S. 229 (1984).
[170] *Id.* at 240.

b. Economic Development Cases. Given that boundless understanding of the police power, the move from blight reduction to economic development as a rationale for using eminent domain is no stretch at all. In fact, the two rationales are intimately connected, for here too, condemnation of whole neighborhoods for reasons of "economic development" usually means replacing "downscale" (sometimes "blighted") properties with "upscale" properties—not through voluntary market transactions but through the force of law.

The quintessential such case, perhaps, came in 1981 from the influential Michigan Supreme Court, *Poletown Neighborhood Council v. City of Detroit*.[171] To make way for a General Motors assembly plant—to build Cadillacs, no less—the city condemned a neighborhood of 4,200 residents, home to generations of Polish immigrants: 1,400 homes, 16 churches, 144 local businesses, several schools, everything, destroying "roots, relationships, solidarity, sense of place, and shared memory,"[172] as Harvard Law Professor Mary Ann Glendon put it. Yet the Michigan Supreme Court upheld the plan. Although the court cautioned, "[t]he power of eminent domain is restricted to furthering public uses *and purposes* and is not to be exercised without substantial proof that the public is primarily to be *benefited*,"[173] such "proof" is invariably speculative. Here, in fact, as nearly always is the case when such grand public-private partnerships supplant market forces, the jobs, increased tax revenue, and other economic benefits touted by the city establishment promoting the project never did materialize as promised.[174]

Given the seminal importance of *Poletown* as a model for other state courts, it was no small matter that in 2004 the Michigan Supreme Court revisited the issue of economic development condemnations, unanimously repudiating its *Poletown* decision in *County of Wayne v. Hathcock*.[175] *Poletown*, the court said, was "a radical departure from fundamental constitutional principles and

---

[171] Poletown Neighborhood Council v. City of Detroit, 410 Mich. 616, 304 N.W.2d 455 (1981).

[172] Mary Ann Glendon, RIGHTS TALK: THE IMPOVERISHMENT OF POLITICAL DISCOURSE 30 (1991).

[173] *Poletown*, 304 N.W.2d at 459 (emphasis added to indicate the court's understanding of "public use").

[174] Interestingly, it seems that General Motors did not initiate or even want the project, as is commonly supposed. Rather, the mayor of Detroit and the federal government, during the oil crisis and recession of 1979, were the principal proponents, and federal money was the lubricant. See William A. Fischel, *The Political Economy of Public Use in* Poletown: *How Federal Grants Encourage Excessive Use of Eminent Domain*, 2004 MICH. STATE L. REV. 929 (Winter 2004).

[175] County of Wayne v. Hathcock, 471 Mich. 445, 684 N.W.2d 765 (Mich. 2004).

this Court's eminent domain jurisprudence."[176] But if that reversal were not enough to give hope to the beleaguered property rights movement, just a month after *Hathcock* came down the U.S. Supreme Court decided to hear a closely watched economic development case from Connecticut, *Kelo v. City of New London*.[177] Since the Court had not taken a public-use case in years, speculation ran high, especially in light of *Hathcock*, that it was ready to revisit and rethink the issue. Alas, the opinion that emerged the following year showed no new thinking at all.[178]

Kelo was a classic redevelopment case involving a comprehensive government plan aimed a revitalizing a distressed part of a New England town that had seen better days. In conjunction with the Pfizer pharmaceutical company's promise to build a new research facility in New London, the city authorized a private development company to redevelop an adjacent 90-acre site by purchasing or acquiring by eminent domain the properties that were located there. The new hotel, stores, and residences planned for the site were to be leased back to private parties on completion of the project. And the usual rationales—employment, increased tax revenue, and the like—were offered in support of the scheme, which was financed originally by a state contribution of 73 million dollars.[179]

Susette Kelo and a few of her neighbors, with the support of the Institute for Justice, a non-profit libertarian litigation organization, decided to resist the city's effort to evict them from their homes. But Justice John Paul Stevens, writing for a 5–4 Court, found nothing wrong with transferring property from one private party to another as long as some "public purpose" justified it. Drawing from an idiosyncratic reading of early cases, he wrote that "when this Court began applying the Fifth Amendment to the States at the close of the 19th century, it embraced the broader and more natural interpretation of public use as 'public purpose.'"[180] And, echoing Justice Douglas in *Berman*, he concluded that "[f]or more than a century, our public use jurisprudence has wisely eschewed rigid formulas and intrusive scrutiny in favor of affording legislatures broad latitude in determining what public needs justify the use of the takings power."[181] In dissent, Justice O'Connor, whose *Midkiff* opinion Stevens employed, attempted to distinguish the two cases; but her main concern was

---

[176] *Id.* at 787.
[177] Kelo v. City of New London, 268 Conn. 1, 843 A. 2d 500 (2004).
[178] Kelo v. City of New London, 125 S. Ct. 2655 (2005). For a critical review of the case, see Ely, *supra* note 6, at 53–65.
[179] Kate Moran, *With Vacant Lots and Cash Needs, NLDC Reaches a Crucial Juncture*, THE DAY, Jan. 18, 2004, at A1.
[180] *Kelo*, 125 S. Ct. at 2662.
[181] *Id.* at 2664.

that "[u]nder the banner of economic development, all private property is now vulnerable to being taken and transferred to another private owner, so long as it might be upgraded—*i.e.*, given to an owner who will use it in a way that the legislature deems more beneficial to the public—in the process."[182]

The public reaction to the *Kelo* decision was immediate, intense, and widespread, surprising even those who were close to the case—all the more surprising because, in truth, the Court had done little more than continue its long line of cases weakening property rights. But the idea that government could take a person's home or business and transfer it to another who might, in the government's eye, make better use of it, focused the public mind in a way that previous cases seem not to have done. Federal and state legislators ran to the microphones, hearings were called, and bills to address the problem were introduced. It seems not to have occurred to most that those very same legislators who had enacted the economic development schemes in the first place were the problem.[183] Nevertheless, to date, some 47 states have strengthened their protections against eminent domain abuse, either through legislation, constitutional amendment, or state supreme court decisions, all aimed at limiting economic development takings.[184] On July 26, 2006, for example, the Ohio Supreme Court, echoing the Michigan Supreme Court two years earlier, handed down a ringing unanimous rebuke to a local municipality, holding that "economic or financial benefit alone is insufficient to satisfy the public-use requirement" of the Ohio Constitution, and adding that "the courts owe no deference to a legislative finding that [a] proposed taking will provide financial benefit to a community."[185]

In the limited realm of full eminent domain condemnations, therefore, there is a glimmer of hope for owners, at least at the state level. But notice that state legislatures and courts are coming at the issue from the back, as it were. These are not head-on challenges to the expansive reading of the police power, with a substantial burden placed on the government to justify its actions. In fact, the blight rationale for eminent domain remains alive in most of the bills and court decisions. What we see, rather, is the economic development rationale carved out, with heightened scrutiny required in those cases. That is a start—a move

---

182   *Id.* at 2671 (O'Connor, J., dissenting).
183   See Roger Pilon, Testimony in the U.S. House of Representatives, Strengthening the Ownership of Private Property Act of 2005: Hearing on H.R. 3405 Before the H. Comm. On Agriculture, 109th Cong. (Sept. 7, 2005), https:// www.cato.org/testimony/strengthening-ownership-private-property-act-2005.
184   For details, see Eminent Domain, INST. FOR JUST., http://www.castlecoalition.org/legislation/index.html.
185   City of Norwood v. Horney, No. 2005–0227, 2006 Ohio LEXIS 2170, at *69 (Ohio July 26, 2006).

in the right direction—but there is much more to do before we can say that property rights have the status of human rights.

3. Procedural Justice. Dispiriting as the Court's substantive treatment of property rights may be, there is perhaps no clearer indication of the second-class status of those rights than can be found in the Court's procedural law. As outlined earlier, the root of the problem is the modern presumption against use, occasioned by the rise of the regulatory state and the need to obtain a permit, or several permits, before use, changes in use, or development can begin.[186] If the agency issuing permits is disinclined to see change, as it often is, the grueling process of trying to obtain one can take years, exhausting most owners long before it is finished. But only after a "final denial" has been issued can the owner go to state court to seek compensation for a taking. And, until very recently, only after compensation has been denied may the owner appeal to a federal court.[187] Once he satisfies that two-prong test, however, he will then find that the federal Full Faith and Credit Act,[188] encompassing *res judicata*, precludes his case being heard in federal court.

The two-prong test emerged in 1985 from *Williamson County Regional Planning Commission v. Hamilton Bank*,[189] another complex factual and procedural case. In brief, in 1973 the bank's predecessor in interest, a Tennessee land developer, obtained the planning commission's approval for residential development under then existing zoning regulations. But in 1977 the county rewrote its zoning law, reducing the allowable density in the process, which the commission applied against the developer in 1979. Thereafter the commission disapproved development of the remainder of the tract, whereupon the developer brought suit in federal district court, alleging a taking without compensation. When the Supreme Court took the case, it declined to address the merits the complex litigation below had addressed. Instead, the Court held that the bank's claim was not "ripe." Although the developer's plan had been rejected (under the new regulations), he had not sought variances and so had not obtained a "final decision."[190] Moreover, the Court held the bank's

---

[186]   Thus, at issue here are "as applied" challenges. Facial challenges to statutes will be entertained by federal courts, where they will almost always fail due to the Court's presumption of constitutionality.

[187]   See Timothy V. Kassouni, *The Ripeness Doctrine and the Judicial Regulation of Constitutionally Protected Property Rights*, 29 CAL. W. L. REV. 1 (1992). But see *infra* note 198.

[188]   THE NATION, *supra* note 63.

[189]   Williamson Cnty. Reg'l Plan. Comm'n v. Hamilton Bank, 473 U.S. 172 (1985).

[190]   *Id.* at 190–94.

claim premature because the developer had not sought compensation under an inverse condemnation action in state court.[191]

The principle underlying ripeness rules is sound enough: appellate courts should avoid premature adjudication. But in practice the rules work great injustice in regulatory takings cases—due, again, to the way the presumption on behalf of the government plays out in fact. Recalcitrant planning and zoning agencies are notorious, for example, for stalling and for avoiding issuing a "final decision." Under that prong of the *Williamson County* test the owner must apply for a specific use; if rejected, he has to apply again for another specific use, responding to agency comments in the process. Or he may ask for a variance—an exception from a rule following a denial based on the rule— all of which can go on forever. Planners are skilled at delay. In one Supreme Court opinion Justice William Brennan cited a California city attorney advising fellow attorneys: "[i]f all else fails, merely amend the regulation and start over again."[192]

The cases exhibiting such delays are legion. Recall *Tahoe-Sierra* above,[193] which went on for over two decades. In *Del Monte Dunes*,[194] also mentioned above, the U.S. Supreme Court brought an end to a struggle that had gone on for 18 years, during which time the company had tried repeatedly to obtain permission to build homes. Although the zoning law allowed more than 1,000 homes to be built on the company's property, in 1981 the company applied to build only 344 homes. What followed was a long history of rejected proposals, each with fewer and fewer homes, forced exactions, and finally an agreement for 190 homes. But that agreement was later rejected because the land was then said to be habitat for an endangered butterfly. Fortunately, this is a case the Court got right, in 1999, albeit with multiple complex opinions.[195]

But again, even if an owner does make it through all the *Williamson County* hurdles, when he finally gets to federal court he will find, even if the state supreme court has wrongly denied him compensation, that the federal court's doors are closed by the federal Full Faith and Credit Act. In 2005 the

---

[191]   *Id.* at 194–95.

[192]   San Diego Gas & Elec. Co. v. City of San Diego, 450 U.S. 621, 655 n.22 (quoting Longtin, *Avoiding and Defending Constitutional Attacks on Land Use Regulations (Including Inverse Condemnation)*, in 38B NIMLO [NAT'L INST. OF MUN. L. OFFICERS] MUN. L. REVI. 192–93 (1975)).

[193]   Tahoe-Sierra Pres. Council, Inc. v. Tahoe Reg'l Plan. Agency, 535 U.S. 302 (2002).

[194]   City of Monterey v. Del Monte Dunes at Monterey, Ltd., 526 U.S. 687 (1999).

[195]   For a brief account of the case, see Eagle, *supra* note 133, at 19. For many examples of property rights horror stories, see TIMOTHY SANDEFUR, CORNERSTONE OF LIBERTY: PROPERTY RIGHTS IN THE 21ST CENTURY (2006).

Supreme Court visited that issue in *San Remo Hotel v. City and County of San Francisco*,[196] here again an exceedingly complex case that has run on for years. Around 1990 the plaintiffs, owners of a partly residential hotel in San Francisco, petitioned the city for a permit to operate as a tourist hotel. The city granted the permit, but only on several conditions, including payment to the city of a $567,000 "conversion fee." Lengthy administrative and judicial proceedings followed in both state and federal courts, the plaintiffs alleging a regulatory taking without compensation. Having finally satisfied the *Williamson County* two-prong ripeness test after losing the compensation claim in state court, the plaintiffs made it at last to the Supreme Court, where the Court agreed to decide the narrow question of whether it should grant an exception to the Full Faith and Credit Act and allow federal court review of Takings Clause claims.

Justice Stevens, writing for a unanimous Court on the holding, declined to grant an exception without a congressional change in the law. More interesting, however, was the concurrence of Chief Justice Rehnquist for himself and three other justices. Although he agreed with the Court's holding, he urged the Court to revisit the second prong of *Williamson County*, an opinion he had joined in 1985, because "further reflection and experience" had led him "to think that the justifications for its state-litigation requirement are suspect, while its impact on takings plaintiffs is dramatic."[197] And he added that the Court had not explained why it should "hand authority over federal takings claims to state courts ... while allowing plaintiffs to proceed directly to federal court in cases involving, for example, challenges to municipal land-use regulations based on the First Amendment, or the Equal Protection Clause."[198] We have here, in short, just one more example of the Court's second-class treatment of property rights under the Fifth Amendment's Takings Clause.[199]

---

[196]   San Remo Hotel v. City of San Francisco, 125 S. Ct. 2491 (2005).
[197]   *Id.* at 2509–10 (Rehnquist, C.J., concurring).
[198]   *Id.* at 2509 (Rehnquist, C.J., concurring) (citations omitted).
[199]   For a fuller treatment of *San Remo*, see Ely, *supra* note 6, at 66–69. For a discussion of yet another of the government's procedural ploys—the so-called Tucker Act Shuffle whereby plaintiffs are bounced between the U.S. Court of Federal Claims, if they are seeking compensation for a *federal* taking, and a U.S. district court, if they are seeking an injunction against a federal taking—see Roger J. Marzulla and Nancie G. Marzulla, *Regulatory Takings in the United States Claims Court: Adjusting the Burdens That in Fairness and Equity Ought to Be Borne by Society as a Whole*, 40 CATHOLIC UNIV. L. REV. 566 (1991).
      Fortunately, in its October 2018 term, in *Knick v. Township of Scott, Pennsylvania*, the Supreme Court revisited and then overturned its 1985 *Williamson County* decision. Knick v. Twp. of Scott, 139 S. Ct. 2162 (2019). See

CONCLUSION

Because language has its limits, a constitution that aims at striking a principled balance between powers granted and liberties retained can go only so far in achieving that end. It is crucial, therefore, that when judges interpret and apply constitutional language to cases before them, they do so with an eye to the larger theory behind the language and the principles the theory entails, as reflected in both the document's text and as a whole.

As this review of the Supreme Court's treatment of property rights has shown, we Americans have grown ever less conversant with the principles our Constitution was meant to secure, to say nothing of the theory behind those principles. The police power especially has been severed from its roots in the theory of natural rights, becoming largely a reflection of the will of those wielding political power at any given time. The cumulative effect is a growing body of public law that in far too many cases trumps the private law of property and contract, reducing it to a subsidiary role in the American legal system. Yet several of the Court's more recent decisions offer hope for a gradual return to America's founding principles.

Ilya Somin, Knick v. Township of Scott: *Ending a Catch-22 that Barred Takings Cases from Federal Court,* 2018–2019 Cato Sup. Ct. Rev. 153.

2. The right to use private property

Ilya Somin

INTRODUCTION

The right to use is a central element of property rights. Indeed, most property loses the vast bulk of its value if the owner is not allowed to use it, as opposed to merely excluding others from it. However, it is an under-analyzed aspect of the right to private property protected by the Takings Clause of the Fifth Amendment, which requires the government to pay "just compensation" whenever it takes "private property" for public use.[1] Modern Supreme Court jurisprudence provides only modest protection for the right to use and does not treat it as a major distinct element of property rights.

This chapter makes the case for a strong right to use under the Takings Clause. Part I outlines the importance of the right to use property in the real world. For most types of property, that right is an essential element of the "bundle of sticks" possessed by the owner. This is particularly true of both residential and commercial property in land. But it is also true for most personal property, and for land used for conservation purposes.

Part II makes the originalist case for a strong right to use under the Takings Clause. William Blackstone—a major influence on early American conceptions of property law and on the leading American Founders—regarded the right to use as a central element of property rights. The same was true of leading court decisions and legal theorists around the time when the Takings Clause and the rest of the Bill of Rights became "incorporated" against state and local governments in 1868. That is significant for theories of originalism that regard the original meaning of 1868 as the one relevant for applications of the Bill of Rights to the states.

Part II also gives a brief overview of the "police power" exception to Takings Clause liability and its relevance to the right to use. That exception would deny compensation in cases where the use restricted poses a significant threat to public health or safety. But it could not do so in other situations. The

---

[1]   U.S. Const. Art. V.

government could, however, still restrict use if it were willing to pay compensation to the owner.

Elsewhere, Joshua Braver and I have argued that the Takings Clause should also be interpreted as protecting the right to use against most exclusionary zoning regulations that restrict the amount and type of housing that can be constructed on private property.[2] In this chapter, I only focus on the original meaning and argue that it protects the right to use even beyond residential uses. I hope to consider living constitution theories' relationship to a broader right to use in future publications.

I.   THE CENTRALITY OF THE RIGHT TO USE

The right to use is a central component of property rights. Indeed, it is probably the most important element of the "bundle of sticks" for most properties. Scholars and judges often understand ownership as a "bundle of sticks" of different rights, such as the right to exclude trespassers, the right to transfer property, and others.[3] Of these sticks, the right to use is surely among the most important. In many situations, it is probably more important than any other stick.

For purposes of clarification, I define the right to use property as the prerogative to employ it for whatever purposes the owner chooses, subject to constraints created by the property and liberty rights of others. In the case of real property in land, that includes using it for commercial or residential purposes, building new structures on it, and more. It can also include relatively passive uses, such as creating a conservation area or simply enjoying peace and quiet.

The bundle of sticks associated with "personal" property (usually understood as property rights in movable and intangible objects),[4] also includes a

---

[2]   See Joshua Braver and Ilya Somin, *The Constitutional Case Against Exclusionary Zoning*, 103 TEX. L. REV 1 (2024), available at https://papers.ssrn.com/sol3/papers.cfm?abstract_id=4728312.

[3]   See, for example, Kaiser Aetna v. United States, 444 U.S. 164, 176 (1979) (referring to "sticks in the bundle of rights that are commonly characterized as property") and United States v. Craft, 535 U.S. 274, 278 (2002) ("A common idiom describes property as a 'bundle of sticks'"). On the "bundle of sticks" metaphor to describe property rights, see, for example, Robert C. Ellickson, *Two Cheers for the Bundle-of-Sticks Metaphor, Three Cheers for Merrill and Smith*, 8 ECON JOURNAL WATCH 215 (2011), available at https://papers.ssrn.com/sol3/papers.cfm?abstract_id=1977286; for criticism, see, for example, Thomas W. Merrill and Henry Smith, *What Happened to Property in Law and Economics*, 111 YALE LAW JOURNAL 357 (2001).

[4]   Cf., Michael Bridge et al., THE LAW OF PERSONAL PROPERTY ch. 1 (3rd ed. 2023); Michael Bridge, PERSONAL PROPERTY LAW ch. 1 (4th ed. 2015) (describing

right to use. For example, the owner of a tool has a right to use it to make or repair things. The owner of clothing has the right to wear it. And so on. In this chapter, however, I focus primarily on real property in land.

A.   The Value of the Right to Use

The fundamental importance of the right to use should not be hard to grasp. For most property owners, most of the time, the right to use is the main benefit of having the property to begin with. Thus, the main advantage of owning residential property is the right to live there or to rent it out to tenants for the same purpose. For commercial property, it is the right to use it to operate a business of one sort or another (or, again, to rent it out).

This is also true of less conventional property rights. For example, the main value of extraction rights—the right to mine oil, precious metals, and other valuable deposits—is the right to use the property for mining. Even a "passive" employment of property, such as for conservation easements,[5] still derives its value from the right to use. In that situation, the owner of the easement is using the property to provide a protected habitat for wildlife.

The significance of the right to use goes far beyond its importance to individual property owners. Restrictions on that right have an enormous impact on society more broadly. In recent American history, that is most obvious in the case of exclusionary zoning, which limits the types of housing that can be built in vast areas of the country.[6] Such zoning restrictions greatly increase housing costs and prevent millions of people from "moving to opportunity," thereby impeding economic growth and innovation.[7] Exclusionary zoning also has a

---

definitions of personal property).

[5]   See Federico Cheever and Nancy McLaughlin, *An Introduction to Conservation Easements in the United States: A Simple Concept and a Complicated Mosaic of Law,* I JOURNAL OF LAW, PROPERTY, AND SOCIETY 107 (2015) (overview of conservation easements and their uses).

[6]   For a recent overview, see Braver and Somin, EXCLUSIONARY ZONING.

[7]   See, for example: Richard D. Kahlenberg, EXCLUDED: HOW SNOB ZONING, NIMBYISM, AND CLASS BIAS BUILD THE WALLS WE DON'T SEE (2023); Robert C. Ellickson, AMERICA'S FROZEN NEIGHBORHOODS: THE ABUSE OF ZONING (2022); James Burling, NOWHERE TO LIVE: THE HIDDEN STORY OF AMERICA'S HOUSING CRISIS (2024); Council of Economic Advisers, ECONOMIC REPORT OF THE PRESIDENT ch. 4 (2024) (extensive review of relevant literature and evidence); Bryan Caplan, BUILD, BABY, BUILD: THE SCIENCE AND ETHICS OF HOUSING REGULATION (2024); Philip Hoxie, et al., *Moving to Density: Half a Century of Housing Costs and Wage Premia from Queens to King Salmon*, 222 J. PUB. ECON. 17 (2023) (finding zoning restrictions greatly reduce labor mobility); Edward Pinto and Tobias Peter, *How Government Policy Made Housing Expensive and*

long history of being used to exclude the poor and racial ethnic minorities from areas populated by relatively affluent whites.[8] A recent study estimates that the abolition of zoning restrictions in seven major US urban areas would increase per capita US output by almost 8 percent.[9]

Other restrictions on the right to use also often have major consequences, as in the case of the right to use property for commercial rather than residential purposes. In addition, they can have a major impact in reducing economic growth and preventing property from being used for the most valuable available purposes.[10]

Scarce, and How Unleashing Market Forces Can Address It, 25 CITYSCAPE 123 (2023) (summarizing extensive evidence and history); Edward Glaeser and Joseph Gyourko, *The Economic Implications of Housing Supply,* 32 J. ECON. PERSPECTIVES 3 (2018) (extensive literature review); Vicki Been, et al., *Supply Skepticism Revisited,* NYU Law & Econ. Res. Paper 24. 12 (2023), available at https://papers.ssrn.com/sol3/papers.cfm?abstract_id=4629628 (literature review and critique of reasons for "supply skepticism"); David Schleicher, *Stuck! The Law and the Economics of Residential Stability,* 127 YALE L. J. 78 (2018); Joseph Gyourko, et al., *The Local Residential Land Use Regulatory Environment Across U.S. Housing Markets: Evidence from a New Wharton Index,* NBER Working Paper No. 26573 (Dec. 2019), available at https://www.nber.org/papers/w26573; Ezra Rosser, *The Euclid Proviso,* 96 WASH. L. REV 811, 824–49 (2021) (reviewing extensive evidence); Edward Glaeser, *Reforming Land Use Regulations,* Brookings Institution, Apr. 24, 2017, available at https://www.brookings.edu/research/reforming-land-use-regulations/amp/; Gilles Duranton and Diego Puga, *Urban Growth and its Aggregative Implications,* NBER Working Paper No. 26592 (Dec. 2019); and Alex Horowitz and Ryan Canavan, *More Flexible Zoning Helps Contain Rising Rents,* Pew Research Ctr., Apr. 17, 2023, available at https://www.pewtrusts.org/en/research-and-analysis/articles/2023/04/17/more-flexible-zoning-helps-contain-rising-rents.

[8] For extensive overviews see Richard Rothstein, THE COLOR OF LAW: THE FORGOTTEN HISTORY OF HOW OUR GOVERNMENT SEGREGATED AMERICA (2017); Jessica Trounstine, SEGREGATION BY DESIGN 85–100 (2018).

[9] Gilles Duranton and Diego Puga, *Urban Growth and its Aggregate Implications,* unpublished paper, June 2023, available at https://diegopuga.org/papers/hcgrowth.pdf.

[10] See Fil Babalievsky, et al., *The Impact of Commercial Real Estate Regulations on U.S. Output,* NBER Working Paper No. 31895 (Nov. 2023), available at https://www.nber.org/papers/w31895.

B.   Why Use May be Even More Fundamental than Other Elements of Ownership

The right to use is so foundational that it may well be more significant than other attributes of ownership, including the right to exclude and the right to transfer property rights to a new owner.

The right to exclude is often seen as the "sine qua non" of ownership, as famed property scholar Thomas Merrill put it.[11] "Give someone the right to exclude others from a valued resource," he avows, "and you give them property."[12] Deny someone the right to excludeand they do not have property. William Blackstone famously described "the right of property" as "that sole and despotic dominion which one man claims and exercises over the external things of the world, in total exclusion of the right of any other individual in the universe."[13] This is usually taken to imply the centrality of the right to exclude, though Blackstone stopped short of saying it is more important than other attributes of property.

The US Supreme Court has also at times indicated that the right to exclude is central to property rights, calling it "'one of the most treasured' rights of property ownership,"[14] asserting that it is "universally held to be a fundamental element of the property right," and "one of the most essential sticks in the bundle of rights that are commonly characterized as property."[15] This doesn't quite say that the right to exclude is more important than any other element of property, but it comes close.

The right to exclude does indeed have great importance. But it is nonetheless generally less fundamental than the right to use. Consider why it is that owners want to exclude those who would enter without permission. In most cases, it is because they want to protect their right to use the property as they see fit. For example, a residential property cannot be used as intended if trespassers can disturb the occupants anytime they want. The same goes for most commercial uses. If trespassers can disrupt the operations of a store, restaurant, or factory, its value may be greatly diminished or even totally destroyed.

The same is true even of "passive" uses, such as conservation. If, for example, I own a conservation easement for the purpose of protecting wildlife, the right to exclude hunters and others who might kill or disturb the protected

---

[11]   Thomas W. Merrill, *Property and the Right to Exclude*, 77 NEB. L. REV 730, 730 (1998).

[12]   Id.

[13]   2 William Blackstone, COMMENTARIES ON THE LAWS OF ENGLAND 2 (1766).

[14]   Cedar Point Nursery v. Hassid, 594 U.S. 139, 149 (2021).

[15]   Kaiser Aetna v. United States, 444 U.S. 164, 176, 179–80 (1979).

animals is important to me only insofar as it protects the right to use the land for the purpose I intend.

In this way, the value of the right to exclude largely arises from its function in protecting the owner's right to use. The former has little value without the latter. To be sure, if I am forbidden to use my land myself, I might still derive some value from a right to exclude, as people might pay me for permission to enter. But that is only likely to be true if they have some use for that right, even if I do not, which in turn means they would be using the property. For example, perhaps they might pay the owner of an ocean-side property to come on the land to see the view or enjoy the fresh air.

What is true of the right to exclude is also true of the right to transfer, which is also often seen as a key element of property, though usually not to the same extent as the right to exclude.[16] As famed judge and law and economics scholar Richard Posner puts it, property should generally be "freely transferable" in order to "facilitate the transfer of resources from less to more valuable uses."[17]

As Posner suggests, the right to transfer derives its value from the fact that it enables the property to be acquired by those who have "more valuable uses" for it. Without the right to use, the right to transfer—like the right to use— would have little value. When people acquire property, they generally do so because they want to use it, or transfer it again to someone else who does.

There are situations where people want to exercise the right to exclude or the right to transfer for reasons other than facilitating use. For example, we might exclude some would-be guests out of spite, or as a means of pressuring them to do something unrelated to the property, as such. Similarly, a transfer might be undertaken for non-use purposes, such as rewarding a friend or relative— though in such cases, its value to the recipient is still a function of the right to use that he or she acquires.

In sum, the right to use is probably the most fundamental and valuable aspect of property rights. Other parts of the "bundle of sticks"—like the right to exclude and the right to transfer—derive most of their value from facilitating use. Without the right to use, the rights of exclusion and transfer are largely empty shells. They protect an asset that has little or no value.

Despite its enormous significance, modern Supreme Court Takings Clause jurisprudence offers little protection for the right to use. Most restrictions on use are evaluated under the Court's 1978 *Penn Central* decision, which sets out three factors that must be weighed in determining whether a regulatory action

---

[16] For an overview, see, for example, Michael D. Kirby, *Restraints on Alienation: Placing a 13th Century Doctrine in 21st Century Perspective*, 40 BAYLOR L. REV. 413 (1988) ("Without doubt, the concept of free alienability is a cornerstone of modern Anglo-American civilization").

[17] Richard A. Posner, ECONOMIC ANALYSIS OF LAW 75 (6th Ed. 2003).

that doesn't involve a physical invasion or occupation of property qualifies as a taking: "[t]he economic impact of the regulation on the claimant," the "extent to which the regulation has interfered with distinct investment-backed expectations," and the "character of the government action."[18] Significantly, none of the three factors is dispositive by itself.

Penn Central cases are often difficult to evaluate because of the vagueness of the criteria and the lack of clear guidance on how to weigh them against each other. Nonetheless, courts generally apply the test in ways that favor the government.[19] In 2002, the Supreme Court indicated that the *Penn Central* test had become the "polestar" of its regulatory takings jurisprudence largely because it shielded from judicial invalidation "numerous practices that have long been considered permissible exercises of the police power."[20]

By contrast, the right to exclude gets much stronger protection. In *Cedar Point Nursery v. Hassid* (2021), the Supreme Court ruled that even temporary physical intrusions on property are *per se* takings, automatically requiring compensation.[21] That is also the longstanding rule for permanent physical occupations,[22] and for regulations that deprive the owner of "all economically beneficial or productive use" of his property.[23]

This relative judicial neglect of the right to use should be reconsidered.

Penn Central built in part on the Supreme Court's 1926 ruling in *Euclid v. Ambler Realty Co.*,[24] which upheld exclusionary zoning against a challenge based on the Due Process Clause of the Fourteenth Amendment. While *Euclid* did not directly address the Takings Clause, it has traditionally been seen as a precedent blocking judicial review of zoning more generally.[25]

---

[18]   Penn Central Transp. Co. v. City of New York, 438 U.S. 104, 123 (1978).

[19]   See, for example, Eric R. Claeys, *The Penn Central Test and Tensions in Liberal Property Theory*, 30 HARV. ENV. L. REV. 339, 340, 344 (2006) (arguing that the majority of the Court's justices apply the *Penn Central* test in a way that is generally deferential to the government and noting that the "conventional wisdom" among "land-use lawyers" interprets the Court's application of the test that way); Robert Meltz, *Takings Law Today: A Primer for the Perplexed*, 34 ECOLOGY L.Q. 307, 333 (2007) (noting that property owners rarely prevail in the Supreme Court under the *Penn Central* test).

[20]   Tahoe-Sierra Pres. Council v. Tahoe Reg'l Planning Agency, 535 U.S. 302, 326 n.23 (2002) (quotation omitted).

[21]   594 U.S. 139 (2021).

[22]   Loretto v. Teleprompter CATV Corp., 458 U.S. 419, 426 (1982).

[23]   Lucas v. S. Carolina Coastal Council, 505 U.S. 1003, 1015 (1992).

[24]   272 U.S. 365 (1926).

[25]   For a discussion of Euclid and its impact, see, for example, Braver and Somin, EXCLUSIONARY ZONING, at 6–9.

II.   THE RIGHT TO USE AND THE ORIGINAL MEANING OF THE TAKINGS CLAUSE[26]

In this part, I outline reasons why the original meaning of the Takings Clause of the Fifth Amendment protects a substantial right to use property, not just a right to exclude trespassers or to prevent the government from physically appropriating the land. Modern originalists disagree on whether the relevant original understanding of provisions of the Bill of Rights applied against the states is that of 1791 or 1868. I do not attempt to resolve that dispute here.[27] Instead, I consider both periods. Both suggest that the relevant property rights included a right to use, not merely a right against physical seizure of property by the state. And any plausible right to use surely includes a right to build housing. This conclusion is relevant not only for claims that use rights are left unprotected because of a narrow definition of "property," but also for those who claim that the meaning of "take" encompasses only physical acquisitions or occupations.[28]

The right to use, protected by the original meaning of the Takings Clause, is not completely unlimited. It is subject to the "police power" exception for measures that protect the public against significant threats to health and safety. Although the police power exception has never been precisely defined, it generally applies to regulations that protect against significant threats to health and safety, such as fire, flooding, environmental harms, and disease.

A.   The Original Meaning of 1791

The iconic definition of "property" known to Founding-era American jurists was that of William Blackstone. As we have seen, Blackstone emphasized the

---

[26]   Some elements of this part are adapted from Braver and Somin, EXCLUSIONARY ZONING.

[27]   Focusing on 1791 is the more traditional approach. For the view that 1868 is the relevant timeframe, see, for example, Akhil Reed Amar, THE BILL OF RIGHTS: CREATION AND RECONSTRUCTION chs. 7–12 (1998); and Michael Rappaport, *Originalism and Regulatory Takings: Why the Fifth Amendment May Not Protect Against Regulatory Takings, But the Fourteenth Amendment May,* 45 SAN DIEGO LAW REVIEW 729 (2008).

[28]   See, for example, John F. Hart, *Colonial Land Use Law and its Significance for Modern Takings Doctrine,* 109 HARV. L. REV. 1252 (1996); John F. Hart, *Land Use Law in the Early Republic and the Original Meaning of the Takings Clause,* 94 Nw. U. L. REV. 1099 (2000) [hereinafter Hart, *Original Meaning*]; William Treanor, *The Original Understanding of the Takings Clause and the Political Process,* 95 COLUM. L. REV 782, 799 (1995).

importance of the right to exclude.[29] But he also famously wrote that "[t]he third absolute right, inherent in every Englishman, is that of property: which consists in the free use, enjoyment, and disposal of all his acquisitions, without any control or diminution, save only by the laws of the land."[30] The qualification that property might be limited by the "law of the land" may be seen as potentially nullifying the right to "use" in any situation where the state has enacted a law restricting it. But to the extent that this qualification nullifies takings liability as applied to "use," it equally does so with respect to "enjoyment" and every other aspect of property, as defined by Blackstone here. Such a thoroughgoing pure "positivist" theory of property rights was recently unanimously repudiated by the Supreme Court in *Tyler v. Hennepin County*, where the Court ruled that state law is "one important source of property rights ... But state law cannot be the only source. Otherwise, a State could sidestep the Takings Clause by disavowing traditional property interests in assets it wishes to appropriate."[31]

John Locke, whose understanding of property rights was a major influence on many thinkers of the Founding era, famously argued that the right to property arose from "*appropriation* of any parcel of *Land*, by improving it."[32] And, once appropriated through "improvement," the owner could continue further construction and improvement. If improving previously unowned land creates a property right, the owner logically has a right to make further improvements now that he or she has acquired the land. Such additional improvements might even further cement the owner's rights over the land.

Blackstone's definition of "property" as including "use" was widely cited by jurists and framers of the Constitution.[33] For example, James Wilson, a key framer of the Constitution and later a Supreme Court justice, described property as the "right to possess, to use, and to dispose of a thing."[34] James Madison, the primary framer of the Takings Clause,[35] advocated an even

---

[29] See discussion in Section I.B.

[30] 1 William Blackstone, COMMENTARIES 134 (1765).

[31] 598 U.S. 631, 638 (2023) (quotation omitted).

[32] John Locke, *Second Treatise on Government* ch. 5 § 33 (1689) (emphasis added). On the influence of Lockean property theory in the Founding era, see, for example, Johnathan O'Neill, *Property Rights and the American Founding: An Overview*, 38 J. SUPREME COURT HISTORY 309, 310–22 (2013) (summarizing its impact).

[33] Eric Claeys, *Takings, Regulations, and Natural Property Rights*, 88 CORNELL L. REV 1549, 1567–68 (2003).

[34] 2 THE WORKS OF JAMES WILSON 711 (Robert G. McCloskey, ed. 1967).

[35] On Madison's key role in drafting and enacting the Takings Clause, see Akhil Reed Amar, THE BILL OF RIGHTS: CREATION AND RECONSTRUCTION (1998), 77–78.

broader definition of property rights in his famous 1792 essay "On Property." After quoting Blackstone, he wrote that "[i]n its larger and juster meaning," the term "embraces every thing to which a man may attach a value and have a right; and which leaves to every one else the like advantage."[36] That surely encompasses the right to use and build.

In the 1790s, as today, building housing was a crucial ordinary aspect of the "use" of property, as also were a wide variety of commercial uses. Indeed, in a nation with a rapidly growing population, new housing construction and the expansion of commerce were especially important. If the right to "use" was part of the definition of "property" protected by the Takings Clause, using land to build housing and engage in commerce was part of the right to use.

In introducing what became the Bill of Rights to Congress, James Madison originally included a preamble stating that "Government is instituted and ought to be exercised for the benefit of the people; which consists in the enjoyment of life and liberty, with the right of acquiring and *using* property."[37] The preamble never became part of the Constitution and is not binding law. But, as Andrew Gold points out, it "suggests that Madison believed his proposed Bill of Rights would function to protect the right of using property, and by implication, this meant the Takings Clause would help to protect that right where regulations were concerned."[38]

These points have implications for arguments about the meaning of "take" as well as those focused on the meaning of "property." The Takings Clause would provide little or no protection for Madison's "right of acquiring and using property" if it were limited to physical invasions and appropriations.[39] In that event, the government could abrogate or even completely eliminate those rights simply by enacting regulations forbidding transfer and use, even in the absence of any physical seizure or invasion. As Laurence Tribe puts it, "telling [a property owner] 'you can keep it, but you can't use it' — is at times

---

[36] James Madison, *Property* [1792], in THE FOUNDERS CONSTITUTION, VOL. 1 (Philip Kurland and Ralph Lerner eds., 1987), 598. It is not entirely clear what Madison meant by "leaves to every one else the like advantage." But presumably, it requires that each person must allow others to exercise similar control over their own property.

[37] 1 ANNALS OF CONGRESS 433 (Joseph Gales ed., 1789) (emphasis added).

[38] Andrew S. Gold, *Regulatory Takings and Original Intent: The Direct, Physical Takings Thesis "Goes Too Far,"* 49 AM. U. L. REV. 181, 195 (1999).

[39] 1 ANNALS OF CONGRESS 433 (Joseph Gales ed., 1789).

indistinguishable, in ordinary terms, from grabbing it and handing it over to someone else."[40]

Some prominent scholars have nonetheless argued that the 1791 original meaning of the Takings Clause encompasses only a right against physical appropriation of property by the state.[41] They contend that extensive regulation of property rights by state and local governments undercuts the notion that the Takings Clause could apply to restrictions on use.

However, the Takings Clause initially applied only to the federal government—which may not have even had a power of eminent domain except in federal territories—and therefore there was little occasion to use it to constrain state and local takings.[42] This point undercuts claims that state and local regulations during the colonial period and early Republic delineate the scope of the Takings Clause protection for property rights.[43] In addition, as Nicole Garnett has emphasized, "unlike many other provisions of the Constitution, the Takings Clause had no colonial or British antecedents."[44] This makes it difficult to infer its scope from prior and contemporaneous practices.[45] It is a mistake to assume that any forms of state regulation prevalent in the colonial era or early Republic were necessarily immune from takings liability, if enacted by a jurisdiction subject to the Fifth Amendment, which—until incorporation—only constrained the federal government. Moreover, the fact that some uncompensated restrictions were permitted in order to protect the health, safety, and morals of the public, under the police power, does not suggest that all restrictions on use were exempt from takings liability. The natural rights understanding adopted from Blackstone and Locke was understood to allow uncompensated restrictions in cases of threats to the public but not a general power to do so.[46] This understanding was at the root of the "police power" exception to takings liability, discussed later in this chapter.

---

[40]   Laurence Tribe, AMERICAN CONSTITUTIONAL LAW § 9–3 at 593 (2d edn. 1988).

[41]   See, for example, Hart, *Original Meaning*; William Michael Treanor, *The Original Understanding of the Takings Clause and the Political Process*, 95 COLUM. L. REV. 782 (1995).

[42]   For a detailed overview of this point, see William Baude, *Rethinking the Federal Eminent Domain Power*, 122 YALE L.J. 1738 (2013).

[43]   See Nicole Stelle Garnett, *"No Taking Without a Touching?" Questions from an Armchair Originalist*, 45 SAN DIEGO L. REV 761, 762–63 (2008) (emphasizing this point).

[44]   Id. at 766.

[45]   Id. at 766–67.

[46]   On this point, see Claeys, *Takings*, 1553–70; see also Andrew S. Gold, *Regulatory Takings and Original Intent: The Direct, Physical Takings Thesis*

In addition, some regulations that James Madison apparently supported—and that are cited by advocates of a narrow definition of takings rights—actually were not limitations on use but constraints on property owners who chose *not* to use their land. For example, John Hart cites Madison's support of Virginia and Kentucky laws penalizing landowners who chose not to improve their land within a certain period of time.[47] But, of course, penalizing lack of use is compatible with the Lockean view of property rights as arising from use and "improvement."[48] The same point applies to Hart's reliance on Madison's seeming approval of three early federal laws that imposed penalties on owners who failed to use or improve their land.[49] Indeed, Hart acknowledges that Madison and others at the time believed that "acquisition and use of land enjoys a higher degree of constitutional protection than speculative, passive ownership."[50]

B.   The Original Meaning of 1868

The evidence that the "property" protected by the Takings Clause included a right to use is even stronger for the original meaning, as of 1868, when the Fourteenth Amendment was enacted, applying the Takings Clause against state and local governments.

During the early nineteenth century, many state courts applying state takings clauses interpreted them in the narrow way as applying only to the physical appropriation of property.[51] But by the 1850s and 1860s, courts had begun to shift to an understanding of property rights as including protection against damage and restrictions on use.[52]

In 1871, just three years after the enactment of the Fourteenth Amendment, the Supreme Court decided the famous case of *Pumpelly v. Green Bay Co.,* one of the most widely cited early takings precedents.[53] The Court reasoned that "there are numerous authorities to sustain the doctrine that a serious interruption to the common and necessary use of property may be ... equivalent to the taking of it, and that under the constitutional provisions it is not necessary

---

"Goes Too Far," 49 AM. U. L. REV. 181 (1999). See also the discussion in Section II.C.

[47]   Hart, *Original Meaning*, at 1127–30.
[48]   See discussion above.
[49]   Hart, *Original Meaning*, at 1140–43.
[50]   Id., at 1136.
[51]   Stuart Banner, AMERICAN PROPERTY: A HISTORY OF HOW, WHY, AND WHAT WE OWN (2011), 46–53.
[52]   Id. at 58–59.
[53]   Pumpelly v. Green Bay Co., 80 U.S. (13 Wall.) 166 (1871).

that the land should be absolutely taken."[54] In addition, the Court rejected the idea that takings liability is limited to cases of physical appropriation, emphasizing that:

> It would be a very curious and unsatisfactory result, if in construing a provision of constitutional law, always understood to have been adopted for protection and security to the rights of the individual as against the government, ... it shall be held that if the government refrains from the absolute conversion of real property to the uses of the public it can destroy its value entirely, can inflict irreparable and permanent injury to any extent, can, in effect, subject it to total destruction without making any compensation, because, in the narrowest sense of that word, it is not *taken* for the public use.[55]

While this decision construed the Takings Clause of the Wisconsin state constitution, rather than the federal one, Justice Miller emphasized that "the court rests its decision upon the general weight of authority and not upon anything special in the language of the Wisconsin bill of rights," thus holding that the reasoning was a general principle of takings law.[56]

In the less famous case of *Yates v. Milwaukee,*[57] decided a year before *Pumpelly,* the Supreme Court also suggested that the property rights protected by takings principles include a right to use. In *Yates,* an agency of the City of Milwaukee sought to force the owner of riparian property bordering a river to remove a wharf he had built on his land, citing authority granted by a Wisconsin state law.[58] The Supreme Court ruled that Yates was "entitled to the rights of a riparian proprietor whose land is bounded by a navigable stream, and among those rights are access to the navigable part of the river from the front of his lot, *the right to make a landing, wharf or pier for his own use or for the use of the public*, subject to such general rules and regulations as the legislature may see proper to impose for the protection of the rights of the public".[59] Justice Samuel Miller's opinion for the Court went on to say that "[t]his riparian right is property, and is valuable" and that "the owner can only be deprived in accordance with established law, and if necessary that it be taken for the public good, *upon due compensation.*"[60] The Court also emphasized that, if Milwaukee could bar a wharf merely by declaring it to be a nuisance,

---

54   Id. at 177.
55   Id. at 177–78.
56   Id. at 180.
57   470 U.S. 497 (1870).
58   Id. at 497–500.
59   Id. at 504 (emphasis added).
60   Id (emphasis added).

"[t]his would place every house, every business, and all the property of the city at the uncontrolled will of the temporary local authorities."[61]

As in *Pumpelly*, the Court clearly assumed that the right to use is part of the "property" protected by the state and federal takings clauses. Otherwise, barring a riparian owner from operating a wharf on his land would not require "due compensation."[62] In warning that a contrary ruling would threaten "all property in the city,"[63] the Court also highlighted the importance of use rights to the protection of private property generally.

Some scholars have cited *Yates* as an early indication of the Court's endorsement of the idea of "regulatory" takings.[64] Here, I call attention to it as a further indication that the property protected by the Takings Clause included the right to use. Unlike in *Pumpelly*, here that right was applied to a situation where there was no physical invasion, seizure, or destruction of the owner's land—just a purely regulatory restriction on use.

In *Eaton v. Boston, Concord & Montreal Railroad*, a highly influential decision issued just one year after *Pumpelly*,[65] the Supreme Court of New Hampshire ruled that "[p]roperty is the right of any person to possess, use, enjoy, and dispose of a thing."[66] The court emphasized that the right to use "is an essential quality or attribute of absolute property, without which absolute property can have no legal existence," and therefore "[f]rom the very nature of these rights of use and of exclusion, it is evident that they cannot be materially abridged without, *ipso facto*, taking the owner's property."[67]*Eaton* involved the flooding of property caused by the construction of a state-authorized railroad.[68]

Some argue that the principles of *Pumpelly* were undermined by *Northern Transportation Co. v. City of Chicago*, an 1878 decision where the Supreme Court held that "acts done in the proper exercise of governmental powers, and

[61] Id. at 505.
[62] Id. at 504.
[63] Id. at 505.
[64] See, for example, James W. Ely, Jr., *"to protect all the essential elements of ownership:" Late Nineteenth Century Emergence of the Regulatory Takings Doctrine*, 13 BRIGHAM-KANNER PROPERTY RIGHTS J. 267–295 (2024); Kris W. Kobach, *The Origins of Regulatory Takings: Setting the Record Straight*, 1996 UTAH L. REV. 1211, 1267 (1996); Andrew S. Gold, *Regulatory Takings and Original Intent: The Direct, Physical Takings Thesis Goes Too Far*, 49 Am. U. L. Rev. 181, 235 (1999).
[65] On *Eaton's* influence, see BANNER, at 60–63.
[66] 51 N.H. 504, 511 (1872).
[67] Id.
[68] Id. at 513.

not directly encroaching upon private property, though their consequences may impair its use, are universally held not to be a taking within the meaning of the constitutional provision."[69] But *Northern Transportation Co.* is distinguishable from *Pumpelly* and *Yates* because in the former case there was neither a direct physical invasion of property (as in *Pumpelly*) nor a regulatory restriction on use (as in *Yates*).[70] In *Northern Transportation*, the construction of a tunnel temporarily blocked access to neighboring private property.[71] But it did not damage or destroy that property, nor did it take away any of the owners' legal rights to use it. Thus, "[a]ll that was done was to render for a time its use more inconvenient."[72] The Court did not hold that direct regulatory restrictions on use were not takings.[73] Nor did it consider the possibility of a permanent indirect impediment to use.

Eaton and *Pumpelly* were "enormously influential" rulings that reflected the dominant legal views of the time.[74] They were embraced and echoed by state court decisions, and by leading legal treatises and theorists.[75]

While these two cases and *Yates* were decided two to four years after the ratification of the Fourteenth Amendment in 1868, there is no reason to think there was a sea change in attitudes during that period. Michigan Supreme Court Justice Thomas Cooley's influential 1868 work *A Treatise on the Constitutional Limitations Which Rest Upon the Legislative Power*

---

[69]   99 U.S. 635, 642 (1878). For the view that *Northern Transportation* undermines *Pumpelly*, see, for example, Ely, at 6 (suggesting that in the later case "the Court confined *Pumpelly* to permanent and physical invasions").

[70]   The *Northern Transportation* decision distinguishes *Pumpelly* and *Eaton* on the grounds that: "In those cases, there was a physical invasion of the real estate of the private owner, and a practical ouster of his possession. But in the present case, there was no such invasion. No entry was made upon the plaintiffs' lot." *Northern Transportation*, 99 U.S. at 642. However, it does not indicate that a regulatory restriction on use wouldn't qualify as a taking; it merely suggests a "physical invasion" is necessary in cases where there isn't such a constraint. Cf. John Groen, *Takings, Original Meaning, and Applying Property Law Principles to Fix Penn Central,* 39 Touro L. Rev. 4, Art 4 (2024), at 56–58, available at https://papers.ssrn.com/sol3/papers.cfm?abstract_id=4444574 (explaining why *Northern Transportation* doesn't impose a general rule that a physical invasion is required for takings liability).

[71]   Northern Transportation, 99 U.S. at 636–38.

[72]   Id. at 642.

[73]   For a more detailed explanation of the reasons why *Northern Transportation* does not undermine *Pumpelly's* protection of the right to use, see Groen, *Takings,* at 56–58.

[74]   Banner, at 61.

[75]   For an overview, see id. at 61–64.

of the States of the American Union was published in the same year as the Fourteenth Amendment was ratified. In his discussion of the Takings Clause in that work, he wrote, "any injury to the property of an individual which deprives the owner of the ordinary use of it is equivalent to a taking, and entitles him to compensation."[76] Housing is pretty obviously part of the "ordinary use" of property, both in Cooley's time and today.

In his later 1880 treatise, *The General Principles of Constitutional Law in the United States of America*, Cooley wrote that "[t]he property which the Constitution protects is anything of value which the law recognizes as such, and in respect to which the owner is entitled to a remedy against anyone who may disturb him in his enjoyment."[77] Once again, the right to build housing surely qualifies.

Cooley's work is notable because of its great influence and because it came out in the very year the Fourteenth Amendment was ratified. Other leading treatise writers of the era also adopted broad interpretations of the Takings Clause as protecting the right to use.[78] For example, Christopher Tiedeman, in an influential 1886 treatise, wrote that "[w]henever the use of land is restricted in any way ... it constitutes as much a taking as if the land itself has been appropriated."[79] In his 1879 treatise on eminent domain, Henry Mills similarly emphasized that any "encumbrance on property" qualifies as a "taking within the meaning of the constitution."[80] John Lewis, author of an influential 1888 treatise on the same subject, wrote that the property rights protected by the Takings Clause included the "right of user [sic], the right of exclusion and the right of disposition," and that "when a person is deprived of any of those rights, he is to that extent deprived of his property, and, hence, that his property may be taken, in the constitutional sense, though his title and possession remain undisturbed."[81]

---

[76] Thomas M. Cooley, TREATISE ON THE CONSTITUTIONAL LIMITATIONS WHICH REST UPON THE LEGISLATIVE POWER OF THE STATES OF THE AMERICAN UNION 544 (1868). For discussions of Cooley's extensive influence, see Alan Robert Jones, THE CONSTITUTIONAL CONSERVATISM OF THOMAS MCINTYRE COOLEY: A STUDY IN THE HISTORY OF IDEAS (1987); and James W. Ely, Jr., *Thomas Cooley, "Public Use," and New Directions in Takings Jurisprudence*, 2004 MICHIGAN STATE LAW REVIEW 845, 845 (2004).

[77] Thomas Cooley, THE GENERAL PRINCIPLES OF CONSTITUTIONAL LAW IN THE UNITED STATES OF AMERICA 336 (1880).

[78] See Banner, PROPERTY, at 61–65.

[79] Christopher Tiedeman, A TREATISE ON THE LIMITATIONS OF THE POLICE POWER IN THE UNITED STATES 397 (1886).

[80] Henry E. Mills, A TREATISE ON THE LAW OF EMINENT DOMAIN 33 (1879).

[81] John Lewis, A TREATISE ON THE LAW OF EMINENT DOMAIN 41, 45 (1888).

To the extent that the relevant original public meaning is that understood by leading lawyers and jurists, the views of Cooley, the Supreme Court in *Pumpelly*, and state court judges like those that decided the *Eaton* case are highly relevant. Many originalists contend that original meaning should be understood as that of either legally sophisticated contemporaries or hypothetical readers who are assumed to have a high degree of legal knowledge.[82] On this view, the understanding of prominent legal elites is highly probative.

It is worth noting, also, that the decisions in cases like *Pumpelly* and *Eaton* and treatise writers like Cooley and Tiedeman did not rigorously differentiate between the meanings of "property" and "take," suggesting that a narrow definition of the latter could vitiate the broad definition of the former. Tiedeman specifically noted that "it is not necessary that there should be an actual or physical taking of the land" for takings liability to be incurred.[83] Cooley wrote that takings liability applies to government restrictions of both "tangible" and "intangible" interests.[84] He gives abrogation of an exclusive "franchise" for a "turnpike" as an example of the latter and notes there is a taking if the state abrogates such a franchise by allowing a competitor to enter the market (though not if the original franchise wasn't supposed to be exclusive).[85] By definition, such "intangible" interests cannot be physically invaded or appropriated. Cooley clearly did not believe that such appropriation or invasion was necessary for there to be a taking.

Similarly, the *Eaton* court noted that "[f]rom the very nature of these rights of user [sic] and of exclusion, it is evident that they cannot be materially abridged without, *ipso facto,* taking the owner's 'property.'"[86] This suggests that the means of the "material abridgement" is irrelevant, whether it involves physical invasion or not. The court also emphasized that "[t]he framers of the constitution intended to protect rights which are worth protecting; not mere empty titles, or barren insignia of ownership, which are of no substantial value."[87] If the Takings Clause does not protect against restrictions on use that do not involve physical invasion, the government could easily turn a property right into an "empty title," one that is hardly "worth protecting."[88]

---

[82]   For examples, see Ilya Somin, *Originalism and Political Ignorance*, 97 Minnesota Law Review 625, 633–37 (2012).

[83]   Tiedeman, at 397.

[84]   Cooley, General Principles, at 369.

[85]   Id. at 369–70.

[86]   Eaton, 51 N.H. at 511.

[87]   Id. at 512.

[88]   Id.

To be sure, *Eaton* itself involved a case of physical invasion—the deliberate flooding of property.[89] The court noted that the infliction of a "physical injury to the land itself" was one of the two factors that distinguish this case from those where regulations merely impose "a mere personal inconvenience or annoyance to the occupant."[90] But the second distinguishing factor noted by the court was that the interference with property rights in question "would clearly be actionable if done by a private person without legislative authority."[91]

That point also applies to restrictions on building and commercial uses. If a private individual used the threat of force to prevent owners from building housing on their land, he or she could surely be held liable for doing so. The same applies to using force to block a commercial use of the land, such as preventing its use as a store or factory. Such coercion would also "clearly be actionable if done by a private person without legislative authority."[92]

Some original meaning originalists focus on the actual understanding of the general public at the time.[93] For example, Justice Antonin Scalia wrote, in his majority opinion for the Supreme Court in *District of Columbia v. Heller,* that "normal meaning" is preferable to "secret or technical meanings that would not have been known to ordinary citizens in the founding generation."[94] We do not have any systematic data on what ordinary people in 1791 and 1868 believed to be the proper scope of compensation under the Takings Clause. But it is worth noting that the idea that property includes a right to use your land and build on it is highly intuitive, and fits normal lay understandings of the notion. John Lewis directly addressed this point in his 1888 treatise, arguing that the term "property" in the Takings Clause should be interpreted in accordance with ordinary meaning, and that the ordinary meaning includes a "bundle of rights," including the right to "use and disposition," not just security against physical appropriation.

> ["Property"] should be given a meaning that accords with the ordinary usage and understanding of the people who made the instrument. We do not refer to the small body of persons who actually formulated the instrument, but the large body of citizens who gave it vitality by their votes. The sovereign people say to their agents and servants, the executive and legislative officers of the State: We delegate to you all

---

[89] Banner, at 60.

[90] Eaton, 51 N.H. at 513.

[91] Id.

[92] Id.

[93] See, for example, Robert H. Bork, THE TEMPTING OF AMERICA 144 (1990).

[94] District of Columbia v. Heller, 554 U.S. 570, 577 (2008). See also *United States* v. *Sprague*, 282 U.S. 716, 731 (1931) ("The Constitution was written to be understood by the voters; its words and phrases were used in their normal and ordinary as distinguished from technical meaning").

of our sovereign powers, but you must not take our private property for public use without making us a just compensation therefor. What did they mean by property? The dullest individual among the people knows and understands that his property in anything is a bundle of rights.[95]

Moreover, it is also important to emphasize that a key reason why the drafters of the Fourteenth Amendment sought to impose the Takings Clause against the states was to prevent southern states from undermining the property rights of white southerners who had remained loyal to the Union during the Civil War. As Representative John Bingham,[96] the leading congressional framer of the Fourteenth Amendment, explained, the purpose was "to protect the thousands and tens of thousands and hundreds of thousands of loyal white citizens of the United States whose property, by State legislation, has been wrested from them under confiscation."[97] The property rights of both blacks and white loyalists in the South were threatened by hostile state and local authorities.[98]

If states retained a free hand to restrict the use of property, so long as they did not physically appropriate it, they could use that power to persecute loyal property owners, even if they could not seize the property outright. As the *Eaton* court recognized,[99] severe restrictions on use could be almost as onerous as total confiscation, and indeed effectively amount to such. This would be true regardless of whether the restrictions on use were upheld based on a narrow definition of "property" or a narrow definition of "take."

An ordinary citizen aware of this goal of incorporation would therefore likely assume that states were barred from uncompensated abrogation of use rights, as well as outright seizure. At the very least, this would be true of severe restrictions like those imposed by exclusionary zoning or by major constraints on other common land uses.

---

[95]   Lewis, 55–56.

[96]   For an account of Bingham's crucial role in drafting the Amendment and shepherding it through Congress, see Gerard Magliocca, AMERICAN FOUNDING SON: JOHN BINGHAM AND THE INVENTION OF THE FOURTEENTH AMENDMENT.

[97]   John Bingham statement, 39th Congress, 1st Session, CONGRESSIONAL GLOBE 1065 (1866).

[98]   See, for example, Erik Mathesen, *"It Looks Much Like Abandoned Land": Property and the Politics of Loyalty in Reconstruction Mississippi* in AFTER SLAVERY: RACE, LABOR, AND CITIZENSHIP IN THE RECONSTRUCTION SOUTH (Bruce Baker and Brian Kelly eds., 2013).

[99]   See discussion earlier in this part.

C.   The Police Power Exception

From early on, it has been understood that some government actions that might otherwise be considered takings are exempt from the requirement to pay "just compensation" because they are exercises of the "police power."[100] But, as Bradley Karkkainen notes, the scope of this exception has always been unclear because "[t]he police power was always a spongy, indefinite concept; courts readily acknowledged that its uncertain contours could never be fully specified."[101] In this section, I refer to the police power "exception," but recognize that it can also be considered a background principle of property law;[102] I use the term "exception" because it is simpler and more intuitive. I do not attempt to definitively resolve the issue of the scope of the police power exception, merely to explain why any plausible originalist understanding of it would provide for a broad right to use.

The Reconstruction-era Supreme Court defined the "police power" as including "the protection of the lives, the health, and the property of the community against the injurious exercise by any citizen of his own rights."[103] Later, courts also added a nebulous category of protection of the "public welfare" to the scope of the police power.[104]

But if this later broad expansion of the police powers were correct, and any legislation or regulation that might enhance the health or welfare of the public in some way were exempt from takings liability, then the Takings Clause and its state equivalents would be virtually nullified. After all, any use of property of any kind might potentially pose at least a small threat to public health or safety. If new housing construction or some other use of land leads to even a small increase in population, for example, it is always possible that one of the new residents might commit a crime, spread a contagious disease, or otherwise pose a threat to health or safety. Similarly, almost any new housing could potentially reduce public "welfare" by a variety of means, such as increasing

---

[100]   For overviews of this debate, see, for example, Joseph Sax, *Takings and the Police Power*, 74 YALE L.J. 36 (1964); D. Benjamin Barros, *The Police Power and the Takings Clause*, 58 U. MIAMI L. REV. 471 (2004); Bradley C. Karkkainen, *The Police Power Revisited: Phantom Incorporation and the Roots of the Takings 'Muddle,'* 90 MINN. L. REV. (2006), at 893–905; William B. Stoebuck, *Police Power, Takings, and Due Process,* 37 WASHINGTON & LEE L. REV 1057 (1980); and Arvo Van Alstyne, *Taking or Damaging by Police Power: The Search for Inverse Condemnation Criteria,* 44 SO. CAL. L. REV. 1 (1970).

[101]   Karkkainen, at 893.

[102]   Id. at 894–95.

[103]   *Patterson v. Kentucky*, 97 US 501, 504 (1879).

[104]   Karkkainen, at 895–96.

congestion or lowering the prices of at least some nearby properties. The same goes for virtually any other land use. Commercial, religious, and charitable uses might all also potentially attract additional people, thereby creating at least a small risk of congestion, crime, disease, or other danger.

But the scope of the police power was not generally understood to be this broad around the time of the framing and ratifying of the Fourteenth Amendment. Chancellor Kent, a highly influential antebellum legal theorist, wrote in his *Commentaries on American Law* that the police power was limited to "general regulations [that] interdict such uses of property as would create nuisances and become dangerous to the lives, or health, or peace, or comfort of the citizens."[105] Kent's view became the dominant one in antebellum police power jurisprudence.[106] In his influential 1868 treatise on constitutional law, Justice Thomas Cooley likewise emphasized that the police power could only be used to restrict "a particular use of property" that was previously lawful if it had become a "public nuisance, endangering the public health and the public safety."[107] Here, "public nuisance" is used as a broad concept encompassing activities threatening to public health and safety.[108]

There is no evidence that the use of land for housing purposes, including multi-family housing, could in and of itself be considered a public nuisance or any kind of serious threat to health and safety, even if it could be argued that it increased some types of risks at the margin. The same goes for most ordinary commercial uses. As examples of what might qualify as such a "nuisance," Cooley listed the use of church lands for cemeteries (presumably because of the health risks created by dead bodies), "[t]he keeping of gunpowder in unsafe quantities in cities and villages, the sale of poisonous drugs, unless labeled [sic]; allowing unmuzzled dogs to be at large when danger of hydrophobia is apprehended; or the keeping for sale unwholesome provisions."[109] These uses obviously create far greater risks than the construction of multi-family housing. Cooley also noted that property uses can be restricted to protect "public morals," by means such as banning the sale of "indecent books or

---

[105]   2 James Kent, COMMENTARIES ON AMERICAN LAW 534 (John M. Gould ed., 14th ed. 1896).
[106]   Karkkainen, at 894–95.
[107]   Cooley, LIMITATIONS, at 595.
[108]   Cf., Thomas W. Merrill, *Public Nuisance as Risk Regulation*, 17 J. L. ECON. & POL'Y 347, 348–50 (2022), describing the history of "public nuisance" law as a tool for regulating activities that impose "a risk of harm on the general public."
[109]   Cooley, LIMITATIONS, at 595–96.

pictures" and banning gambling.[110] Housing, including multi-family housing, obviously does not pose any such danger to "morals."[111]

In a famous 1887 Supreme Court decision in *Mugler v. Kansas*, Justice John Marshall Harlan's opinion for the Court held that the police power allowed the government to ban "noxious" uses of property without paying compensation, but not "unoffending" ones.[112] The line between the two is far from a clear one, but it seems unlikely that mere use of property for ordinary commercial and residential purposes would qualify as "noxious." Harlan indicated that the "noxious" uses are those that are "prejudicial to the health, the morals, or the safety of the public,"[113] which is similar to other formulations of the scope of the police power exception described above.

These understandings of the scope of the police power are similar to Randy Barnett's interpretation of Reconstruction-era evidence as supporting the view that the police power included "prohibiting wrongful and regulating rightful private behavior that may injure the rights of others, [and also that] the state may also manage government controlled public space so as to enable members of the public to enjoy its use."[114] By contrast, they probably allow more regulation to fall within the police power exception than Richard Epstein's theory that the exception should be limited to measures that "protect liberty and private property against all manifestations of force and fraud," which he interprets as including regulation of common-law nuisances, but not most types of environmental regulations.[115]

As we have seen,[116] prominent nineteenth-century takings decisions required compensation even in some cases where the government action at issue protected safety and welfare far more clearly than exclusionary zoning could be said to do. The influential 1872 *Eaton* decision required compensation in a situation where the government flooded a farmer's land in order to

---

[110]   Id. at 596. "Hydrophobia" is a somewhat archaic word for rabies, a deadly disease spread by animal bites.
[111]   On the history of the "morals" element of the police power, see, for example, Santiago Legarre, *The Historical Background of the Police Power*, 9 J. CONSTITUTIONAL LAW 745, 760–71 (2007).
[112]   Mugler v. Kansas, 123 U.S. 623, 679 (1887).
[113]   Id.
[114]   Randy E. Barnett, *The Proper Scope of the Police Power*, 79 NOTRE DAME L. REV. 429, 493 (2004). See also Randy E. Barnett and Evan D. Bernick, THE ORIGINAL MEANING OF THE 14TH AMENDMENT: ITS LETTER AND SPIRIT 306–13 (2021) (expounding on this idea in detail).
[115]   Richard A. EPSTEIN, TAKINGS: PRIVATE PROPERTY AND THE POWER OF EMINENT DOMAIN 112, 113–25 (1985).
[116]   See the discussion in Section II.B.

facilitate the construction of a railroad.[117] Railroad construction undeniably benefits the public welfare, especially in an era when railroads were the principal means of relatively fast transportation by land, and played a vital role in economic development.[118]

In *Pumpelly v. Green Bay Co.*, discussed above, the Supreme Court required payment of liability in a situation where land was flooded in order to facilitate the construction of a canal.[119] Like railroads, canals were crucial to public welfare, given their vital importance to the nineteenth-century economy.

Modern regulatory takings doctrine has also required liability in situations where the benefit to public safety and welfare was far clearer than in the case of exclusionary zoning. Most famously, in the landmark case of *Pennsylvania Coal Co. v. Mahon*, the Supreme Court ruled that compensation was required for a regulation that restricted mining in order to protect surface property from subsidence and collapse.[120] More recently, in *Arkansas Game and Fish Commission v. United States*,[121] the Supreme Court unanimously ruled that takings liability is possible in a case where the Army Corps of Engineers flooded property in order to reduce flooding elsewhere, and thereby enable farmers in the region to have a longer growing season.[122] Reducing flooding harmful to agriculture clearly benefits public welfare and safety, yet that did not lead the Court to rule there was an exception from takings liability.[123]

To the extent that the original meaning of the Takings Clause should be interpreted in accordance with "ordinary meaning" as understood by members of the general public,[124] that also argues against the idea that the police power exception is broad enough to encompass exclusionary zoning and restrictions on ordinary commercial use. Such a broad exception would also cover almost any restriction of land use, thereby massively undermining the whole point of having a Takings Clause in the first place. It seems unlikely that ordinary

---

[117] Eaton, 51 N.H. at 505–10.

[118] See, for example, Robert Fogel, RAILROADS AND AMERICAN ECONOMIC GROWTH: ESSAYS IN ECONOMETRIC HISTORY (1964) (a well-known account of the role of railroads in nineteenth-century economic growth).

[119] Pumpelly v. Green Bay Co., 80 U.S. 166, 178–79 (1871).

[120] Pennsylvania Coal Co. v. Mahon, 260 U.S. 393 (1922).

[121] 568 U.S. 23 (2012).

[122] Id. at 26–27.

[123] The Court did not definitively rule there was a taking, but merely established some criteria for assessing whether repeated flooding qualifies as a taking. Id. at 32–37. The Federal Circuit did find a taking upon remand. See Arkansas Game & Fish Commission v. United States, 736 F.3d 1364 (Fed. Cir. 2013).

[124] See the discussion of this possibility in Section II.B.

people would understand the Takings Clause as having an exception so broad as to largely swallow the rule.

Along related lines, an expansive police power exception would also undermine the immediate purpose of incorporating the Takings Clause against state governments, which was to protect the property rights of white southerners loyal to the Union against hostile southern state governments.[125] Such a broad exception could easily have been used to target the property of these groups, under the pretext of promoting public health or welfare in some way.

The police power exception might apply to unusual cases where a commercial use or the construction of new housing creates a serious risk of flooding or land subsidence, or some other similar significant threat to health. But it could not justify large-scale exclusionary zoning or sweeping restrictions on more conventional commercial uses.

The exception does have stronger applicability to unusually dangerous uses. Most obviously, uses that spread dangerous pollution or toxic waste are much more plausibly regarded as threats to public health and safety than housing is. The Supreme Court recently reaffirmed the notion that health and safety inspections are exempt from Takings Clause liability, even in situations where they entail physical intrusions on property that would otherwise qualify as per se (automatic) takings.[126] The police power exception would also likely encompass public-health sanitation requirements and building-code regulations to prevent the spread of fire.

State and local governments could still impose restrictions on use that do not fall within the police power exception. But they would have to pay "just compensation," as required by the Takings Clause, generally interpreted as the fair market value of the property right taken by the government.[127] Government officials could still impose restrictions they considered worth the expenditure of resources for compensation. But the requirement of payment would make it difficult for them to impose massive large-scale restrictions on the right to use, such as those involved in exclusionary zoning.[128]

---

[125] See the discussion in Section II.B.

[126] Cedar Point Nursery v. Hassid, 139 U.S. 149 (2021).

[127] For an overview and critique of this standard, see Yun-Chien Chang, PRIVATE PROPERTY AND TAKINGS COMPENSATION: THEORETICAL FRAMEWORK AND EMPIRICAL ANALYSIS (2013).

[128] For a detailed discussion of the significance of this constraint, see Braver and Somin, EXCLUSIONARY ZONING, Part IV.

CONCLUSION

The right to use is a central element of the right to private property. It is also part of the "private property" protected by the Takings Clause of the Fifth Amendment, at least under the original meaning. For those reasons, it deserves much stronger judicial protection than it currently gets.

3.   Judicial abdication

Jan G. Laitos

The American system of constitutional government contains an odd and anomalous feature—the ability of a private party to successfully challenge a law in court seemingly in violation of the country's constitution depends on the nature of the harm inflicted by the offending law. If the harm involves the right of speech or assembly, or the right to not be discriminated against on the basis of race or sex or gender, or the right to participate in the electoral process, or the right to bear arms, or the right to marry, reviewing courts will closely and strictly examine whether the challenged law is in violation of the U.S. Constitution. On the other hand, if the law seems to violate one of the enumerated constitutional rights that protect an individual's right to own, use, and dispose of private property, or if the law regulates a person's choice to participate in the American economic market,[1] constitutional review of that law is subject to a form of *non-review*, called "rational basis" review, where the court typically, and robotically, defers to the wishes and choices of the law-maker.

This two-tiered system of judicial review means there are two types of judicial review available to litigants raising a constitutional claim: (1) deferential review for property and economic harms, and (2) serious meaningful review for other harms. Such bifurcated judicial review appears to be at odds with the Declaration of Independence, which famously begins with these stirring words: "We hold these truths to be self-evident, that all men are created equal ...." The two tiers of judicial review also seem contrary to the text of the Equal Protection Clause of the Constitution's Fourteenth Amendment, which

---

[1]   There are four enumerated property-protective clauses in the American Constitution that are available to property owners and owners of economic interests:

the Takings Clause of the Fifth Amendment;
the Due Process Clause of the Fifth and Fourteenth Amendments;
the Contracts Clause of Article I, Section 10; and
the Equal Protection Clause of the Fourteenth Amendment.

commands that no government actor may "deny to any person within its jurisdiction the equal protection of the laws."

Instead of all interest holders having an equal chance of successfully resisting laws by seeking protection of constitutional rights in court, the two tiers
mean that there will be winners and losers. The losers are property owners
and persons wishing to exercise economic liberties. These classes are not able
to seek redress from possibly unreasonable and unconstitutional laws in court,
because for these "commercial" harms, courts will not engage in any analysis
or examination of whether the law is unconstitutional. Instead, the courts simply, routinely, and inevitably defer to the wishes and choices of the lawmaker.

The case that first established this unsettling, and discriminatory, system
of disparate levels of judicial review was a 1938 United States Supreme Court
decision—*United States v. Carolene Products Co.*[2] After *Carolene Products*,
most reviewing courts, both federal and state, at appellate and trial levels,
embraced highly deferential "rational basis" review whenever constitutional
defenses were raised to defeat government regulation of social, economic,
and property interests. For almost ninety years, these reviewing courts have
abdicated any notion of meaningful judicial constitutional review with regard
to laws regulating economic and property claims. The working principle
for courts post-*Carolene Products* is that "legislative judgment" is not to be
judicially disturbed. Rather, the legislative-regulatory judgment is presumed
always to be supported by "facts either known, or which could reasonably be
assumed."[3]

This obeisance to the police power has largely removed reviewing courts as
an affirmative check or limit on legislative or regulatory restrictions on economic, commercial, or property interests held by private parties. The United
States Supreme Court has warned lower courts considering constitutional challenges to economic regulations to never substitute their predictive judgments
for those of elected legislatures or expert agencies.[4] Even when the property
owner or commercial plaintiff raises an enumerated property-protective clause
in the Constitution as a defense, the Supreme Court applies highly deferential
rational basis review to sustain the regulation.[5] This withdrawal from meaningful judicial review when private economic interests are at stake has also

---

[2]   304 U.S. 144 (1938).

[3]   *Id.* at 152, 154.

[4]   *Lingle v. Chevron*, U.S.A, 544 U.S. 528, 544 (2005).

[5]   See, for example, *Williamson v. Lee Optical of Oklahoma*, 348 U.S. 483
(1955) (Due Process Clause) and *Nordlinger v. Hahn*, 505 U.S. 1 (1992) (Equal
Protection Clause); *Keystone Bituminous Coal Co. v. DeBenedictis*, 438 U.S. 104,
124 (1978) (Contracts Clause).

been enthusiastically followed by trial and appellate courts.[6] The universal acceptance of deferential rational basis review when economic and property interests assert constitutional defenses to regulation has deterred litigation; property owners and their attorneys have come to realize that judicial challenges to police power regulations are likely futile.

A near ninety-year tradition of refusing to provide meaningful judicial review to a single class of plaintiffs—owners of property and economic interests— seems contrary to the intention of the Founders who originally drafted the American Constitution. There is no evidence that those who wrote and ratified the Constitution wanted the judiciary to exclude certain stakeholders (for example, property owners or those with commercial interests) from the protections afforded persons seeking judicial review of actions by the legislative or executive branches. Instead, the authors of the Constitution repeatedly emphasized the critical role of the courts as a countervailing check and limit on all lawmakers within the political branches. There were no exceptions suggesting that private parties with economic interests should be denied meaningful judicial review.[7]

What follows is an analysis of why it was, and is, wrong for the *Carolene Products* rule to foreclose courts from considering certain constitutional defenses. This rule of non-review prevents serious and heightened examination when the injured litigants are raising harm to property and economic interests. Failure to provide judicial review to private parties who find their properties, businesses, or economic enterprises subject to police power regulations is contrary to the purpose, history, and rationale of the concept of judicial review. The judiciary should not have license to discriminate against plaintiffs simply because their injury is to a constitutional right that has "economic" underpinnings.[8] A private interest in property, or in an activity that has economic, commercial, or marketplace worth, should not disqualify that interest from meaningful judicial review and constitutional protection.

Moreover, the text of the Constitution itself carefully and explicitly lists certain economic interests that should be constitutionally protected. The

---

[6]   See, for example,: *Michael Mogan v. City of Chicago*, 2024 WL 4249160, 115 F.4th 841 (7th Cir, 2024); *74 Pinehurst LLC v. New York*, 59 F.4th 546 (2d Cir. 2023); *Schnuck v. City of Santa Monica*, 935 F.2d 171, 174–75 (9th Cir. 1991); *Salt Lake City v. Utah State Tax Commission*, 548 P.3d 865, 871 (Utah 2023); and *Woodstone Limited Partnership v. City of Saint Paul*, 674 F. Supp. 3d 571 (D. Minn. 2023).

[7]   The Federalist No. 78, at 525–27 (Alexander Hamilton) (Jacob E. Cooke ed. 1961). See also Sotirios A. Barber, *Judicial Review and "The Federalist"*, 55 U. Chi. L. Rev 836 (1988).

[8]   Louise Weinberg, *Unlikely Beginnings of Modern Constitutional Thought*, 15 Journal of Constitutional Law 323, 327 (2012).

Constitution prohibits state laws that impair "contracts." The Constitution requires just compensation when laws "take private property." The Constitution demands that governments not deprive persons of "property" without due process. The Constitution did not ignore commercial marketplace interests.

I.   THE SIGNIFICANCE OF JUDICIAL REVIEW

When the original Thirteen Colonies considered the formation of a unified nation, a "United States," a threshold question was who, or what, would "make" the laws here? The formal structure of this new nation would be a united federal democratic republic, organized under a constitution. This form of government was unprecedented in 1787–88. This meant that the Founders, in effect, invented a new system for law-making. The political structure selected to make the law was a *legislative* body, comprised of properly chosen representatives founded on majoritarian democratic rule. In theory, a government with a majoritarian legislative body would make laws "which will protect all parties, the weaker as well as the more powerful."[9] Such a law-making system founded on majoritarian representative democratic rules should, in theory, act in a way that is consistent with the public good and public welfare.[10]

However, regardless of the genius of this legislative system that would create and drive the laws of the new nation, the Founders realized that legislative miscalculations about an amorphous public welfare might still occur. A legislature not subject to some "higher law," some law superior to itself, could insulate itself from demands for change in the law. If groups were wrongly excluded from political power, a legislature could be unresponsive to their grievances. Lawmakers governed by majority rule could be insensitive to minorities needing protection. Moreover, systems founded on democratic rule for self-interested legislation by the most powerful faction could "trample on the rules of justice."[11] In order to ensure that legislatures would not run amuck with no self-control, the American government that emerged after the Revolutionary War imposed two exogenous limits on all laws: (1) All political branches of government, especially the legislative branch, and including the executive branch, were subject to the freshly drafted United States Constitution; (2) the judicial branch, particularly the United States Supreme Court, had the power to "review" the decisions of the political branches to determine if the laws from the branches were consistent with the Constitution.

---

[9]   The Federalist No. 51 (James Madison) at 352 (Jacob E. Cooke ed. 1961).
[10]   The Federalist No. 10 (James Madison), *id.* at 61.
[11]   *Id.* at 60.

These two countervailing checks on political power were confirmed early in our country's constitutional history, in the landmark Supreme Court case, *Marbury v. Madison* (1803).[12] In *Marbury*, Chief Justice Marshall famously announced that "an act, repugnant to the Constitution, [cannot] become the law of the land ...."[13] And he confirmed that it is "emphatically the province and duty of the judicial Department to say what the law is."[14]

Marbury ratified an important and uniquely American invention that serves to limit government power, such as the police power regulating private choices about privately owned property. That "invention" is *constitutionalism*, enforced by *judicial review*.[15] A constitution cabins the power of the political, lawmaking branches of government. Judicial review ensures that a law not consistent with the Constitution can be declared unconstitutional by the judiciary and therefore unable to become "the law of the land."[16] This idea of judges being constitution-enforcers authorized to declare laws unconstitutional is nowhere expressly stated in the Constitution. Nonetheless, after *Marbury*, the twin powers of (1) constitutionalism and (2) meaningful judicial review have been constant limitations on police power exercises which seek to limit and regulate private initiative.

This dynamic between *property owner, government police power and reviewing court* was thoughtfully and succinctly outlined by Justice Holmes in the famous case of *Pennsylvania Coal v. Mahon* (1922).[17] Justice Holmes summarized how each of the above three actors serves as a check on the power exercised by each of the other actors. The property owner initially asserts a common law right to use the private property; the government then limits that right by imposing police power conditions on the private right for a public benefit; a reviewing court may in turn limit the police power if that power violates the Constitution. Justice Holmes briefly encapsulated this checking function of differing legal powers in the *Pennsylvania Coal* case: "[S]ome values [associated with private property ownership and use] are enjoyed under an implied limitation and must yield to the police power. But obviously the implied limitation [of the police power] must have its limits ...."[18] The "limit" on the

---

[12] *Marbury v. Madison,* 5 U.S. 1, Cranch 137 (1803).

[13] *Id.* at 176.

[14] *Id.* at 177.

[15] See generally Keith E. Whittington, *An "Indispensable Feature"? Constitutionalism and Judicial Review*, 6 LEGISLATION AND PUBLIC POLICY 21 (2002).

[16] Alexander M. Bickel, THE LEAST DANGEROUS BRANCH: THE SUPREME COURT AT THE BAR OF POLITICS 14–17 (1962).

[17] 260 U.S. 393 (1922).

[18] *Id.* at 413–14.

"implied limitation" [of the police power] is the *power of judicial review.* This power enables reviewing courts to strike down police power actions and regulations that violate the Constitution.[19]

When the power/limit/limit-on-limit interplay unfolds in the way envisioned by Justice Holmes, no one power becomes dominant. Each exercise of legal power becomes limited by a higher power. The owner's common law right and power to use property may be limited by the government's police power, hopefully exercised to advance the general welfare. But that police power limit may in turn be limited by the power of judicial review if the property owner's constitutional rights have been violated. However, if the power of judicial review is meaningless, or superficial, which occurs when courts simply defer, then the police power is unchecked and without effective constitutional limits. Justice Holmes reminds us that while the private property right must "yield" to the dictates of the police power, the police power must also yield to a court finding the police power regulation to violate the Constitution. If the reviewing court ceases to be a viable limit on the police power limitation, the police power is limited only by political and social pressures, not the Constitution.

Unfortunately, by the 21st century, instead of reviewing courts providing meaningful review of regulations affecting property and other economic interests, the judiciary engages in "deferential review." Courts that defer to the judgments of lawmakers and regulators are providing a form of non-review. Deference permits the reviewing court to avoid asking hard questions about the viability of the law or the value of the private interest affected by the law. A deferring court instead recites an array of platitudes about how reviewing courts should not offer meaningful review to challenged laws affecting "social and economic interests," including private property rights. In other words, the normal judicial review limit on the police power is missing when property owners challenge police power limits on their use of property. There is, then, an invidious double standard of constitutional review—courts are vigilant in upholding constitutional protections in cases involving personal "civil rights," but deferential towards legislation and police power exercises involving economic or property interests.[20]

The question then becomes, if such judicial abdication of meaningful review of economic and property rights is not consistent with the rationale behind judicial review, then why did the judiciary choose to relinquish its power of review? Why did the judicial branch grant to lawmakers, and the

---

[19]   Charles Grove Haines, THE AMERICAN DOCTRINE OF JUDICIAL SUPREMACY (1959).

[20]   James E. Ely, Jr., THE GUARDIAN OF EVERY OTHER RIGHT: A CONSTITUTIONAL HISTORY OF PROPERTY RIGHTS 133 (2d ed. 1998) and Steven J. Eagle, REGULATORY TAKINGS 79 (1996).

political-regulatory branches, unchallengeable, inviolable power to limit and affect private commercial and economic choices? It appears that the Supreme Court's rejection of meaningful review for one class of police power actions (those affecting private property and private economic interests) can largely be traced back to a case decided in the 1930s. Perhaps one should take another look at that case and its underlying rationale.[21]

II. THE DEMISE OF JUDICIAL REVIEW OF REGULATIONS AFFECTING ECONOMIC AND PROPERTY INTERESTS

Between 1938 and the 21st century, a nearly 90-year period, reviewing courts have chosen not to act as a "limitation" on the police power limiting private property uses. Instead of checking the police power, courts have deferred to it, especially when that power is exercised in the form of regulations affecting property uses. Courts have not become a viable and countervailing third actor in the (1) property owner, (2) police power regulator, and (3) reviewing court three-party dynamic. The judiciary has, instead, decided to team up with the regulator wielding the police power, creating a *de facto* coalition. As a result of this court-regulator coalition, the affected property owner is left without meaningful judicial recourse to check the police power.[22] Contrary to Holmes' syllogism in *Pennsylvania Coal*, the "implied limitation" of the police power does *not* itself experience realistic "limits" from checking courts. Constitutional provisions protecting property owners are then, to use Holmes' words, "gone."

This judicial decision to remove reviewing courts as a limit-on-the-limit can be traced to three choices made by the United States Supreme Court in the 1930s. First, the Supreme Court was winding down a quite controversial era in the Court's history—the *Lochner* era.[23] During this *Lochner*-era time between the 1890s and 1936, the Court had invalidated almost 200 federal and state

---

[21]   See, for example, Peter Linzer, *The Carolene Products Footnote and the Preferred Position of Individual Rights: Louis Lusky and John Hart Ely vs. Harlan Fiske Stone*, 12 CONSTITUTIONAL COMMENTARY 277 (1995) and Felix Gilman, *The Famous Footnote Four: A History of the Carolene Products Footnote*, 46 S. TEXAS L. REV. 163. (2004).

[22]   Richard E. Levy, *Escaping Lochner's Shadow: Toward a Coherent Jurisprudence of Economic Rights*, 73 N.C.L. REV. 329 (1995) and Robert McCloskey, *Economic Due Process and the Supreme Court: An Exhumation and Reburial*, 1962 SUP. CT. REV 34 (1962).

[23]   The *Lochner* era was named after the period's paradigm case, *Lochner v. New York*, 198 U.S. 45 (1905).

economic regulations for interfering with various property-protective constitutional rights, such as the right to contract and substantive due process.[24] In the early 1930s, the Court used *Lochner*-era reasoning to invalidate some of the central laws of President Franklin Roosevelt's New Deal. A combination of pressure from Roosevelt and changes in the composition of the Court saw the Court dramatically change its direction by 1937.[25] A decision was made by the majority of the justices that judicial review should not encompass a constitutional examination of legislative choices affecting economic, commercial, and property-related transactions. The thinking of these appellate judges was that the constitutional propriety of such economic legislation was solely for the Congress and state legislatures and other political branches of government, but not the courts.[26]

A second choice followed from the first choice to abandon judicial review of economic regulations and legislation involving social welfare and property use. If courts were to be out of the business of closely reviewing economic and property regulations, a choice needed to be made about what business the courts should be in. An otherwise obscure case decided in 1938—*United States v. Carolene Products Co.*—made that choice. That case also defined the agenda for the judiciary for nearly a century.[27] The *Carolene Products* case confirmed that judicial review should not entail a court reexamination of legislative judgments made regarding economic- or property-related regulations.[28]

---

[24]   Noah Feldman and Kathleen M. Sullivan, CONSTITUTIONAL LAW 518 (21st ed. 2022). See, for example: *Weaver v. Palmer Bros.*, 270 U.S. 402 (1926); *Adkins v. Children's Hospital*, 261 U.S. 525 (1923); *Hammer v. Dagenhart*, 247 U.S. 251 (1918); and *Adair v. United States*, 208 U.S. 161 (1908). For a summary of these cases, see Benjamin F. Wright, THE GROWTH OF AMERICAN CONSTITUTIONAL LAW 148–79 (1942).

[25]   William E. Leuchtenburg, THE SUPREME COURT REBORN: THE CONSTITUTIONAL REVOLUTION OF THE AGE OF ROOSEVELT 132–34, 213–36 (1995). The turning point in the rejection of *Lochner*-era judicial activism in invalidating economic legislation seemed to be the 1937 decision *West Coast Hotel Co. v. Parrish*, 300 U.S. 379, 386–87, 400 (1937), where the Court overruled a *Lochner*-era decision and upheld a state law establishing a minimum wage for women.

[26]   See Christopher Dodrill, *In Defense of "Footnote Four": A Historical Analysis of the New Deal's Effect on Land Regulation in the United States Supreme Court*, 72 LAW AND CONTEMPORARY PROBLEMS 191 (2009); Barry Cushman, RETHINKING THE NEW DEAL COURT: THE STRUCTURE OF A CONSTITUTIONAL REVOLUTION 21 (1998); and Howard Gillman, THE CONSTITUTION BESIEGED: THE RISE AND DEMISE OF LOCHNER ERA POLICE POWERS JURISPRUDENCE 200–201 (1993).

[27]   *Carolene Products Co., supra* note 2.

[28]   *Id.* at 148–51.

Rather *Carolene Products* Deference should apply, where the "existence of facts supporting the legislative judgment is to be *presumed* [because] regulatory legislation affecting ordinary commercial transactions is not to be pronounced unconstitutional unless [facts are present] to preclude the assumption that the [regulation] rests upon some rational basis ...."[29] In other words, *Carolene Products* definitively announced that the *Lochner*-era time of meaningful judicial review of economic regulations was over. It would be replaced by judicial *deference* to legislative judgments authorizing police power regulation of private decisions about economic transactions and property use.[30]

A third choice made by the Supreme Court and lower courts between the late 1930s and the early 21st century was to combine the first choice (end the *Lochner*-era) and the second choice (embrace the *Carolene Products* rationale), which meant that meaningful judicial review would cease for a discrete class of cases. Henceforth, reviewing courts would routinely uphold virtually all exercises of the police power involving economic and property legislation. The judicial explanation for this default to the police power has been repetitive and robotic: (1) property owners limited by the police power have no viable right to resist the regulation because the property right itself is not considered to be "fundamental,"[31] and (2) the police power is largely immune from judicial review because it is being exercised as part of the larger political process to promote and protect the public welfare.[32]

---

[29] *Id.* at 152.

[30] Rebecca L. Brown, *The Art of Reading Lochner*, I N.Y.U.J.L. & LIBERTY 570, 589 (2005).

[31] See, for example: *PBT Real Estate, LLC v. Town of Palm Beach*, 988 F.3d 1274 (11th Cir. 2021); *Van Sant & Co. v. Town of Calhan*, 83 F.4th 1254 (10th Cir. 2023); *Rondigo, LLC. v. Town of Richmond*, 641 F.3d 673, 682 (6th Cir. 2011); *Fair Rates v. New Mexico Pub. Regul. Comm'n*, 503 P.3d 1138 (N.M. 2022); and *Pratt Land & Dev., LLC v. City of Chattanooga*, 581 F. Supp. 3d 962 (E.D. Tenn. 2022).

[32] See, for example: *F.C.C. v. Beach Comm'rs, Inc.*, 508 U.S. 307, 314 N. 6, 315 (1993); *Hobbs v. City of Pacific Grove*, 85 Cal. App. 5th 311 (2022); *Lent v. Cal. Coastal Comm'r*, 62 Cal. App. 5th 812 (Cal. App. 2d Dist. 2021); *Monagham Farms v. Bd. of Cnty. Comm'rs*, 527 P.3d 1195, 1218–19 n. 14 (Wyo. 2023); and *Dodd v. Hodd River Cnty*, 855 P.2d 608 (Or. 1993).

III.   DEVALUATION OF COURTS AS DECISION-MAKERS, AND THE TRIUMPH OF HIGHLY DEFERENTIAL RATIONAL BASIS JUDICIAL REVIEW

The post-*Carolene Products* era transformed our assumptions about courts and judicial review. There has been an effective loss of a judicial "limit" on the police power "limitation" of property rights. In cases involving economic conflicts and property use disputes, judges' review powers have become degraded to the point where they are rarely perceived by litigants as performing a realistic checking function on regulators. This degradation of the judicial review function is because courts have embraced a standard of review that is so hyper-deferential to police power regulators that it is a "review" in name only, but without any substance. The adoption of "rational basis review" has meant not only that police power regulations are presumed to be constitutional, but also that an insurmountable burden has been placed on the property owner. Any challenger attacking the law must negate any factual, conceivable, and hypothetical basis which might support it.[33]

The Diminished Institutional Stature of the Judiciary. By the 21st century, courts had concluded that the judiciary was, as a decision-maker, unfit to review and strike down laws affecting economic and property interests. The United States Supreme Court summarized this assumption in *Lingle v. Chevron USA* (2005):[34] "[C]ourts [should not] scrutinize the efficacy of a vast array of state and federal [property and economic] regulation—a task for which courts are not suited."[35] Lower courts have been equally eager to disqualify themselves when asked to strike down economic legislation; judges have deemed themselves unworthy to interject judicial power as a check on police power exercises affecting property or other economic interests.[36]

Ironically, throughout the 19th and early 20th centuries, the courts assumed that as an institution they were well-equipped and intentionally designed to judicially review police power actions of the legislative and executive branches.[37] But by the 1940s, the courts instead began to defer to the presumed wisdom and judgments of both elected officials and regulatory agencies when challenged laws affected economic interests. This abandonment of a meaningful judicial role has, in large part, been due to several assumptions about

---

[33]   See, for example, *Armour v. Indianapolis*, 566 U.S. 673, 685 (2012).
[34]   *Lingle v. Chevron*, 544 U.S. 528 (2005).
[35]   *Id.* at 544.
[36]   See, for example, *Big Tyme Inv., L.L.C. v. Edwards*, 985 F.3d 456, 470 (5th Cir. 2021) and *Browne v. Indus. Claim Off.*, 495 P.3d 973, 983 (Colo. App. 2021).
[37]   See notes 17–19 and accompanying text, *supra*.

the competence of courts and regulators regarding property uses and the police power.

First, there was concern that judicial constitutional protection of property rights adversely affected by the police power would interfere with a separate branch's "political decision" to promote a redistribution of wealth (from economically better-off property owners to those who are less well-off).[38] Second, it was presumed that politicians, planners, and regulators had better on-the-ground expertise about property issues than judges.[39] Third, property owners were thought not to need judicial help because the existing political process protected them adequately.[40] And, *Carolene Products* judicial deference was consistent with the growing 20th-century belief that judicial restraint was critical to ensure that the "least dangerous branch" would not be perceived as encroaching on democratic political processes.[41]

The Judicial Embrace of Rational Basis Review. The *Carolene Products* case itself, not Footnote 4, had warned future reviewing courts that "for regulatory legislation affecting ordinary commercial transactions ... the facts supporting legislative judgment [are] to be presumed [and] not to be pronounced unconstitutional unless ... it rests upon some [non]rational basis ...."[42] This is a statement of legislative infallibility when property owners, or owners of economic interests, have the temerity to challenge police power regulations affecting "commercial transactions." The *Carolene Products* case is telling reviewing courts to adopt and apply what is known as "rational basis" review as the applicable standard of review. A court applying rational basis review does not consider whether the plaintiff's economic interests are worthy or subject to constitutional protection. Rather, rational basis is an invitation for the reviewing court to mechanically uphold the regulations. The court needs only to recite a canonical statement that (1) the regulation is "presumed" to be constitutional, and (2) the regulation does not "rest upon some [non]rational basis," since it could possibly, hypothetically, be related to a conceivable public

---

[38]   Daniel Cole, *Political Institutions, Judicial Review, and Private Property: A Comparative Institutional Analysis*, 15 Sup. Ct. Econ. Rev. 141 (2007) and Barbara Fried, THE PROGRESSIVE ASSAULT ON LAISSEZ-FAIRE 71–107 (1998).

[39]   See, for example, *Kelo v. City of New London*, 545 U.S. 459, 488 (2005).

[40]   Christopher Serkin, *Local Property Law: Adjusting the Scale of Property Protection*, 107 COLUM. L. REV. 883 (2007).

[41]   Alexander Bickel, THE SUPREME COURT AND THE IDEA OF PROGRESS 38 (1970).

[42]   *Carolene Products, supra* note 57 at 2.

purpose.[43] Supporting empirical evidence justifying this conclusion does not have to be considered by a reviewing court.[44]

Since *Carolene Products*, the Supreme Court and lower courts have consistently applied highly deferential rational basis review to defeat constitutional challenges to police power regulation. These deferential courts ignore property owners who have argued that the offending law has violated the due process clause,[45] the equal protection clause,[46] the contracts clause,[47] or the takings clause.[48] Such cases insist that the judicial branch should *not* act as a check on legislative or executive power because policy choices about economic and property matters should not be made or overturned by judges.[49]

CONCLUSION

There is, in the United States, an odd and unsettling double standard that applies when plaintiffs seek judicial review. For plaintiffs whose affected interests do *not* encompass economic, commercial, or property issues, courts will take a hard look at the law in question. Courts will ask if some provision in the Constitution has been violated, if the law is seeking to accomplish some problematic goal, or if the law is so poorly drafted that it cannot ever achieve its goal. However, for cases where the plaintiff's injury involves government actions affecting property or economic interests, courts embrace a policy of non-review for such cases, where they simply *defer* to the lawmaker responsible for the offending regulation. This deference takes the form of the court applying a standard of review, rational basis review, where the court basically rubber stamps the choices of the regulator. For the first class of plaintiffs, there is some chance of success when a private party seeks judicial review of a regulation. For the second class of plaintiffs, there is little or no chance of success in court.

In effect, when reviewing courts merely defer to the regulator and apply rational basis review to the suspect law, plaintiffs with commercial or property

---

[43]   Nicolas Walter, *The Utility of Rational Basis Review*, 63 Vⁱˡˡ. L. Rᴇᴠ. 79, 80 (2018).

[44]   *Birchansky v. Clabaugh*, 955 F.3d 751, 757 (8th Cir. 2020) ("Rational basis is not a particularly high bar: 'The law's rational relation to a state interest need only be conceivable ....'").

[45]   *Williamson v. Lee Optical of Okla.*, 34 U.S. 483 (1955).

[46]   *Nordlinger v. Hahn*, 505 U.S. 1 (1992).

[47]   *Keystone Bituminous Coal Ass'n v. DeBenedictis*, 480 U.S. 470, 503 (1987).

[48]   *Penn Central Transp. Co. v. City of New York*, 438 U.S. 104, 124 (1978); see also *Lingle*, 544 U.S. at 545.

[49]   *Big Tyme L.L.C. v. Edwards*, 985 F.3d at 470 (5th Cir. 2021).

interests fighting the regulators in court face the modern-day equivalent of Dante's message to those passing through the Gates of Hell: "Abandon all hope, ye who enter here!" This admonition should be heeded by property lawyers expecting meaningful judicial review from courts tasked with deciding whether to serve as a limit on the implied limitation of the police power.[50] That limitation may exist in theory, and be applied when the interest asserted involves personal matters like reproductive autonomy, or racial or gender-based discrimination, or free expression; but the judicial limitation on the police power limit on property uses does not, in fact, meaningfully occur anymore.

ACKNOWLEDGEMENTS

Professor Laitos wishes to acknowledge the help provided by Professor Nancy Leong and Makayla Shoults in the drafting and production of this chapter. Professor Laitos also wishes to acknowledge the financial backing provided by Neil and Susan Ray, who made possible the April 2024 Private Property Rights Conference, during which this paper was initially delivered as a conference presentation.

---

[50] Erwin Chemerinsky, *The Rational Basis Test is Constitutional (and Desirable)*, 14 GEO. J. OF LAW. & PUB. POL'Y 401, 410 (2016).

PART B

The necessity and legitimacy of public land-use regulations

4. Property, public health, and the liberal virtue of political contestation

Daniel Cole

INTRODUCTION

Every public health crisis reveals a fundamental tension between individual liberty interests and public health protection.[1] At the height of the 2020–22 COVID-19 pandemic, serious questions were raised about the scope and locus of governmental authority to impose temporary business closures, quarantine, and masking requirements.[2] Civil libertarians justifiably worry about the potential for government overreach and the possibility that supposedly temporary government powers might endure long beyond the immediate crisis. According to Erwin Chemerinsky and Michele Goodwint, "there is every reason to fear that the pandemic could be used as a justification for a massive deprivation of rights and abuses."[3] Indeed, autocrats (and would-be autocrats) around the world seized on the opportunity to acquire sweeping new powers

---

[1] See, for example: J. Alexander Navarro and Howard Markel, *Politics, Pushback, and Pandemics: Challenges to Public Health Orders in the 1918 Influenza Pandemic*, 111 AMER. J.PUB. HEALTH 416 (2021); Jonathan Pugh, *The United Kingdom's Coronavirus Act, Deprivations of Liberty, and the Right to Liberty and Security of the Person*, 7 J.L. & BIOSCIENCES 1 (2020); George C. Thomas III and Erica C. Pulford, *Civil Liberties in the Age of COVID-19*, 72 RUTGERS U.L. REV 1457 (2019–2020); Nadja Durbach, *"They Might As Well Brand Us": Working-Class Resistance to Compulsory Vaccination in Victorian England*, 13 SOCIAL HIST. MED. 45 (2000); and James G. Hanley, HEALTHY BOUNDARIES: PROPERTY, LAW AND PUBLIC HEALTH IN ENGLAND AND WALES, 1815–1872 (2016).

[2] See, for example, Efthimios Parasidis, *COVID-19 Vaccine Mandates at the Supreme Court: Scope and Limits of Federal Authority*, HEALTH AFFAIRS FOREFRONT, Mar. 8, 2022 and K.D. Ewing, *COVID-19: Government by Decree*, 31 KING'S L.J. 1 (2020).

[3] Erwin Chemerinsky and Michele Goodwint, *Civil Liberties in a Pandemic: The Lessons of History*, 106 CORNELL L.REV. 815, 818 (2021).

that curtailed freedom of speech (in Jordan and Hungary), censored the media (in Thailand and Hungary), delayed elections (in Bolivia and Hungary), shut down the courts (in Israel), suspended existing laws (in Hungary), and gave one person the power to rule by decree during the crisis, along with sole authority to determine when the emergency ended (in Hungary).[4]

In the face of such abuses, one might be forgiven for concluding that it is simply too dangerous to allow governmental authorities the power to impose regulations to prevent or mitigate public health crises. We must bear in mind, however, that simply allowing a pandemic to "run its course" would also be extremely dangerous and would allow risk-taking citizens to externalize costs to more risk-averse citizens. Many more people would die. It is also easy to overestimate the risks of government overreach. During the COVID-19 pandemic, the vast majority of advanced, industrial democracies, including some that had been moving in an illiberal direction, such as Poland, did not impose measures that were extreme, unprecedented, or permanent.

In denouncing public health measures as "government overreach," conservatives and libertarians also play fast and loose with "the classical-liberal tradition." In fact, neither "the classical-liberal tradition," the federal constitution, state constitutions, nor principles of the common law mandate *"laissez-faire et laissez passer"* in normal circumstances, let alone during public health emergencies. As a practical matter, people look to governments, at one level or another, to protect them from harms they cannot control through other forms of collective action. Social-contract theorists from Locke to America's founders conceived of civil society and "the state" as collective-choice arrangements to deal with collective-action problems.

While the "rhetoric of reaction"[5] against pollution-control regulations and other public-health measures remains a powerful force, scant evidence exists to support a claim that the "regulatory state" has led us down "the road to serfdom."[6] Property rights remain strongly protected in the USA and other advanced industrial democracies, thanks in part to constitutional policy innovations like the "regulatory takings" doctrine.[7] According to Freedom House, which "rates people's access to political rights and civil liberties in 208 countries and territories,"[8] the UK remains a "free" country despite its nationalized system of health care and myriad other features of a modern welfare state. The

---

[4]   Selam Gebrakidan, *For Autocrats, and Others, Coronavirus Is a Chance to Grab Even More Power,* NEW YORK TIMES, April 14, 2020.
[5]   Albert Hirschman, THE RHETORIC OF REACTION (1991).
[6]   Friedrich von Hayek, THE ROAD TO SERFDOM (1944).
[7]   See *Pennsylvania Coal Co. v. Mahon,* 260 U.S. 393 (1922).
[8]   https://freedomhouse.org/countries/freedom-world/scores.

UK also ranks high on the Cato Institute's Human Freedom Index,[9] which assesses countries using 86 indicators of personal and economic freedom in areas that include rule of law, legal system and property rights, and regulation. This despite the fact that Parliament can (a) lawfully expropriate land from private landowners with or without compensation and (b) heavily regulate land uses, greatly reducing their value, without giving rise to "compulsory purchase." That is because the UK's unwritten constitution includes neither a "just compensation" requirement nor a doctrine similar to "regulatory takings." Yet, parliament rarely expropriates land and, when it does so, it always pays compensation. This consistent practice has given rise to a constitutional "convention" according to which parliament is presumed to intend to pay compensation unless it expressly denies such intent.[10] According to the Freedom Index and the Cato Institute, the UK is both a regulatory state and a free country. Oddly, it is often rated as freer than the USA, even though the USA has constitutional protections for property that the UK lacks.

Section I of this chapter reviews the "classical-liberal" literature and more recent works in that tradition to show that modern property and liberty claims against public health measures, especially in exigent circumstances, such as pandemics, find very limited support among "classical liberals." Scholars including Adam Smith, Friedrich von Hayek, Karl Popper, and Milton Friedman recognized a government's obligation to provide public goods, expressly including basic sanitation to protect public health. Section II then provides historical support for the proposition that governments have an inherent duty to protect public health. A concise survey reveals that public health measures, ranging from basic sanitation to epidemic management and pollution control, have been ubiquitous throughout the history of human settlements. Section III briefly recounts the evolution of constitutional jurisprudence relating to emergency powers of the states. Unsurprisingly, courts have been more willing to give leeway to the states during the early days of a public health emergency, but as time goes on, courts become more concerned about private rights, to the point that public health measures are sometimes eroded or ended before crises are over. Although, by the end of COVID, the Supreme Court's jurisprudence indicated that, in future emergencies, states will be on a shorter judicial tether from the outset. Section IV argues that any search for a simple legal or constitutional rubric to strike the "right" balance between protecting public health and private liberty and property is doomed to fail. It will always

---

[9] Ian Vasquez et al., THE HUMAN FREEDOM INDEX 2023: A GLOBAL MEASUREMENT OF PERSONAL, CIVIL, AND ECONOMIC FREEDOM (2023), https://www.cato.org/human-freedom-index/2023.

[10] Daniel H. Cole, *Political Institutions, Judicial Review, and Private Property: A Comparative Institutional Analysis*, 15 SUP. CT. ECON. REV. 141 (2007).

remain a matter of trial, error, political contestation, and correction. This is as it should be in a liberal-democratic system. As the Conclusion observes, liberal theory does not provide all the answers to our problems because it has no teleology – no predetermined vision of *the* desirable end(s) that society should be organized to attain. It accepts as a premise that individuals within a liberal-democratic commonwealth will disagree about both ends and means. And it seeks to respect those differences, within disputable constitutional guardrails, not by declaring permanent victory for one view, which is somehow determined to be the most consistent with liberal principles, over any others, but by establishing organizational mechanisms and legal processes in which disagreements can be resolved *for the time being* and without violence. Mistakes are inevitable but there are no panaceas.

I.   PUBLIC HEALTH AND THE "CLASSICAL-LIBERAL" TRADITION

Though it is often presented as a monolith, the "classical-liberal tradition" in political economy comprises a diverse set of opinions and principles about the proper limits of governmental authority over individuals' behavior. The tradition rules out authoritarianism on the one hand and state socialism on the other, but liberals disagree among themselves about where to draw the line between those two extremes. Conservative, moderate, and progressive liberals all share fundamental commitments to the rule of law, multi-party representative democracy, and political equality under law, but those principles allow plenty of room for disagreements about specific public policies and, more generally, the limits of government power.

John Locke is often portrayed as the founding father of political liberalism.[11] His theories of property and governance undeniably influenced later classical-liberal thinkers, including Adam Smith, Jeremy Bentham, James Mill, and his son, John Stuart Mill. Locke famously wrote that "government has no other end but the preservation of property."[12] The only reason people would agree to leave the state of nature to live in a governed society is for "the enjoyment of their properties in peace and safety."[13] This is the Locke loved

---

[11] See, for example, Michael P. Zuckert, LAUNCHING LIBERALISM: ON LOCKEAN POLITICAL PHILOSOPHY (2002) and Duncan Bell, REORDERING THE WORLD: ESSAYS ON LIBERALISM AND EMPIRE 73 (2016).

[12] John Locke, SECOND TREATISE OF GOVERNMENT, OF CIVIL GOVERNMENT: BOOK 185 (1824). In Locke's use, the term "property" encompassed individual liberty. See *id.* at 204 ("… lives, liberties, and estates, which I call by the general name, property").

[13] *Id.* at 208.

by libertarians. But Locke also recognized that, once in a system of civil governance, individuals must be prepared to relinquish some of their liberty and property for the common good. That included paying taxes to support legitimate state functions and suffering reasonable regulation of their liberty and property to protect public health and welfare. The importance of public health protection for Locke is underscored by the 1669 constitution he co-wrote for England's Carolina colony in America. In it, Locke and his co-author the Earl of Shaftesbury gave Carolina's governors "a broad power to take care of all 'corruption or infection of the common air or water, and all things' necessary to protect 'the public commerce and health.'"[14]

More generally, Locke's strong commitment to the protection of private property was vitiated by his belief that, in a commonwealth, the legislature holds the "supreme authority" to act in any way that advances the public good. Its decisions have the *tacit* consent of all property owners, as exercised by their elected representatives (whether or not the property-owner voted for his or her legislator).[15] In a commonwealth, Locke held, the landowner's power to grant or withhold consent is transferred to his elected representative in parliament, which operates according to majority rule. So, even if the landowner's representative votes against a measure that affects the landowner's property, the landowner is taken to have consented to the new law. Most libertarians simply ignore Locke's notion of *tacit* consent, but some classical-liberal scholars have criticized him for it, arguing that it allows Leviathan in through the back door.[16] In theory, tacit consent might allow a legislative body, such as parliament, to run roughshod over individual liberty and property in the name of some alleged common good. However, the actual history of parliamentary sovereignty in England suggests the fear is overblown.

While Locke is often treated as if he conjured the theory of tacit consent out of thin air, the theory predated him by at least a century in English jurisprudence and political theory. It was an historically established principle of English constitutional governance, which conservative-liberals like Hume and Burke would probably have acknowledged as conventional or traditional.

---

[14] John Fabian Witt, AMERICAN CONTAGIONS: EPIDEMICS AND THE LAW 15 (2020).

[15] Locke, *supra* note 12, at 26, Locke's notion of tacit consent appears also in his state of nature, when everyone tacitly consents to everyone else's appropriation (through labor) of land and other gifts of nature. He makes clear that the idea of tacit consent in the state of nature is to minimize what are now known as transaction costs. Perhaps the same purpose is served by the adoption of tacit consent in civil society, but he does not expressly say so.

[16] Richard Epstein, TAKINGS: PRIVATE PROPERTY AND THE POWER OF EMINENT DOMAIN 14–15 (1985).

Writing a century before Locke, Queen Elizabeth I's Secretary of State, Sir Thomas Smith declared that:

> [E]very Englishman is intended to be present [in parliament], either in person or by procuration and attorneys, of what preeminence, state, dignity or quality soever he be, from the prince, be he king or queen, to the lowest person in England. And the consent of the parliament is taken to be every man's consent.[17]

Sir Edward Coke's famous phrase, "common consent in parliament," from the 1628 Petition of Right, reflects the same idea.[18] Indeed, writers in the Tudor era were agreed that parliamentary decisions had the "universal consent" of all "members of the realm ... because their community was represented," notwithstanding the fact that, at that time, the political system was still far from democratic.[19]

Writing approximately a century after Locke, Adam Smith is often mistaken for a proponent of *laissez-faire*. In fact, like Locke, he was far from a property and market absolutist. In his *Lectures on Jurisprudence*, Smith observed that "[g]overnment was established to defend the property of the subjects, but if it come to be of a contrary tendency, yet they must agree to give up a little of their right...."[20] Though he generally disapproved of government intervention in markets, he supported public regulation of banks and monopolies, while also proposing state grants of temporary monopolies for public purposes, such as expanding trade. More generally, Smith believed the state served three purposes: (1) administration of justice, including, of course, protection of liberty and property interests; (2) national defense; and (3) provision of public goods, including infrastructure, encompassing not only roads, bridges, and canals but also parks for public recreation.

> The third and last duty of the sovereign or commonwealth is that of erecting and maintaining certain public works and certain public institutions, which it can never be for the interest of any individual, or small number of individuals, to erect and maintain; because the profit could never repay the expense to any individual or small number of individuals, though it may frequently do much more than repay it to a great society.[21]

---

[17]   Quoted in F.W. Maitland, THE CONSTITUTIONAL HISTORY OF ENGLAND 255 (1908).

[18]   3 How. St. Tr. 59, 222–24.

[19]   G.R. Elton, THE RULE OF LAW IN SIXTEENTH-CENTURY ENGLAND 280 (1974).

[20]   Adam Smith, LECTURES ON JURISPRUDENCE 324 (1982 [1772–3; 1776]). Smith was not the actual author of the LECTURES, which comprise two sets of student notes taken from his lectures.

[21]   Adam Smith, THE WEALTH OF NATIONS 779 (1994 [1776]).

Smith supported government provision of public goods for both commercial and noncommercial purposes. Improvements in public transportation were mainly for advancing commerce. But Smith also called for the government to finance mandatory education for the young and moral instruction for all ages. He supported public ownership and management of lands for purposes of public recreation and pleasure.[22] His reference to recreation implies a concern for public health, which he explicitly raises elsewhere in *The Wealth of Nations*. Specifically, in arguing for public funding of compulsory education as a public good, Smith writes that the dangers of an uneducated populace "deserve the most careful attention of government; in the same manner as it would deserve its most serious attention to prevent a leprosy or any other loathsome and offensive disease, though neither mortal nor dangerous, from spreading itself among them."[23] In his *Lectures on Jurisprudence* Smith explicitly recognized that governments are responsible for enacting sanitation regulations. He considered "the police," by which he meant the power of government to regulate social interactions, necessary for preserving "the cleanliness of roads, streets, etc., and to prevent the bad effects of corrupting and putrifying substances."[24]

Smith's close friend David Hume concurred that government existed for protection and security, including of private property, but Hume rejected natural law explanations of property in favor of positive explanations based on conquest or convention.[25] He was more suspicious of state interference in private matters than either Locke or Smith. He believed the proper scope and scale of formal governance was a matter of historical convention. Hume expressly recognized the need for government to support collective action at scales larger than a single neighborhood. For example, Hume supported the establishment of a state bank to control the quantity of paper money.[26] However, Hume never wrote anything about issues of local governance, or its role in protecting public health through sanitation and pollution-control measures. His historical and philosophical writings, like those of his contemporary and fellow conservative-liberal Edmund Burke, focused on the constitutional level of governance, the level of kings, parliaments, and empires.

---

[22]   *Id.* at 887.

[23]   *Id.* at 845.

[24]   Adam Smith, *supra* note 20, at 331. Also see *id.* at 486.

[25]   David Hume, *Of the Origin of Government*, in David Hume, ESSAYS MORAL, POLITICAL, AND LITERARY 37, 37–41 (1985 [1777]) and David Hume, *Of the Coalition of Parties*, in David Hume, ESSAYS MORAL, POLITICAL, AND LITERARY 493, 495–6 (1985 [1777]).

[26]   David Hume, *Of Money*, in David Hume, ESSAYS MORAL, POLITICAL AND LITERARY 281, 285 (1985 [1777]).

There is good reason to believe that Hume did not oppose municipal land-use and pollution-control regulations if only because they were *conventional* in Britain and Europe long before he was born. In 1505, magistrates and the town council first hired an individual to clean city streets. In 1584, the Dean of Guilt Court was granted exclusive jurisdiction over neighborhood disputes, including sanitation nuisances. By the 1620s, Edinburgh's High Street had drains running down either side of the street. In 1672, the town council resolved to improve the city's water supply. Ten years later, it appointed a "constant committee," which met weekly, to oversee a street cleaning team of 30 "muckmen." In 1686, Edinburgh enacted a street-cleaning ordinance, which was funded by taxes on all inhabitants, burgesses, and others in the town and its suburbs.[27] All of this before Hume was born in 1711, and public regulation of urban environmental problems continued throughout his life. In 1749, for example, the Edinburgh Town Council enacted the "Nastiness Act," which allowed the dumping of household waste only between the hours of 10 pm and 7 am. Any person dumping waste onto the street was supposed to yell "Gardyloo" to alert pedestrians and bystanders so they would not get soiled. During Hume's life, several disease epidemics, including smallpox, swept through Edinburgh.[28]

In 1774, two years before Hume's death, the UK's parliament passed "An Act for preserving the Health of Prisoners in Gaol and preventing the Gaol Distemper."[29] "Gaol-distemper" was actually typhus, which broke out not only in prisons but also in the criminal courts, where prisoners were kept in crowded quarters underneath or alongside courtrooms. Contagions swept through courthouses often enough to give rise to the label "Black Assizes." One typhus outbreak, at London's famous Old Bailey court in 1750, killed 40 criminals, lawyers, judges, and city officials.[30] According to the

---

[27]   Leona J. Skelton, SANITATION IN URBAN BRITAIN, 1560–1700 21, 69, 71, 73, 150 (2015).

[28]   *Gardyloo: The Grim Story of Unsanitary Edinburgh*, THE SCOTSMAN, March 16, 2016.

[29]   14 George 3 c. 59 (1774), https://statutes.org.uk/site/the-statutes/eighteenth-century/1774-14-george-3-c-59-health-of-prisoners-act/. The classical-liberal thinker Edmund Burke was a Whig MP when the Prisoners' Health law was enacted. However, he evidently gave no speech on the issue. At least, there is no record of one in the parliamentary record (34 JOURNAL OF THE HOUSE OF COMMONS (1774)). At that time, he was, of course, preoccupied with attempts to mend parliament's relations with its American colonies, whose independence he ultimately supported.

[30]   Roy Porter, *Cleaning Up the Great Wen: Public Health in Eighteenth-century London*, Supp. 11 MEDICAL HISTORY 61, 63 (1991).

nineteenth-century medical historian and doctor William A. Guy, the 1774 statute gradually improved jail conditions and was ultimately effective in eradicating "jail distemper."[31] The 1774 statute holds two other distinctions: (1) it appears to be the first statute parliament enacted in the area now known as public health; and (2) it was both the start and the limit of parliament's interest in public health before the nineteenth century. Until the 1830s, England's "Statute-Book contained no general law of sanitary intention," aside from one other Quarantine statute."[32] Public health protection remained mainly the province of municipalities.

A contemporary of both Smith and Hume, the jurist William Blackstone had impeccable classical-liberal credentials. A thoroughgoing Lockian, Blackstone argued that "the principle aim of society is to protect individuals in the enjoyment of those absolute rights, which were vested in them by the immutable laws of nature."[33] "This natural liberty consists properly in a power of acting as one thinks fit, without any restraint or control, unless by the law of nature."[34] Of course, natural liberty includes private property, which Blackstone famously defined as "that sole and despotic dominion which one man claims and exercises over the external things of the world, in total exclusion of the right of any other individual in the universe."[35]

Upon entering society, according to Blackstone, the individual "gives up a part of his natural liberty, as the price of so valuable a purchase; and in consideration of receiving the advantages of mutual commerce, obliges himself to conform to those laws, which the community has thought proper to establish."[36] The individual remains "master of his own conduct except in

---

[31]   William A. Guy, PUBLIC HEALTH: AN INTRODUCTION TO SANITARY SCIENCE 190 (1870).

[32]   John Simon, ENGLISH SANITARY INSTITUTIONS: REVIEWED IN THE COURSE OF THEIR DEVELOPMENT, AND IN SOME OF THEIR POLITICAL AND SOCIAL RELATIONS 166. (1890).

[33]   William Blackstone, COMMENTARIES ON THE LAWS OF ENGLAND, BOOK THE FIRST 120 (1765).

[34]   *Id.* at 121.

[35]   William Blackstone, COMMENTARIES ON THE LAWS OF ENGLAND, BOOK THE SECOND 2 (1766). Blackstone's definition is plainly inaccurate as a description of common law real property, which he makes clear in the rest of Book II of the *Commentaries*. The largest estate in land, *fee simple absolute*, is not allodial property, but subject to various restrictions of neighbors, as described by nuisance and trespass law, and public authorities under their police powers (*for example*, public nuisance law) or pursuant to eminent domain (in the USA) or compulsory purchase (in the UK).

[36]   *Id.* at 121.

those points wherein the public good requires some direction or restraint."[37] Positive law can "restrain" persons from "doing mischief to his fellow-citizens, though it diminishes the natural liberty," in order to increase "the civil liberty of mankind."[38] While restrictions on or takings of private property require voluntary consent of the landowner, that consent can be either personal "or that of his representatives in parliament."[39] Blackstone, thus, explicitly adopts the pre-Lockian notion of tacit consent. That said, Blackstone, more clearly than Locke, limits government regulation of private behavior: "[P]rivate vices ... are not, cannot be, the object of any municipal law any farther than as by their evil example or other pernicious effects they may prejudice the community."[40] This is Blackstone's precursor to Mill's "Harm Principle." Among the private vices that Blackstone argued should not be deemed offenses against public order were private drunkenness and lying (unless it amounted to libel, slander, or fraud).

The civil liberties individuals possess under English private law, Blackstone argued, include a broad "right of personal security"[41] one incident of which is a right to "*health.*"[42] That right is protected against acts that might "prejudice or annoy it." In addition to the private right of health held by individuals, Blackstone observed that English common law also protected public health. He devoted an entire chapter of his *Commentaries* to "Offenses against the Public Health, and the Public Police or Œconomy." The chapter's first paragraph observed that a plague victim who violates quarantine commits a felony, likewise, someone who sells "unwholesome provisions, including corrupted wine, contagious or unwholesome flesh...." These amounted to "offenses which may properly be said to respect the public health."[43]

Blackstone held an expansive view of the police power as "due regulation and domestic order of the kingdom," according to which "individuals ... are bound to conform their general behavior to the rules of propriety, good neighborhood, and good manners."[44] Violation of those duties would amount to "common nuisances..., a species of offences against the public order and œconomical regimen of the state," which annoy the king's subjects." In this context, Blackstone uses the term "common" in contradistinction to the term

---

[37] *Id.* at 122.

[38] *Id.* at 121–2.

[39] *Id.* at 135.

[40] William Blackstone, COMMENTARIES ON THE LAWS OF ENGLAND, BOOK THE FOURTH 41 (1769).

[41] Blackstone, COMMENTARIES, BOOK THE FIRST, *supra* note 33, at 125.

[42] *Id.* at 130.

[43] *Id.* at 161–2.

[44] *Id.* at 162.

"private," which makes it synonymous with modern common law's notion of "public nuisance."[45] His list of nuisances includes one that Blackstone might have listed among measures designed to protect public health: "[c]orrupting the air with noisome smells." He refers to a common law case in which a property owner was held liable for nuisance because he built a lead smelter "vapor and smoke" from which killed the neighbor's corn and grass and damaged his cattle.[46]

In 1859, John Stuart Mill published *On Liberty*, thought by some to be the *locus classicus* of liberal theory.[47] His motivation in writing it was "an increasing inclination to stretch unduly powers of the society over the individual, both by the force of opinions and even by that of legislation." The effect was to "strengthen society ... and diminish the power of the individual."[48] Mill sought to rectify this not by elevating the individual above all social considerations but by delimiting the circumstances under which an individual's freedom of action might be constrained. Mill was equally concerned that too much individual liberty would dominate "the social principle."[49] A balance was needed, and to that end Mill introduced the "Harm Principle," according to which "the only purpose for which power can be rightfully exercised over any member of a civilized community, against his will, is to prevent harm to others. His own good, either physical or moral, is not a sufficient warrant."[50] The phrase "civilized community" introduces an important caveat. Mill believed some polities, such as India, were not yet sufficiently civilized for liberty.[51] To some extent, this reflected the prejudices of his time; but that should not excuse Mill, who had no problem transcending the prejudices of his time to argue in favor of women's suffrage. His bias with respect to India was likely influenced by the political position he held overseeing the activities of the East India Company.[52]

In contrast to Hume and Burke, Mill was skeptical about customs and traditions, which sometimes did more harm than good in society. He wrote that "[t]he despotism of custom is everywhere the standing hindrance to human

---

[45]   *Id*. at 166–7.

[46]   William Blackstone, COMMENTARIES ON THE LAWS OF ENGLAND, BOOK THE THIRD 217 (1768).

[47]   John Stuart Mill, ON LIBERTY (1947 [1859]).

[48]   *Id*. at 14.

[49]   *Id*. at 60.

[50]   *Id*. at 57. While Mill is usually credited with innovating the "Harm Principle," it was already present in Locke and Blackstone. See LOCKE, *supra* note 12, at 133; Blackstone, COMMENTARIES, BOOK THE FOURTH, *supra* note 40, at 41.

[51]   Blackstone, *id*., at 10.

[52]   R.J. Moore, *John Stuart Mill at East India House,* 20 HIST. STUD. 497 (2009).

advancement."[53] Traditional or customary constraints on individual behavior that prevented material harm to others were warranted. But constraints on behavior that did not harm others were despotic. So, for example, a tradition of religious discrimination against Catholics or Jews did not warrant the continuation of religious conformity requirements to vote or hold elective office. Similarly, a tradition of subjugation of women provides no *reason* to continue treating them as second-class citizens. Mill advocated for women's suffrage, under the intellectual influence of his remarkable spouse Harriet Taylor.[54] For Mill "the appropriate region of human liberty" included conscience, thought, opinion (including in matters of religion), expression, association, and "framing the plan of our life to suit our own character." For the state or any private individual or group to obstruct others from exercising their rightful liberties is itself harmful, and therefore not a proper exercise of liberty.[55]

Mill's theory of liberty unquestionably provides room for government intervention to prevent harm, including local government regulation for the purposes of sanitation and pollution control, which prevent material harms to the health and well-being of practically all members of the public. Mill's writings on political economy predated theories of "externalities" and "social costs," but he certainly would have recognized that an individual disposing of waste in derogation of local sanitation rules was not only violating law but imposing harm on others. In *On Liberty*, Mill considered the "proper limits of what may be called the functions of police":

> It is one of the undisputed functions of government to take precautions against crime before it has been committed, as well as to detect and punish it afterwards. The preventative function of government, however, is far more liable to be abused, to the prejudice of liberty, than the punitory function.... Nevertheless, if a public authority, or even a private person, sees any one evidently preparing to commit a crime, they are not bound to look on inactive until the crime is committed, but may interfere to prevent it.[56]

For reasons of justice, Mill's theory of liberty requires government to police harm-causing individual acts so as to protect those who are or might be harmed by it. But government action to protect public health and well-being is also justified under Mill's theory of utilitarianism – a revised version of Jeremy Bentham's "Happiness Principle" incorporating individual virtue and social

---

[53] MILL, ON LIBERTY, *supra* note 47, at 70.
[54] John Stuart Mill, ON THE SUBJECTION OF WOMEN (1869).
[55] Mill, ON LIBERTY, *supra* note 47, at 12.
[56] *Id.* at 97.

justice as important elements of the utility calculus.[57] In *Principles of Political Economy* (1865), Mill's utilitarianism is plain to see. Like Adam Smith, he generally deplored government interference in markets, while noting several important exceptions:

> There is a multitude of cases in which governments, with the general approbation, assume powers and execute functions for which no reason can be assigned except the simple one, that they conduce to general convenience. We may take as an example the function (which is a monopoly too) of coining money. This is assumed for no more recondite purpose than that of saving to individuals the trouble, delay, and expense of weighing and assaying. *No one, however, even those most jealous of state interference, has objected to this as an improper exercise of the powers of government.* Prescribing a set of standard weights and measures is another instance. Paving, lighting, and *cleansing the streets and thoroughfares,* is another; whether done by the general government, or, as is more usual, and generally more advisable, by a municipal authority.[58]

Later in the same volume, Mill expressly supports government provision of public goods:

> [A]nything which it is desirable should be done for the general interests of mankind or of future generations, or for the present interests of those members of the community who require external aid, but which is not of a nature to remunerate individuals or associations for undertaking it, is in itself a suitable thing to be undertaken by government.

That public health was among the "general interests of mankind" unlikely to be provided by the market is implied in an 1858 report Mill authored on the East India Company's operations in India. He lauded "[m]easures ... taken for many years, and with much success, for the diffusion of vaccination not only in

---

57   See, John Stuart Mill, Utilitarianism (1863). Mill's libertarian and utilitarian principles can be reconciled by observing that (a) individual liberty general promotes social welfare, but (b) harmful abuses of liberty (*i.e.,* licentiousness) reduces social welfare. See, for example, D.G. Brown, *Mill on Liberty and Morality,* 81 Phil. Rev 133 (1972) and Oskar Kurer, *John Stuart Mill: Liberal or Utilitarian?,* 6 Eur. J. Hist. of Econ. Thought 200 (2999). Mill also believed that small-s, nonstate "socialism" (such as that advocated by Charles Fourier) was fully consistent with individual liberty because it would involve purely voluntary associations of individuals conducting "experiments in living." Mill, On Liberty, *supra* note 47, at 56; John Stuart Mill, Socialism (1891).
58   John Stuart Mill, Principles of Political Economy, Vol. 2 482 (1858) (emphasis added).

the British territories, but also in the native states."[59] Though he vociferously opposed the UK's Contagious Disease Acts of 1866 and 1869,[60] that was only because they discriminated against women. To this day, Millian utilitarianism is considered "the lynchpin for good public health policies...."[61]

Twentieth-century liberals in the classical tradition, including Friedrich von Hayek, Karl Popper, and Milton Friedman, were no less supportive of public health protections, including basic sanitation and pollution control, than their eighteenth- and nineteenth-century predecessors. Popper and Hayek both reacted to that century's crisis of liberalism, represented by both Nazism and Communism, by publishing polemics against the Utopian idealism and totalitarianism of state socialism. In his *The Road to Serfdom* (1944), Hayek warned against increasing state power, which threatened the liberty of individuals. He particularly opposed government redistributions of wealth as illiberal. But he supported a substantial "welfare state" on grounds that many of its activities were not detrimental to individual liberty, noting that "[t]he range and variety of government action ... reconcilable with a free system is ... considerable."[62]

In *The Constitution of Liberty* (1960), Hayek wrote:

> All modern governments have made provision for the indigent, unfortunate and disabled and have concerned themselves with questions of *health* and the dissemination of knowledge. There is no reason why the volume of these pure service activities should not increase with general growth of wealth. There are common needs that can be satisfied only by collective action and which can be thus provided for without restricting individual liberty. It can hardly be denied that, as we grow richer, that minimum of sustenance which the community has always provided for those not able to look after themselves, and which can be provided outside the market, will gradually rise, or that government may, usefully and without doing any harm, assist or even lead in such endeavors. There is little reason why the government should not also play some role, or even take the initiative,

[59]   John Stuart Mill, MEMORANDUM OF THE IMPROVEMENTS IN THE ADMINISTRATION OF INDIA DURING THE LAST THIRTY YEARS 87–8 (1858). https://www.google.com/books/edition/Memorandum_of_the_Improvements_in_the_Ad/SICBzx3h7OsC?hl=en&gbpv=1&dq=mill+memorandum+improvements+india&printsec=frontcover.

[60]   *The Evidence of John Stuart Mill Taken Before the Royal Commission of 1870 on the Administration and Operation of the Contagious Diseases Acts of 1866 and 1869, Reprinted Verbatim from the Blue Book* (1871).

[61]   Tim Lang and Geof Rayner, *Beyond the Golden Era of Public Health: Charting a Path from Sanitarianism to Ecological Public Health*, 129 PUB. HEALTH 1369 (2015).

[62]   F.A. Hayek, THE CONSTITUTION OF LIBERTY: THE DEFINITIVE EDITION 340 (R. Hamowy, ed., 1960).

in areas such as social insurance and education, or temporarily subsidize certain experimental developments.[63]

Hayek restated Mill's Harm Principle and supported measures to prevent crimes of violence, fraud, unsafe housing and factory conditions, use of poisonous substances, unsanitary conditions, and production of immoral and dangerous products.[64] He also supported the licensing of certain professions to ensure competence,[65] compulsory military service, mandatory education (including public schools), and tax payments to fund necessary state operations (but not for the purpose of redistributing wealth). He did not oppose public subsidies for agriculture and the private construction of housing, so long as market entry by non-subsidized enterprises was not restricted.[66] Among welfare-state initiatives, Hayek supported "an equal minimum income for all,"[67] "protection against risks common to all,"[68] local government provision of "parks and museums, theaters and facilities for sport,"[69] "social security,"[70] legal mandates requiring private health insurance,[71] and "uniform minimum unemployment insurance."[72] Hayek generally opposed "town planning" (for example, zoning), believing that markets led to rational land-use decisions. As a matter of both theory and practice, this was short-sighted.

Interestingly, in his discussion of town planning Hayek paid no attention to pollution and sanitation, other than noting the problem of "neighborhood effects" (externalities), which justifies government intervention in accordance with conventional welfare economics. But in a subsequent chapter on "Economic Policy and the Rule of Law," Hayek expressly includes "sanitation and health services" among the "fields in which the desirability of government action can hardly be questioned."[73] In the same chapter, Hayek argues:

---

[63] *Id.* at 374.

[64] F.A. Hayek, THE ROAD TO SERFDOM: THE DEFINITIVE EDITION 38–40 (B. Caldwell, ed., 1944).

[65] Hayek, THE CONSTITUTION OF LIBERTY, *supra* note 62, at 336–7.

[66] *Id.* at 381.

[67] *Id.* at 376. Needless to say, this would require a substantial redistribution of wealth, though Hayek never explained why redistribution was warranted for this purpose but not others.

[68] *Id.* at 375.

[69] *Id.* at 375–6.

[70] *Id.* at 405–6.

[71] *Id.* at 421.

[72] ID. at 426.

[73] *Id.* at 332–3.

> The destroying of a farmer's cattle in order to stop the spreading of a contagious disease, the tearing down of houses to prevent the spreading of a fire, the prohibition of an infected well, ... and the enforcement of safety regulations in buildings undoubtedly demand that the authorities be given some discretion in applying general rules.[74]

The government must even have discretion to impose economically unwise regulations, so long as they do not significantly impact individual liberty.[75]

Hayek's contemporary Karl Popper held an even more expansive view of government power and responsibility consistent with individual liberty and the notion of a free and "open society." Popper was less opposed than Hayek to the regulation of economic activity in the public interest. But Popper strenuously opposed state socialism, communism, and other forms of totalitarian rule that involved, among other things, public ownership of economic enterprises and central planning of economic activity. His famous 1945 book *The Open Society and Its Enemies* condemned communism and socialism as inimical to both individual liberty and social justice. Popper's political views were informed by his philosophy of science, according to which science proceeds by a series of conjectures about tentative solutions to theoretical puzzles and the elimination of tentative solutions by refutations. Scientific theories can never be proven correct (though we may act as if they are) but always remain subject to potential refutation based on additional information.[76] Scientific progress – the movement from worse (less explanatory) to better (more explanatory) theories – depends on widespread dissemination of information, freedom to experiment, and the ability to question existing dogmas.[77] These requirements are met in "open societies" but not in "closed societies," where science comes under the political control of rulers who turn politically preferred scientific theories into dogmas that cannot be questioned. A prime example is Lysenkoism, named for the Soviet biologist, Trofim Lysenko, who rejected theories of genetics and science-based agriculture. In 1948, Lysenko's theory was declared by Stalin to be "the only correct theory." It became the "official biology," and works that contradicted Lysenko were condemned as "bourgeois" or "fascist." Research in cell biology and other fields was banned, and thousands of scientists were

---

[74]   *Id.* at 335.

[75]   *Id.* at 334.

[76]   Karl Popper, THE LOGIC OF SCIENTIFIC DISCOVERY (1959); Karl Popper, CONJECTURES AND REFUTATIONS: THE GROWTH OF SCIENTIFIC KNOWLEDGE (1963).

[77]   Popper, CONJECTURES AND REFUTATIONS, *supra* note 76, at 216–17.

dismissed from their positions or imprisoned for failing to toe the party line.[78] Russian science and society both suffered as a consequence.

Moving to the realm of politics, Popper adapted his philosophy of science to public policy: all policies are provisional and subject to repeal, replacement, or improvement based on further evidence. Popper never precisely defined the attributes of the "open society," but one of his critics, Ronald Levinson, has neatly encapsulated Popper's meaning: "an association of free individuals respecting each other's rights within the framework of mutual protection supplied by the state, and achieving through the making of responsible rational decisions, a growing measure of humane and enlightened life."[79] In a 1972 paper, "On Reason and the Open Society," Popper wrote, "[w]e evolve theories for the elimination of social ills, try to work out the consequences critically, and then assess our theories accordingly."[80] This can happen in open societies that, by definition, allow unfettered criticism and continual contestation, creating a political culture that favors experimentation and improvement. While in closed societies the only way to change policy is via regime change, open societies allow for what Popper called "piecemeal reforms," which he contrasted to the "Utopian social engineering" of revolutionaries.[81]

Popper's preference for policy experimentation and piecemeal reform connects him directly to Mill, though Popper was less distrustful than Mill of democracy. Popper's belief in social progress and well-being also tracked Mill's. Both men staunchly opposed state-socialism. But Popper believed in a more active government committed to reducing immiseration, even if that required a modicum of paternalism and redistribution. Mill was primarily concerned with state interference in individual lives, but Popper was concerned about both abuse of government power and abuses of individual liberty: "We need freedom to prevent the state from abusing its power, and we need the state to prevent the abuse of freedom.... We must not allow our love of freedom to blind us to the problems of its abuse."[82]

Despite Popper's toleration for a more active state, he was no statist. He agreed with Mill that the government should not intervene to prevent people from harming themselves However, he observed that, when individuals accept risks, those risks often end up involving others. He offered a revision of Mill's

---

[78]   Nils Roll-Hansen, *Wishful Science: The Persistence of T.D. Lysenko's Agrobiology in the Politics of Science*, 23 OSIRIS 166 (2008).

[79]   Ronald B. Levinson, IN DEFENSE OF PLATO 17 (1953).

[80]   Karl Popper, *On Reason and the Open Society*, in Karl Popper, AFTER THE OPEN SOCIETY 275, 285 (2008).

[81]   Karl Popper, THE OPEN SOCIETY AND ITS ENEMIES, VOL. I, at 1 (1945).

[82]   Karl Popper, THE LESSON OF THIS CENTURY: KARL POPPER INTERVIEWED BY GIANCARLO BOSETTI 73 (P. Camiller ed., 1997).

Harm Principle according to which "[e]veryone should be free to be happy or unhappy in their own way so long as this does not endanger a third party, but the state has a responsibility to ensure that uninformed citizens do not incur avoidable risks that they themselves are unable to evaluate."[83] Ultimately, "[t] he political demand for piecemeal (as opposed to Utopian) methods corresponds to a decision that the fight against suffering must be considered a duty, ... Pain, suffering, injustice, and their prevention, these are the eternal problems of public morals, the 'agenda' of public policy."[84]

Popper did not address the question of whether or not people were happier in liberal societies because he did not agree with Bentham's (and Mill's) Happiness Principle. For Popper, the purpose of public policy was not to maximize happiness but to minimize misery:

> Avoidable misery, such as economic misery, is the responsibility of everybody, and therefore of society, or the state. It is the primary task of public policy. But we should neither attempt to make people happy or better, nor expect that we can do so. Human happiness and human goodness are terribly important, but they should be regarded as objects of private initiative rather than as objects of public policy.[85]

Popper believed liberal societies were better at reducing immiseration than other governance systems. And he celebrated the advances in both liberty and fairness made by the welfare state during the twentieth century:

> We abolished slavery, we are fighting against poverty all over the world. We are richer, to be sure, than all previous societies, but this is not the reason why I call our free society the best that there has ever been. I believe, rather, that our free societies are *morally* better than any of their predecessors.[86]

In addition, "[p]eople are no longer driven by the fear of starvation to accept terrible conditions of work. Chronic unemployment still exists, but there is unemployment relief, and most people who are really anxious and able to work do work. A great deal has also been done to bring medical help to everybody, although with varying success in different countries."[87] Popper did not address sanitation or pollution control in detail, but he wrote that "the fundamental problems of our time" include "the pollution of lands and seas by the

---

[83]   *Id.* at 78.

[84]   Karl Popper, THE OPEN SOCIETY AND ITS ENEMIES, VOL. 2, at 237 (1945).

[85]   Karl Popper, *For a Better World*, in Karl Popper, AFTER THE OPEN SOCIETY 288, 291 (2008).

[86]   Karl Popper, *The Open Society and the Democratic State*, in Karl Popper, AFTER THE OPEN SOCIETY 231, 248 (2008).

[87]   Popper, *For a Better World*, *supra* note 85, at 294.

products of industry." He was not especially sanguine about humanity's ability to solve such problems. At some times, he worried that "all political and legislative measures in this direction constitute[d] a *very grave* danger to human freedom."[88] At other times, he downplayed that concern:

> It is perfectly true that some problems – air pollution, for example – may require special legislation. There are ideological worshippers of the so-called 'free market' (to which we naturally owe a great deal) who think that such legislation limiting market freedom is a dangerous step down the road to serfdom.... But that again is ideological nonsense.[89]

Ultimately, he pinned his hopes on engineers and scientists: "Our only possibility for saving ourselves is that all of us, especially scientists and technical people, learn to recognize as our primary task the obligation to save our beautiful earth and to keep it as pure and clean as the houses we live in."[90]

Popper's philosophy of science – in particular, his solution of the demarcation problem based on testability, according to which scientific theories are falsified by negative experimental or empirical test outcomes but merely corroborated, rather than proven correct, by positive outcomes – has influenced scientific theories relating to public health, such as epidemiology. His influence in that field has also been criticized.[91] His work has also been used to both support and critique governmental policy responses to the COVID epidemic of

---

[88] Karl Popper, *Was Ist Liberal?*, in Karl Popper, AFTER THE OPEN SOCIETY 273 (2008) (italics in original).

[89] Karl Popper, *All Life is Problem Solving*, in Karl Popper, ALL LIFE IS PROBLEM SOLVING 99, 101 (P. Camiller, trans. 1999).

[90] Popper, *Was Ist Liberal?*, *supra* note 88, at 274.

[91] See, for example, Mervyn Susser, *The Logic of Sir Karl Popper and the Practice of Epidemiology*, 124 AM. J.EPIDEMIOLOGY 711 (1986) and L.R. Karhausen, *The Poverty of Popperian Epidemiology*, 24 INT. J.EPIDEMIOLOGY 869 (1995). More generally, Popper's anti-inductivist theory of scientific progress by falsification has long been criticized as an errant explanation of how science is done. See, for example, Sven One Hansson, *Falsificationism Falsified*, 11 FOUNDATIONS SCI. 275 (2006). But falsificationism also has its defenders. See, for example, Miloš Taliga, *Why the Objectivist Interpretation of Falsification Matters*, 46 PHIL. SOC. SCI. 335 (2016).

2020–22.[92] And Popper has been invoked on both sides of scientific debates about anthropogenic climate change.[93]

Last, but by no means least, the economist and classical liberal Milton Friedman spent most of his long career strenuously advocating for free markets and freedom of choice for individuals. He distrusted government more than he distrusted privately held power because government has a (supposed) monopoly on the use of force.[94] But he was by no means a doctrinaire libertarian, let alone an anarcho-capitalist.[95] Unlike them, he was a welfare-consequentialist. He deplored the modern "welfare state," though more for its outcomes than its intentions.[96] That is to say, he believed the welfare state had negative consequences for social welfare, which was the aggregation of all individuals' private welfare functions.

As a social-welfare economist, Friedman understood perfectly well that markets could not be expected to (1) provide public goods, i.e., goods characterized by low rivalry in consumption and high costs of exclusion or (2) correct negative externalities, including pollution costs (which he referred to as "neighborhood effects). In his 1962 paper on "The Role of Government in a Free Society," Friedman wrote: "If a technical monopoly is of a service or commodity that is regarded as essential and if its monopoly power is sizable, even the short-run effects of private unregulated monopoly may not be tolerable and either public regulation or ownership may be a lesser evil." Later in the same paper, he addressed "neighborhood effects:"

> An obvious example is the pollution of a stream. The man who pollutes the stream is in effect forcing others to exchange good water for bad. These others might be willing to make the exchange at a price. But it is not feasible for them, acting individually, to avoid the exchange or to enforce appropriate compensation.[97]

---

[92] See, respectively, Tuomo Peltonen, *Popper's Critical Rationalism as a Response to the Problem of Induction: Predictive Reasoning in the Early Stages of the COVID-19 Epidemic*, 22 PHIL. MGMT. 7 (2023) and Michael Esfeld, *From the Open to the Closed Society: Reconsidering Popper on Natural and Social Science*, 137 FUTURES 102919 (2022).

[93] David Mercer, *Why Popper Can't Resolve the Debate over Global Warming: Problems with the Uses of Philosophy of Science in the Media and Public Framing of the Science of Global Warming,* 27 PUB. UNDERSTANDING SCI. 139 (2016).

[94] Milton Friedman, *The Role of Government in a Free Society*, in Milton Friedman, CAPITALISM AND FREEDOM 22, 29 (1982).

[95] In *The Role of Government, id.* at 34, he wrote, "The consistent liberal is not an anarchist."

[96] See generally Milton Friedman and Rose Friedman, FREE TO CHOOSE (1980).

[97] Friedman, *supra* note 94, at 30.

In such a circumstance, state intervention is warranted to protect the victims of the externality from a forced transaction. On the other hand, Friedman cautioned that government intervention could create neighborhood effects of its own, including impositions on individual liberty. Those effects needed to be weighed against the market's neighborhood effects by policymakers.[98]

How much should government intervene to control externalities? According to Friedman, "[o]ur principles offer no hard and fast line on how far it is appropriate to use government to accomplish jointly what it is difficult or impossible for us to accomplish separately through strictly voluntary exchange... [W]e must make up a balance sheet."[99] Thus, Friedman called for cost–benefit analysis in policymaking to provide public goods and regulate negative externalities. Later, in his 1980 book (co-authored with his wife, Rose) *Free to Choose*, Friedman reiterated his view of pollution as a classic externality that warrants state intervention.[100] But he would limit state intervention to the imposition of pollution taxes on the presumption that they are less coercive and dislocating of economic activity than quantity-based regulations.[101] Ideally, the tax rate should set at a level that corrects the market failure by internalizing the negative externalities.[102] This result would be both economically efficient and just.

Neither Friedman nor any other of the classical liberals reviewed in this section believed that individual liberty and property were the sole legitimate maximands of civil society and the state. In economic terms, they all believed in the existence of a "social welfare function," a phrase that can encompass Locke's "common good" and Blackstone's "public good." Most of them expressly supported public provision of public goods, including public health, and none of them wrote a word against government initiatives to improve public sanitation.

---

[98]   *Id.* at 31–2.

[99]   *Id.* at 32.

[100]   Friedman and Friedman, FREE TO CHOOSE, *supra* note 96, at 214.

[101]   *Id.* at 217–18.

[102]   Although he never did so explicitly, Friedman presumably would have accepted Coase's marginal correction that only inefficient externalities should be internalized, *i.e.*, externalities should be externalized up to the point at which the cost of additional internalization would exceed the benefits. Ronald H. Coase, *The Problem of Social Cost*, 3 J.L. & ECON. 1 (1960).

II.   FROM BASIC SANITATION TO POLLUTION AND PANDEMICS: A SELECTIVE HISTORY OF PUBLIC HEALTH REGULATION FROM THE EARLIEST TIMES

Having established that some amount of public regulation of sanitation and pollution to protect public health is consistent with classical-liberal theory, we next turn to a historical analysis of public regulation to show that governments (especially local governments) have always treated the protection of public health as a fundamental obligation, even if the measures taken have often been controversial.

Sanitation is among the very first collective-action problems faced by the earliest human settlements (whether permanent or seasonal) that emerged *ca.* 12,000 years ago. Those communities, mostly small but sometimes quite large – by around 8000 BCE, some ancient cities had as many as a hundred thousand inhabitants – had to control, as best they could, infestations, malodors, and corruption of water supplies for their own preservation. They could not have survived otherwise. As the Victorian medical historian John Simon observed:

> Human sanitary endeavor has subsisted continuously from the earliest to latest times, and ... mankind, in no stage, however early, of existence, can ever have been without glimmerings of health-protective purpose.... The pangs of dying by hunger and thirst, the poisonousness of certain foods and waters, the fatality of certain sites, the hardships and dangers of extreme heat and extreme cold, the destructiveness of floods, the sterilizing effects of droughts, such, in various combination, may be supposed to have been familiar conditions to the beginners of the human race: the primordial field of physical evil, where man first became conscious of inclination to escape disease, and learnt ways by which he partially could do so.[103]

Through trial and error, early humans gained some understanding of how pollutants affected health.[104] Although the germ theory of disease only emerged toward the end of the nineteenth century,[105] humans always had a keen sense of smell and disgust. Indeed, the sense of smell was "a key factor influencing sanitation behaviors of millions of people across cultures and socio-economic

---

[103]   John Simon, *English Sanitary Institutions* 2 (1890).

[104]   The term "pollution" is of modern vintage, but it is practically synonymous with the older term "corruption," which implied conditions of moral turpitude as well as what we now call pollution. See, for example, John Copeland Nagle, *The Idea of Pollution*, 43(1) U.C. Davis L. Rev 1 (2009).

[105]   John Waller, The Discovery of the Germ: Twenty Years That Transformed the Way We Think About Disease (2002).

contexts."[106] It was a rough-and-ready indicator of health threats, though hardly foolproof. Soot deposits in early cave dwellings of hunter-gatherers indicate high levels of indoor air pollution.[107] Depending on the fuel source, cave dwellers' sense of smell might not have detected danger. Burning wood, for example, emits dangerous small particles and toxic chemicals (such as benzene), but is not generally speaking malodorous. The sense of sight might have played a somewhat more useful role in that case because high concentrations of visible smoke from wood-burning would have been bothersome. Cave dwellers responded rationally by locating fires in areas of caves with the best air circulation to minimize smoke accumulation.[108]

Around 2000 BCE, when people in most places were still defecating on streets or in open cesspits, villages and cities as far apart as Minoan Crete and the Indus Valley were already using advanced techniques for disposing of human waste. In Minoan communities, "carefully planned" and "well-developed sewerage and drainage systems … carr[ied] away sewage and rainwater, including storm waters."[109] An early twentieth-century visitor to the ancient Minoan village of Hagia Triada observed that sewers built four thousand years earlier were still "function[ing] perfectly" in the twentieth century.[110] Between 1650 and 1450 BCE, rainwater, collected for domestic uses, was treated through filters of sand before it reached cisterns at the bottom of dwellings.[111] Rudimentary sewage treatment methods for removing suspended solids from water by the use of small sedimentation tanks were also in use.[112] We do not

---

[106]   Thilde Rheinländer et al., *Smell: An Overlooked Factor in Sanitation Promotion*, 32(2) WATERLINES 106, 110 (2013).

[107]   L. Makra and P. Brimblecombe, *Selections from the History of Environmental Pollution, with Special Attention to Air Pollution, Part 1*, 22(6) INT. J. ENVT. AND POLLUTION 641 (2004) and László Makra, *Anthropogenic Air Pollution in Ancient Times*, in Philip Wexler, ed., HISTORY OF TOXICOLOGY AND ENVIRONMENTAL HEALTH: TOXICOLOGY IN ANTIQUITY, VOL. II 21 (2015).

[108]   Yafit Kedar, Gil Kedar, and Ran Barkai, *The Influence of Smoke Density on Hearth Location and Activity Areas at Lower Paleolithic Lazaret Cave, France*, 12 SCI. REP 1469 (2022).

[109]   Andreas N. Angelakis et al., *Sustainability of Water, Sanitation, and Hygiene: From Prehistoric Times to the Present Times and the Future*, 15 WATER 1614 (2023).

[110]   A.N. Angelakis, D. Koutsoyiannis, and G. Tchobanoglous, *Urban Wastewater and Stormwater Technologies in Ancient Greece*, 39 WATER RESEARCH 210, 214 (2005).

[111]   A.N. Angelakis, K.S. Voudouris, and G. Tchobanoglous, *Evolution of Water Supplies in the Hellenic World Focusing on Water Treatment and Modern Parallels*, 20(3) WATER SUPPLY 773, 775 (2020).

[112]   Angelakis et al., *Urban Wastewater*, *supra* note 109, at 215.

know anything about the governance system for drinking water supply and sewage disposal on Crete. But some governance system, however informal, had to exist for construction and maintenance within a village.

Indus Valley Civilizations (IVCs), established as much as 1,000 years before Crete's Minoan civilization, had "the most advanced sanitation systems of the ancient world."[113] These systems were "designed to prevent the spread of disease by keeping waste separate from living areas and by ensuring that waste was quickly and efficiently removed from the cities."[114] IVCs were planned cities, built for tens of thousands of residents. Nearly all houses had separate water supply basins and wastewater drainage systems of terracotta pipes, which were connected to the city's sewer system consisting of pipes that ran on one or both sides of each street. Those sewers drained into cesspits for sedimentation before the wastewater flowed out of the city.[115] IVCs also had a regular trash removal system to pick up household waste from bins located outside each residence.[116] In a city of tens of thousands, this would have required collective action at a scale requiring more than everyone "doing the right thing." It would have required sanitation workers (perhaps including ordinary householders) but also managers to ensure proper maintenance of water supply and sewage systems. Unfortunately, when the Indus Valley Civilization collapsed around 1300 BCE (after nearly 2,000 years of existence), "sanitary engineering science vanished from India, to be replaced by open latrines and open defecation."[117]

The *Torah* (a.k.a., Old Testament), which appeared in about the sixth or seventh century BCE, contained some of the earliest written injunctions concerning sanitation and public health. The Book of Deuteronomy forbids open latrine pits, requiring human excrement to be buried outside the camp.[118] The punishment for disobeying this or other sanitation and hygiene rules was severe: "He will bring back upon you all the diseases of Egypt...."[119] The Book of Leviticus also contained injunctions that included community health measures such as incineration of waste and prevention of the spread of fungal

---

[113] Angelakis, et al., *Sustainability of Water, Sanitation, and Hygiene, supra* note 108, at 1618.

[114] *Id.*

[115] Saifullah Khan, *Sanitation and Wastewater Technologies in Harappa/ Indus Valley Civilization (ca. 2600–1900 BC)*, in Andreas N. Angelakis and Joan B. Rose, eds., EVOLUTION OF SANITATION AND WASTEWATER TECHNOLOGIES THROUGH THE CENTURIES 25, 35–6 (2014).

[116] *Id.* at 36.

[117] Angelakis et al., *Sustainability of Water, Sanitation, and Hygiene, supra* note 108, at 1620.

[118] Deuteronomy 23:13–14, https://www.chabad.org/library/bible_cdo/aid/9987.

[119] *Id.*, 28:60, https://www.chabad.org/library/bible_cdo/aid/9992.

disease, including by inspecting, even destroying, households and imposing quarantines.[120] According to Sir Lionel Whitby, the Regius Professor of Physic at Cambridge and one-time president of the British Medical Association, "Leviticus and Deuteronomy could be regarded as the first textbooks in preventative medicine, and Moses their first medical officer of health."[121]

Around 500 BCE, in Classical Athens, philosophers and natural scientists such as Alcmaeon of Croton and Hippocrates begin laying the scientific foundations for public sanitation and pollution control. Alcmaeon (ca. 470 BCE) was the first to observe in writing that water quality could affect human health. Not long after (ca. 400 BCE), Hippocrates published a treatise on *Air, Water, Places* which provides "an account of the other kinds of waters, namely, of such as are wholesome and such as are unwholesome, and what bad and what good effects may be derived from water; for water contributes much towards health."[122] It is in Classical Athens that the "miasma" theory of disease first appears in writing, with its hypothesis that "bad air" causes sickness.[123] "Bad air" could arise naturally from swamps or sewers. In a letter to the Emperor Trajan, Pliny the Younger complained about a river that flowed through the city of Amastris that it was "not only an eyesore because it is so disgusting to look at, but it is a danger to health from its shocking smells." Trajan responded: "It stands to reason, my dear Pliny, that the stream which flows through the city of Amastris should be covered over, if by remaining uncovered it endangers the public health."[124]

The works of Hippocrates and Alcmaeon would have been known to the Romans, who considered themselves the inheritors of Athenian traditions. By the late Republic, Rome had become the world's first city to reach one million inhabitants. It was increasingly congested and polluted. Sanitation had a hard time keeping up with the city-state's growth. Those who lived in apartments above the streets simply dumped waste buckets out of their windows. Water

---

[120] Leviticus 4:12. https://www.chabad.org/library/bible_cdo/aid/9905; 13:4, 26, 31, 33, 46, 54. https://www.chabad.org/library/bible_cdo/aid/9914; 14:8, 36, 38, 45, 46. https://www.chabad.org/library/bible_cdo/aid/9915.

[121] Sir Lionel Whitby, *The Sir Charles Hastings Lecture: On Prevention of Disease*, Brit. Med. J. 1272, 1273 (Dec. 2, 1950).

[122] Hippocrates, Airs, Waters, and Places 23 (1881). https://www.google.com /books/edition/Hippocrates_on_Airs_Waters_and_Places/0s5fAAAAMAAJ?hl =en&gbpv=1&bsq=kinds%20of%20water.

[123] Caroline Hannaway, *Environment and Miasmata*, in W.F. Bynum and Roy Porter, eds, Companion Encyclopedia of the History of Medicine, Vol. 1, 292 (1993).

[124] Pál Sáry, *The Legal Protection of Environment in Ancient Rome*, 29 J. Ag. & Envtl. L. 199, 205 (2020).

sources became contaminated. Filth and contagion spread.[125] In addition, lead-lined aqueducts brought contaminated water into city. Lead also leached into wine stored in large vessels.[126] Because lead poisoning impairs cognitive functions, questions have been raised about the extent to which chronic and widespread lead poisoning might have contributed to the downfall of the Republic and, later, the Western Roman Empire.[127]

By Rome's Imperial era, problems resulting from lead poisoning were beginning to be understood by scientists. Vitruvius (d. 15 CE) wrote:

> Water conducted through earthen pipes is more wholesome than that through lead; indeed that conveyed in lead must be injurious, because from it white lead [now known as lead carbonate] is obtained, and this is said to be injurious to the human system. Hence, if what is generated from it is pernicious, there can be no doubt that itself cannot be a wholesome body. This may be verified by observing the workers in lead, who are of a pallid colour; for in casting lead, the fumes from it are fixing on the different members, and daily burning them, destroy the vigour of the blood; water should therefore on no account be conducted in leaden pipes if we are desirous that it should be wholesome. That the flavour of that conveyed in earthen pipes is better, is shewn at our daily meals, for all those whose tables are furnished with silver vessels, nevertheless use those made of earth, from the purity of the flavour being preserved in them.[128]

Air pollution levels were also very high in Rome. Residents of the city referred to its *gravioris cæli* ("heavy heaven") and *infamis ær.*[129] In 61 CE, the philosopher and statesman Seneca wrote about the "reek of smoking cookers," "cloud[s] of ashes," and "all the poisonous fumes" of the city.[130] Some urban fumes came from metals mines and smelting processes located near the city. The Codex Theodosianus includes a statute declaring: "All of the lime kilns in the entire vicinity of the seacoast between the amphitheater and the port of the Divine Julian we order abolished, in the interest of the health of this enormous

---

[125]   Filip Havlíček and Miroslav Morcinek, *Waste and Pollution in the Ancient Roman Empire*, 9(3) J. LANDSCAPE ECOL. 33 (2016).
[126]   F.P. Retief and L. Cilliers, *Lead Poisoning in Ancient Rome*, 26(2) ACTA THEOLOGICA, SUPPLEMENTUM 7 147 (2005).
[127]   S.C. Gilfillan, *Lead Poisoning and the Fall of Rome*, 7(2) J. OCCUPATIONAL AND ENVTL. MED. 53 (1965).
[128]   Joseph Gwilt, trans., THE ARCHITECTURE OF MARCUS VITRUVIUS POLLIO 255 (1826).
[129]   Sanja Rajagopalan, Robert D. Brook, and Sadeer Al-Kindi, *Air Pollution and Flooding in the Lungs: Modern Insights into Ancient Problems*, 42 EURO. HEART J. 1592, 1592 (2021).
[130]   Quoted in O.F. Robinson, ANCIENT ROME: CITY PLANNING AND ADMINISTRATION 97 (1922).

city and due to the proximity to our palace: no one shall be granted permission to burn lime in these places.[131]

Roman law was primarily concerned with private law issues of property and contract, rather than public law issues like sanitation.[132] Private disputes about pollution did arise from time to time. Close to the beginning of the first century CE, the jurist Labeo (d. 10–11 CE) issued an interdict against polluting another person's well.[133] A century later, Titius Aristo (d. ca. 120 CE) ruled that:

> [smoke could not lawfully] be discharged from a cheese shop into buildings above it, unless they are subject to a servitude to this effect. .... It is not permissible to discharge water or any other substance from the upper onto the lower property: one is only permitted to carry out operations on his own premises to this extent, that he discharges nothing onto those of another; smoke may be a pollution just as water.[134]

Ulpian (d. 228 CE) discussed Aristo's ruling,[135] but also noted another case decided by Sextus Pomponious (who lived during the first half of the second century CE) according to which no case would lie if the neighbor were producing only a "moderate" amount of smoke on his own premises.[136]

Private actions were not, however, the only sources of sanitation and pollution control in Rome. The Roman Senate introduced a law in the first century of the Common Era prohibiting air pollution: *"Aerem corrumpere non licet."*[137] A similar law was enacted to protect the quality of waters supplied by aqueduct: "No one shall with malice pollute the waters where they issue publicly. Should anyone pollute them, his fine shall be ten thousand sestertii."[138] Rome also engaged in land-use zoning to remove heavily polluting industrial activities from residential neighborhoods. We have already seen that lime kilns nearby the city were shut down. Tanneries were required to relocate in the

---

[131] Quoted in Havlíček and Morcinek, *supra* note 124, at 42.
[132] Andreas Wacke, *Protection of the Environment in Roman Law?*, 6 FUNDAMINA 1, 4 (2000).
[133] *Id.* at 11.
[134] THE DIGEST OF JUSTINIAN, VOL. I, BOOK EIGHT SERVITUDES 269 (Alan Watson, trans. 2009).
[135] *Id.* at 270.
[136] *Id.*
[137] Makra and Brimblecombe, *supra* note 106, at 641.
[138] Sáry, *supra* note 123, at 207.

fourteenth region *trans Tiberium*, putting the river between them and upscale residences.[139] Glass-making operations were moved to the suburbs.[140]

To deal with human and animal wastes Roman engineers constructed advanced drainage systems. Stone and mortar sewers were located six feet under sidewalks and connected by clay pipes to public and private buildings. They were topped by stone slabs that could be removed for maintenance.[141] The sewers emptied into "*cloacae* (tunnels that were large enough for a man to walk upright in)," which carried the waste away from the city to a nearby swamp or river.[142] Funding for construction and maintenance (including cleaning) of sewer systems was split between the treasury and a tax assessed on landowners. During the Republican era, *aediles* and *censors* were charged with operating and maintaining sewer systems; in the Imperial era, special *curators* were appointed. One time, when a sewer cleaner was forcefully prevented from carrying out his task, the case came before Ulpian for an opinion. He noted that "[t]he praetor has taken care by means of ... interdicts for the cleaning and the repair of drains. Both pertain to the health of civitates and to safety. For drains choked with filth threaten pestilence of the atmosphere and ruin, if they are not repaired."[143]

In the tenth century, writers in the Middle East were expressing concerns over pollution and public health. The Jerusalem-born Arab scholar Muhammad al-Tamimi (early tenth century – 990) wrote about "air spoilage" in his book, *The Extension of Life by Purifying the Air of Corruption and Guarding Against the Evil Effects of Pestilences*.[144] More famously, Ibn Sina (Avicinna, ca. 980–1037) wrote a textbook that became the standard throughout the Middle East and Europe for several hundred years. His book promoted the miasma theory of disease, discussing "coal smoke" as a prime example. He also addressed water pollutants such as arsenic and ammonia.[145] In the twelfth century, the Jewish scholar Maimonedes wrote about Cairo's serious smog problem.[146]

---

[139] Wacke, *supra* note 131, at 9.
[140] Peter Brimblecombe, *Early Episodes*, in Peter Brimblecombe, ed., AIR POLLUTION EPISODES, 6 AIR POLLUTION REVIEWS 11, 13 (2018).
[141] RONALD E. ZUPKO AND ROBERT A. LAURES, STRAWS IN THE WIND: MEDIEVAL URBAN ENVIRONMENTAL LAW 62 (1996).
[142] *Id.*
[143] Sáry, *supra* note 123, at 205.
[144] *Māddat-ul-Baqā' fi Iṣlāḥ Fasad il-Ḥawā w-al-taḥarruz min Ḍarar-il-Awbā*, discussed in Lutfallah Gari, *Arabic Treatises on Environmental Pollution up to the End of the Thirteenth Century*, 8(4) ENVT. & HIST. 479–80.
[145] *Id.* at 80–81.
[146] Makra and Brimblecombe, *supra* note 106, at 644.

By the High Middle Ages, European populations and economies were grow-ing again, after a long period of stagnation following the fall of the Western Roman Empire.[147] Academics at the University of Bologna, Europe's first uni-versity, discovered Roman law in the eleventh century. Within two centuries after that, both the English common law and the *ius commune*, an interna-tional body of law combining Roman law and ecclesiastical law of the Roman Catholic Church, emerged. By the twelfth to fourteenth centuries, documen-tary evidence of sanitation and pollution rules in small villages and large cities alike becomes abundant. That evidence reveals that "[m]edieval people were driven to create an environment as clean and healthy as their technology, pri-orities, and civilization permitted."[148] The water and land pollution standards they adopted "tend to reflect modern norms because the effects of pollutants were perceptible to the regulators and had an immediate impact upon the phys-ical and financial well-being of the town's citizens."[149]

In small English village communities, for example, manorial by-laws included provisions regarding sanitation and pollution. The by-laws of the Village of Elmley Castle from 1390 included the rule that "no one shall place cadavers in a certain lane called Parsoneslane under pain for each one so doing of 20*d*."[150] In 1430, the town of Wistow in Huntingdonshire enacted a by-law prohibiting any one from putting "anything noxious in the water from Burybyghton to Gerholme under pain of 6*d*." Elmley Castle enrolled a simi-lar by-law in 1469. These rules may have been adopted in village plebiscites, assemblies including all free villagers, but by-laws did not require majority voting, let alone unanimous approval. Often by-laws were written into the manorial rolls by the Lord of the Manor after consultation with a relatively few prominent freeholders and the local cleric.[151]

In medieval European cities, regulations to protect public health were, not surprisingly, more extensive than in village communities. With larger and more densely packed populations to protect from health threats arising

---

[147]   See generally William Chester Jordan, EUROPE IN THE HIGH MIDDLE AGES (2001).

[148]   ZUPKO AND LAURES, *supra* note 140, at 33.

[149]   *Id*. at 34.

[150]   Warren Ault, COMMON-FIELD FARMING IN MEDIEVAL ENGLAND: A STUDY OF VILLAGE BY-LAWS 110 (1972). The currency unit *d*. is *denarius*, a legacy of Roman occupation. It was equivalent to the Anglo-Saxon penny. A fine of 20*d* was by no means an insignificant amount in that era, when the Statute of Laborers (22 Ed. 3) of 1351 set wages for reapers of corn at 2*d* for the first week and 3*d* for subsequent weeks. AULT at 32.

[151]   Chris Wickham, THE INHERITANCE OF ROME: ILLUMINATING THE DARK AGES 400–1000 211–12 (2009).

from an increasing number of polluting activities, cities had to deal with all the same basic sanitation issues as village communities, such as disposal of human and animal waste, but on a far larger scale.[152] In addition to effluents from residential chimneys, beer production, and blacksmiths, urban residents were also exposed to pollution from larger industrial and commercial sources including tanneries, smelters, brickmakers, butchers, and clothmakers.[153] In addition, pollution from industrial activities taking place beyond city limits exacerbated urban air and water pollution problems. The mining of metals, including gold, silver, lead, tin, and copper increased during the High Middle Ages. The mining of coal increased to meet the demands of urban residents for heat, as well as the needs of industrial producers. Coal use in the City of London already presented a serious public health threat in the 1200s. In addition, city granaries attracted all kinds of pests, including rodents that eventually became disease vectors for plagues which wiped out large swaths of urban and rural populations.[154]

Medieval cities enacted ordinances to deal with various sanitation and pollution problems. Human and animal waste, for example, required "proper" disposal at designated locations.[155] Cities had a special incentive to enforce these rules because the collected human and animal waste could be sold as fertilizer for use on agricultural fields outside of the cities.[156] Butchers, who were among the most recalcitrant polluters in medieval cities, simply dumped waste in the city streets "until the city fathers banned the practice; then they dumped the waste products into vacant fields until that practice was also banned and the butchers were explicitly told to take the waste products out of the city."[157] Cities did not only regulate how and where butchers disposed of waste, they

[152]   Norman Pounds, THE MEDIEVAL CITY XXVII–XXIX (2005).

[153]   John Aberth, AN ENVIRONMENTAL HISTORY OF THE MIDDLE AGES: THE CRUCIBLE OF NATURE 32 (2013).

[154]   Richard C. Hoffman, AN ENVIRONMENTAL HISTORY OF MEDIEVAL EUROPE 218–22 (2014).

[155]   Dolly Jørgensen, *What to Do with Waste? The Challenges of Waste Disposal in Two Late Medieval Towns*, in Mattias Legnér and Sven Lilja, eds, LIVING CITIES: AN ANTHOLOGY IN URBAN ENVIRONMENTAL HISTORY 34, 42, 51 (2010).

[156]   Either the "invisible hand" did not lead private entrepreneurs to grasp these profit opportunities, or there was not enough profit in the enterprise to make it worth their while. Or, it might be that city ordinances crowded out private enterprise. We just do not know. However, the historical record (as far as this author has been able to discover) does not reveal evidence of private waste collection firms in Medieval Europe.

[157]   ZUPKO AND LAURES, *supra* note 140, at 35, 101.

also prohibited them from "selling diseased meat, carrion, ... entrails, or animals killed by wild beasts."[158]

In English and Northern Italian cities some polluting activities, including clothmaking and tanning, were ultimately zoned out of the city proper. Clothmaking involved dangerous chemicals, including stale urine, lye-water, flax, various detergents, sulfur, and dyes.[159] Tanning required the use of "toxic chemicals, including such exotic solutions as slaked lime, a chicken-, pigeon-, and dog-dung mixture, tannic acid, and a mildly acidic concoction derived from fermenting bran."[160] Initially, these activities were regulated within city limits. For example, in 1287, the Northern Italian City of Ferrara required tanners to keep their activities away from the town's cesspool and the River Po.[161] Other towns kept them as far as possible from commercial and political centers, especially the town market, because of the stench.[162] Some of the chemicals used in clothmaking and tanning, such as flax, were subject to specific regulations governing their retention and use.[163] Local officials – in Bergamo they were called "lords judges of the streets – were appointed to monitor and enforce these land-use requirements.[164] Nevertheless, chemical wastes still found their way into city sewers and rivers. Moreover, citizens complained about the incessant, obnoxious smells emitted by clothmakers and tanneries, which permeated entire sections of town. Such emissions were considered "bad air" under the "miasma" theory of disease and, therefore, presumed to be unhealthy. For these reasons, many cities ended up zoning their producers out of town completely.[165]

In addition to zoning, cities enacted special ordinances for dealing with epidemic disease. For example, after the Black Death (bubonic plague) swept

---

[158] *Id.* at 179.

[159] To some extent, this shifted the problem to other cities, towns, and villages downstream, but over the course of some distance pollutants washed out into wetlands or settled into sediment. Albert Edwin Cooper, Evelyn Ashley Cooper, and Joseph Alan Heward, *On the Self-Purification of Rivers and Streams*, 13(4) BIOCHEM. J. 24 (1919). However, in times of drought pollutants move downstream slowly, if at all.

[160] Zupko and Laures, *supra* note 140, at 36.

[161] *Id.* at 36, 81.

[162] *Id.* at 37.

[163] *Id.* at 38, 87.

[164] *Id.* at 104.

[165] Of course, excluding such activities from the city was cheaper and easier than regulating or otherwise treating the effluents of clothmakers and tanners within city limits.

through Milan in 1350, Viscount Bernabo Visconti, Lord of Milan, decreed in 1374 that:

> Every plague-patient was to be taken out of the city into the fields, there to die or to recover. Those who attended upon the plague-patient were to remain apart for ten days. The priests were to examine the diseased, and point out to special commissioners the persons infected, under punishment of the confiscation of their goods, and of being burned alive. Whoever imported the plague, the State [i.e., the City-State] condemned his goods to confiscation. Finally, none except those who were appointed for the purpose, were to attend plague-patients, under penalty of death and confiscation.[166]

In 1485 a special council of health was appointed in Milan, and places of quarantine (*lazerettos*) were established on islands far removed from the city. Before strangers could enter the city, they first had to quarantine. If this failed to prevent plague from entering the city, infected residents were to be taken out to a special *lazaretto*. If they survived, they would be sent to another island to quarantine for 40 days before they could return to Milan.[167] "Health boards" were established in many urban communities of Europe during the fifteenth century.[168]

Like the Italian city-states, medieval London enacted municipal ordinances to deal with rampant pollution and sanitation problems. In 1297, owners were required to keep the streets in front of their tenements clean. From that time, roaming pigs would be forfeited to the city (as a corporate entity), which would then sell them to finance the building of city walls and gates. In 1283, tallow-melting was no longer allowed in Chepe. In 1309, the City prohibited the dumping of trash from houses onto the streets; instead, the garbage was to be dumped in the River Thames. The effect on the river was predictable. In 1310, tailors could no longer scour furs in river water during daytime (with exceptions). In 1371, Plumbers in Eastcheap were required to raise chimneys from the furnaces they employed for solder-melting, so as to carry away the smoke. A Royal Order from the same year banished from the city the slaughtering of oxen, sheep, swine, and other large animals.[169] In 1345, London hired four workers to cleanse the Thames docks at Dowgate.

The city was not the only government that regulated pollution in London. In 1306, King Edward I prohibited the burning of "sea coal" in London. "Sea coal" was a soft and heavily polluting bituminous coal. It was called "sea coal" because it arrived in London on ships from Newcastle. Even including shipping

---

[166]   William A. Guy, PUBLIC HEALTH 53 (1870).
[167]   *Id.* at 54.
[168]   Aberth, *supra* note 152, at 64.
[169]   John Simon, ENGLISH SANITARY INSTITUTIONS 39–40 (1890).

costs, it was much less expensive than locally available anthracite coal, a less-polluting hard coal with a higher content. Anthracite was far more difficult to extract, and therefore cost a great deal more. By 1228, London already had a designated street for buying sea coal, called Sacole Lane, now Old Seacoal Lane, located a block north of Fleet Street at Ludgate Circus.[170]

The earliest recorded complaint about the malodor from burning "sea coal" came in 1257 from Eleanor of Provence, wife of King Henry III (r. 1216–1272), while she was staying at Nottingham Castle, 127 miles north of London. The stench of sea-coal fumes, assumed dangerous under the miasma theory of disease, caused her to flee the area to preserve her health.[171] But just 12 years later Henry III requisitioned a boatload of sea coal to be delivered, "without delay," to Windsor Castle, located on the River Thames only 23 miles West of London.[172] By that time, the amount of sea coal fueling industries and home hearths made it the primary source of London's already infamous smog. The 1306 Royal prohibition required a switch to the more expensive, locally mined anthracite coal. Not surprisingly, compliance with the ban was low, so the king reissued the order in 1309, this time including severe penalties. First time offenders would be subject to heavy fines. Second time offenders would have their furnaces destroyed. Later, the law was amended once more to impose the death penalty for repeat offenders. One person was reportedly executed for violating the statute,[173] but that story might be apocryphal. In any case, despite various prohibitions and severe penalties, sea coal remained a major part of the city's air pollution problems into the second half of the twentieth century. In the sixteenth century, Queen Elizabeth complained about "sea-cooles." A century later, King Charles I complained about sea coal. By then, England was one of the "world's leading industrial cities," thanks in large measure to inexpensive sea coal.[174]

The rise of environmental regulations in the High and Late Middle Ages in England reflected general concern with threats to public health. The regulations focused on cleanliness and sanitation. "In late-medieval English towns and cities, the condition of one's health was intimately tied to the conditions of

---

[170] Peter Brimblecombe, The Big Smoke: A History of Air Pollution in London Since Medieval Times 7 (1987).

[171] *Id.* at 8.

[172] *Id.* at 7.

[173] *Id.* at 9.

[174] William H. Te Brake, *Air Pollution and Fuel Crises in Preindustrial London, 1250–1650*, 16(3) Tech. & Culture 337, 341–2 (1975).

the environment."[175] A 1349 royal order from King Edward III to the Mayor of London is a clear example:

> Order to cause the human feces and other filth lying in the streets and lanes of that city and its suburbs to be removed with all speed to places far distant from that city and to cause the city and suburbs to be cleansed from all odour and to be kept clean … so that no great cause of mortality may arise from such smells, as the king has learned how the city and suburbs, which are under the mayor's care and rule, are so foul by the filth thrown out of the houses both by day and night into the streets and lanes where there is a common passage of men that the air is infected, the city is poisoned to the danger of men passing, especially in the mortality by the contagious sickness which increases daily [a reference to the bubonic plague that arrived in England the year before].[176]

Eight years later, Edward III instructed the Mayor and Sheriffs of London to issue an ordinance that would eliminate pollution of the Thames River. The king noted that the river was overloaded with all manner of "'dung … and other filth,'" resulting in "fumes and other abominable stenches," which created "great peril … to persons dwelling in the said city as [well as] to the nobles and others passing along the river." He instructed the mayor and sheriffs to implement a new prohibition on the "throwing or putting of rubbish or filth into the Thames or its tributary, the Rivers Thames and Fleet."[177] Similar Royal Orders were issued in 1379 and 1383 by Edward III's successor, Richard II. In 1388, parliament enacted a water pollution statute for London, imposing a £20 fine on anyone dumping "harmful matter, dung, offal, entrails and other ordure into ditches, rivers, waters, or other places."[178]

The common law, which first emerged in written form from the pen of King Henry II's Chief Justiciar Ranulf de Glavill in the twelfth century, included anti-pollution rules to protect public health in the form of trespass and nuisance complaints under the Assize of Novel Disseisin. In the 1498 *Prior of Southwark's Case*,[179] the prior complained that his neighbor, a glovemaker, had polluted a stream that ran across the prior's land. The prior (and his tenants) used the stream for drinking water, garden irrigation, watering livestock, etc. The glovemaker had dug a lime pit so close to the common boundary that separated his land from the prior's land and so close to the stream that

---

[175]   N.J. Ciecieznski, *The Stench of Disease: Public Health and the Environment in Late-Medieval English Towns and Cities*, 4(1) HEALTH CULTURE & SOC. 92, 101 (2013).

[176]   Quoted in *id.*

[177]   William Alfred Brend, HEALTH AND THE STATE 5 (1917).

[178]   Quoted in Aberth, *supra* note 152, at 65.

[179]   (1498) YB Trin., 13 Hen. 7, f.26, pl. 4.

chemicals leached from his lime pit into the stream. The court ruled that the glovemaker had committed a trespass on the case. A little more than a century later, the king's court ruled that a smelly pigsty located near a neighbor's house constituted an unlawful nuisance. One property owner has:

> no right to maintain a structure upon his own land which, by reason of disgusting smells, loud or unusual noises, thick smoke, noxious vapours, the jarring of machinery, or the unwarrantable collection of flies, renders the occupancy of adjoining property dangerous, intolerable, or even uncomfortable to its tenants.[180]

Importantly, these two landmark cases, one about water pollution, the other about air pollution, did not portend active judicial involvement in policing pollution. They were at the time, and remained for a long time after, exceptional.

When Europe finally passed out of the Middle Ages and into the Modern Era, sanitation, pollution control, and other public health concerns only grew more serious, especially as industrialization exploded in the eighteenth and nineteenth centuries. In the cities of Britain's North American colonies, "the streets reeked with waste, wells were polluted, and deaths from epidemic disease mounted rapidly."[181] In both England and the colonies, common law and city ordinances were used to control threats to public health. In the colonies, the earliest quarantine regulations and sanitation measures date from the seventeenth century.[182] The first sanitation law in Massachusetts is from 1630. In 1647–8, after news reached Boston of a "major epidemic" in the Caribbean, the Massachusetts General Court ordered all vessels arriving from the West Indies to remain at anchor in the harbor until they were cleared.[183] New York followed this example and began inspecting arriving vessels for "pestilential diseases."[184]

In 1669, the English political philosopher John Locke and his employer the Earl of Shaftsbury co-wrote a constitution for the Colony of Carolina that included "a broad power to take care of all 'corruption or infection of the common air or water, and all things' necessary to protect 'the public commerce and health.'"[185] The legal codes of several colonies authorized town officials to isolate persons infected or suspected of being infected with

---

[180]   *Aldred's Case* (1610) 9 Co Rep 57b; (1610) 77 ER 816, [1558–1774] All ER Rep 622.
[181]   Martin Melosi, GARBAGE IN THE CITIES: REFUSE REFORM AND THE ENVIRONMENT 11 (1981).
[182]   John Duffy, THE SANITARIANS: A HISTORY OF AMERICAN PUBLIC HEALTH 15 (1992).
[183]   *Id.* at 15.
[184]   *Id.* at 15–6.
[185]   WITT, *supra* note 14, at 15.

smallpox, and to charge the family for the costs of quarantine and treatment.[186] In 1685, New York City hired a doctor for five pounds a year to care for the "deserving poor."[187] Eventually, all colonial towns hired doctors for the same purpose. It was a form of public health insurance, albeit on a very small scale. By the end of the seventeenth century, all American colonies had temporary quarantine rules for disease outbreaks, food inspection regulations, and other basic sanitation laws.[188]

Local government intervention increased in the American colonies during the seventeenth century, mainly in response to rapidly growing populations and higher levels of population density. The first public water supply systems appeared along with public wells and aqueducts. Regulation of food, water, and sanitation "became both more specific and more comprehensive." Quarantine rules did to some extent reduce the spread of contagious diseases including smallpox, yellow fever, diphtheria, and malaria. In 1712, Charleston, Carolina hired a quarantine commissioner to its port authority. Sick sailors arriving from the West Indies and other places were quarantined on Sullivan's Island in Charleston Harbor. In the middle of the eighteenth century, the Colony of Carolina enacted a permanent quarantine law for Charleston. Similarly, the Provincial Council of New York in 1755 passed a law empowering the governor to appoint a health officer to oversee the protection of the public from contagious diseases. New York City's first "pesthouse" for quarantine opened on Bedlow's Island in 1760.[189] Just 16 years later, after the start of the Revolutionary War, General George Washington issued a mandatory vaccination order for American Army troops during the Revolutionary War to prevent smallpox outbreaks, even though it was known at the time that the vaccine killed 2 percent of those inoculated.[190]

Following the war, the newly independent American states began enacting public health statutes. In New York, the state legislature authorized the governor to establish quarantines to prevent "yellow fever 'or any other contagious Distemper.'"[191] In 1793, Pennsylvania established a state health officer to protect the city of Philadelphia "from the introduction of pestilential and contagious diseases."[192] That city's corporate charter, enacted by the state a few years earlier, specified among the city's basic purposes the "advancement of

---

[186] *Id.* at 15–16.
[187] Duffy, *supra* note 182, at 117.
[188] *Id.* at
[189] *Id.* at 26.
[190] *Id.* at 28.
[191] Witt, *supra* note 14, at 16.
[192] *Id.* at 17.

health."[193] In 1795, Virginia authorized quarantines at "'any place within this commonwealth' that 'shall become infected with a malignant distemper.'"[194] In 1801, Philadelphia became the first American city to construct a waterworks and municipal water distribution system, which was "sophisticated even by European standards."[195] In 1824, the US Supreme Court, in *Gibbons v. Ogden*,[196] confirmed that state police powers included the power to quarantine individuals or groups to deal with public health threats. In 1830, the Vermont Supreme Court ruled that, when faced by even the possibility of contagion, "it becomes the duty of the selectman [a member of the governing board of a city or town] to take the most prudent measures to prevent the spreading of the disease."[197] This was a rare assertion by a state court in an era when states believed they were protecting "real liberty by granting broad deference to elected and appointed officials who acted (or failed to act) to protect the public's health."[198]

In 1827, Boston began requiring children to be vaccinated against smallpox before attending school. In 1833, the small town of Chicago was incorporated as a city with an estimated population of about 330 inhabitants. That same year, Chicago's City Council enacted "sweeping sanitary provisions to fend off cholera, including street cleaning, removal of nuisances, prohibiting the dumping of animal carcasses into the river, and regulating the disposal of other waste.[199] That ordinance proved ineffective for reasons the City Council could not possibly have predicted. Chicago was about to experience one of the greatest population explosions in world history. In the 100 years from 1830 to 1930, Chicago's population increased from approximately 250 people to just under 3.4 million. Unsurprisingly, Chicago's government could hardly track, let alone keep up with, such a massive influx. As it grew into the "Hog Butcher for the World,"[200] practically the entire city turned into a waste heap. "'[D]eath fogs' emanated from piles of odure" that were "so vile that 'the very

---

[193] *Id.* at 11, 15, and 18.

[194] *Id.* at 18.

[195] Martin U. Melosi, THE SANITARY CITY: ENVIRONMENTAL SERVICES IN URBAN AMERICA FROM COLONIAL TIMES TO THE PRESENT 19 (Abridged edn., 2000).

[196] 22 U.S. 1 (1824).

[197] *Hazen v. Strong*, 2 Vt. 427, 433 (1830).

[198] Wendy E. Parmet, CONSTITUTIONAL CONTAGION: COVID, THE COURTS, AND PUBLIC HEALTH 122 (2003).

[199] Witt, *supra* note 14, at 19.

[200] Carl Sandburg, Chicago, 3 POETRY: A MAGAZINE OF VERSE I (March 1914).

swine turn up their noses in disgust.'"[201] Lack of proper sanitation led to all kinds of disease outbreaks, including at least four deadly cholera outbreaks in 1849, 1850, 1866, and 1867. Those epidemics likely were caused by untreated sewage, which was dumped untreated into Lake Michigan, contaminating the city's water supply. Arguably, the great fire that destroyed most of Chicago in 1871 was the best thing that could have happened for the long-term health of the population, though its immediate consequences were awful with 300 dead and 100,000 left homeless.

In 1851, the Supreme Judicial Court Massachusetts concluded, in *Commonwealth v. Alger*,[202] that, under its state constitution, the state and its subdivisions had a full panoply of police powers. Those powers authorized the state and its cities to "prohibit buildings from being used for hospitals for contagious diseases, or for the carrying on of noxious or offensive trades; to prohibit the raising of a dam, and causing stagnant water to spread over meadows, near inhabited villages, thereby raising noxious exhalations, injurious to health and dangerous to life."[203] All private property was subject to police-power regulations because they were an inherent power of the government. "State courts sustained broad authority to clean the streets to remove waste, to condemn and destroy dangerous buildings or infectious property, and to prohibit the slaughtering of animals in cities. Courts upheld mandatory vaccination and reasonable waiting times for [quarantined] commercial vehicles at the ports."[204] What was true in Massachusetts was true throughout all the states. After Michigan gained statehood in 1837, one of its legislature's first acts created local health boards throughout the state "empowered to order the removal of 'all nuisances, sources of filth, and causes of sickness,' including sick people themselves, 'that may in their opinion be injurious to the health of the inhabitants within their township.'" The local boards also had the power to quarantine sick people and required family members to report cases of smallpox. Failure to do so could result in a $100 fine, a great deal of money in the first half of the nineteenth century.[205]

In 1850, the Massachusetts Sanitary Commission issued a defense of increased regulation that spoke to both community and liberty, stressing the importance of Mill's Harm Principle: "Every person has a direct or indirect interest in every other person. We are social beings – bound together by indissoluble ties." The Commission cited "Cicero's ancient legal dictum, *'salus*

---

[201]   Ben Wilson, Metropolis: A History of the City, Humankind's Greatest Invention 220 (2020).
[202]   61 Mass. 53 (1851).
[203]   Id. at 86.
[204]   Witt, *supra* note 14, at 23.
[205]   *Id.* at 18.

populi supreme lex, to protect one set of human beings from being the victims of disease and death through the selfish cupidity of others.'"[206] Urban sanitary codes around the country began to swell.[207] City residents, especially elites, demanded them. But city sanitary and health regulations still struggled to keep pace with growing populations and increasing population-densities. Local pollution problems were also increasing rapidly in the wake of the Industrial Revolution, which began in England in the middle of the eighteenth century and a century later in the USA and Germany. In 1866, New York state created a new Metropolitan Board of Health for Manhattan and the other boroughs. Various local boards of health and other public officials were subordinated to the metropolitan board, which was well funded and staffed. The board's powers during health emergencies were almost unlimited. When New York faced "great and imminent peril to the public health," the board could take any measures it deemed necessary, even without express authority of the state legislature.[208]

By the middle of the nineteenth century, inadequate urban sanitation was taking a serious toll on public health. Average life expectancy for whites, which ranged between 51 and 56 years from 1720 to 1830, fell to under 46 by 1850; unfortunately, accurate statistics on Black lives were not kept until the twentieth century. Most economic historians attribute the decline in life expectancy to infectious diseases, poor sanitation, or both. In the opinion of the Nobel laureate Robert Fogel, the decline was due to reductions in net nutrition that, in turn, were due to malaria and other diarrheal diseases.[209] Death rates from diseases proliferated in conditions of increasing urbanization and industrialization along with poor sanitation.[210] It is worth noting in this context that the first state-level board of health was not instituted until 1869 in Massachusetts.[211] At the federal level, a Sanitary Commission was established during the Civil War to deal with disease outbreaks, which caused twice as many combatant deaths

---

[206]   *Id*. at 16.

[207]   *Id*.

[208]   *Id*. at 20.

[209]   Robert W. Fogel, THE FOURTH GREAT AWAKENING AND THE FUTURE OF EGALITARIANISM 164–5 (2000).

[210]   Michael Haines, Lee Craig, and Thomas Weiss, *The Short and the Dead: Nutrition, Mortality, and the "Antebellum Puzzle" in the United States*, 63(2) J. ECON. HIST. 385 (2003). Also see Robert Floud, Robert W. Fogel, Bernard Harris, and Sok Chul Hong, THE CHANGING BODY: HEALTH, NUTRITION, AND HUMAN DEVELOPMENT IN THE WESTERN WORLD SINCE 1700 (2011).

[211]   The Massachusetts legislature was first urged to create a state board of health in 1850 but declined.

as battles.[212] Despite the federal Sanitary Commission's efforts and subsequent state measures to improve sanitation, white life expectancy in the USA hovered between 47 and 49 years for the rest of the nineteenth century. It did not reach 50 years again until 1900.[213]

Even before the industrial revolution took hold in the USA, black smoke was pouring from furnaces and boilers in big cities like New York, Chicago, and Detroit. It hung over the cities like a "great cloud." To industrialists, its acrid odor was the "smell of prosperity," [214] but the chemicals in the smoke were a "direct menace to the public health." A visitor described the city of Pittsburgh, during an 1868 atmospheric inversion, as "hell with the lid taken off."[215] Epidemiologists already correlated smoke emissions and the increasing incidence of lung diseases.[216] Unfortunately, before 1880, common law public nuisance suits against air polluters were of little avail as the legal process became an adjunct to economic development and growth.[217] In response, city residents, local smoke abatement committees, and others advocated for municipal ordinances to control smoke pollution.

The earliest municipal smoke ordinances, enacted in St. Louis (1867) and Pittsburgh (1869), sought to restrict the use of bituminous coal and build higher smokestacks.[218] Chicago's first air pollution ordinance, enacted in 1881, defined smoke as a "public nuisance,"[219] and appointed a city smoke inspector. Ten years later, local Chicago businessmen created a Society for the Prevention

---

[212]   The USA was following the example set by the UK during the Crimean War, during which Florence Nightingale's sanitary interventions reduced the annualized noncombat mortality rate of 1,174 per 1,000 soldiers to 13 per 1,000. Rebecca J. Anderson, Florence Nightingale: The Biostatistician, 11(2) REFLECTIONS: SCI. IN THE CULTURAL CONTEXT 63, 67 (2011).

[213]   Hoyt Beakley, Louis P. Cain, and Sok Chul Hong, *Health Disease, and Sanitation in American Economic History*, in L.P. Cain, ed., THE OXFORD HANDBOOK OF AMERICAN ECONOMIC HISTORY 53, 56, Table 2.1 (2018).

[214]   Thomas O. McGarity, POLLUTION, POLITICS, AND POWER: THE STRUGGLE FOR SUSTAINABLE ELECTRICITY 46 (2019).

[215]   Quoted in David Stradling and Peter Thorsheim, *The Smoke of Great Cities: British and American Efforts to Control Air Pollution, 1860–1914*, 4(1) ENVTL. HIST. 6, 8 (1999).

[216]   See Frederick Law Olmstead and Harlan Page Kelsey, THE SMOKE NUISANCE 4 (2d ed. 1908).

[217]   Jan G. Laitos, *Legal Institutions and Pollution: Some Intersections between Law and History*, 15 NAT. RESOURCES J. 423, 430.

[218]   Noga Morag-Levine, CHASING THE WIND: REGULATING AIR POLLUTION IN THE COMMON LAW STATE 103 (2003).

[219]   *Id.* at 112.

of Smoke, which pushed for additional measures to control smoke.[220] A 1903 ordinance for the first time required greater combustion efficiency in furnaces, forges, and boilers.[221] By 1915, 23 of the 28 biggest cities in the USA had some form of smoke control ordinance. Kansas City's ordinance prohibited as a nuisance:

> dense black or thick grey smoke, issuing from any chimney, flue, smokestack, or from any other sources within the corporate limits of Kansas City in such quantities or in such manner as to be deleterious or offensive to health, or productive of physical discomfort, or so as to detract from the ordinary enjoyments of life, or be damaging to property, or impair the enjoyment thereof....[222]

Enforcement was a major problem for these municipal ordinances,[223] but some cities proved more adept than others in controlling smoke emissions, at least in the short run. St. Louis's ordinances were relatively successful for a couple of reasons. First, the city required polluters to build taller smokestacks. That requirement was easily monitored and likely to resolve pollution in the immediate vicinity of the city. Taller smokestacks emitted effluents higher into prevailing winds, removing them from the area. It was a tried and tested method of reducing urban smoke, which had been around since at least the fifteenth century in England. By the late seventeenth century, it was a judicial remedy to nuisance claims. In 1691, a court in London ordered a defendant to abate a smoke nuisance by building a chimney "soe high as to convey the smoke clear of the topps of houses."[224]

St. Louis was also able to enforce a requirement to "wash" bituminous coal in order to reduce the amount of soot, sulfur dioxide and nitrogen oxides emitted upon combustion.[225] However, even relatively successful state and local smoke ordinances merely slowed emission increases and reductions in air

---

[220] Christine Meiner Rosen, *Businessmen against Pollution in Late Nineteenth Century Chicago*, 69(3) THE BUS. HIST. REV 351 (1995). In St. Louis and Pittsburgh, women's groups had lobbied for smoke ordinances. Stradling and Thorsheim, *supra* note 213, at 13.

[221] Paul P. Bird, REPORT OF THE DEPARTMENT OF SMOKE INSPECTION, CITY OF CHICAGO 15, Feb. 1911, https://www.google.com/books/edition/Annual_Report/j2M0AQAAMAAJ?hl=en&gbpv=1&dq=chicago+1881+smoke+ordinance+pdf&pg=PA12&printsec=frontcover.

[222] Quoted in Adam Rome, *Coming to Terms with Pollution: The Language of Environmental Reform, 1865–1915*, 1 Envt'l Hist. 6, 18 (1996).

[223] Laitos, *supra* note 215, at 435.

[224] Quoted in Brimblecombe, *supra* note 169, at 96.

[225] Frederick S. Mallette, *Legislation on Air Pollution*, 71(11) PUB. HEALTH REP. 1069, 1070 (1956).

quality. In cities where smoke proved ineffective, "[a]fter each unsuccessful attempt a feeling of apathy descended on the community. For a period of 3 to 5 years nothing would be done, then conditions would become so severe that small groups of citizens would again become aroused and a new attempt would be made."[226] In the meantime, the common law courts were altering the rules again. Before 1880, the courts insulated air polluters from liability to protect economic growth. After 1880, they "favored the interests of plaintiffs over those of polluters."[227] "Law, which had previously been used to help private economic growth, was now called upon to regulate it," and "[l]aw, not the market, was seen as the prime tool with which the air pollution problem might be corrected."[228] At least some judges grasped that holding polluters liable would not disrupt efficient economic growth but merely internalize to relevant markets the pollution costs of economic development. For example, in 1880, Pennsylvania's high court awarded an injunction against a polluter, but with the proviso that the polluter could avoid the injunction by installing a $10,000 smoke prevention device.[229] That same year, California's supreme court overturned prior court decisions barring property owners along a light rail line from suing for harms from smoke, noting the city could not grant a franchise that included a right "to materially injure the plaintiffs in their property rights."[230] By enforcing the private property rights of plaintiffs, public health might be protected from pollution. The US Supreme Court capped off this trend in 1916, ruling in *Northwestern Laundry v. Des Moines* that:

> So far as the Federal Constitution is concerned, we have no doubt the state may itself, or through authorized municipalities, declare the emission of dense smoke … a nuisance … and that the harshness of such regulation, or its effect on business interests, short of a merely arbitrary enactment, are not valid constitutional objections.[231]

Judicial decisions upholding state and municipal regulations and protecting private property from pollution harm were important for the development of pollution-control law. But from a public health perspective they were not the most important developments of the nineteenth century's last two decades. More important was the science of germ theory, which had begun establishing definitive causal links between diseases and exposure to solid and toxic

---

226   Quoted in Morag-Levine, *supra* note 216, at 115.
227   Laitos, *supra* note 215, at 431.
228   *Id.*
229   *Price v. Philip Carey Manufacturing Co.*, 165 A. 849 (Pa. 1933).
230   *Tuebner v. California Street Railroad Co.*, 4 P. 1162 (Cal. 1884).
231   239 U.S. 486, 491–2 (1916).

wastes.[232] This ultimately revolutionized sanitation and public health protection, though not immediately. Germ theory took some time to displace miasma theory, especially in the USA. When the Scottish surgeon Joseph Lister toured the USA in 1876, giving lectures in New York, Boston, and Philadelphia, American doctors "struggled to understand the relationship between bacteria and disease."[233] Even after the scientific and medical communities grudgingly accepted the mounting evidence supporting germ theory, it remained controversial in policy circles because it increased the political tension between public health and economic growth. As always, advancements in science enabled, but did not guarantee, more effective responses to public health problems, including sanitation/pollution and disease epidemics. Suffice it to say that it took New York's Metropolitan Board of Health, created in 1866, one hundred years to finally rid the city of pigs, which regularly contaminated the city's water supply.[234]

In 1918–19, an influenza pandemic killed 30 million people worldwide and 500,000 in the USA. As is nearly always the case when outbreaks of infectious diseases occur, it took time for public authorities to recognize the seriousness of the outbreak and take emergency measures. The first public measure was to spread information about the disease and precautions that could be taken against it. The US Post Office, Federal Railroad Administration, and the Red Cross distributed posters nationwide.[235] That was practically as much as the federal government could do at the time. The United States Public Health Service (USPHS) "did not have legal power to quarantine influenza, … measles, whooping cough, or any other common and usually mild disease."[236] The federal government's warnings were to little avail as influenza continued its march across the country. Despite the federal warnings, some state public health officers "were cautious, skeptical, and poorly informed."[237]

Emergency measures were eventually put into place at local and state levels, but always belatedly. For example, the City of Philadelphia closed all schools, churches, theaters, and other places of "public amusement." Pennsylvania's Acting State Commissioner of Health immediately extended the order to the

---

[232] MELOSI, THE SANITARY CITY, *supra* note 193, at 76–7; Mervyn Susser and Zena Stein, ERAS IN EPIDEMIOLOGY: THE EVOLUTION OF IDEAS 107–22 (2009).

[233] Ira Rutkow, *Joseph Lister and his 1876 tour of America*, 257(6) ANN. SURG. 1181 (2013).

[234] WITT, *supra* note 14, at 21.

[235] Alfred W. Crosby, AMERICA'S FORGOTTEN PANDEMIC: THE INFLUENZA OF 1918 49 (2003).

[236] *Id.* at 31.

[237] *Id.* at 73.

entire state.[238] The *Philadelphia Inquirer* newspaper called the ban tyrannical, arguing that "places of amusement" should never have been closed.[239]
However, the day after Pennsylvania shut down public gatherings, the Surgeon
General of the USPHS sent telegrams to each state's public health officer rec-
ommending they adopt the same policy. Officials in "hundreds and probably
thousands of communities" took the advice, but not everywhere.[240]

Unlike Philadelphia, San Francisco had full warning that the epidemic
was heading its way. But many local public health officials in California were
remarkably complacent and slow to act. But when the death rate began to
rise above normal rates of death from influenza, their complacency quickly
turned to panic. Health officials throughout California shut down places of
public gathering, including schools and churches, just as had been done in
Philadelphia (among other eastern cities). Unlike Philadelphia, San Francisco
also issued the following mask ordinance:

> Every person appearing on the public streets, in any public place, or in any assem-
> blage of persons or in any place where two or more persons are congregated, except
> in homes where only two members of the family are present, and every person
> engaged in the sale, handling or distribution of foodstuffs or wearing apparel shall
> wear a mask or covering except when partaking of meals, over the nose and mouth,
> consisting of four-ply materials known as butter-cloth or fine mesh gauze.[241]

Even before that ordinance took effect, an estimated 99 percent of San
Franciscans were already masking. But some called the masking mandate "a
humiliating and unconstitutional interference with personal liberty."[242] Not
surprisingly, the epidemic began to wind down soon after the mask mandate
took effect. But as the rate of new infections subsided, many city residents
decided not to wait for the Board of Health to withdraw its mandates. In the
final two months of the year, rates of infection began increasing again.

When the epidemic resumed, San Francisco's Public Health Officer recommended reimposing social isolation regulations and a mask mandate. His
recommendation was supported by the Red Cross and Affiliated Catholic
Charities, but many San Franciscans were weary of social isolation and mandatory masking. Christian Scientists publicly opposed the revival of the masking ordinance on the grounds that it was "subversive to personal liberty and
constitutional rights."[243] Other civil libertarians, "whose sensitivity on the

---

238   *Id.* at 74.
239   *Id.* at 85.
240   *Id.*
241   *Id.* at 102.
242   *Id.* at 105.
243   *Id.* at 109.

topic of tyranny exceeded their fear of flu, agreed: 'If the Board of Health can force people to wear masks, then it can force them to submit to inoculation, or any experiment or indignity.'"[244] The *San Francisco Chronicle* weighed in against renewing mask mandates, but acknowledged that the order was lawful and "would not be just cause for rebellion."[245] Then, California's State Board of Health announced that the flu's return was not severe enough to warrant masking mandates.[246] That decision proved premature. Within a month, the increasing rate of infections forced San Francisco's Board of Supervisors to reimpose a mask mandate. Once again, this was followed by a reduction in the rate of infections and deaths, but enforcement became a problem. Despite the strong correlation between masking and reductions in infections, many had started doubting that masking made any difference. The police arrested hundreds for violating the mask mandate.

In the wake of the 1918–19 influenza epidemic, it was clear that state governments needed to prepare more seriously for future outbreaks.[247] But complacency returned just a few years later. The federal government, meanwhile, was somewhat less complacent, at least during Franklin Roosevelt's four terms in office. In 1935, the Social Security Act became law.[248] It included a federal grant-in-aid program for maintaining state public health services and training public health officers. In 1944, Congress unanimously passed the Public Health Service Act (PHSA),[249] which gathered the disparate powers established in previous statutes under one umbrella agency comprised of health officers, researchers, and specialists to deal with *national* and international health problems. The statute, which has been amended a dozen times since 1944, expressly recognized the federal government's authority to impose interstate quarantines. Pursuant to the PHSA, the Centers for Disease Control was established in 1946 and the National Center for Health Statistics in 1960. By the 1970s, the National Institute of Health contained an Institute for Environmental Health Sciences. In the last fifty years, it has been the basis for more direct federal involvement in public health crises, including the HIV-Aids epidemic, SARs, and most recently COVID-19. However, the federal government's public health powers and agencies have been geared mainly toward

---

[244]   *Id.*

[245]   *Id.* at 109–10.

[246]   *Id.* at 110.

[247]   Rebecca Bratspies, *The Great Catastrophe: Bungling Pandemics from 1918 to Today*, 30 MICH. ST. INT'L L. REV. 189, 192–3 (2022).

[248]   42 USC §§ 301–1397.

[249]   42 USC § 201 *et seq.*

scientific research and information collection,[250] while the states maintain primary regulatory authority.

Throughout the twentieth century, urban pollution problems worsened, despite the fact that more states enacted pollution-control statutes. Many of those efforts were minimal, but a few states, such as California, meant business. World War II had contributed to the rapid industrialization of the Los Angeles basin, giving rise to both local and regional air pollution concerns. In 1945, the *Los Angeles Times* used the word "smog" for the first time to describe the "brownish haze that settled over the Los Angeles basin, lowering visibility, irritating eyes, and leaving some residents short of breath."[251] In 1947, the State of California enacted the Air Pollution Control Act, which created county-wide air pollution control districts to implement a permit system for industrial sources. To receive a permit, sources had to install available pollution-control technology. The Los Angeles County Office of Pollution was the first agency in the USA "whose jurisdiction extended beyond smoke to gases,"[252] but results were not fast in coming.[253]

Shortly after California enacted its Air Pollution Control Act, a major pollution incident in Donora, Pennsylvania served as a "catalytic event" for policy. It aroused national indignation after Walter Winchell broadcast news about it on his national radio program.[254] In October 1948, 20 residents of Donora and nearby Webster, Pennsylvania died and thousands were made ill by emissions from local steel and zinc factories, which were trapped for several days near the ground by an atmospheric inversion. When lawsuits started, Carnegie Steel claimed it was an act of God.[255] "In the two years following Donora, the U.S. Public Health Service received more than thirty official requests for help in evaluating localized pollution risks in response to worried and often

---

[250] Committee for the Study of the Future of Public Health, Division of Health Care Services, THE FUTURE OF PUBLIC HEALTH 66–9 (1988). https://www.ncbi .nlm.nih.gov/books/NBK218224/.

[251] Morag-Levine, *supra* note 216, at 125.

[252] *Id.*

[253] *Id.* at 125–6.

[254] Lynne Page Snyder, *The Death-Dealing Smog over Donora, Pennsylvania: Industrial Air Pollution, Public Health Policy, and the Politics of Expertise, 1948–1949*, 18(1) ENVTL. HIST. REV 117, 121 (1994) and Michael E. Kraft, *U.S. Environmental Policy and Politics: From the 1960s to the 1990s*, 12(1) J. POLICY HIST. 17, 18 (2001).

[255] Lorraine Boissoneault, *The Deadly Donora Smog of 1948 Spurred Environmental Protection – But Have We Forgotten the Lesson?*, SMITHSONIAN MAGAZINE, Oct. 26, 2018.

angry complaints from citizens."[256] This led, in 1950, to the first United States Technical Conference on Air Pollution, convened by President Truman. He made clear that the meeting's purpose was protection of public health:

> There is an urgent need to bring to bear on the problem of air pollution all the scientific knowledge at the command of industry, government, and scientific institutions. With the increasing industrialization of the United States, contamination of the air around us has become a serious problem, affecting all segments of our population. Air contaminants exact a heavy toll.... In exceptional circumstances, such as those at Donora, Pa, in 1948, they even shorten human life. The health hazards arising from air pollution, as shown by the Donora disaster, are especially important. We need to find out all we can about the relationship between air contaminants and illness.[257]

This marked the beginning of US federal government involvement in pollution, which at first was restricted to research and financial support to state research efforts. It was not until the 1960s, however, that the federal government began enacting statutes to regulate air and water pollution, starting with the 1963 Clean Air Act, the 1965 Motor Vehicle Air Pollution Control Act, and the 1967 Air Quality Act.[258] Those federal statutes were all based on the presumption that states had primary regulatory authority. But that presumption changed in 1970, when President Nixon signed into law a set of revolutionary amendments to the 1963 Clean Air Act. The amendments were revolutionary because they asserted direct federal authority to regulate polluters jointly with the states, through an exercise of "cooperative federalism."[259] Over time, through subsequent amendments, the federal government's role became dominant, though states continue to play an important role implementing and enforcing federal standards.[260] The 1970 Clean Air Act was quickly followed by the 1972 Clean Water Act,[261] the 1974 Safe Drinking Water Act,[262] the 1976 Toxic Substances Control Act,[263] the 1976 Resource Conservation and Recovery Act,[264] and the

---

[256]   Morag-Levine, *supra* note 216, at 127.

[257]   https://www.trumanlibrary.gov/library/public-papers/101/message-united
-states-technical-conference-air-pollution.

[258]   Those three statutes were subsumed, as amended, in the Clean Air Act Amendments of 1970, 42 USC § 7401 *et seq.*

[259]   42 USC § 7402.

[260]   E. Donald Elliott, Bruce A. Ackerman, and John C. Millian, *Toward a Theory of Statutory Evolution: The Federalization of Environmental Law*, 1(2) J. L. Econ. & Org. 313 (1985).

[261]   33 USC § 1151 *et seq.*

[262]   42 USC § 300f *et seq.*

[263]   15 USC §§ 2601–29.

[264]   42 USC § 6901 *et seq.*

1980 Comprehensive Environmental Response, Compensation and Liability Act (the Superfund law).[265]

While those statutes are conventionally referred to as "environmental laws," they are first and foremost public health statutes.[266] The main objective of the US Clean Air Act Amendments of 1970 is to attain national ambient air quality standards for six common air pollutants. Those standards are established (and periodically updated by new science) to "protect public health with an adequate margin of safety," regardless of cost.[267] The primary purpose of the 1974 Safe Drinking Water Act is to protect public health to the extent "feasible" based on available technologies (considering costs).[268] Waters that are not part of drinking water supplies are regulated under the Clean Water Act, which requires the Environmental Protection Agency (EPA), along with state agencies, to develop plans for "improving the sanitary condition of surface and ground waters.[269] The Act further requires the EPA to cooperate with the (then) Secretary of Health and Human Services "to conduct research on … the harmful effects on the health and welfare of persons caused by pollution."[270] Public health is also a primary concern of federal hazardous waste and toxic substances laws.[271]

On other issues relating to public health and safety, states remained generally complacent until the terrorist attacks and anthrax scare of 2001. These events spurred efforts to modernize public health and emergency laws. The national Centers for Disease Control and Prevention (CDC) asked public health experts at Georgetown University and Johns Hopkins University to draft a Model State Emergency Health Powers Act (MSEHPA) for state health officials. MSEHPA defined "public health emergency" broadly and provided

---

[265]   42 USC § 9601 *et seq.*

[266]   In the 1960s and 70s, Congress also enacted a number of statutes that were primarily intended to protect nature and natural resources. They included (among others) the 1964 Wilderness Act, 16 USC § 1131 *et seq.*, the 1966 National Wildlife Refuge System Administration Act, 16 USC § 668dd–ee, and the 1973 Endangered Species Act, 16 USC §§ 1531–44.

[267]   42 USC § 7409(b)(1); *Whitman v. American Trucking Assn.*, 531 US 457 (2001).

[268]   42 USC § 301g–1(a)(2).

[269]   33 USC § 1252(a).

[270]   *Id.* at § 1254(c).

[271]   Resource Conservation and Recovery Act of 1976, 42 USC § 6902(a); Comprehensive Environmental Response, Compensation, and Liability Act of 1980, 42 USC § 9602(a); Toxic Substances Control Act of 1976, 15 USC § 2601(b)(2); and Emergency Planning and Community Right-to-Know Act of 1986, 42 USC §§ 11001–50.

state executive officers with several powers, some of which were traditional: to suspend statutes and regulations, and regulate property; to compel individuals to submit to testing, quarantine, isolation, vaccination, and treatment; to close businesses and roads; and to abate nuisances. However, to protect individual liberty and property rights against government overreach, MSEHPA included a provision obligating states to specify the duration of emergency measures when they are introduced. In addition, isolation or quarantine orders require procedural due process protections, including court hearings, individual danger assessments, and proof that less burdensome measures would not suffice.[272] MSEHPA influenced more than 40 states to modernize their public health and emergency statutes. Forty-two states enacted laws that authorized governors to temporarily suspend laws and regulations that might impede emergency responses.[273] After MSEHPA, only 13 states imposed no time limits on social isolation or quarantine orders. However, emergency declarations that expire can be renewed in most states. Thirty-six give state legislatures a power of veto over executive emergency declarations and orders.[274] Generally speaking, the MSEHPA reflected the "rules of the game" at the time COVID-19 hit.

III.   LIBERTY, PROPERTY, PUBLIC HEALTH, AND THE CONSTITUTION

Taken together, the preceding two sections of this paper establish the following propositions: (1) governments historically have had wide-ranging legal authority to protect public health against known and dangerous threats, even if that requires temporary restrictions on individual rights, and those powers grow in times of emergency; (2) contrary to conventional assumptions, governmental power to regulate for public health is broadly consistent with classical liberal theories; and (3) policies to protect public health are often, if not always, controversial. The obvious question raised is whether and how the government's power to regulate to protect public health be squared with the protection of individual rights. State and federal courts have been trying to answer this question since the founding of the Republic. Federal and state constitutions establish only very broad limits that may be best expressed in the language of Regulatory Taking Doctrine: the power to protect public health cannot go "too far" in limiting private liberty and property rights. But neither can private liberty and property rights expand so far as to undermine the rightful power of

---

[272]   Michelle M. Mello and Lawrence O. Gostin, *Public Health Law Modernization 2.0: Rebalancing Public Health Powers and Individual Liberty in the Age of COVID-19*, 42(3) Health Aff. 318, 319 (2023).
[273]   *Id.*
[274]   *Id.*

public authorities to protect public health. Within those fuzzy limits, however, a wide range of points exist where a balance might be struck.

Traditionally, courts have been very deferential to public authorities during emergency situations. For more than 400 years, common law courts have held that "public necessity" in emergency circumstances, including wars, fires, floods, and epidemics, allows for the destruction of private property without compensation.[275] For example, in 1879, the US Supreme Court ruled, in *Bowditch v. Boston*,[276] that no compensation was required after the city ordered the destruction of privately owned buildings to create a firebreak. In 1952, the Court held, in *United States v. Caltex (Philippines) Inc.*,[277] that no compensation had to be paid to oil companies when the US army destroyed their terminal facilities in Manila, Philippines, during World War II to prevent them from falling into Japanese hands. In 2003, the Washington State Supreme Court ruled, in *Eggleston v. Pierce County*,[278] that police destruction of an individual's home while in pursuit of a criminal suspect was not a compensable taking.

In the absence of emergency circumstances, public necessity will not absolve governments from liability for taking private property. However, the law of public nuisance still applies. Public nuisance doctrine operationalizes Mill's Harm Principle, allowing for the regulation of harmful activities and conditions, whether for economic or moral reasons, without compensation.[279] In 1888 US Supreme Court Justice Harlan explained that "government is organized for the purpose, among others, of preserving the public health and public morals, and it cannot divest itself of the power to provide for these objects... ."[280] Subsequently, in 1894 the Court ruled in *Lawton v. Steel* that the police power "includes[s] everything essential to the public safety, health, and morals, and to justify the destruction ... of whatever may be regarded as a public nuisance."[281] In the early twentieth-century case of *Holden v. Hardy*, [282] the

---

[275] See, for example, *The Case of the King's Prerogative for Saltpetre* (1606) 77 ENG. REP 1294 (K.B.) (holding that King James I could take saltpeter from a private citizen to use for making gunpowder in a time of war) and *Major of New York v. Lord,* 17 Wend. 285 (N.Y. Sup. Ct. 1837) (upholding the city's uncompensated destruction of private property in order to create a firebreak).

[276] 101 U.S. 16 (1879).

[277] 344 U.S. 149 (1952).

[278] 4 P.3d 618 (Wash. 2003).

[279] Jesse Dukeminer et al., PROPERTY 803 (9th ed. 2014).

[280] *Powell v. Pennsylvania*, 127 U.S. 678, 683 (1888).

[281] 152 U.S. 133, 136 (1894).

[282] 169 U.S. 366 (1898).

Court upheld a Utah statute prohibiting miners from working more than eight hours per day, except in emergency circumstances. The statute was in accordance with Article 16 of Utah's constitution, which provided in part that "the legislature shall pass laws to provide for the health and safety of employees in factories, smelters, and mines." The plaintiff challenged the statute under the federal constitution's Contract Clause. In its ruling, the Court acknowledged the federal constitutional right of contract but wrote that it was "subject to certain limitations which the State may lawfully impose in the exercise of its police powers."[283] Here, the Court found that the dangers of mining and the detrimental health impacts on miners warranted "special precautions."[284] Thus the labor conditions were a legitimate exercise of the state's police power to protect public health.

In the first decade of the twentieth century, the US Supreme Court treated epidemics as public nuisances, even though no person caused them: "Upon the principle of self-defense, of paramount necessity, a community has the right to protect itself against an epidemic of disease which threatens the safety of its members."[285] One means by which it might protect itself is mandatory vaccination. In *Jacobson v. Massachusetts,* the Court held that a city ordinance requiring smallpox vaccination, enforced by a fine, was within the "authority of a state."[286] Especially in times of disease outbreaks, states had the authority "to enact quarantine laws and 'health laws of every description,'" only violating the constitution if they were imposed on "particular persons in … an arbitrary, unreasonable manner, or might go … far beyond what was reasonably required for the safety of the public."[287] Ever since *Jacobson,* states have had the power to enforce mandatory vaccinations, regardless of emergency circumstances.

In 1922, Rosalyn Zucht sued the City of San Antonio, Texas, challenging its ordinance that prohibited children from attending school without proof of vaccination. She claimed that: there was no need for vaccination; the ordinance deprived her of her liberty without due process of law by requiring vaccination; and it was void for leaving the city's Board of Health with excessive discretion and not providing safeguards against partiality and oppression. The trial court dismissed the case on the city's pretrial motion to dismiss. Without amending her claim, Zucht appealed to the state court of appeals, which affirmed the trial

---

[283] *Id.* at 391.

[284] *Id.* at 391–2.

[285] *Jacobsen v. Massachusetts,* 197 U.S. 11, 27 (1905). The Supreme Court of Georgia expressly referred to smallpox as a nuisance in *W. & A. R. Co. v. City of Atlanta,* 38 S.E. 996 (Ga. 1901).

[286] *Id.* at 25.

[287] *Id.* at 25, 28.

court's decision. The Texas Supreme Court declined to hear the case. Finally, it came before the US Supreme Court, which upheld the trial court's dismissal on grounds that the plaintiff's constitutional claim was not substantial. The Court treated as "settled that it is within the police power of a state to provide for compulsory vaccination," and that the state could delegate that power to municipal authorities to determine the conditions under which health regulations would become operative. Justice Brandeis wrote, "a long line of decisions by this court had also settled that in the exercise of the police power reasonable classification may be freely applied, and that regulation is not violative of the equal protection clause merely because it is not all-embracing.... [T]hese ordinances confer not arbitrary power, but only that broad discretion required for the protection of the public health."[288]

Today, all states require certain immunizations before children can attend school. Medical exemptions are provided as a matter of course. On the "Harm Principle," it is easy to appreciate why medical exemptions are important. Individuals with contraindications would be at much higher risk for harm than the general population from the vaccine itself. Religious exemptions are provided not because of any higher risk of harm from the vaccine but merely because vaccination conflicts with religious observance. Historically, the courts have looked upon claims for religious exemptions with more suspicion. In 2015, the Supreme Court declined to review an appellate court decision rejecting substantive due process and free exercise challenges to mandatory vaccinations under New York state law.[289] Nevertheless, because of political pressure from religious groups, nearly all states now provide for religious exemptions – as of 2017 only Mississippi and West Virginia did not. Of states allowing religious exemptions, 18 also provide philosophical and personal-belief exemptions.[290] The high number of vaccination exemptions has significantly impacted total population immunity, as exemplified by the measles outbreak that originated at Disneyland in California in 2015. That outbreak sickened 157 people, not a large number but infinitely higher than zero – measles was declared eradicated in the USA at the start of the twenty-first century.[291]

---

[288]   *Zucht v. King,* 260 U.S. 174 (1922).

[289]   *Phillips v. City of New York*, 775 F3d. 538 (2d Cir. 2015), *cert. denied* 136 S.Ct. 104 (2015).

[290]   John Colgrove and Abigail Lowin, *A Tale of Two States: Mississippi, West Virginia, and Exemptions to Compulsory School Vaccination Laws*, 35(2) HEALTH AFF. 348 (2016).

[291]   Marie Killmond, *Why is Vaccination Different: A Comparative Analysis of Religious Exemptions*, 117 COLUM. L. REV. 913, 914, 930 (2017).

Table 4.1   *Covid litigation grounds, number of cases, and plaintiff victories*

Claims and Legal Grounds	Total #	Plaintiff won some or all
Proc. Due Process	430	61
Equal Protection	329	45
Contract and/or Taking Clause	149	16
Second Amendment	27	4
Free Exercise Clause: gatherings	143	37
Free Exercise Clause: vaccinations	81	21

Source: Wendy E. Parmet and Faith Khalik, *Judicial Review of Public Health Powers Since the Start of the COVID-19 Pandemic: Trends and Implications*, 113(3) AMER. J. PUB. HEALTH 280, 282–83 (2023).

In addition to preventing infectious disease outbreaks, the courts have held that governments can protect public health from pollution threats. In two cases decided a year apart in the second decade of the twentieth century, the US Supreme Court declared that laundries emitting excess smoke and livery stables were both public nuisances. As such they could be regulated out of existence without compensation.[292] And no preliminary hearing was required to satisfy the due process clause before shutting them down.[293] Similarly, when chemical spills occur, local government officials have the authority to require mandatory evacuation until the emergency is over.[294]

During the recent COVID-19 outbreak, more than 1,000 lawsuits were filed challenging federal, state, and local restrictions. Five hundred lawsuits challenged social distancing requirements; 242 challenged mask mandates; and 211 challenged vaccine mandates.[295]

The vast majority of legal complaints targeted state mandates; only about 13 percent challenged federal regulations. But nearly 80 percent of claims were filed in federal court.[296] The figures from Table 4.1 indicate that states and

---

[292] *Northwestern Laundry v. City of Des Moines,* 239 U.S. 486 (1916); *Reinman v. Little Rock,* 237 U.S. 171 (1915).

[293] *North American Cold Storage Co. v. City of Chicago,* 211 U.S. 306, 320 (1908).

[294] See, for example, Thomas W. Merrill, *Public Nuisance as Risk Regulation,* 17 J. L. ECON. & POL'Y 347 (2022).

[295] Wendy E. Parmet and Faith Khalik, *Judicial Review of Public Health Powers Since the Start of the COVID-19 Pandemic: Trends and Implications,* 113(3) AMER. J. PUB. HEALTH 280, 281, Fig. 1 (2023).

[296] *Id.* at 281–2.

municipal authorities prevailed completely in approximately 85 percent of all cases. Between May 2020 and January 2022, the US Supreme Court reviewed a total of 18 cases relating to the pandemic. Of those, 10 were free exercise challenges to restrictions on gatherings, three were free exercise challenges to vaccine mandates, and five claimed government agencies exceeded their authority in various ways. On average, plaintiffs did much better before the Supreme Court than in litigation in all courts, receiving at least partial relief in 10 of the 18 cases.[297]

What do all these numbers mean? The win rate of public health regulators indicates that the courts still defer substantially to public officials during public health emergencies. As Chief Justice John Roberts of the US Supreme Court wrote, concurring in one early (2020) pandemic decision, "[o]ur Constitution principally entrusts 'the safety and health of the people' to the politically accountable officials of the States."[298] However, as Wendy Parmet and Faith Khalik note, judicial deference to public health authorities was declining even before COVID-19 struck.[299] And as the COVID-19 pandemic continued into 2021 and 2022, courts, and especially the US Supreme Court, became far less deferential, especially in cases involving alleged violations of religious liberty (free exercise). Interestingly, these judicial decisions correlated to declining popular support for public health measures against COVID-19.[300]

In November 2020, the Supreme Court decided *Roman Catholic Diocese of Brooklyn v. Cuomo*,[301] a 5–4 decision that enjoined New York Governor Andrew Cuomo's executive order restricting attendance at religious services to 10 persons in red zones (for COVID infections) and 25 persons in orange zones. According to the *per curiam* decision, the restrictions on religious service attendance could not be "viewed as neutral because they single[d] out houses of worship for especially harsh treatment." The "minimum requirement of neutrality" to religion was established in *Church of Lukumi Babalu Aye, Inc. v. Hialeah*.[302] Although the *Cuomo* case was a 5–4 decision, the merits of the case were not especially controversial. Among the main reasons for the dissents, including one by Chief Justice Roberts, was that the injunction was unnecessary because Governor Cuomo had already altered the executive order shortly after the case was filed to bring it into alignment

---

[297]   *Id.* at 283, Tab. 1.
[298]   *South Bay United Pentacostal Church v. Newsom*, 140 S.Ct. 1613 (2020) (Roberts, CJ, concurring).
[299]   Parmet and Khalik, *supra* note 292, at 285.
[300]   Wendy Parmet, CONSTITUTIONAL CONTAGION: COVID, THE COURTS, AND PUBLIC HEALTH 3 (2023).
[301]   592 U.S. 14 (2020).
[302]   508 U.S. 520 (1993).

with *Church of Lukumi Babalu Aye.* The other dissenters, Justices Kagan, Sotomayor, and Breyer, argued for greater deference to political authorities during the pandemic.

Just five months later, the Court gave practically no deference to political authorities. In *Tandon v. Newsom*,[303] it enjoined a California state restriction on gatherings in private homes that obstructed bible study groups, even though the same limitations applied to any groups meeting in private homes for any reason. The Court held the restriction violated the Free Exercise Clause of the First Amendment because some secular gatherings in places *outside the home* were restricted less. By comparing apples and oranges – in-home religious gatherings v. secular gatherings in other places – the Court treated the case as one requiring strict scrutiny, rather than rational-basis review. It put the burden on the state to prove that the risks of a certain number of people meeting in a private home exceeded the risks of the same number of people meeting somewhere else. But without any evidence of comparative risks, the Court ruled that, because the state treated some out-of-home secular activities more leniently than in-home religious gatherings, the state had violated the Free Exercise Clause. The *Tandon* ruling is a stark departure from the history of judicial deference to public health officials in emergency circumstances. By treating the case from the outset as one requiring strict scrutiny, the Court's majority not only failed to defer to political authorities but imposed on them extra burdens during an emergency. In effect, the Court held that strict scrutiny is required whenever the state limits a religious activity more than *any*, even non-comparable, secular activity. On the *Tandon* Court's logic, a pandemic regulation that permits 100 people to gather in a hospital emergency room must allow the same number of people to gather for religious services in a space the same size or smaller because the respective congregations of people create similar risks.

In the 2021 case of *Fulton v. City of Philadelphia*,[304] the Court held that if a state allows for individual exemptions from its public health mandates but declines to grant a religious one, that decision is automatically subject to strict scrutiny. The Six Circuit US Court of Appeals, in *Dahl v. Board of Trustees of Western Michigan University*,[305] subsequently applied the *Fulton* rule to apply strict scrutiny in a case where no exemption of any kind had been offered to anyone. In *U.S. Navy Seals 1–26 v. Biden*,[306] a federal district court in Texas found that the US Navy violated the Free Exercise Clause (as well as the Religious Freedom Restoration Act) in failing to provide religious exemptions

---

[303] 593 U.S. 61 (2021).
[304] 593 U.S. 522 (2021).
[305] 15 F. 4th 728 (6th Cir. 2021).
[306] 578 F. Supp. 3d 822 (N.D. Texas 2022), *aff'd,* 72 F. 4th 666 (5th Cir. 2023).

from a rule requiring vaccination before deployment. Fortunately for George Washington, this ruling came nearly 250 years after he ordered mandatory vaccination of all soldiers in the Continental Army, without exception.[307]

Even in cases not involving religious liberty, the Court scrutinized federal and state COVID regulations. In *National Federation of Independent Business v. U.S. Dept. of Labor*,[308] the Supreme Court ruled that the Occupational Safety and Health Act did not authorize the Dept. of Labor to mandate that large businesses require their employees to be tested, masked, or vaccinated during the COVID pandemic. In that same case, however, the Court ruled that the Dept. of Labor could impose such requirements on research facilities and hospitals because of the higher risks encountered there. In a 2022 case, the Supreme Court, on a narrow 5–4 majority, upheld the Biden Administration's rule that all facilities receiving Medicare and Medicaid funding must mandate vaccinations of all staff members, except those with medical or religious exemptions.[309] The dissenters, led by Justice Thomas, argued that "[t]he government has not made a strong showing that this hodgepodge of provisions authorizes a nationwide vaccine mandate."[310] The dissenters would have required a new congressional law to impose a nationwide vaccine mandate. Again, this runs strongly against the tradition of deference to the executive during a national emergency. Some consider this a dangerous power-grab by the Court, which has made it "increasingly difficult for state and federal governments to protect the public's health."[311]

Although plaintiffs attained greater success in the courts as the pandemic wore on, they arguably received more favorable treatment in the political arena than in the courts. States, which "drove the initial policy response,"[312] were, as we would expect, responsive to constituent concerns. Across all states, the stringency of the pandemic response was driven mainly by daily case rates.[313] But Republican-controlled state governments spent fewer days than Democrat-controlled state governments at a high level of stringency relative to similar case rates. The 10 states with the least restrictive response measures were all led by Republican governors.[314] During the first year of COVID, only six US states did *not* issue mandatory stay-at-home orders (SAHOs), and they all had

---

[307]   See *supra* note 189 and accompanying text.

[308]   595 US ___ (2022).

[309]   *Biden v. Missouri*, 595 U.S. 87 (2022).

[310]   595 U.S. at 102 (Thomas, J., dissenting).

[311]   Parmet, *supra* note 297, at 114 (2023).

[312]   Laura Hallas et al., *Variation in US States' Responses to COVID-19, Version 2.0 BSG Working Paper Series*, University of Oxford (Dec. 2020).

[313]   *Id.* at 13.

[314]   *Id.* at 16.

Republican governors.[315] Overall, Republican governors were "significantly less likely to issue a SAHO … and when they did issue one, they were slower to do so."[316] Overall, throughout 2020, Democrat-led states had more stringent COVID policies than Republican-led states.[317] The political scientist Donald Kettl rightly cautions that "it is much too simple to argue that the most important strategic decisions were purely the product of partisanship."[318] But even he acknowledges that "no other major democracy has seen this kind of vicious infighting among their governments." Kettl goes so far as to say that "[f]rom the very beginning, COVID-19 has been more a political than a public health problem." That is a remarkable conclusion, given that COVID killed more than 1.1 million Americans.[319]

During the COVID-19 pandemic, conservatives, libertarians, and business interests complained of state interference with individual, economic, and religious liberty from SAHOs, shut-downs, and restrictions on public and private gatherings. Progressives and public-health advocates were equally unhappy with states they thought did too little too late to control the pandemic. But, as Eric Posner has observed, "while gun owners, churchgoers and property owners can challenge overzealous stay-at-home orders, the elderly, the immune-suppressed and the rest of us have no legal recourse when government fails to protect us. Governors who choose not to impose adequate precautions, for political reasons unrelated to public health, are free to do so."[320] This legal asymmetry is a consequence of the fact that American courts have never recognized a right to public health. Civil, religious, and economic liberty advocates can sue whenever they feel aggrieved by government regulations, including during a health emergency. But "[w]hen the government fails to issue orders, when it underreaches rather than overreaches, citizens have no right to judicial review."[321] Their only recourse is to "throw the bums out" at the next election. It should come as no surprise then that courts appear to favor the rights of individuals at low risk from disease over those of individuals at high risk.[322] This

---

[315] Chan Wang, Yushim Kim, and Karen Mossberger, *Governor's Political Affiliation and Stringent COVID-19 Policy*, 2023 PUBLIC ADMIN. REV 1, 1–2 (2023).

[316] *Id.* at 3.

[317] *Id.* at 30.

[318] Donald F. Kettl, *States Divided: The Implications of American Federalism for COVID-19*, 80(4) PUB. ADMIN. REV 595, 597 (2020).

[319] https://www.statista.com/statistics/1113068/reported-deaths-from-covid-by-place-of-death-us/.

[320] Eric Posner, *You Can Sue to Stop Lockdowns, but Not to Start Them*, WASHINGTON POST, May 10, 2020.

[321] *Id.*

[322] PARMAT, *supra* note 297, at 133.

might be another reason courts should defer more, rather than less, to public health authorities during pandemics.

IV. LIBERAL GOVERNANCE AND THE MESSINESS OF POLITICAL DISAGREEMENT

It is hard to avoid the conclusion that the public health system in the USA failed the test of COVID-19. After all, more than one million Americans died from the disease. Some public health agencies allegedly over-responded with unnecessarily harsh regulations, while others under-responded with containment efforts that were too little and too late. Certainly, public health officials were not helped by misinformation and denialism, which have always complicated public health emergencies.[323] It is, however, unprecedented for the president of the USA to act as denialist-in-chief.[324]

At the same time, state regulatory responses saved many lives. According to one study published in the *Journal of the American Medical Association*, "if all states had imposed COVID-19 restrictions similar to those used in the 10 most ... restrictive states, excess deaths would have been an estimated 10% to 21% ... lower," amounting to a saving of 271,000 to 447,000 additional lives. It would have come at a higher cost to individual liberty in states that chose "weak" protections over "strong" protections. But it is important to bear in mind that all impositions on liberty, nationwide, were only temporary. On May 12, 2022, US COVID-19 related deaths surpassed one million. Exactly one year later, on May 11, 2023, the public health emergency initially declared under Sec. 319 of the Public Health Act expired.[325] As of June 2023, all state public health emergencies had been lifted.[326] Since then, the personal, economic, and especially religious liberty of Americans is more expansive than before the pandemic, thanks to Supreme Court decisions that have reduced the deference shown to public health agencies both during emergencies and in normal circumstances.

---

[323] See, for example, Sabrina L. Jin et al., *Social Histories of Public Health Misinformation and Infodemics: Case Studies from Four Pandemics*, 9(6) THE LANCET INFECTIOUS DISEASE e345 (2024).

[324] See Samuel K. Cohn, EPIDEMICS 49–50 (2018) (discussing the annihilation of Jewish communities throughout continental Europe during and after the Black Death of the fourteenth century based on stories that Jews caused plague by poisoning water sources).

[325] https://www.defense.gov/Spotlights/Coronavirus-DOD-Response/Timeline/.

[326] https://nashp.org/state-tracker/states-covid-19-public-health-emergency-declarations/.

Before condemning the overall public health response to COVID-19, we also must acknowledge that both over-regulation and under-regulation were inevitable. The probability of achieving the "correct" amount of intervention during a major pandemic is effectively zero. In the first place, no consensus ever exists on the "correct" amount of intervention. Even if a consensus existed, the chances of hitting the optimal level of intervention remains infinitesimally low. Policy responses are not like mathematical equations or optimization models in economics – they are never perfect. As Popper observed, policies in liberal governance systems are always experiments.[327] They all fail to some extent. Some fail a little; some fail a lot; and some fail completely. As Ronald Coase observed in a 1964 comment, we are always "choosing between social arrangements which are all more or less failures."[328] Markets, firms, and governments all fail. This cannot be a reason for doing nothing, of course, because a policy that is only partly effective might still be vastly preferable to, and more efficient than, doing nothing. And policies can be improved or abandoned.

Few economists have ever expected markets to provide sufficient public goods or auto-magically correct negative externalities. An invisible hand may lead market actors to minimize their private costs, but not the social costs of their activities; quite the contrary, they have every incentive to externalize as many of their costs as possible. Such market failures provide the original justification for government intervention to provide public sanitation and protect public health. Milton Friedman, who was as anti-government as a social-welfare economist could be, nevertheless acknowledged clear circumstances when government intervention is not just legitimate but desirable. He wrote that "public health measures have contributed to the reduction of infectious disease. Assistance measures have relieved suffering and distress. Local authorities have often provided facilities essential to the life of communities."[329] He had no expectation that markets would provide sufficient public health and environmental protection.

In assessing the success or failure of policies, people employ various "evaluative criteria," including economic efficiency (net benefits over costs), fiscal equivalence (those who pay more, should benefit more), (re)distributional equity (those with less benefit more), accountability (of officials to the public), conformance to general morality (doing the right thing), and adaptability

---

[327] See *supra* notes 60–8 and accompanying text.
[328] Ronald H. Coase, *The Regulated Industries: Discussion*, 54(3) AMER. ECON. REV. 195 (1964).
[329] Milton Friedman, CAPITALISM AND FREEDOM 199 (1962).

(to changing circumstances over time).[330] Needless to say, in any evaluation these criteria might not all point in the same direction. And evaluations always reflect the subjective values of the evaluators. Many of those at special risk from COVID-19 because of age, occupation, or underlying co-morbidities might have thought masking and social distancing restrictions were imposed too late and lifted too soon. Many libertarians thought they never should have been imposed in the first place. Certainly, for some businesses, the economic shut-down was ruinous, despite government assistance.

Given that disagreements are inevitable, is it even possible to attain a stable balance between protecting liberty and protecting public health? Liberal democratic societies have sometimes been able to attain a stable equilibrium after long periods of fundamental disagreement. Today, no serious person would suggest that women should not have the right to vote or that racially restrictive covenants should be enforceable at law. Nevertheless, many policy disputes, especially those pitting individual liberty against religious liberty, seem resistant to any stable resolution. But is that such a bad thing? From a classical-liberal perspective, policy messiness is to be expected. Liberal theory is not geared to permanent, once-and-for-all solutions to essentially contested problems. It is designed for more or less permanent disagreements. Consistent with its openness to various conceptions of the good life, liberalism offers no *telos* or desired end to which all members of society are presumed or required to aspire. Instead, it offers principles, institutions, and procedures for resolving political disagreements, if only for the time being.[331] Policy choices create winners and losers, but as Popper and Mill both stressed, policies are always experiments that may be amended/improved or reversed. Today's losers may be tomorrow's winners. This is borne out empirically in the history of policy and policy change in the USA. Consider, for example, the extent to which environmental policies have changed since 1980 depending on which party holds the White House.[332] Even the US Constitution, which many think is set in stone, changes over time, and not only via the formal amendment process.[333]

---

[330]   Elinor Ostrom, *Institutional Rational Choice: An Assessment of the Institutional Analysis and Development Framework*, in Paul Sabatier, ed., THEORIES OF THE POLICY PROCESS 321, 3–35 (2007).
[331]   See, for example, Daniel H. Cole, Aurelian Craiutu, and Michael D. McGinnis, *Embracing Liberalism's Complexity*, 36(3) CRITICAL REV. 352 (2024).
[332]   See, for example, David M. Shafie, PRESIDENTIAL ADMINISTRATION AND THE ENVIRONMENT (2013).
[333]   See, for example, Cass R. Sunstein, A CONSTITUTION OF MANY MINDS: WHY THE FOUNDING DOCUMENT DOESN'T MEAN WHAT IT MEANT BEFORE (2009).

That process is cumbersome, indeed, but the Supreme Court regularly amends the Constitution simply by (re)interpreting it.[334]

The widespread belief that the classical liberals would resolve all policy questions by reference only to individual liberty and private property is a pernicious myth that disregards their complex and nuanced thinking. Far from advocating Robert Nozick's "nightwatchman state,"[335] let alone anarcho-capitalism, the classical liberals were all social welfarists. Adam Smith has been described, not implausibly, as a "maximin" welfarist, who adjudged policies based mainly on their effects on the working poor.[336] Karl Popper, whose chief focus was on reducing immiseration, might be similarly described. John Locke believed that in the commonwealth the "common good" took precedence over individual rights.[337] Milton Friedman, who stressed individual autonomy more than any of the others, did so in the service of a social-welfare function: "the freedom of people to control their own lives in accordance with their own values is the surest way to achieve the full potential of a great society."[338]

Even classical liberalism's well-justified distrust of the state is most often expressed in social welfare terms. Societies that create institutions to protect liberty, property, and voluntary exchange are materially better off overall than those that do not because they create incentives that facilitate production and exchange.[339] But "property" is an imprecise and variable term that denotes diverse configurations of rights and duties created by governments and their courts.[340] This underscores the all-important point that liberty and governance

---

[334] Examples of Supreme Court decisions that, at least in effect, amounted to amendments of the constitution, include (among many others): *Marbury v. Madison*, 5 U.S. 137 (1803), which established the Supreme Court as final arbiter of the constitution; *Pennsylvania Coal Co. v. Mahon*, 260 U.S. 393 (1922), in which Justice Holmes invented the Regulatory Taking Doctrine; *Roe v. Wade*, 410 U.S. 113 (1973), which created a limited right to terminate pregnancies; *Dobbs v. Jackson Women's Health Organization*, 597 U.S. 215 (2022), which repealed the right created in *Roe*; and, most recently, *Trump v. United States*, No. 23-939, 603 U.S. __, (2024), in which the Court granted presidents absolute immunity to criminal prosecution for "official acts" after they leave office.

[335] See Robert Nozick, ANARCHY, STATE, AND UTOPIA (1974).

[336] Eric Schliesser, ADAM SMITH: SYSTEMATIC PHILOSOPHER AND PUBLIC THINKER Ch. 8 (2017).

[337] See Locke, *supra* note 12 and accompanying text.

[338] Friedman and Friedman, *supra* note 96, at 309–10.

[339] See, for example, Cass R. Sunstein, FREE MARKETS AND SOCIAL JUSTICE 206–7 (1997).

[340] See, for example, Daniel H. Cole and Elinor Ostrom, *The Variety of Property Systems and Rights in Natural Resources*, in Daniel H. Cole and Elinor Ostrom, eds, PROPERTY IN LAND AND OTHER RESOURCES 37 (2012).

are not antithetical categories. It is even possible to reconcile substantial social welfare programs with individual liberty. Economic historians in the classical-liberal tradition have described the welfare state as a relatively low-cost means of "sharing the gains from the market without disrupting it."[341] By reducing social risk, welfare states "reduce the probability of an antimarket political reaction during bad times."[342] No one was more distrustful of the state than the author of *The Road to Serfdom* (1944), but that did not prevent Friedrich von Hayek from endorsing a panoply of welfare-state programs, including social security, based on his understanding that such programs were consistent with individual liberty.[343] Karl Popper advocated for initiatives to reduce immisera-tion, which did not prevent him from railing against the "petty dictators" of local bureaucracies.[344] He believed an open society could, though only imper-fectly, regulate the regulators while bettering the circumstances of the least well off. Adam Smith focused most of his attention in *The Wealth of Nations* (1775) on the harmful consequences for ordinary citizens of unwise govern-ment market interventions. But he also expressed a healthy distrust of market actors: "People of the same trade seldom meet together, even for merriment and diversion, but the conversation ends in a conspiracy against the public, or in some contrivance to raise prices."[345] Far from liberty and property ideo-logues, the classical liberals distrusted *all* concentrations of power, whether public or private.

CONCLUSION

From a classical-liberal perspective, the messiness of our polycentric public health system is, arguably, as it should be. No panacea solution exists for bal-ancing public health and private liberty interests. Traditionally, in times of health emergencies, courts have deferred to the determinations of public health officials. Toward the end of the COVID-19 pandemic, some states maintained that bias, while others leaned more toward protecting individual liberty. The Supreme Court, too, seems to have shifted more in favor of liberty, especially religious liberty. Again, such shifts are to be expected in a liberal society, which cannot promise the kind of stability authoritarian and theocratic sys-tems promise and sometimes achieve. But those systems are also more rigid

---

[341] Douglass C. North, John Joseph Wallis, and Barry R. Weingast, VIOLENCE AND SOCIAL ORDERS: A CONCEPTUAL FRAMEWORK FOR INTERPRETING RECORDED HUMAN HISTORY 122 (2009).

[342] *Id.* at 122–3.

[343] See *supra* notes 68–73 and accompanying text.

[344] Karl Popper, THE LESSON OF THIS CENTURY, *supra* note 82, at 79.

[345] Adam Smith, THE WEALTH OF NATIONS, *supra* note 21, at 148.

and less amenable to policy changes than liberal democracies, which could leave them more vulnerable in fast-changing circumstances.[346] Liberal systems may well be more adaptively efficient.[347]

Liberalism has been declared dead many times since its modern inception in the eighteenth century.[348] Yet, liberal governance systems persist, perhaps in part because they do not set their rules in stone. A great deal of policy space, within broad constitutional limits, exists for policy experiments that weigh public health and liberty considerations differently. The constitutional limits are, of course, crucial, though they too can be flexible. To maximally protect public health, individual liberty and property would have to be permanently sacrificed. As the famous Polish dissident, Jacek Kuroń, once remarked, "The safest state is a police state."[349] On the other hand, maximizing liberty and property would require the establishment of a *laissez-faire* state (if that is not a contradiction in terms) capable of preventing some public bads but incapable of providing sufficient public goods. That might be a libertarian Utopia, but it is not at all what the classical liberals had in mind. It would be an exaggeration to say that any classical liberal from Adam Smith to John Stuart Mill contemplated the kind of welfare state that emerged in the twentieth century. And twentieth century liberals in the classical tradition, who witnessed the rise of the welfare state, had various reactions to it. Milton Friedman deplored the growth of welfare-state policies designed to redistribute wealth because of the incentives and waste they created.[350] But he still favored state interventions to internalize negative externalities, such as pollution, and to provide welfare-enhancing public goods, ranging from standard weights and measures to public health protection. Hayek, too, was generally opposed to redistributive welfare-state policies, but he supported social security.[351] Karl Popper was less opposed than Friedman or Hayek to redistributive policies to reduce immiseration of the least well off in society, though he always maintained a strong

---

[346]   See, for example, Bryan D. Jones, Derek A. Epp, and Frank R. Baumgartner, *Democracy, Authoritarianism, and Policy Punctuations*, 1 INT'L REV. PUBLIC POLICY 7 (2019) and Douglass C. North, UNDERSTANDING THE PROCESS OF ECONOMIC CHANGE Ch. 11 (2005).

[347]   North, Wallis, and Weingast, *supra* note 338, at 252–4.

[348]   See Daniel H. Cole and Aurelian Criautu, *The Many Deaths of Liberalism*, AEON, June 28, 2018. https://aeon.co/essays/reports-of-the-demise-of-liberalism-are-greatly-exaggerated.

[349]   Personal recollection from a presentation Kuroń made at the Hudson Institute in Indianapolis in the early 1990s.

[350]   Friedman and Friedman, FREE TO CHOOSE, *supra* note 96, at 107–8.

[351]   See *supra* notes 69–73 and accompanying text.

distrust of centralized power.[352] He supported an active welfare state while deploring the "petty dictators" who filled government bureaucracies.[353]

The diversity of these views reflects the kind of rational disagreement liberal constitutions are designed to take seriously and resolve according to institutional mechanisms that are fair and consistent, in accordance with due process and the rule of law. That is something all liberals in the classical-liberal tradition would support, along with other basic features of our constitutional system, including the institutions that protect liberty and property, contract and contract-enforcement mechanisms to facilitate exchange in competitive markets, equal protection under the law, political institutions to provide public goods and compensate for market failures, and independent courts to correct private harms and curb government overreach and corruption by regulating the regulators. None of these institutions functions perfectly, ever, including in the context of public health. But they do function, despite the very real tensions that exist between them. Precisely because it takes seriously disagreements about what is "good," allows for reassessments and corrections, and reflects the messiness of human interrelations in the real world, the liberal constitution *is* truly a "common good" constitution.[354]

---

[352] Karl Popper, *For a Better World*, *supra* note 85, at 291; Karl Popper, *The Open Society and the Democratic State*, *supra* note 86, at 248.

[353] Karl Popper, THE LESSON OF THIS CENTURY, *supra* note 82, at 79.

[354] The label "common good constitutionalism" refers to a constitutional system that reflects Roman Catholic values. See Adrian Vermeule, COMMON GOOD CONSTITUTIONALISM (2022). The "common good" is what aligns with Vermeule's religiously informed preferences. It does not take political disagreements seriously and would create permanent winners and losers.

PART II

The unrealized power and promise of private property rights in the 21st century

PART A

Rethinking private property and housing

5. Once more into the rent control abyss

Richard Epstein

INTRODUCTION

Rent control has been a source of controversy and confusion since its constitutionality was first sustained in 1921 by a bare five-to-four vote in *Block v. Hirsh*.[1] Over the next 100-plus years, various permutations on the basic rent control design have been developed by imaginative governments, only to be vigorously attacked on a range of inventive constitutional theories relating to property, contract, and equal protection. In virtually every case, subject to only one minor exception of theoretical interest,[2] the outcome is clear: these counterattacks have been foiled, so that rent control laws today look to be per se legal, no matter their form, origins, or effects.[3]

Yet this uniform triumphant success of rent control statutes should be the source of social anxiety, not jubilation. Today's rent control rules are no longer a minor irritation whose impact will diminish over time. Rent control has grown from its modest origins into a powerful and entrenched system. It is run by multiple state and city administrative agencies, backed by specialized courts, and politically supported by cohesive tenant lobbying groups. Their combined efforts have now demonstrated an increasing capacity to upend housing markets in major cities in both the short and the long term.

The leading example of this regulatory resurgence comes out of New York City, which in 2019 passed its most onerous rent control statute to date.[4] That statute recently survived constitutional scrutiny in *74 Pinehurst LLC v. New*

---

[1]   256 U.S. 135, 159 (1921).

[2]   *Chastleton Corp v. Sinclair*, 264 U.S. 543 (1924).

[3]   See, for example, *RENT ASSN. v. Higgins*, 630 N.E.2d 626 (N.Y. 1993) and *Harmon v. Markus*, 412 Fed. Appx. 420 [2d Cir. 2011], cert. denied, *Harmon v. Kimmel*, 132 S. Ct. 1991 [2012]).

[4]   S. 6458, A 8281, available at https://rentguidelinesboard.cityofnewyork.us /wp-content/uploads/2019/11/Housing-Stability-and-Tenant-Protection-Act-of -2019.pdf.

York,[5] where a unanimous panel of the Second Circuit held the case did not present any serious challenge to the dominant view that rent control and rent stabilization laws are per se legal.[6] One striking feature of that decision is that nowhere does it mention or discuss any of the specific provisions that it sustained. The District Court opinion of Komitee, J. set the tone: "No precedent binding on this Court has ever found any provision of a rent-stabilization statute to violate the Constitution, and even if the 2019 amendments go beyond prior regulations, it is not for a lower court to reverse this tide."[7] It then set out the provisions briefly:

- Cap the number of units landlords can recover for personal use at one unit per building (and only upon a showing of immediate and compelling necessity). N.Y. Reg. Sess. § 6458, Part I (2019).
- Repeal the "luxury decontrol" provisions, which allowed landlords, in certain circumstances, to decontrol a unit when the rent reached a specified value. *Id.* at Part D, § 5.
- Repeal the "vacancy" and "longevity" increase provisions, which allowed landlords to charge higher rents when certain units became vacant. *Id.* at Part B, §§ 1, 2.
- Repeal the "preferential rate" provisions, which allowed landlords who had been charging rates below the legal maximum to increase those rates when a lease ended. *Id.* at Part E.
- Reduce the value of capital improvements—called "individual apartment improvements" (IAI) and "major capital improvements" (MCI)—that landlords may pass on to tenants through rent increases. *Id.* at Part K, §§ 1, 2, 4, 11.
- Increase the fraction of tenant consent needed to convert a building to cooperative or condominium use. *Id.* at Part N.
- Extend, from six to 12 months, the period in which state housing courts may stay the eviction of breaching tenants. *Id.* at Part M, § 2.[8]

These provisions of the 2019 law reflected the transformation in state politics when the Democratic party, dominated by its aggressive progressive

---

[5]   59 F.4th 557 (2d Cir. 2023).

[6]   For the record, I wrote, with the Buckeye Institute, an amicus curiae brief in support of 74 Pinehurst, available to registered users at https://1.next.westlaw.com /Document/I72a42c19149811ee9093e6f084407295/View/FullText.html.

[7]   *Id.*

[8]   *74 Pinehurst LLC v. New York*, No. 19-cv-6447(EK)(RLM), available at https://scholar.google.com/scholar_case?case=13758241797609339451&hl=en &as_sdt=400006.

wing, obtained full control of both the state Senate and Assembly in 2018. The revised statute therefore lost the remaining few balancing mechanisms that survived the introduction of the initial Local Emergency Housing Rent Control Act of 1962.[9] That Act was followed in 1969 by the passage of the original Rent Stabilization Law (RSL), which has since weathered every judicial storm. It was, therefore, no great surprise that the United States Supreme Court refused to hear *74 Pinehurst*. But the next flurry of activity moved quickly into unknown territory when the *Wall Street Journal* published a dispirited editorial and news story that together recounted the sharp decline in the share values of a major lender, New York Community Bancorp (NYCB).[10] NYCB is, or was, a large player in the rent stabilization mortgage market. Recently, its stock price suffered a severe downturn because of the fragile condition of its mortgage portfolio, which became evident after the rent control in *74 Pinehurst* challenge was rejected. Some 14 percent of NYCB's RSL loans are said to be at risk of default, while the buildings on which these loans are secured are now selling at 30 to 60 percent below their purchase price, for a net loss that might exceed $75 billion. In March 2024, it received a $1 billion cash injection that may not be sufficient to meet its current obligations amid market regulatory uncertainties.[11]

The situation could well get worse, for the New York state legislature is now thinking about a statute that is going to provide all renters with the protection of a so-called Good Cause Eviction law, which will brand as unreasonable any rent increase that exceeds 3 percent or 1.5 times the consumer price index, whichever is higher.[12] To charge any additional rents requires a hearing before the housing court, which will cost thousands and may fail in any event. In some cases, the cap may not come into play, but in all too many cases the relevant components of the markets in goods and services could easily exceed the cap, so that the rents cannot keep up with costs. This will introduce a form

---

[9]   Act 21/62, available at https://www.nysenate.gov/legislation/laws/LEH.

[10]   *A New York Rent Control Panic,* WALL STREET JOURNAL, February 11, 2024, https://www.wsj.com/articles/new-york-community-bancorp-real-estate -losses-rent-control-signature-bank-8338b8fb: See also Gina Heeb and Rachel Ensign, *New York Community Bancorp Went From a Crisis Winner to Banking's Next Worry,* WALL STREET JOURNAL, February 10, 2024, https://www.wsj.com/ finance/banking/new-york-community-bank-banking-crisis-663a95af.

[11]   Joy Wildermuth, *NYCB Still Faces Big Challenges After $1 Billion Cash Injection,* March 7, 2024, available at https://www.marketwatch.com/story/nycb -still-faces-big-challenges-after-1-billion-cash-injection-9910f25f.

[12]   WSJ Review and Outlook, *How to Kill New York's Rental Housing Market,* April 1, 2024, available at https://www.wsj.com/articles/albany-democrats-good -cause-eviction-new-york-rent-control-kathy-hochul-f4d8125f.

of universal rent control whose effects will not be experienced only today but also by any future investment. But at this point there is no constitutional safeguard against these risks, or against the further prospect of even more stringent restrictions down the road, given that Justice Thomas's "pro landlord" position in *74 Pinehurst* is sure to shut down the market.[13]

These are not isolated disruptions. Given the anticipated burden of the regulations, many landlords have taken some of their rent-controlled units off the market, finding that they have no viable path for obtaining a satisfactory return on any expenditures for building repairs and improvements. This delicate situation could get worse when the low-interest COVID loans have to be refinanced at today's higher rates, such that NYCB may have to sell off part of its portfolio. The consequences, *The Wall Street Journal* continues, are that greater pressure is exerted in the non-RSL sector, where rents have soared by as much as 30 percent in the last two years. Thus, New York City is now divided into the "haves" which receive ever more comprehensive legal protection, and the "have-nots" that must make peace in the tight unregulated market. And *74 Pinehurst* has had its ripple effects as well, as the Blackstone Corporation abandoned any effort to remove some 5,000 units from rent control in Stuyvesant Town-Peter Cooper Village shortly after *Pinehurst* was decided.[14] It is no wonder, therefore, that New York leads the nation in net population losses, driven in part by the search for cheaper housing for its citizens who are not protected by the RSL.[15] Exit is chosen by the have-nots because they know that a voice strategy is hopeless.[16]

The question here is whether there are any options left to challenge rent control after *74 Pinehurst*. To tackle that question, I begin by criticizing Justice Thomas's statement on the denial of certiorari for *74 Pinehurst* in Part II, pointing out how it fails on both its analysis of the facial and as applied challenges to the RSL. Next, Part III examines the flawed origins and intellectual confusion that surrounds the problem. This stems chiefly from the confusions

---

[13] See *74 Pinehurst* at 4–10.

[14] Aaron Ginsburg, *In Win for Stuy Town Tenants, Blackstone Drops Challenge to Rent Stabilization.* 6SQFT, February 26, 2024, available at https://www.6sqft.com/blackstone-drops-challenge-to-rent-stabilization-stuy-town-apartments/.

[15] Fox5 NY, *New York Sees Largest Population Decline of 50 States in 2023: Census*, available at https://www.fox5ny.com/news/new-york-state-population-2023.

[16] Richard A. Epstein, *Exit Rights Under Federalism*, 55 Law & Contemp. Prob. 147 (Winter, 1992); Richard A. Epstein, *Exit Rights and Insurance Regulation: From Federalism to Takings*, 7 GEORGE MASON L. REV 293 (1999) and Richard A. Epstein, *The Role of Exit Rights: What the Theory of the Firm Says About the Conduct of Brexit Negotiations*, 39 CARDOZO L. REV 825 (2018).

on two fronts. The first is the correct treatment of divided interests in real property, including the landlord's reversion at the end of a lease, and the second is the proper reading of the police power limitation, which must be read into all constitutional guarantees even though it is not explicitly referred to in the text of the Constitution. Finally, Part IV identifies how the RSL violates the core, traditional rights for landlords by distorting at every point the traditional categories of law on such basic matters as possession, use, voluntary and necessity or emergency. Taken altogether, this reexamination of these laws suggests that the perfect success of the RSL in court got matters exactly backwards, for as a matter of first principles the entire scheme is unconstitutional on its face. The serious challenge is to work out a remedial system that allows for a smooth transition to a market economy from its current impaired state, even as the next round of rent control expansions threaten permanent damage to the rental market.

I. FACIAL AND AS APPLIED CHALLENGES TO RENT CONTROL

When the Supreme Court denied certiorari on the RSL cases, Justice Clarence Thomas issued a brief supplemental statement noting that "[t]he constitutionality of regimes like New York City's is an important and pressing question."[17] In the next breath, however, he emphasized that the Court denied certiorari because the pleadings "would complicate our review."[18] He writes that:

> The petitioners' complaints primarily contain generalized allegations about their circumstances and injuries. But, to evaluate their as-applied challenges, we must consider whether specific New York City regulations prevent petitioners from evicting actual tenants for particular reasons. Similarly, petitioners' facial challenges require a clear understanding of how New York City regulations coordinate to completely bar landlords from evicting tenants. The pleadings do not facilitate such an understanding. However, in an appropriate future case, we should grant certiorari to address this important question.[19]

This Thomas opinion purports to offer some compensation to these "owners of small and midsize apartment buildings."[20] In fact, this statement dashes all hope of obtaining any kind of sensible relief in these cases. In his short

---

[17] *74 Pinehurst v. New York*, 601 U.S. ___, 22–1130 slip op. at 1 (2024).

[18] *Id.* at 1–2.

[19] *Id.* at 2.

[20] Christian Britschgi, *After Supreme Court Denies Cases, Clarence Thomas Offers Hope to Rent Control Critics*, Reason Magazine, February 20, 2024, available at https://reason.com/2024/02/20/after-supreme-court-denies-cases -clarence-thomas-offers-hope-to-rent-control-critics/.

opinion, Thomas rejects facial challenges, but favors as applied ones. His analysis of both scenarios is incorrect.

A.   Facial Challenges

Determining compensation. The gist of any strong takings claim is that the decision to rob the owner of its rights to regain possession of the property after the expiration of the lease removes virtually the full value of the property, so that there are no lurking complexities that prevent a final adjudication on the merits. Thus, it is easy to identify the value of the reversion held under the common law rules. For ease of exposition, assume that this right was worth $10,000 a month if the property could be rented out at market prices. The rent control laws do not strip the owner of that property in its entirety, but give him a limited statutory right in exchange for that reversion, which allows the landlord to recapture the property only if a narrow set of conditions are satisfied. Thus:

> the RSL does not compel landlords to refrain in perpetuity from terminating a tenancy. Instead, the statute sets forth several bases on which a landlord may terminate a tenant's lease, such as for failing to pay rent, creating a nuisance, violating the lease, or using the property for illegal purposes.[21]

Concentrate for the moment on the first of these grounds. When a tenant fails to pay rent, the premises can be recovered if the tenant does not pay the allowable below-market rate of rent (say $2,500 per month) that is allowed under the statute. But that right is largely worthless. No sensible tenant will forgo paying $2,500 a month when the subsidy is, at the first approximation, $7,500 per month or about $90,000 per year, which translates into a capital value of close to $1 million per year. So put a value on that limited right to recover at $100. With about 700,000 units renting at below market rates, the total amount of lost landlord revenue equals about $2.1 billion per year. New York City could not possibly pay compensation at that level out of its existing revenue streams for all past takings actionable within the statute of limitations, without imposing crushing financial and administrative burdens to determine and raise compensation owing to each landlord on a case-by-case basis, given the difficulties that surround each individual eviction.

Nonetheless, several points become clear from these simple observations. First, some of the huge losses are transfer payments from landlords to tenants,

---

[21]   *74 Pinehurst*, 59 F. 4th at 564, citing 9 NYCRR § 2524.3.

but others represent serious social losses that stem from the huge misallocation of rental real estate resources under the RSL. These losses will continue at a rising rate if the program is allowed unabated to continue in its present form. Thus, in lieu of vast damages, it might be better to fashion an imperfect remedy that acknowledges unhappily the dangerous settled expectations that have arisen under the current law. Such a remedy could be executed by deciding to forgo the payment of damages in favor of a general system of landlord relief, which raises the permissible rents by, say, 10 percent per year until all rents are at market value.

In this connection, it is important to understand that the RSL is far more intrusive into private arrangements than ordinary price controls that have, at least in wartime, been sustained.[22] The key difference is as follows. A system of simple price controls sets the prices but allows the seller to choose its customers. The RSL, operating as it does only on the renewal of a lease, not only sets the price of renewal, but also identifies the only party entitled to receive that benefit. If the two elements were separated, so that the RSL only sets maximum rents but allowed the landlord to choose a new set of tenants, support for the law would evaporate instantly because the local political forces would never exert their influence to benefit strangers who seek to dispossess them from their homes. The system depends therefore on an explicit state-authorized transfer from this landlord to this tenant that goes far beyond any system of wage or price controls which sets prices but does not dictate the class of preferred purchasers. The status quo is impossible to dislodge politically because rent stabilization is price control with a twist: the key beneficiaries are the sitting tenants who can resist any change in the legal regime as voters. The losers are outsiders seeking to get into New York City who do not have any short-term political clout.

The political forces massed behind the RSL have had even more deleterious consequences than other ill-conceived systems of price controls. In this regard, it is critical to note that there are, as it were, price control systems and price control *systems*—that is, the level of interference does not depend solely on the *form* of the interventions but also on their *extent*. Here is one prominent variation on the same theme. It is impossible in the abstract to make any general statement about the harms associated with the operation of a minimum wage system. Even in the simplest model the impacts of the law depend on the relationship between market wages on the one side, and regulated wages on the other. If the market wage is $20 per hour, and the minimum wage is $15, as a first approximation the minimum wage has no impact because it is too low to alter market behavior. This is not a tepid endorsement of the minimum wage

---

[22]   See *Yakus v. United States*, 321 U.S. 414 (1944).

because wage levels could plunge in difficult (perhaps even COVID) times, such that the minimum wage law again becomes a relevant constraint. Indeed, this change would be highly likely if the minimum wage was set at $19 when the market wage was $20, showing that the possibility of future mischief is real. On the other hand, the minimum wage law can be set above the market level, and here too the magnitude of the gap matters. If the market wage is $20 and the minimum wage is $22, firms could scramble to change other terms of employment so that the employer is still able to recoup the lost $2 per hour. The demand for labor is not constant so that reduction in force is one response, and altering the terms of work, for example the adoption of split shifts for work only in high demand times, is yet another. But raise that number closer to $30 and the market shuts down because these adaptations are no longer feasible.

The same is true with any system of price controls. Thus in *Yakus v. United States*,[23] the initial grant of power was limited to times of "abnormal market conditions,"[24] which was "a war emergency measure."[25] In turn, that grant of power was meant to apply "so far as practicable, to prevailing prices during the designated base period."[26] The Court noted that the situation was quite different from the National Industrial Recovery Act[27] considered in *A.L.A. Schechter Poultry Corp. v. United States*,[28] a decision

> which proclaimed in the broadest terms its purpose "to rehabilitate industry and to conserve natural resources." It prescribed no method of attaining that end save by the establishment of codes of fair competition, the nature of whose permissible provisions was left undefined. It provided no standards to which those codes were to conform.[29]

In other words, the decision in *Schechter* was sensitive to the limitations on delegated power, and did not regard them as irrelevant, but as satisfied.

It is also useful to look at *Bowles v. Seminole Rock & Sand Co*,[30] which involved yet another price control regulation during the Second World War. The dispute arose under a regulation that capped prices at the "Highest price charged during March, 1942"—a phrase defined as "The highest price which the seller charged to a purchaser of the same class for delivery of the article

---

23   321 U.S. 414 (1944).
24   *Id.* at 420.
25   *Id.* at 422.
26   *Id.* at 423.
27   Act of June 16, 1933, 48 Stat. 195.
28   295 U.S. 495 (1935).
29   *Yakus*, 321 U.S. at 424.
30   325 U.S. 410 (1945). For a discussion see RICHARD A. EPSTEIN, THE DUBIOUS MORALITY OF MODERN ADMINISTRATIVE LAW 131–134 (2020).

or material during March, 1942."[31] The vendor insisted that the correct price for its crushed stone was $1.50 per ton, which was the price that had been charged for contracts made during the statutory period, but delivered after the rule went into effect in April 1942.[32] The government contended that the maximum price should be $0.60 per ton, based on deliveries actually made during the relevant period.[33] Note that this regulation did not simply pick some number out of the air, but related it to historical prices that this company had charged in the immediate past. This case was not about the validity of the price control scheme, but rather the choice between two price baselines—$0.60 versus $1.50. The court combined a mixture of plain meaning analysis with a system of deference, which was not needed in this case to hit the right note. The anticipation of future shortages raised the bids in the March contract, so that the lower price for current deliveries under past contracts was correct as the proper means to void price-gouging, within the framework of this system—which looks much more like early rent control systems and not the 2019 reform.

The same logic is needed to account for the error costs in both directions. Set the rent control too low, and little harm is done. This relationship held before the 2019 legislation for much of the rent-stabilized market where rents were below the state-established maximum. Hence, the cost of high maximum rent control laws are minimal, but the error costs of low minimum rents (as induced by the 2019 legislation) are disastrous. Why? Because the below-market rental levels discourage investment in renovation and repairs. The high administrative costs create delays, uncertainty, and animosity. The mispricing of units prevents the orderly turnover of apartments to their highest and best use, but induces sitting tenants to stay far longer in their protected units than is healthy for the continued stability of local neighborhoods, which depend on fresh infusions of people and businesses to renew business and social vitality. The odd mix of regulated and unregulated units creates a two-tiered system of rental housing that favors incumbents and makes it more difficult for New York City to attract the best and the brightest to its ranks. Yet the program has no intelligible distributive function, for longevity of occupation, not wealth or need, is the sole determinant of who benefits from the RSL.

The remedial issue here is tough, given that this is a long-standing system of rent regulation. On this regard, the key step to a successful transition is to impose a fixed and certain rule that allows for the increase of rents in all stabilized units by some figure, like 10 percent per year. Under that regime, some

---

[31] *Bowles*, 325 U.S. at 414.
[32] *Id.* at 412.
[33] *Id.* at 412–413.

of the rent stabilized units will reach market rates in one year; others may take a bit longer. But the clear rule will allow tenants to plan on how to respond to the changes, and landlords to make investments in their property that are justified under the new rent structure. The removal of price controls will be system wide, which will exert downward pressure on prices as the superior utilization of the available space will act as an increase in the overall supply of housing units.

Other grounds blocking facial challenges. Justice Thomas also thinks that these RSL cases "require a clear understanding of how New York City regulations coordinate to completely bar landlords from evicting tenants."[34] Again, he does not mention any such regulations, but it is obvious that rental units are subject to constant forms of inspection on one kind of issue or another. The most recent rule is New York Local Law 97, which purports to control the level of emissions from large (over 25,000 sq ft) buildings that are thought to contribute to climate change, which is the target of Local Law 97.[35] This comprehensive initiative is creating massive dislocations in rental markets, given that the costs of retrofitting are too prohibitive to implement but imposing the default taxes will cripple the finances of all middle-class housing.[36]

The basic structure of that law requires expensive renovations to reduce emissions or, alternatively, the payment of a heavy tax that drives down revenues. The potential disruption in New York is legion and already delays in enforcement are very much on the agenda. The net regulatory burden on local real estate for some insignificant global benefit will surely risk both landlord and tenant solvency because there is no place to hide. Thus an effort to supply Justice Thomas with a "clear understanding" of the larger mosaic of regulations is utterly irrelevant to understanding and removing the huge level of transfer payments that are now the *raison d'être* for rent control. The knowledge of other looming disasters is no reason to make a simple question more complicated here.

B.   As Applied Challenges

Excusing circumstances. Justice Thomas also explains why he favors a case-by-case approach to deal with rent control cases: he thinks that the Court "must consider whether specific New York City regulations prevent petitioners

---

[34]   *74 Pinehurst*, 22–1130 slip op. at 2.
[35]   Available at https://www.nyc.gov/assets/buildings/local_laws/ll97of2019.pdf.
[36]   Richard A. Epstein, *Bankrupted by Green Follies*, DEFINING IDEAS, June 26, 2023, available at https://www.hoover.org/research/bankrupted-green-follies.

from evicting actual tenants for particular reasons."[37] But what is gained by moving from the wholesale to the retail level? Unfortunately, there is no hint in what Justice Thomas writes, nor to my knowledge in the entire vast literature on rent control, that fills in the blanks of some general equation on what should be done when the rent is late. But imagine some reasons: medical illness is one, but of what severity? And for parties with health care insurance of some uncertain amount? And for people with second homes bought on rent control savings? Any mention of a catalogue offers no information on what should be done with the infinite variety of circumstances when cases are reviewed one-by-one on a granular basis.

Or suppose one asked whether rent control applies to the surviving spouse, or to some children or grandchildren? Again, such claims open up another line of inquiry, but do nothing whatsoever to justify the current accommodations for these successors in title. New York has already passed a law that makes these rights partially inheritable, by protecting any surviving spouse against eviction, including life partners, or a family member who had been living with the tenant.[38] Subsequent regulations have extended the definition of family member to cover any other person "who can prove emotional and financial commitment, and interdependence between such person and the tenant or permanent tenant,"[39] which leads to yet another administrative morass by extending the number of years that the unit will rent for below-market rates.[40] To dispute any feature of the current landlord/tenant system will of course take time and money, which could easily eat up a huge portion of the landlord's potential recovery if he wins, and could devastate the landlord if some tenant-friendly housing court, which has exclusive jurisdiction over these cases, proves partial to the tenant.[41]

Nuisance-like exceptions. The Court in *74 Pinehurst* also noted that a residential tenant could be evicted for creating a nuisance.[42] A moment's reflection should confirm the obvious point that no residential tenant will engage on the premises in such foolish activities, from which he could gain little, but from which he could lose huge amounts of value attached to the below-market

---

[37] *Id.* at 2.

[38] 9 NYCRR 2104.6 [d] (1964); 2204.6 [d] (1984).

[39] See Rent and Eviction Regulations (9 NYCRR 2204.6 [d] [3] [i] (1984)).

[40] For a sampler of the rules, see NYC Guidelines, *Succession Rights* https://rentguidelinesboard.cityofnewyork.us/resources/faqs/succession-rights/.

[41] A TENANT'S GUIDE TO THE NEW YORK CITY HOUSING COURT, https://www.nycbar.org/pdf/report/tenantsguide.pdf.

[42] *74 Pinehurst*, 59 F.4th at 563 ("[The RSL] sets forth several bases on which a landlord may terminate a tenant's lease, such as for failing to pay rent, creating a nuisance, violating the lease, or using the property for illegal purposes").

rental rates. Nonetheless, Justice Thomas seeks to pump some life into that exception by citing *Heights Apartments, LLC v. Walz*,[43] which does nothing to bolster his case.[44] That COVID-order imposed a moratorium on the eviction of residential tenants, but the exception allowed the eviction of tenants who "seriously endanger[ed] the safety of other[s]" on the premises of the leased residential property, rather than just the safety of other tenants.[45] In this case, the landlords sought to evict tenants who did not pay their rent and who created a ruckus that disturbed other tenants. Thus they violated the two major prohibitions that retained force after the 2019 legislative amendments. It is therefore impossible to see how this ruling offers any way, direct or indirect, to undermine the basic rule that permits both those exceptions. In sum, the real question here is how many rent-stabilized tenants have been evicted via the narrow exceptions under recently enacted New York laws.

C.   Ad Hoc Versus Simple Rules

Ultimately, the fatal mistake in Justice Thomas's concurrence in *74 Pinehurst* connects to a larger methodological point, which relates to the theme of Simple Rules for a Complex World.[46] Most relevant to the intellectual disaster of rent control are the endless decisions that try to make sense of the standard balancing test applicable *in Penn Central Transportation Co. v. City of New York*.[47] The issue in that case was whether the City of New York owed compensation for the air rights taken when it refused to authorize the construction of a Breuer tower over Grand Central Station. The tower would have impaired the views up and down Park Avenue, which were already compromised by the Pan Am building that straddled Park Avenue on the North Side of the Terminal. The simple answer is that these air rights were protected under New York law and they had a recognized market value. That value was greater if the City insisted that it obtained the right to build in their air space once held by the Penn Central company. But the compensation owed would be smaller if it only wanted a restrictive covenant that prevented the company and anyone else from using those air rights. The discount was likely to be steep because

---

[43]   30 F. 4th 720 (8th Cir. 2022).

[44]   *74 Pinehurst*, 22–1130 slip op. at 1.

[45]   *Id.* at 724.

[46]   Richard A. Epstein, SIMPLE RULES FOR A COMPLEX WORLD (1995).

[47]   438 U.S. 104 (1978). It does not help that Justice William Brennan misread every precedent on which he relied. Richard A. Epstein, *Disappointed Expectations: How the Supreme Court Failed to Clean up Takings Law in* Murr v. Wisconsin, 11 NYU J LAW & LIB 151 (2017) (discussing *Murr v. Wisconsin*, 137 S.Ct. 1933 (2017)).

the preservation of view rights was probably quite valuable. Indeed, the market differential for two comparable apartments, one with a view and the other not, often runs to about 30 percent, which is a tidy sum that should never be overlooked.

Yet once the deprivation of either set of air rights is compensable, all the incentives are properly aligned and the public can decide which mix of restriction and compensation is best. The only role for the courts is now to supervise the valuation once the decision has been made. The eminent domain law thus puts market prices on the government initiative, just as it does when the entire fee simple (including ground rights) is taken. Rightly understood, *Penn Central* fades into history as a nonevent. But Justice Brennan gave it an unwarranted new life by anticipating the mistake in Thomas's short statement. In Brennan's view, there were no per se rules in this complex area, so he invented a balancing test with these fatal words:

> The question of what constitutes a "taking" for purposes of the Fifth Amendment has proved to be a problem of considerable difficulty. While this Court has recognized that the "Fifth Amendment's guarantee ... [is] designed to bar Government from forcing some people alone to bear public burdens which, in all fairness and justice, should be borne by the public as a whole," Armstrong v. United States, 364 U.S. 40, 49 (1960), this Court, quite simply, has been unable to develop any "set formula" for determining when "justice and fairness" require that economic injuries caused by public action be compensated by the government, rather than remain disproportionately concentrated on a few persons....
>
> In engaging in these essentially ad hoc, factual inquiries, the Court's decisions have identified several factors that have particular significance. The economic impact of the regulation on the claimant and, particularly, the extent to which the regulation has interfered with distinct investment-backed expectations are, of course, relevant considerations. So, too, is the character of the governmental action. A "taking" may more readily be found when the interference with property can be characterized as a physical invasion by government, than when interference arises from some public program adjusting the benefits and burdens of economic life to promote the common good.[48]

The sure sign that an opinion has gone off the rails is that it uses quotation marks around key terms, which here is done twice with the word "taking," which now takes on a mysterious meaning. Yet no one in the 46 years since has offered a coherent account of those "ad hoc factual inquiries" that make for a "taking." The range of factors continues to multiply such that the judgments are contingent and continuous, which violates one fundamental tenet of all legal systems. Liability rules should be yes/no determinations, which is why

---

[48] *Penn Central*, at 123–4.

we put bright lines down the middle of the road.[49] Damages can be continuous because the harms are continuous as well.

In this passage, Justice Brennan distinguishes *Armstrong* for the worst possible reason—because it embodied a simple rule that works. That case involved a mechanics lien that was placed on two United States vessels that were brought to Maine waters for repairs. The general contractor did not pay the subcontractors, from whom he did not obtain the lien waivers needed under standard restitution principles to block any lien on the property.

Historically, the purpose of such a lien is to make sure that the project owner does not foist a large portion of the cost onto someone who does not receive the benefit of the work. This principle, which is well established in private law, does not miss a beat when carried over to situations where the government, instead of some corporation, partnership, or individual, owns the property in question. In the ordinary course of business, therefore, the lien (like any ordinary mortgage) may be foreclosed so that the lienor gets paid its principal, interest, and costs. After that, the remainder of the money is paid over to other claimants in the order of their priority, with the property owner being the residual claimant—last on the list. And thus the famous sentence in *Armstrong* that tries to demarcate the line between government and private costs:

> The Fifth Amendment's guarantee that private property shall not be taken for a public use without just compensation was designed to bar Government from forcing some people alone to bear public burdens which, in all fairness and justice, should be borne by the public as a whole.[50]

In this case, the United States sought to rupture the connection between the lienor and the vessels by sailing them into international waters, at which point the lien was dissolved by operation of law. There were three dissenting justices (Harlan, Frankfurter, and Clark), who thought that the principle of sovereign immunity governed the case,[51] in part because the case did not involve the standard application eminent domain condemnation procedures. But at this point the anticircumvention principle of constitutional, statutory, and contract law takes over. No one can use a close, if unanticipated, ruse to achieve with no

---

[49]   A more complete statement of the rule has to account for the limited circumstances where a rule of reason has to take over. No one is allowed to remain indifferent when someone else violates the rules, but people must act reasonably and in good faith to avoid peril, which they routinely do as they have no reason to court extra danger. For discussion see Richard A. Epstein, *Rules and Reasons, Public and Private: On the Use and Limits of Simple Rules 25 Years Later*, 52 EUROPEAN JOURNAL OF LAW AND ECONOMICS 363 (2021).

[50]   *Id.* at 49.

[51]   *Id.* at 50.

cost to itself a forbidden outcome, which is exactly what happened here (given that the ruse was, for the government, a perfect substitute for stripping the materialmen of their lien). All one needs to do to avoid constitutional disaster is insist that the same tactics used by the Court to prevent the government from eviscerating materialmen's liens also be used to protect the air rights that were removed in *Penn Central*. In both cases, pay for what you take.

II.   HISTORICAL AND JUDICIAL ORIGINS OF RENT CONTROL LAWS

A.   The Roots of Rent Control in Block and Feldman

To understand the current disputes, it is critical to look historically at the shifting rationale for the rent control law. The opening salvo was *Block v. Hirsh*,[52] which upheld a Washington D.C. rent control law, favoring Block (the tenant) over Hirsh (the landlord), albeit only by a five-to-four vote.[53] Justice Holmes wrote for the majority and Justice McKenna wrote for the dissent. The case arose out of an October 1919 federal statute, which was enacted to address skyrocketing rents in Washington D.C. *after* the end of World War I, as large numbers of new workers into Washington D.C. transformed the once sleepy southern town into a bustling hub of a global power. The new trend led predictably to a surge in rental prices, as landlords sought to capitalize on the post-war boom.

In response, Congress enacted a statute that organized a new Commission which temporarily capped rents in the District for two years. By its terms, this cap allowed for a fair and reasonable rate of return—adopting the language that was commonly used in dealing with rate regulation statutes. It allowed the owner to retake the property for use by himself and his family on 30 days' notice. It cited the emergencies stemming from the recently concluded war as a reason for its passage. Landlords challenged the act, alleging that its cap on rents was an uncompensated taking of their property. In upholding the statute, Holmes did not necessarily disagree with the landlords' claim that the statute under other circumstances might effectuate a compensable taking. But in the aftermath of the First World War, he accepted that "[t]he general proposition to be maintained is that circumstances have clothed the letting of buildings in the District of Columbia with a public interest so great as to justify regulation

---

[52]   256 U.S. 135 (1921).

[53]   For the majority—Holmes, joined by Brandeis, Clarke, Pitney, Day. The dissenter was McKenna, joined by White, Van Devanter, and McReynolds. The two surprises were Pitney and Day for the majority.

by law."[54] Holmes allowed, however, that "circumstances may so change in time or so differ in space as to clothe with such an interest what at other times or in other places would be a matter of purely private concern."[55] It is another version of the "affected with the public interest" standard used to justify rate regulation after the famous Supreme Court decision in *Munn v. Illinois*.[56]

Justice Holmes then went out of his way to stress the limited reach of his opinion:

> Congress has stated the unquestionable embarrassment of Government and danger to the public health in the existing condition of things. The space in Washington is necessarily monopolized in comparatively few hands, and letting portions of it is as much a business as any other. Housing is a necessary of life. All the elements of a public interest justifying some degree of public control are present. The only matter that seems to us open to debate is whether the statute goes too far. For just as there comes a point at which the police power ceases and leaves only that of eminent domain, it may be conceded that regulations of the present sort pressed to a certain height might amount to a taking without due process of law.[57]

As emergency legislation the Title is to end in two years unless sooner repealed.

> No doubt it is true that a legislative declaration of facts that are material only as the ground for enacting a rule of law, for instance, that a certain use is a public one, may not be held conclusive by the Courts. [Citations omitted]. But a declaration by a legislature concerning public conditions that by necessity and duty it must know, is entitled at least to great respect. In this instance Congress stated a publicly notorious and almost world-wide fact. That the emergency declared by the statute did exist must be assumed, and the question is whether Congress was incompetent to meet it in the way in which it has been met by most of the civilized countries of the world.[58]

A spirited dissent was both direct and succinct:

> The grounds of dissent are the explicit provisions of the Constitution of the United States; the specifications of the grounds are the irresistible deductions from those provisions and, we think, would require no expression but for the opposition of those whose judgments challenge attention.[59]

---

[54] *Id.* at 155.
[55] *Id.*
[56] 94 U.S. 113 (1876).
[57] *Block* 256 U.S. 135, 156 (1921).
[58] *Id.* at 154.
[59] *Id.* at 159 (McKenna, J., dissenting).

The dissent further insisted on a fundamental mismatch of means and ends of rent control schemes, noting that while the majority justifies the intrusion on the landlord's property rights "because 'space in Washington is limited' and 'housing is a necessary of life' ... A causative and remedial relation in the circumstances we are unable to see."[60]

It is useful to unpack Holmes's arguments. First, he was clearly incorrect in claiming that the market in Washington was "necessarily monopolized." The number of landlords was too great to constitute a housing monopoly, for what he saw was not an increase in concentration on the landlord side, but an exogenous shift in demand that pushed the price upward, while inducing some increase in available units, as doubtless some people saw the influx as a reason to sublet a spare upstairs bedroom. Holmes also failed to realize that the high rates and low vacancy rates were an invitation to new entry, at least in the absence of any limiting zoning ordinance that would become standard only a decade later.[61] Thus, in a famous study by Milton Friedman and George Stigler of the rebuilding after the destruction of the San Francisco earthquake of April, 1906, they concluded that there was an active rental market a month after the San Francisco earthquake left 250,000 homeless.[62] That successful pattern was *not* repeated in 1946, though, when San Francisco's rent control statute sharply reduced the number of properties for rent, creating the same long-term shortage that the RSL was supposed to alleviate in New York City. Friedman and Stigler's explanation for the return of the housing market to normal after 1906 stresses all the features of private housing markets that are systematically disregarded under the RSL.

Given the evident strength of these competitive forces, Holmes was also wrong descriptively to make an implicit reference to the rate regulation cases that typically offered a fair and reasonable rate of return on investment for public utilities and common carriers that did have some measure of monopoly

---

[60] *Id.* at 161 (McKenna, J., dissenting).

[61] See for discussion *American Planning Association Standard State Zoning Enabling Act and Standard City Planning Enabling Act*, available at https://www.planning.org/growingsmart/enablingacts/ Note that Herbert Hoover, in his then role of Secretary of Commerce, was the driving force behind the program, which was promoted in an advisory capacity because the federal government at that time had no jurisdiction over local land-planning decisions. At the same time, in *Euclid v. Ambler Realty,* 272 U.S. 365 (1926), the Supreme Court recognized vast state and local powers to enact zoning ordinances.

[62] Milton Friedman and George Stigler, ROOFS OR CEILINGS: THE CURRENT HOUSING PROBLEM, at 7, and explained at 9, Foundation for Economic Education (1946), , available at https://fee.org/resources/roofs-or-ceilings-the-current-housing-problem.

power.[63] That approach has to fail in this context because the current rents were competitive and necessarily must be reduced below a competitive rate if costs are increased on the one side and revenues are reduced on the other. But Holmes never addressed this argument; instead, in an obvious adumbration of his famous opinion, *Pennsylvania Coal v. Mahon*,[64] he settled on a "too far" test that, analytically, just had to be incorrect. As noted above, liability—whether for tort or for eminent domain proceedings—should always be governed by on/off switches, and by not matters of degree. That *Pennsylvania Coal* was right in demanding compensation or an injunction rests on the simple fact that the statute required the transfer, without compensation, of the support estate from the coal company that had reserved under the 1878 statute individual conveyances of the surface lands, usually to employees of the mining company.[65] It is also noteworthy that Holmes referred to earlier cases that took uneven approaches to the monopoly problem.[66]

The immediate sequel to *Block, Marcus Brown Holding Co. v. Feldman*,[67] involved another short-term rent control law that took effect in early 1920 and lasted only to November 1, 1922. Unlike *Block, Feldman* considered a state law for New York that could also be pitched as an impairment of the obligation of contract under Article I, Section 10 of the Constitution. The relevant principles track those of both the Takings Clause and the Fourteenth Amendment, especially on the scope of the police power. Much of the case was disposed under *Block*, but the Court made no mention of any parallel "emergency" (so called) of an influx of people in the aftermath of World War I. A bare declaration had to do the work of the detailed account in *Block*.

---

[63]   See *Smyth v. Ames*, 169 U.S. 466 (1898). For a discussion of these rate cases, see Richard A. Epstein, *The History of Public Utility Regulation in the United States Supreme Court: Of Reasonable and Nondiscriminatory Rates*, 38(1) J. SUPREME COURT HISTORY 345 (2013).

[64]   260 U.S. 393 (1922).

[65]   For my discussion see Richard A. Epstein, Pennsylvania Coal v. Mahon: *The Erratic Takings Jurisprudence of Justice Holmes*, 86 GEO. L.J. 875 (1998).

[66]   *German Alliance Insurance Co. v. Lewis,* 233 U.S. 389; irrigation, in *Clark v. Nash*, 198 U.S. 361, and mining, in *Strickley v. Highland Boy Gold Mining Co.*, 200 U.S. 527. *German Alliance* is the odd one out because it tied rate regulation to the size of the insurance market not the existence of monopoly power. *Clark* and *Strickley*, both involved bilateral monopoly holdout problems where the holders of low-value property sought holdout power. These cases were cited in *Kelo* by Justice Stephens, in *Kelo v. New London* 545 U.S. 469, 481 n. 11 (2005) and by Justice O'Connor *id.* at 516. The problem was the converse of the issue in *Block*— too little competition, not too much.

[67]   256 U.S. 170 (1921).

Feldman introduced yet another feature that survived the end of the case: it applied to "a city of a population of one million or more," i.e. a code word for New York, suggesting that the evil to be met was a very pressing want of shelter in certain crowded urban centers. From that time forward, it became possible to divide New York into two zones, which reduced the resistance to the passage of these rent control laws by not offending smaller communities opposed to these laws. In dissent, Justice McKenna castigated this bifurcation as an abuse of the police power.[68] Indeed, he was right to say there is no reason to treat a low vacancy rate as evidence of major social unrest—a contention that grows in importance over time.

Whatever the flawed nature of Holmes's arguments, Holmes did *not* deny, especially in *Block*, that a taking had occurred. Instead, he pitched his entire case on the emergency justification. Indeed, Holmes was true to his word, for in *Chastleton Corp. v. Sinclair*,[69] he refused to accept at face value a legislative declaration that a second two-year extension of the original Washington D.C. rent control law was needed: "A law depending upon the existence of an emergency or other certain state of facts to uphold it may cease to operate if the emergency ceases or the facts change, even though valid when passed."[70] And he noted further:

> It is a matter of public knowledge that the government has considerably diminished its demand for employees that was one of the great causes of the sudden influx of people to Washington, and that other causes have lost at least much of their power. It is conceivable that, as is shown in an affidavit attached to the bill, extensive activity in building has added to the ease of finding an abode. If about all that remains of war conditions is the increased cost of living, that is not, in itself, a justification of the Act.[71]

And so the first burst of rent control laws came to a close—but the rejection of any government initiative was not to occur again.

B.   The RSL in Historical Context

The next round of rent control regulation was sustained on far different grounds, centering on the combined application of the Takings Clause, the Due Process Clause and the Contracts Clause. To see how this overall argument unfolds,

---

[68] *Id.* at 201–202.
[69] *Chastleton Corp. v. Sinclair*, 264 U.S. 543 (1924).
[70] *Id.* at 547–548.
[71] *Id.* at 548.

it is first necessary to review the tangled history of rent control law that long antedated the adoption of the RSL.[72]

The RSL was first put into effect in 1969, as the successor to New York's 1943 rent control statute. In its most rigid form, this statute limited the landlord to a 15 percent increase in rent, but only when a new tenant replaced a prior one. This practice led to leases of uncommon duration, leading landlords in some cases (for example, my own) to actively seek out college students, who were far more likely to leave on graduation, as I indeed did.[73] The RSL, however, does not require a turnover in tenants to trigger a rent increase. Those increases are typically allowed annually to reflect the increase in costs, but the intention is *not* to allow increases that are the result of a greater market demand for the property. Conversely, the law did not cushion the blow caused by the case where the market value of these properties decline. And of course, the mandatory increases were not defined by divine ordinance but were determined after extensive hearings, in which all matters were contested, before a government board that retained discretion to reduce the size of the increase below the statutory minimum in cases of tenant hardship.

In its 1969 version, the RSL applied only to some rental housing completed prior to that date. In 1974, the RSL was modified to bring within its scope rental housing constructed between 1969 and 1974, and brought back under the RSL some 200,000 units that had been exempt from coverage under the initial 1969 RSL. At no point has the RSL ever been applied to new rental housing, because otherwise, such units would not be constructed in large quantities. But under the current state of law, the legislature could subject any rental housing built after 1974 to a modified version of the RSL, as it did in the 2019 legislature amendments.

Under current law, the New York State Division of Housing and Community Renewal (DHCR) authorizes New York City to impose its RSL on covered units. Under the RSL, sitting tenants have the right to have their leases renewed at the stabilized rent set by the City's rent control board. At present, New York City has about one-half of its rental units, or about 1,000,000 apartment units, subject to the RSL. In large portions of Brooklyn, the Bronx, and Queens, the market rate rents were (at least before the 2019 legislative revisions) well below the maximum allowable rents, so that the RSL had no practical effect. But at the inception of RSL, in certain neighborhoods—most notably in the

---

[72]   (N.Y.C. Admin. Code Sections 26-501 to 26-520), available at http://tenant.net/Rent_Laws/RSC/rsctoc.html; see also S. 6458, A 8281, available at https://rentguidelinesboard.cityofnewyork.us/wp-content/uploads/2019/11/Housing-Stability-and-Tenant-Protection-Act-of-2019.pdf.

[73]   See Richard A. Epstein, *Rent Control and the Theory of Efficient Regulation*, 54 BROOK. L. REV 741, 741 (1988).

core areas of Manhattan and Brooklyn—the law created an enormous wedge between the fair market value of the units and their rent-stabilized rents, which were often as little as a quarter or a third of their market value. Until the 2019 law, the system of vacancy decontrol allowed units that rented for more than $2,500 per month to be rented at market rates, but even before 2019, various dodges were used to postpone decontrol, which only widened the difference in rents for controlled and market units.[74]

The market value issue here gives rise to two distinct cases. In the first, the market value is determined by allowing any given unit to rent outside the RSL while other units remain subject to that law. In those cases, decontrol results in substantial increases given the paucity of units in the unregulated market. A full repeal of the RSL would vastly increase the effective housing stock, so that rent increases would in all likelihood be far smaller.

The RSL only applies to units in New York City, according to action by the City Council, which before the adoption of the 2019 law regularly adopted a declaration of a housing emergency every three years, based on a single figure—a city-wide vacancy rate below 5 percent on all units whether or not covered by the RSL.[75] Recently, vacancy rates for all rental units were 4.54 percent in 2021.[76] Vacancy rates in stabilized units were 4.57 percent in 2021. The vacancy rates in private unregulated units were higher, at 4.61 percent in 2011 and 5.60 percent in 2014.[77] If the aggregate vacancy rates were to exceed 5 percent in any given year, nothing would prevent the state and city from concluding that a housing emergency existed with vacancy rates below, say, 6 per cent.

---

[74] For an evaluation of the many adverse short- and long-term effects, see NBER, *The End of Rent Control in Cambridge*, http://www.nber.org/digest/oct12/w18125 .html D.H. Autor, C.J. Palmer and P.A. Pathak, HOUSING MARKET SPILLOVERS: EVIDENCE FROM THE END OF RENT CONTROL IN CAMBRIDGE MASSACHUSETTS (2012), http://www.nber.org/papers/w18125.pdf.

[75] McKinney's Uncons Laws of NY § 8585 [1] [Emergency Housing Rent Control Law § 5 (1)] [1946]; Administrative Code § 26–408 [a], formerly § Y51-6.0 [1962].

[76] https://www.nyc.gov/assets/hpd/downloads/pdfs/services/2021-nychvs -selected-initial-findings.pdf at 25.

[77] See Table 6, Vacant for Rent Units and Vacancy Rates by Rent Regulation Status New York City 2011/2014, *Selected Initial Findings of the 2011/2014 New York City Housing and Vacancy Survey*, NYC Dept. of Housing Preservation and Development (2012/2015).

III.   THE THREE LINCHPINS OF THE MODERN SYSTEM

Three issues are relevant here. The first is the right to evict any holdover tenant at will. The second deals with the so-called "emergency" justification for lease extension, in the style of *Block v. Hirsh*. The third stresses that rent control helps present speculation in real-estate markets. Modern systems of rent control, exemplified by the New York revisions, offer no reason to accept any of these purported justifications.

A.   The Right to Evict a Holdover Tenant at Will

The entire system of private rights in rental housing can only work because the common law in every jurisdiction emphatically allows the eviction of any tenant who *holds over* after the expiration of a lease, without landlord consent, as a common trespasser. The customary rule is:

> As a general rule, a tenancy from year to year is created by the tenant's holding over after the expiration of a term for years and the continued payment of the yearly rent reserved. * * * By remaining in possession of leased premises after the expiration of his lease, a tenant gives the landlord the option of treating him as a trespasser or as a tenant for another year....[78]

In the famous case of *Board of Regents v. Roth*,[79] Justice Potter Stewart addressed the analogous case of whether a teacher on a term employment contract could be given a renewal. In denying that claim, his logic spoke to the rent control laws:

> It is a purpose of the ancient institution of property to protect those claims upon which people rely in their daily lives, reliance that must not be arbitrarily undermined. It is a purpose of the constitutional right to a hearing to provide an opportunity for a person to vindicate those claims.
> Property interests, of course, are not created by the Constitution. Rather, they are created and their dimensions are defined by existing rules or understandings that stem from an independent source such as state law—rules or understandings that secure certain benefits and that support claims of entitlement to those benefits.[80]

Indeed, it would hardly do for the state to announce that its property law had changed such that all tenants were entitled to remain on the premises without

---

[78]   3 THOMPSON ON REAL PROPERTY § 1024, at 65–66 (1959). See also, *Crechale & Polles, Inc. v. Smith*, 295 So. 2d 275 (Miss. 1974).

[79]   408 U.S. 564, XXX (1972) (termination of teacher employment allowed at expiration of the contract).

[80]   *Roth*, 408 U.S. at 577.

paying any rent at all. So in the case of the RSL, it is also necessary to pay close attention to the terms of the lease contracts, none of which contain the slightest suggestion that the tenant can stay after the expiration of the lease, from which it follows that these holdover tenants have no procedural rights to the complex RSL hearings. The principles of renewal are the same for leases and employment markets. Thus if a stranger walks into your home, you may get an immediate eviction, or treat him at your option as a tenant at will. So too a tenant who overstays his lease.

There have been only a few instances in which automatic renewal does apply to properties not yet listed in the rental market, and they have led to its elimination. Thus in England and Washington, D.C., where the lease renewal requirement has been applied to owner-occupied single homes,[81] the legislative refusal to follow the common law rule barring forced renewal of the lease has led to the collapse of the short-term rental market. Landowners refuse, at great social cost, to lease their property to any strangers, including foreign academics, lest they are unable to ever regain its possession. Commercial landlords, of course, do not have the option to leave their premises vacant. But that is no reason force them into involuntary relations that go far beyond the scope of the original consent. Given the widespread rejection of forced renewals by ordinary homeowners, the RSL can only work in commercial residential markets.

The RSL is a form of legislative intervention that offers bargain rates for the tenant who is now entitled by legislative fiat to hold over beyond the stipulated lease term, which is why constitutional protection against takings in all forms is a necessary curb against the dangers of faction and discord. That constitutional protection, moreover, has to apply to two situations with equal force. The first covers cases where the government takes over the property for its own use, as in *United States v. General Motors Corp.*[82] The same principle carries over with equal force to the RSL, where the government never takes possession of the property itself, but simply *authorizes* the tenant, backed by government force, to remain in possession. Just that situation arose when a New York statute authorized a cable company to put its equipment on the roof of a privately owned apartment unit. In *Loretto v. Teleprompter Manhattan CATV Corp.*,[83] the Supreme Court concluded that "a permanent physical occupation *authorized by government* is a taking without regard to the public interests that it may serve."[84] Put otherwise, the government cannot evade

---

[81] See http://www.lawhelp.org/dc/resource/frequently-asked-questions-by -landlords (no eviction at the end of the lease).

[82] 323 U.S. 373 (1945).

[83] 458 U.S. 419 (1982).

[84] *Id.* at 426 (italics added).

its constitutional obligations by refusing to go into possession when it orders that others be allowed to remain. Such a transaction is properly characterized as one in which the government first takes the property for the duration of the renewal period from the owner, and then transfers that possession to the tenant, who is then instructed to pay the rent in question. The government's obligations under the takings law cannot be skirted by a strategic decision not to first enter into possession of the property or take title thereof.[85]

B.   The Emergency Justification for Rent Control

As was evident in both *Block* and *Feldman*, the initial constitutional rationalization for rent control did not deny that it was a taking of the landlord's property, but insisted that the taking was justified by a national emergency. That determination was iffy because there was no threat to life and limb by external forces and no evidence of any civil disruption or disorder, in either Washington D.C. or New York, that fell within the ordinary definition of any emergency. Instead, the move taken in Section 26-501 of the 1969 RSL was an announcement, made with uncommon prescience, that the "serious public emergency" in New York "will continue to exist after April first, 1974." That initial declaration of emergency was not a one-time event, as the New York City Council before 2019 made the emergency perpetual. Like clockwork, it reiterated the supposed emergency every three years when renewing its adoption of statutory rent protections, and it will continue in perpetuity on a pro forma basis unless stopped by some sort of judicial intervention. Yet at no point did the New York City Council seek to justify that conclusion by proffering, as it did in 1943 with the adoption of its first rent control statute, any independent evidence of a natural disaster or war that could disrupt the operation of rental markets. Nor has New York ever advanced any credible outside evidence to support its dramatic conclusion.

---

[85]   See *Pumpelly v. Green Bay Co.*, 80 U.S. 166, 177–178 (1872): "It would be a very curious and unsatisfactory result if in construing a provision of constitutional law always understood to have been adopted for protection and security to the rights of the individual as against the government, and which has received the commendation of jurists, statesmen, and commentators as placing the just principles of the common law on that subject beyond the power of ordinary legislation to change or control them, it shall be held that if the government refrains from the absolute conversion of real property to the uses of the public it can destroy its value entirely, can inflict irreparable and permanent injury to any extent, can, in effect, subject it to total destruction without making any compensation, because, in the narrowest sense of that word, it is not taken for the public use."

We are thus a long way from the historical definition of an emergency—or as it is sometimes said, a public or private necessity—which allows for the suspension of private property rights without compensation. The applicable rule is of long historical vintage, and was well stated in the *Mayor of New York v. Lord*[86] in 1837, which involved the great fire of December 1835 in which private property "was destroyed by order of the mayor and two aldermen, to prevent the spreading of the conflagration."

> In all cases of the kind, the individual concerned in the taking or destroying of the property is not personally liable. If the public necessity in fact exists, the act is lawful. Thus, houses may be pulled down, or bulwarks raised for the preservation and defence of the country, without subjecting the persons concerned to an action, the same as pulling down houses in time of fire; and yet these are common cases where the sufferers would be entitled to compensation from the national government within the constitutional principle (Const. U. S. Art. 5, of the Amendments).

That basic principle has been followed faithfully in subsequent cases. Thus in *United States v. Caltex, Inc.,*[87] the Supreme Court refused to compensate private oil companies whose terminal facilities in the Philippines were destroyed on orders of General Douglas MacArthur in late December 1941 to prevent them from falling into the hands of the invading Japanese. The Court refused to order compensation, relying explicitly on the constitutional framework that was defined by the common law rules, and further noted that "the common law had long recognized that in times of imminent peril—such as when fire threatened a whole community—the sovereign could, with immunity, destroy the property of a few that the property of many and the lives of many more could be saved."[88]

A projected market failure four years down the road does not count as an "imminent peril." No desperate property owner calls out the police or the national guard to deal with it. And no emergency lasts indefinitely. The situation is far removed from the use of martial law when, after Pearl Harbor, the writ of habeas corpus was suspended and martial law was declared. Martial law is invoked, and then only on a temporary basis, when civil order has broken down.[89] At the state level, martial law has been limited to '[u]prisings,

---

[86] 17 Wend. 285 (1837).

[87] 344 U.S. 149 (1952),

[88] *Id.* at 154, citing *Bowditch v. Boston,* 101 U.S. 16, 18–19 (1879). See also *Respublica v. Sparhawk,* 1 U.S. 357 (1788).

[89] See *Duncan v. Kahanamoku,* 327 U.S. 304, 311–312 (1946).

political protests, labor strikes and riots."[90] Even under the War Powers Act,[91] the periods for emergency action are stunningly short. The President is supposed to notify the Congress within 48 hours after he commits armed forces to action, and the use of armed forces in combat for a period of longer than 90 days is forbidden without Congressional authorization. The term emergency as used in the RSL bears no relationship to its recognized use elsewhere. Martial law has not been imposed since 1969.

C.   The Antispeculation Rationale

The last rationale for the RSL claims that it is justified "in order to prevent speculative, unwarranted and abnormal increases in rents; that there continues to exist an acute shortage of dwellings which creates a special hardship to persons and families occupying rental housing."[92] The passage was part of the original rent control law of 1943, at which time it fell squarely under *Block v. Hirsh*, wholly without regard to any 5 percent vacancy rule, which could apply in times of war or peace. That particular conclusion is then elaborated as follows:

> such action is necessary in order to prevent exactions of unjust, unreasonable and oppressive rents and rental agreements and to forestall profiteering speculation and other disruptive practices tending to produce threats to the public health, safety and general welfare; that the transition from regulation to a normal market of free bargaining between landlord and tenant, while still the objective of state and city policy, must be administered with due regard for such emergency.[93]

But the constant repetition of these assertions long after the end of World War II rests on no historical or economic foundations. Instead, this language makes it appear as though a "normal" market can never emerge. Most obviously, the quoted passage purporting to justify the RSL offers no explanation of why or how these conditions are satisfied. Of course, an increase in overall demand will work to raise rents above their previous level. But this welcome change is the antithesis of any speculative, unwarranted, or abnormal increase in rents. Instead, it represents only the most common and welcome of social phenomena: as demand for a given product increases, the price of that commodity will increase to reflect its higher scarcity value. To be sure, some tenants on short-term leases may be forced to pay higher rents if they want to remain on

---

[90]   See legal dictionary, http://legal-dictionary.thefreedictionary.com/Martial +Law.

[91]   50 U.S.C. §§ 1541–1548.

[92]   See, Findings 1969.

[93]   Section 501. Findings of Emergency.

the premises, or they may choose to leave, which will be easier to do if there is a large set of market-rate units available, which is frustrated when a large fraction of the (un)available units are tied up under rent control.

It is, however, completely myopic to assume these private tenant losses signal in any way, shape, or form a decline in overall social welfare. Rather, the RSL's unduly solipsistic view of the economic landscape ignores two other factors that point sharply in the opposite direction. First, even within the existing supply, the willingness of new tenants to occupy those premises at a higher rent is evidence that the rental property is now being put to a higher-valued use than it was before. Second, the existence of higher rents has the positive effect of inducing new owners to enter the rental market at all economic levels, which in turn will both reduce shortages and spur the construction of new units. Some fraction of that added supply will, moreover, remain in place even when the short-term emergency passes and demand goes back to lower levels. Just that happened when all the wartime rent control statutes were phased once hostilities ended. The situation under rent control is the exact opposite, for as Friedman and Stigler noted back in 1946:

> The advantages of rationing by higher rents are clear from our [earthquake] example:
>
> 1. In a free market, there is always some housing immediately available for rent—at all rent levels.
> 2. The bidding up of rents forces some people to economize on space. Until there is sufficient new construction, this doubling up is the only solution.
> 3. The high rents act as a strong stimulus to new construction.
> 4. No complex, expensive, and expansive machinery is necessary. The rationing is conducted quietly and impersonally through the price system.

The RSL helps create and preserve the "acute shortage of housing units" that it purports to counteract. If a statute runs against its stated purpose, it should not be able to survive even under a sensible rational basis test. This analysis thus helps explain why the statutory reference to the traditional police power arguments of protecting health and safety are in this context incorrect. There is nothing whatsoever about the rent control regulations that deal with matters concerning the physical safety of the various premises. The extensive web of laws that governs these safety issues remains outside the scope of these challenges. Yet there is not one word in the finding as to how the imposition of rent controls, which reduce the amount of money that landlords have to invest in local improvements, can improve safety when they place a financial constraint on repairs and improvements. Nor could it be possibly said that the possible displacement of some sitting tenants poses a systematic threat to public health and safety, given that the more efficient allocation of existing units, and the expansion of supply from new units should result in a widespread improvement of the overall housing stock. Nor should anyone take seriously, 47 years down the road, the claim that the RSL is a temporary measure designed to hold only in the "transition" to an unregulated market. The game is rigged to guarantee that such a transition will never happen, so that the current shortfalls of the RSL on matters of health and safety will be magnified as well.

Nonetheless, in dealing with this issue, many modern courts (see, for example, *Birkenfeld v. City of Berkeley*)[94] have insisted that the tough standards announced and enforced by Justice Holmes no longer apply after the due process revolution ushered in by such cases as *Nebbia v. New York*,[95] with its low, rational basis standard of review with respect to general price control regulations. But that conclusion is wrong for several reasons. First, the Court in *Nebbia* never discusses, let alone rejects, *Block v. Hirsh*. The only reference in *Nebbia* to *Block* is in the dissent of Justice McReynolds, who cautions against giving it a broad reading.[96] Analytically the two cases are distinguishable because the argument in *Birkenfeld* misses the central distinction, noted above, between a general system of price controls under which an owner of property is entitled to exit the market, and the RSL, which forces a landlord to let any tenant remain in the market against his will. The more relevant decision for these purposes is *Wolff Co. v. Industrial Court*,[97] which invalidated a labor statute that required compulsory adjudication before a Kansas labor court of all issues relating to the employment relationship. There is nothing in the decision of *Nebbia* and like cases that undercuts the decision in *Wolff* to ban those kinds of forced relationships in ordinary markets which are not common carriers. Indeed, the decision in *Nebbia* did not stop the Supreme Court in *Federal Power Commission v. Hope Natural Gas*,[98] which insisted on some constitutional limitations on regulated rates.

---

[94] 550 P.2d 1001 (Cal. 1976).
[95] 291 U.S. 502 (1934).
[96] *Id.* at 539 (McReynolds, J., dissenting).
[97] 262 U.S. 522 (1923).
[98] 320 U.S. 591 (1944).

IV.   A CLOSE ANALYSIS OF THE DECIDED CASES
       UNDER THE TAKINGS AND DUE PROCESS
       CLAUSES CONFIRMS THAT THE RSL WORKS AN
       UNCONSTITUTIONAL TAKING

A.   How Divided Property Interests Work

To see why all RSLs are per se unconstitutional—the very proposition that
Justice Thomas rejected in *74 Pinehurst*—compare step-by-step the current
system with a sensible alternative of broad application beyond the particulars
of New York law.

Under the modern law of *Penn Central*, the clause is largely eviscerated
by the refusal to use the same basic framework to discuss all takings, total or
partial, physical or regulatory, with the same framework. The insistence that
all regulations (broadly defined) survive and the government position will be
sustained so long as the fraction taken is below some unknown line. There is
no textual foundation to that approach, which appears to be based more on the
fear that it will block modern schemes than on any textual or structural interpretation of the broader reading.

It is opposition to this formless, ad hoc, approach that I have championed
in my book *Takings* and elsewhere. Here the approach is to follow the stated
logic of the clause. The initial task, therefore, is to answer, in clear sequence,
the four basic questions that the Takings Clause presented. The Clause reads,
of course, "nor shall private property be taken for public use, without just
compensation." This formulation of the issue raises three of the four issues in
takings jurisprudence. There is, of course, no textual reference to the police
power in any of the quoted provisions, but the police power exception is
needed to *narrow* its potential application and to avoid an intolerable trunca-
tion of government powers over all private activities—including deleterious
consequences to neighbors such as odors, microbes, stench, and other forms of
pollution. The basic historical proposition that no one should use his property
to harm another is a necessary part of takings law. The real challenge is to give
that proposition specific content to allow the government to govern, but not so
broad as to allow it to swallow up private rights. That point in the abstract was
recognized by Justice Holmes in *Pennsylvania Coal, Inc.,* even though he was
unable to explain where that "too far" line should be drawn: "As long recognized, some values are enjoyed under an implied limitation and must yield to
the police power. But obviously the implied limitation must have its limits, or
the contract and due process clauses are gone."[99]

---

[99]   260 U.S. 393, 413 (1922).

Hence there are four key elements in this constitutional project. The first asks what it means for the government to take private property; the second asks what are the police power justifications that can be used to limit the right of any property owner to claim compensation from the government; the third asks whether the government has supplied just compensation for the property taken; and the last asks the question of whether the taking may take place at all, even with just compensation.

The conceptual difficulties under the current law begin with the way in which it defines the taking of private property. The great genius of both the Roman and the common law is that they permit private parties by voluntary arrangements *to divide up unitary ownership into constituent parts* that allow for huge gains from trade among various parties. Over time, no one has ever denied that the outright taking of the entire piece of property and all the rights associated with it, counts as a prima facie taking, which the government has to either justify under the police power or supply compensation in cash or kind, so that the provision does not become an idle guarantee, a mere form of words that can be evaded by the glib rationalizations used to defend the RSL.

The analytical challenges under the Takings Clause begin once owners divide interests in all forms of property, either real or personal. It is this division of interests that allows private parties through voluntary means to unlock value by transacting to increase their joint value by an amount in excess of the transaction costs needed to put those deals into place. The types of transformation of property are legion. Here is a summary of the kinds of interests that have been created at common law and in equity. First, the doctrine of "estates" divides land along the plane of time.[100]

> The theory of estates, a peculiarity of Anglo-American law, is based on the concept of ownership measured in terms of time. "Property rights in land are ... projected upon the plane of time. The category of quantity, of duration is applied to them." The maximum allowable interest, the state in fee simple is of potentially infinite duration; a life estate or an estate for years, on the other hand, is an estate of finite duration.

The application of that principle allows for the creation of legal life estates, for leases for terms of years *and* for legal remainders and reversions, which fall into possession at the expiration of all prior estates in possession. Today, legal life estates are generally not used because, for family purposes, they have largely been displaced by the trust, which allows for the more flexible

---

[100]   Frederick Pollock and Frederic W. Maitland, THE HISTORY OF ENGLISH LAW BEFORE THE TIME OF EDWARD I, 10 (2d ed. 1911).

management and distribution of assets to the trust beneficiaries. But commercial and residential leases are of great value for the reasons noted above.

The division of basic interests in property is not limited to present and future interests. In addition, voluntary mortgages and involuntary liens play a critical economic role because they allow for the secured financing of long-term projects that would otherwise take place. Under the modern form of a mortgage or lien, at the outset the creditor takes a security in interest in lieu of going into possession of the property, so that the borrower can continue to make efficient use of the property with the borrowed funds. Foreclosure rules were put into place to cover those situations when the borrower was in default on the underlying debt. Partial interests in land also include mineral rights, oil and gas rights, air rights, easements, and restrictive covenants, all of which have generated their share of Takings and Contract Clause challenges. It is also well understood that these transactions can only take place if the grantor and grantee have the security of expectations that their original deal will be honored, not only between the parties to it, but against all successors in title to both sides of the transaction.

B.   The Constitutional Protection of Divided Interest Private Property Does Not Compromise the Ability of the State to Protect Health and Safety Under the Police Power

Unfortunately, the constitutional cases do not build on the common law of private property, but instead resort to the incoherent distinction between physical takings and "regulatory takings." Return again briefly to *Pennsylvania Coal Co. v. Mahon*, described above,[101] where the simple and direct approach treats this as a taking of the support estate from the mining company for which just compensation should be provided, preferably from the surface owners who benefited from the shift, and not from the public as a whole, which has no stake in the transaction. But Justice Holmes confused the matter mightily when he opined: "The general rule at least is, that while property may be regulated to a certain extent, if regulation goes too far it will be recognized as a taking." The conceptual difficulty with this approach is, as noted earlier, that it wrongly turns the yes/no takings question into a question of degree for which there is no obvious answer.[102] The case, moreover, does not fall into the police power dealing with matters of health and safety because the actions in question did not create any risk of a nuisance to third persons. The only harm in this case was to individuals who had explicitly and unambiguously agreed to take the

---

[101]   *Pennsylvania Coal Co,,* supra at 17.
[102]   *Id.* at 11.

risk when they acquired the property in question. The nuisance law is critical to understanding the scope of the police power in its relation to the protection of public health and safety. But it has no role to play in *Mahon*. Nor, most emphatically, does it have any role whatsoever to play in this challenge to the RSL. The correct rule remains the one in *Armstrong*[103] that requires the government to pay for the partial interests it takes.

This general proposition carries over rent control cases. As Justice Scalia wrote in *Pennell v. San Jose*,[104] "The politically attractive feature of regulation is not that it permits wealth transfers to be achieved that could not be achieved otherwise; but rather that it permits them to be achieved 'off budget,' with relative invisibility and thus relative immunity from normal democratic processes."[105] The "off-budget" nature of the exaction makes it difficult to have these private costs taken into account in the political process. The just compensation requirement does not forestall examination of this problem. Instead, it has the salutary effect of forcing the political branches to take into account the full set of consequences of their actions, so that their deliberations will be fully informed. The same rules apply to liens, air rights, and reversions in real estate.

As noted earlier, Justice Thomas in his short opinion in *74 Pinehurst* endorsed the ad hoc *Penn Central* balancing test that neutralized the air rights over Grand Central Station.[106] Justice Brennan's punch line was: "The Landmarks Law's effect is simply to prohibit appellants or anyone else from occupying portions of the airspace above the Terminal, while permitting appellants to use the remainder of the parcel in a gainful fashion." Unfortunately, the word "simply" glosses over the enormous impact that the rule has insofar as it reduces the value of those air rights to zero. The action is a partial taking of the entire real estate, no different in principle from a rule that prohibits a property owner by fiat and without compensation from entering one half of his land because he is still free to enter the other.

In dealing with these interests, the correct formula is, as stated by Justice Holmes in *Boston Chamber of Commerce v. Boston*,[107] that in all takings cases "the question is what has the owner lost, not what the taker has gained."[108] The logic behind that proposition, largely obscured in *Penn Central*, is unexceptionable. The purpose of the Takings Clause is to make sure that government's use of the eminent domain power is for the public benefit. If the rule were other

---

[103]   See *Id.*

[104]   485 U.S. 1 (1988).

[105]   *Id.* at 15 (Scalia, J. concurring).

[106]   438 U.S. 104 (1978), discussed supra.

[107]   217 U.S. 189 (1910).

[108]   *Id.* at 195.

than Holmes stated it, then the government could take a plot of land worth $1,000 to its owner and compensate him at $100 if that were the value of the government's use, leading to a systematic loss of social value. The point of the Holmes formula is to put the proposal back on-budget, so as to force the government to decide whether it thinks that the land in question is worth $1,000 or more, for otherwise social welfare is best served if the private property in question is *not* taken for public use.

In addition, overturning *Penn Central* does not limit the ability of the state to protect the "health and safety" of the public at large, *without* any payment of compensation. In practice, that strong form of government intervention is needed to counter the trespasses and nuisances created by private parties. But it cannot be invoked against conduct that falls short of these or similar forms of tortious behavior. This distinction between a taking for public use and the police power is absolutely necessary for developing any coherent body of takings law, for there must be some way to determine which government actions require compensation and which do not. Working off the private law offers the only appropriate guideline for in all instances the government action operates as the agent of the citizens it protects. There is no general rule that just allows one person to enjoin by self-help or legal action the activities of his neighbors of which he disapproves. Payment must be made, as when what is required is a restrictive covenant that restricts the size, use, or location of activities on the servient tenement, which is what the New York City Council did in *Penn Central*. But those limitations can be done as of right, in order to prevent the overflow of stench, odors, or noise coming from one parcel to another.

This distinction rightly entrenched itself into takings law from the earliest days, when *Fertilizing Company v. Hyde Park*[109] enjoined the defendant from transporting waste material over public streets to protect neighbors from smells, infestations of insects, and other potential dangers, none of which are remotely involved in either *Penn Central* or under the RSL. As Justice Rehnquist noted in his *Penn Central* dissent:

> In essence, Appellees are not prohibiting a nuisance. The record is clear that the proposed addition to the Grand Central Terminal would be in full compliance with zoning, height limitations, and other health and safety requirements. Instead, appellees are seeking to preserve what they believe to be an outstanding example of beaux arts architecture. Penn Central is prevented from further developing its property basically because *too good* a job was done in designing and building it.[110]

---

[109]   97 U.S. 659 (1878).
[110]   *Id*. at 145–146.

Systematically, the core difficulty with the majority opinion in *Penn Central* is its unexplained rejection in the context of partial takings of the conceptual framework used in other total takings. Under the general body of law, the police power allows the state to restrict the creation and maintenance of common law nuisances as an agent for the private parties who have been wrongfully injured by that conduct. When that is done, the background norms of private law are perfectly respected, given that each landowner has the right to be free of nontrespassory invasions by neighbors. Public enforcement of the laws in these cases works wonders. In addition, it is perfectly appropriate for the state to impose regulations on land use that work for the average reciprocity of advantage of all property owners.[111] In these instances each party that is burdened by the regulation will lose if that burden is viewed in isolation. But the similar burdens imposed on neighbors *by the same statute* work for his advantage, which means that *on net*, each owner is fully compensated by receiving his aliquot share of the social gains generated by the rules.

In dealing with the air rights in *Penn Central*, neither of the proper grounds for limiting state action are available. The ordinary exercise of air rights could never be condemned as a nuisance and there is no average reciprocity of advantage in imposing regulations that impact only select properties for the benefit of the public large, and this through an administrative process that allows public officials the luxury of deciding which parcels should be subject to these burdens and which not.[112]

C.   The Structural Errors in Penn Central Carry Over to the Rent Control Law

The importation of *Penn Central* into rent control cases undermines the notion that the landlord is entitled to the full value of the reversion. There are two major conceptual mistakes that upend the entire structure of property rights. The first of these is the claim that the takings law does not protect private property, but only "investment backed expectations," a phrase never defined. The second error is that takings law should treat "the parcel as a whole" and not as a set of separate interests, each of which is entitled to protection to the

---

[111]   *Pennsylvania Coal, Co. v. Mahon*, 260 U.S. 393, 415 (1922).

[112]   Note that the Rehnquist dissent observes that "normal zoning restrictions" are far less likely to involve singling out particular persons for special treatment. *Penn Central*, 438 U.S. 140. The point is true, but overstated. In many cases, general zoning laws have exactly that impermissible redistributive effect. The key point in all cases is to allow anyone who challenges any zoning ordinance to make out the net loss in value that does not happen whenever there is an average reciprocity of *advantage*.

extent of its value. The sole reason why *Penn Central* introduces the notion of investment-backed expectations is to reduce the value of the air rights to zero. "So the law does not interfere with what must be regarded as Penn Central's primary expectation concerning the use of the parcel. More importantly, on this record, we must regard the New York City law as permitting Penn Central not only to profit from the Terminal but also to obtain a "reasonable return" on its investment."[113] There is no explanation as to why only the primary expectation should be taken into account, while all other expectations embedded and protected under state law could be blithely ignored. The standard form of valuation for complex property interests is to take each component separately and then to sum their value, taking care to worry about any interactions, positive or negative, in the value of the separate interests, as for example with "damages and enhanced benefits to the retained portion."[114] The Court's interjection of the term "primary expectation" illicitly excludes the full range of available uses that are normally covered by the compensation formula, without any explanation as to why any owner of property would not expect to realize all elements of value from the government when he could surely recover them from a private purchaser. The situation with rent control may look different but the internal logic is the same because it offers the same shabby treatment of the landlord's revision that *Penn Central* does to air rights. The separation of unitary ownership into parts should not diminish the value of the whole, when the private transactions have increased its value.

This recurrent valuation error falls prey to Holmes's trenchant observation that the proper measure of compensation *in all cases* is the extent of the loss to the owner. But after *Penn Central* the law now looks at the *ratio* between the value of the property interest taken (the "numerator") relative to the value of the parcel as a whole ("the denominator"), without any explanation for this radical shift in approach. That approach to regulatory takings is flatly inconsistent with the general injunction in *Roth* that state law rules set the entitlements by which a taking is done, which requires that the law pay full respect to *all* the interests that are so created.

The dangers imposed by the ad hoc formula used in *Penn Central* provoked a modest backlash in *Loretto v. Teleprompter Manhattan CATV Corp.*,[115] which held that "a permanent occupation of property is a taking,"[116] which in turn generates a per se obligation to compensate for the losses in question. In principle, this proposition should be dispositive of the entire matter, for as a matter of both law and common sense, the ability of the tenant to stay in pos-

---

[113] *Penn Central*, at 136.
[114] See *United States v. Miller*, 317 U.S. at 376.
[115] 458 U.S. 419 (1982).
[116] *Id.* at 441.

session after the expiration of the lease has in principle to count as a physical taking to which *Loretto's* per se compensation rule applies. But its internal doctrinal confusion dulls its impact.

Loretto arose after the New York state legislature passed Section 828 of the Executive Law which provided that no landlord could "interfere with the installation of cable television facilities upon his property or premises." The effect of that rule was to abrogate the existing contracts that Teleprompter "routinely" entered into with property owners, under which the property owners would receive "a standard rate of 5% of the gross revenues that Teleprompter realized from the property."[117] Unfortunately, the opinion of Justice Thurgood Marshall implicitly ignored the doctrine of estates by tying the obligation to compensate to the "permanent" use of the property, even though a cable box has a short useful life. Thus that box is never permanent in its literal sense of "perpetual" or "forever," for as Justice Blackmun pointed out in his dissent, the deal remains in effect "only for as long as she uses her building for rental purposes, and as long as Teleprompter maintains its equipment in compliance with the statute."[118]

Indeed, flaws in Justice Marshall's analysis cut far deeper, to the issue of why possessory takings cases rely on the idea of permanence at all. Suppose that Section 828 authorized Teleprompter's use of the space for only ten years. Must someone make an "ad hoc" judgment under *Penn Central* on compensation? No, the correct answer is that any occupation for any time counts as a taking, and the variations in length only go to the level of compensation owing, which, as noted earlier, is always a continuous function, like standard tort damages. The Takings Clause does not mandate some lump-sum payment that is difficult to estimate with any accuracy. Instead, the proper approach in these leasehold condemnation cases is to require payment of a *periodic* rental, which means that Teleprompter's continued use of the space need not be subject to some speculative once-and-for-all initial determination about how long the equipment will be kept in place. That rule is routinely followed when the government condemns for its own use lease of property for an uncertain duration.[119]

Once this point is understood, it follows that the decision on remand to the New York Courts in *Loretto v. Teleprompter Manhattan CATV Corp* to award the plaintiffs only $1 in damages is both wrong and irrelevant.[120] The decision is wrong because the true loss to the plaintiff there was not the trivial occupation of its space by Teleprompter, but the legislative abrogation of its existing

---

[117]   *Id.* at 423.
[118]   *Id.* at 455.
[119]   See *United States v. Miller*, 317 U.S. 369 (1943).
[120]   446 N.E.2d 428 (N.Y. 1983).

contractual right to 5 percent of Teleprompter's rentals. Once the income stream is lost, Loretto cannot recoup it by raising rents to her tenants because their bills are not reduced by the legislation.

The utter confusion in *Loretto* is brought to the fore by the hopeless confusion that surrounded the recent divided opinions in *Cedar Point Nursery v. Hassid*.[121] In *Cedar Point Nursery*, the statute administered by the Agricultural Labor Relations Board (ALRB), the California Agricultural Labor Relations Act, decreed that labor union representatives were entitled to enter any employer's property for three hours per day for 120 days per year to solicit union support. Cedar Point, an agricultural grower, originally acquiesced, but then demanded that the union representatives leave the premises for "distracting" and "intimidating" its employees. The court struck down the ALRB regulation, holding that it amounted to an unconstitutional taking of the grower's private property rights. In this key passage it wrote:

> Government action that physically appropriates property is no less a physical taking because it arises from a regulation. The essential question is not, as the Ninth Circuit seemed to think, whether the government action at issue comes garbed as a regulation (or statute, or ordinance, or miscellaneous decree). It is whether the government has physically taken property for itself or someone else—by whatever means—or has instead restricted a property owner's ability to use his own property.[122]

It should be noted that this passage does not contain the word "permanent" and thus marks a break from *Loretto*. It also downplays the distinction between regulation and physical takings and thus undercuts the logic of the distinction drawn in *Penn Central*. Since no compensation had been offered for the intrusion—which should include not just the loss of space, but the consequential damages for any union recruitment effectuated by the taking, the only question was whether the injunction was correct, and here the correct rule does not turn on the length of time that the unconnected episodes took but only on the size of the loss, which need not be calculated when no compensation is offered. Indeed, rightly understood, the decision in *Cedar Point* should cast doubt on one of the subordinate conclusions in *Loretto*, namely that its strictures on permanent takings does not apply to rent control laws:

> This Court has consistently affirmed that States have broad power to regulate housing conditions in general and the landlord-tenant relationship in particular without paying compensation for all economic injuries that such regulation entails.[123]

---

[121]   141 S.Ct. 2063 (2021).
[122]   *Id.* at 2072.
[123]   *Loretto*, at 440, citing cases starting with *Block*.

Yet Justice Marshall offered no reasoning to support this conclusion. But it became sacred text in *Yee v. Escondido*,[124] which stands for the proposition that a tenant in possession under rent control does not have 'possession' but only "use" of the property that, presumably, he does not possess:

> The government effects a physical taking only where it *requires* the landowner to submit to the physical occupation of his land. Here, petitioners have voluntarily rented their land to mobile home owners, and are not required to continue to do so by either the city or the State. On their face, the laws at issue merely regulate petitioners' *use* of their land by regulating the relationship between landlord and tenant. Any transfer of wealth from park owners to incumbent mobile home owners in the form of submarket rent does not, itself, convert regulation into physical invasion.[125]

It is all frivolous. The renting was voluntary for the period of the lease, but did not cover any holdover period. It is not the submarket rental which allows the tenant to keep the gain in property value *after* the expiration of the lease that makes the transaction a taking. It is the refusal to surrender the property on time.

V.   CONCLUSION

The decision in *Yee* shows how the perverse effort to retain rent control statutes bowdlerizes the English language and just involves the creation of legal fictions and verbal gymnastics used to address these statutes. The initial error is that hard cases require multi-factor tests that work far less well than simple rules which define the interests in land as divided by time and space. Once the glorification of complexity takes place, it is only a matter of time before all subordinate judgments are infected by that original premises. Reversions and air rights cease to be property interests. Emergencies become a permanent state of affairs. All competitive markets become exploitative. The police power is no longer confined to protecting against serious risks to health and safety, but becomes a cure-all nostrum to be invoked whenever the public interest that protects tenants and excludes landlords becomes enshrined doctrine. But all these machinations can if left unchecked overpower the ability of private ingenuity to beat back the ignorant forces of interest groups who equate their constituencies with the public at large. *74 Pinehurst* highlights the downward cycle. Only time will tell whether that trend is reversible or not.

---

[124]   503 U.S. 519 (1992).
[125]   *Id.* at 519–520.

But here the writing is on the wall. Rent control can only be sustained by a series of verbal fictions that require a total divergence between the private law that makes sense and the public law that does not. If one looks at the current debacle with *74 Pinehurst* and the disintegration of the New York rental market, the answer is the same. Rent control should have been killed at birth, and should be declared per se unconstitutional today, so that rents can be raised over time until they reach market levels, and so that New York City can look like other places where rental markets are allowed to work.

6. Land use reform and property rights: the need for caution

Vicki Been

Over the past few years, the affordable housing crisis afflicting cities, suburbs, and rural areas across the United States[1] has resulted in a fairly radical rethink of the wisdom of our current land use regulatory regime. Many discussions about revisiting land use restrictions are centered on political coalitions that have secured reforms in progressive states like California, Oregon, Washington, and Massachusetts, as well as blue cities like Minneapolis.[2] In

---

[1] *The State of the Nation's Housing 2024*, Joint Center for Housing Studies of Harvard University, https://www.jchs.harvard.edu/sites/default/files/reports/files/Harvard_JCHS_The_State_of_the_Nations_Housing_2024.pdf (finding that 23.2% of homeowners and approximately 50% of all renters are burdened by rising housing costs); *The Gap: A Shortage of Affordable Homes*, National Low Income Housing Coalition, Mar. 2024, https://nlihc.org/gap (finding that "[e]xtremely low-income renters in the U.S. face a shortage of 7.3 million affordable and available rental homes, resulting in only 34 affordable and available homes for every 100 extremely low-income renter households").

[2] See, for example: Megan Kimble and Kriston Capps, *Zoning Reform, Now a Bipartisan Cause, Tries to Build a Bigger Tent*, BLOOMBERG (Mar. 7, 2024), https://www.bloomberg.com/news/articles/2024-03-07/at-austin-s-yimbytown-fans-of-zoning-reform-seek-common-ground?srnd=citylab-housing; Hillary Borud, *Oregon Lawmakers Push "Transformational" Bipartisan Plan to Speed Housing Construction by Streamlining Local Rules*, OREGONIAN (Feb. 24, 2023), https://www.oregonlive.com/politics/2023/02/oregon-lawmakers-push-transformational-bipartisan-plan-to-speed-housing-construction-by-streamlining-local-rules.html; David Gutman, *WA Senate Passes Bill Allowing Duplexes, Fourplexes in Single-Family Zones*, SEATTLE TIMES (Apr. 11, 2023), https://www.seattletimes.com/seattle-news/politics/wa-senate-passes-bill-allowing-duplexes-fourplexes-in-single-family-zones/; and Emily Hamilton, *Bipartisan Hope for Affordable Housing Emerges in the West*, GOVERNING (Jun. 20, 2023), https://www.governing.com/housing/bipartisan-hope-for-affordable-housing-emerges-in-the-west. For a discussion of bipartisan land use reform initiatives at the federal level, see Nolan Gray,

these places, the political pitch for land use reform—based on evidence of the links between restrictive regulation and racial injustice, economic inequality, climate change, and other environmental harms[3]—has invoked progressive priorities like desegregation, affordability, and equity.[4] In those jurisdictions, owners of already developed property have often been regarded as a barrier to pro-housing reforms, as suburban homeowners have opposed zoning reforms,[5]

The Growing Federal Push for Zoning Reform, BLOOMBERG (Jun. 25, 2024), https:// www.bloomberg.com/news/articles/2024-06-25/-yimby-zoning-reform-is-finding -fans-at-the-federal-level and Jerusalem Demsas, *The Only Force Stronger Than Polarization? Rising Home Prices*, THE ATLANTIC (Mar. 10, 2024), https://www .theatlantic.com/ideas/archive/2024/03/yimby-housing-bipartisan-zoning/677704/.

[3]   See generally Vicki Been, Ingrid Gould Ellen and Katherine O'Regan, *Supply Skepticism Revisited*, 35 HOUS. POLY. DEBATE 96 (2024) and Vicki Been, Ingrid Gould Ellen and Katherine O'Regan, *Supply Skepticism: Housing Supply and Affordability*, 29 HOUS. POLY. DEBATE 25 (2019) for surveys of the research about how increased housing supply affects housing prices, rents, and neighborhood change. For a discussion of the links between restrictive regulation and racial, as well as economic inequality, see Jessica Trounstine, *The Geography of Inequality: How Land Use Regulation Produces Segregation*, 114 AM. POL. SCI. REV 443 (2020) (finding that cities with more restrictive land use regulation "remain whiter over time") and Whitney Airgood-Obrycki, Magda Maaoui and Sophia Wedeen, *Rental Deserts, Segregation, and Zoning,* Joint Center for Housing Studies of Harvard University, Jun. 2024, https://www.jchs.harvard.edu/sites/default/files/ research/files/harvard_jchs_rental_deserts_airgood-obrycki_etal_2024.pdf (finding an association between areas where rental units make up less than 20% of the housing stock and restrictive land use regimes, as well as the lack of racial and economic diversity). For a discussion of the links between restrictive regulation and climate harms, see Adie Tomer et al., *We Can't Beat the Climate Crisis Without Rethinking Land Use*, Brookings Institute, May 2021, www.brookings.edu/articles /we-cant-beat-the-climate-crisis-without-rethinking-land-use/ and Jacob Korn et al., *Why State Land Use Reform Should Be a Priority Climate Lever for America*, Feb. 16, 2024, Rocky Mountain Institute, rmi.org/why-state-land-use-reform-s hould-be-a-priority-climate-lever-for-america/; see also *infra* nn. 137–38.

[4]   See, for example, Kriston Capps, *Why Minneapolis Just Made Zoning History*, BLOOMBERG (Mar. 7. 2023), https://www.bloomberg.com/news/articles /2018-12-07/how-minneapolis-mayor-jacob-frey-scored-a-rezoning-win   (interview with Minneapolis Mayor on Minneapolis 40 Plan, the city's comprehensive zoning plan, which emphasizes affordability and racial equity) and Desegregate Connecticut, *Why Are We "Pro-Homes"?,* https://www.desegregatect.org/pro -homes (advocacy organization arguing that zoning reform is necessary to achieve racial equity).

[5]   Suburban homeowners are opposing land use reform from coast to coast, see, for example, Luis Ferré-Sadurní and Mihir Zaveri, *A Plan to Force More*

and owners of rental properties have pushed back against the proposals for tenant protections sometimes included in land use reform packages.[6]

However, as the nation's housing affordability crisis has grown, the politics of land use reform has taken on a new dimension. In the last few years, a "small but growing number of Republicans" have embraced pro-housing land use reforms based on a libertarian conception of property rights.[7] Rather than posing a barrier to pro-housing reforms, property rights have been used to create a wider coalition for reforms in blue states and have been the major argument for reforms in purple and red states such as Arizona, Montana, and Utah.

From the libertarian perspective, "modern zoning and building regulations are a direct infringement on the foundational human right of citizens to control their own land."[8] As a result, some conservative advocates across the country are supporting ambitious zoning reforms aligned with progressive YIMBY (Yes In My Backyard) priorities but rooted in "radically different rhetoric."[9] For example, while progressives might frame a bill repealing restrictions on accessory dwelling units (ADUs) as a means to improve equity and sustainability, libertarians are increasingly supporting identical legislation, but on the grounds that it violates "property owners' rights to build housing."[10] Put

---

Housing Development in New York Has Failed, N.Y. TIMES, Apr. 21, 2023, https://www.nytimes.com/article/nyc-housing-hochul-long-island-westchester.html and Ellie McLogan, *NYC Mayor Eric Adams' "City of Yes" Proposal Sparks Debate at Lengthy Public Hearing. One Opposing Voice Calls It "Apocalyptic,"* CBS NEWS, Jul. 11, 2024, https://www.cbsnews.com/newyork/news/city-of-yes-new-york-city-proposal-opposition/.

[6] See, for example, Peter Tomao and Sam Mellins, *Landlord Legislators Carved Themselves Out of Good Cause Evictions,* N.Y.S. FOCUS, May 13, 2024, https://nysfocus.com/2024/05/13/good-cause-eviction-landlord-legislators.

[7] Brandon Fuller and M. Nolan Gray, *Where Are All the Republican YIMBYs?*, CITY JOURNAL (Apr. 17, 2019), https://www.city-journal.org/article/where-are-all-the-republican-yimbys; see also Vanessa Brown Calder, *Zoning Reform Is for Conservatives, Too,* CATO INSTITUTE (Feb. 28, 2019), https://www.cato.org/blog/zoning-reform-conservatives-too.

[8] Kendall Cotton, *The Conservative Case for Affordable Housing*, Frontier Institute (Nov. 30, 2021), https://frontierinstitute.org/the-conservative-case-for-affordable-housing.

[9] M. Nolan Gray, *YIMBY Zoning Reform Sweeps the Mountain West*, BLOOMBERG (Mar. 7. 2023), https://www.bloomberg.com/news/articles/2023-03-07/yimby-zoning-reform-sweeps-mountain-west-as-housing-costs-rise.

[10] *Allowing Accessory Dwelling Units Would Contribute to Housing Affordability in Virginia, Before the H. of Del., Cntys., Cities, and Towns Comm., Land Use Subcomm.,* 2019 Leg., (Va. 2019) (testimony of Emily Hamilton, Research Fellow, Urbanity Project, Mercatus Center at George Mason University)

another way, "why should the government have the authority to tell homeowners that they can't renovate their garages into granny flats, or tell small businessmen that they can't convert their laundromats into apartment buildings?"[11]

The practical impact of libertarian support for land use reform movements has varied. In some blue states, discussion of property rights is being used to reach across partisan lines.[12] Federal GOP legislators have embraced some of the rhetoric.[13] But arguments that regulatory reform is needed to protect property rights are finding the most traction in state legislatures in the Southwest and Mountain West—where skyrocketing housing prices and a libertarian ethos have propelled land use reforms. Recent battles in Arizona, Montana, and Utah illustrate the property rights arguments being used.

However, the appeal of using property rights as one of the motivations for land use reform comes with some dangers. Those who oppose the reforms are also invoking property rights—the rights of existing residents who own homes that they consider to be threatened by the reforms being discussed and adopted. The political block that Professor William Fischel referred to as "homevoters" is a powerful force.[14] Through public discourse and in the courts, those homevoters are advancing arguments that could give them even more power to affect land use patterns in their neighborhoods.

Part I of this article uses the examples of several states in which coalitions of property rights proponents and pro-housing advocates have recently helped to secure sweeping land use reforms to explore how property rights arguments

---

https://www.mercatus.org/research/state-testimonies/allowing-accessory-dwelling-units-would-contribute-housing-affordability.

[11]   Fuller and Gray, *supra* n. 7.

[12]   See Elliott Wenzler, *Colorado Democrats are Turning 2023 into the Year of Housing. But Should the State Wade into Local Land Decisions?*, THE COLORADO SUN (Feb. 13, 2023), https://coloradosun.com/2023/02/12/colorado-housing-local-control-density/ (quoting the state's Democratic Governor Jared Polis as saying, "We have to break down government barriers, expand private property rights and reduce regulations to actually construct more housing to provide housing options at a lower cost so that all Coloradans can thrive").

[13]   See, for example, Todd Young and Tim Phillips, *More Affordable Housing? Yes, in My Backyard*, NATIONAL REVIEW (Aug. 6, 2021), https://www.national-review.com/2021/08/more-affordable-housing-yes-in-my-backyard/ (op-ed by GOP Senator and right-leaning think tank president advocating for a proposed federal bill to discourage exclusionary land use policies) and Nolan Gray, *When the Federal Government Takes on Local Zoning*, BLOOMBERG (Aug. 20, 2018) (discussing GOP HUD Secretary Ben Carson's openness to land use reform).

[14]   William A. Fischel, THE HOMEVOTER HYPOTHESIS: HOW HOME VALUES INFLUENCE LOCAL GOVERNMENT TAXATION, SCHOOL FINANCE, AND LAND-USE POLICIES (2001).

have been used to justify land use reforms. Part II then turns to how home-owners who fear that such reforms may decrease the value of their proper-ties are invoking property rights to make *their* claims. Part III then explores how land use law has sought to balance the interests of existing homeown-ers with a community's need for change and the rights of landowners who seek to develop their properties within the community. It assesses what we can learn about the viability of neighbors' challenges by looking at existing judicial decisions about protest statutes; "spot zoning;" claims that the govern-ment's authorization of a neighbor's land use that decreases the value of the claimant's own property effects an unconstitutional taking; attacks on "right to farm" laws and other legislative restrictions on nuisance suits; and challenges to legislative decisions to override private covenants. Part IV concludes with some suggestions about how to minimize the danger that courts will prioritize the property rights claims of existing homeowners over the interests of those who have not yet been able to build housing on their land and those who do not have access to affordable homes as a result of the shortage of housing in many areas across the country.

I. PROPERTY RIGHTS AS AN ARGUMENT FOR LAND USE REFORM

Recent battles in Arizona, Montana, and Utah illustrate the property rights arguments being used and the results those arguments are achieving.

A. Arizona

After the 2008 subprime mortgage crisis, Arizona faced a growing housing shortage as homebuilders cut back on production even though people contin-ued to move to the Southwest.[15] The shortage had grown to between 67,000 and 200,000 housing units by early 2024.[16] Not surprisingly, therefore, rental prices across Arizona surged by 53% between 2017 and 2023 (and renters in

---

[15] Katherine Davis-Young, *Phoenix Had a Housing Crisis Before; The Pandemic Could Make It Worse*, KJZZ (Jun. 6, 2020), https://www.kjzz.org/2020 -06-06/content-1589405-phoenix-had-housing-crisis-pandemic-could-make-it -worse.

[16] Glenn Farley and Kamryn Brunner, *Housing Affordability in Arizona: Quarter 1 2024 Update*, COMMON SENSE INSTITUTE ARIZONA (Mar. 19, 2024), https://commonsenseinstituteaz.org/quarter-1-2024-housing-affordability/   and Gloria Rebecca Gomez, *Facing a Housing Crisis, Arizona Lawmakers Propose Overriding City Control*, AZMIRROR (May 4, 2023), https://azmirror.com/2023 /05/04/facing-a-housing-crisis-arizona-lawmakers-propose-overriding-city

Tucson, Mesa, Glendale, and Phoenix faced even higher increases).[17] The cost of homeownership also skyrocketed: "a family earning \$55,000 would have been able to afford the monthly mortgage payment on an average entry-level home in 2017, but a family would have to earn \$99,500, to afford the monthly payment for the same home" by 2023.[18]

Many critics blamed overly restrictive regulations for the slow provision of housing and the accompanying skyrocketing costs. The criticism built upon an earlier movement to limit land use regulation that resulted in Arizona voters adopting Proposition 207—the "Private Property Protection Act"—in 2006.[19] The Act primarily addresses local governments' use of eminent domain, but also provides that:

> [whenever] existing rights to use, divide, sell or possess private real property are reduced by the enactment or applicability of any land use law enacted after the date the property is transferred to the owner and such action reduces the fair market value of the property the owner is entitled to just compensation from this state or the political subdivision of this state that enacted the land use law.[20]

The Act is similar to one passed in Oregon and ones rejected in California, Idaho, and Washington.[21] While there has been surprisingly little litigation under the Act,[22] some observers claim that the law has deterred local governments from adopting regulations intended to protect the public interest in historic preservation, water resources, and other public goods.[23] Others have

---

-control/#:~:text=Arizona%20is%20short%20more%20than,from%20cities %20across%20the%20state.

[17] Alex Horowitz and Tushar Kansal, *Restrictive Zoning Is Raising Housing Costs and Homelessness in Arizona*, PEW CHARITABLE TRUSTS (Dec. 7, 2023), https://www.pewtrusts.org/en/research-and-analysis/articles/2023/12/07/restric-tive-zoning-is-raising-housing-costs-and-homelessness-in-arizona#:~:text=From %20August%202017%20to%20August,more%20of%20income%20on%20rent.

[18] *Id.*

[19] Jeffrey L. Sparks, Note, *Land Use Regulation in Arizona After the Private Property Rights Protection Act*, 52 AZ L. REV 211 (2009).

[20] Ariz. Rev. Stat. Ann. § 12-1134(A) (2006).

[21] Sparks, *supra* n. 19, at 217 and Hannah Jacobs, Note, *Searching for Balance in the Aftermath of the 2006 Takings Initiatives*, 116 YALE L.J. 1518, 1520, 1522–27, 1542–43 (2007).

[22] See, for example, Patel v. City of Holbrook, https://www.goldwaterinstitute .org/wp-content/uploads/2024/02/Verified-Complaint.pdf and *Protecting a Small Business Owner's Private Property Rights: Patel v. City of Holbrook*, GOLDWATER INSTITUTE (Feb. 1, 2024), https://www.goldwaterinstitute.org/case/protecting-a -small-business-owners-private-property-rights/.

[23] Sparks, *supra* n. 19, at 219–22.

celebrated what they point to as victories for property owners stymied by local regulations.[24] Further, the support for the ballot proposition indicates that property rights arguments are persuasive to Arizona voters. Indeed, the Goldwater Institute, a significant national pro-property rights litigation and advocacy organization that has championed moves to restrict "regulations that make it prohibitively expensive to build, improve, or own housing," is based in Arizona.[25]

In 2022, Republican State Senator Steve Kaiser and Democratic State Representative Cesar Chavez introduced a bill that would have allowed the construction of up to eight single-family homes or 12 two-family units per acre on any land zoned for single-family or agricultural use.[26] The bill would also have permitted more multifamily development, increased housing density, prohibited design review of new homes, and substantially revised the process developers use to secure land use approvals.[27] The bill failed to make it out of committee, and Kaiser and Chavez turned their focus to securing the passage of legislation establishing a bipartisan study commission to recommend a way forward. That commission held meetings across the state to hear from stakeholders and experts before issuing a report in December 2022 with recommendations about the reforms necessary to make land use processes more effective in addressing the state's housing needs.[28]

Senator Kaiser then introduced SB 1117, adopting the commission's recommendations to rein in the limits local governments could impose on residential development.[29] First, his bill would have prevented larger local governments

---

[24]   *Property Ownership Fairness Act (A Decade of Success)*, GOLDWATER INSTITUTE (Aug. 24, 2023), https://www.goldwaterinstitute.org/policy-report/property-ownership-fairness-act/.

[25]   Christina Sandefur, *Governments Should Ease Up on Zoning Restrictions*, GOLDWATER INSTITUTE (Dec. 26, 2018), https://www.goldwaterinstitute.org/governments-should-ease-up-on-zoning-restrictions/.

[26]   See H.B. 2674, 55th Leg., 2d. Reg. Sess. (Ariz. 2022), https://www.azleg.gov/legtext/55leg/2R/bills/HB2674P.pdf; see also BEX Staff, *The Deeper Dive: HB 2674*, BEX AZBEX (Feb. 8, 2022), https://azbex.com/trends/the-deeper-dive-hb-2674/ and AZRE, *New Legislation Eliminates Barriers to New Housing Construction Across Arizona,* AZ BIG MEDIA (Feb. 7, 2022), https://azbigmedia.com/real-estate/residential-real-estate/new-legislation-eliminates-barriers-to-new-housing-construction-across-arizona/.

[27]   H.B. 2674, *supra* n. 26.

[28]   Ariz. Housing Supply Study Comm., FINAL REPORT (Dec. 2022), https://homefront.azhousingforall.com/wp-content/uploads/2023/01/Housing-Supply-Study-Committee-Final-Report-2022.pdf.

[29]   S.B. 1117, 56th Leg., 1st Reg. Sess. (Ariz. 2023), https://legiscan.com/AZ/text/SB1117/id/2747053/Arizona-2023-SB1117-Engrossed.html;   see   also   S.

from issuing minimum lot size and setback requirements in areas zoned for single-family housing. Second, it would have required those jurisdictions to allow ADUs and manufactured homes in all residential zones and to establish zones for duplexes, triplexes, and single-room occupancy housing. Third, it would have prohibited all municipalities from imposing design standards on residential construction. Fourth, the bill would have placed deadlines on jurisdictions' review of applications for rezonings, changed the standard and burden of proof required to reject such applications,[30] and required the local government to identify the "least restrictive means" of mitigating any externality used to justify a rejection.[31] Finally, the bill would have required each municipality to estimate its housing needs every five years and file an annual report on its progress in meeting those needs and its plans for addressing unmet needs. While Senator Kaiser was able to build some support for the bill among both Republicans and Democrats, and both developers and local governments, the bill ultimately failed by a 9 to 20 vote in the Senate, with only one Democrat voting in favor, and Republicans split evenly between opposition and support.[32]

In the 2024 legislative session, the Senate and House majority leaders—both Republicans—sponsored identical bills, known as the Arizona Starter Homes Act (ASHA), that would have banned restrictions on design standards, lot sizes, lot coverage, and setbacks—similar to what Kaiser's bill proposed.[33] The starter homes bill passed with bipartisan support in the House and in the Senate.[34] Democratic Governor Katie Hobbs vetoed the bill in March 2024, citing concerns raised by the Department of Defense and Arizona's firefighters association, along with opposition from a wide range of local governments.[35]

Research, S.B. 1117 S. Fact Sheet (Mar. 13, 2023), https://www.azleg.gov/legtext/56leg/1R/summary/S.1117COM_ASPASSEDCOW.pdf.

[30] Ariz. SB 1117, 9–462.10 (D).

[31] *Id.*

[32] See *Roll Call Senate Vote: AZ SB1117*, LegiScan (2023), https://legiscan.com/AZ/rollcall/HB2570/id/1404011; see also Lauren Gilger, *Why His Arizona Housing Bill Failed, and Why He Thinks This Year's Will be Successful*, KJZZ (Jan. 31, 2024), https://www.kjzz.org/2024-01-31/content-1869924-why-his-arizona-housing-bill-failed-and-why-he-thinks-years-will-be-successful.

[33] S.B. 1112, 56th Leg., 2d Reg. Sess. (Ariz. 2024), https://www.azleg.gov/legtext/56leg/2R/bills/SB1112P.pdf.

[34] See *Roll Call House Vote: AZ HB2570*, LegiScan (2024), https://legiscan.com/AZ/rollcall/HB2570/id/1392073; see also *Roll Call Senate Vote: AZ HB2570*, LegiScan (2024), https://legiscan.com/AZ/rollcall/HB2570/id/1404011.

[35] Letter from Katie Hobbs, Governor of Ariz., to Ben Toma, Speaker, Ariz. House of Representatives (Mar. 18, 2024), https://azgovernor.gov/sites/default/files

Both Republicans and Democrats criticized the veto, arguing that failing to address the gap in the supply of housing would lock Arizonians out of homeownership.[36]

Later in the session, the legislature and Governor Hobbs approved two bills that included some of the reforms recommended by the study commission and included in the earlier bills. One requires municipalities with a population over 75,000 to allow ADUs in residential zones and limits the municipalities' ability to regulate them.[37] The second, the Arizona Starter Homes Act, requires those municipalities to allow the construction of missing middle housing (duplexes, triplexes, townhomes) within 1 mile of the municipality's central business district and to allow such homes to make up at least 20% of any new development of more than 10 contiguous acres.[38]

Advocates repeatedly invoked property rights arguments in favor of the various bills. The sponsors of the various bills repeatedly invoked property rights. Senate Majority Leader Sonny Borrelli justified the passage of the Starter Homes Act by noting that "local municipalities are overstepping their authority by trying to control private property rights, instead of focusing their attention on valid rules and regulations protecting against nuisance and safety issues."[39] Representative Michael Carbone, a Republican who sponsored both

---

/hb_2570.pdf; see also Joe Duhownik, *Arizona Governor Blocks Bill to Increase Starter Home Affordability*, Courthouse News Service (Mar. 18, 2024), https://www.courthousenews.com/arizona-governor-blocks-bill-to-increase-starter-home-affordability/.

[36] Press Release, Analise Ortiz, Representative, Ariz. House of Representatives, Rep Ortiz Responds to Gov. Hobbs Veto of HB 2570 (Mar. 18, 2024), https://www.azhousedemocrats.com/post/press-release-rep-ortiz-responds-to-gov-hobbs-veto-of-hb-2570.

[37] H.B. 2720, 56th Leg., 2nd Reg. Sess. (Ariz. 2024), www.azleg.gov/legtext/56leg/2R/laws/0196.pdf.

[38] H.B. 2721, 56th Leg., 2nd Reg. Sess. (Ariz. 2024), https://legiscan.com/AZ/text/HB2721/id/3002004/Arizona-2024-HB2721-Chaptered.html; see also H.B. 2721, 56th Leg., 2nd Reg. Sess., S. Engrossed (Ariz. 2024), https://www.azleg.gov/legtext/56leg/2R/summary/H.HB2721_050824_SENATEENGROSSED.pdf.

[39] Daniel Stefanski, *Arizona Legislature Passes Housing Affordability Bill*, AZ Free News (Mar. 9, 2024), https://azfreenews.com/2024/03/arizona-legislature-passes-housing-affordability-bill/; see also Bob Christie, *Hurdles Remain for Republicans to Pass Affordable Housing Zoning Measure*, Daily Independent (Feb. 29, 2024), https://www.yourvalley.net/stories/hurdles-remain-for-republicans-to-pass-affordable-housing-zoning-measure,481321 (Rep. Barbara Parker, reacting to the defeat of a bill she sponsored: "This tiny homes cottage home act would have made it easier for rural property owners to build on their own land

bills, called their success "a win for property rights" and added, "it's not going to happen overnight, but hopefully we will see a significant increase in permitting …. as far as single-family homeowners being able to build a casita in their backyard."[40] Arizona House Democrat Analise Ortiz agreed, arguing that prior to the ADU bill's enactment, cities "had ordinances in place that really were not strong enough to protect people's private property rights."[41]

B.   Montana

An influx of migration during the pandemic, coupled with lagging housing production, resulted in falling vacancy rates and spiraling home prices across Montana early in this decade. While the population increased by 40,000 between 2020 and 2023, the housing supply grew by only 8,700, and prices jumped by 60%.[42] In 2021, Republican Governor Greg Gianforte made the resulting crisis a central plank in his agenda and quickly issued an executive order establishing a 30-member housing task force charged with suggesting "short- and long-term recommendations and strategies ... to increase the supply of affordable, attainable workforce housing."[43] Within months, the Task Force issued a set of recommendations focused on encouraging local land use reform and "broadly restoring the rights of landowners throughout Montana cities to build attainable forms of housing."[44] The Task Force recognized that "some property owners will express opposition to other owners exercising property

---

without the interference of excessive and intrusive government regulation, because property rights are human rights").

[40]   Bob Christie, *Arizona Gov. Hobbs Signs Bill to Allow Casitas and More Dense Housing in Larger Cities*, KAWC (May 22, 2024), https://www.kawc.org/news/2024-05-22/arizona-gov-hobbs-signs-bill-to-allow-casitas-and-more-dense-housing-in-larger-cities.

[41]   Serena O'Sullivan, *Arizona House Democrat Explains How "Casita Bill" Can Help Fight the State's Housing Shortage*, KTAR NEWS (May 17, 2024), https://ktar.com/story/5574017/arizona-house-democrat-explains-how-casita-bill-can-help-fight-housing-shortage/.

[42]   Susan Shain, *Has Montana Solved its Housing Crisis?*, HIGH COUNTRY NEWS (Nov. 20, 2023), https://www.hcn.org/issues/55-12/housing-has-montana-solved-its-housing-crisis/.

[43]   Executive Order 5–2002, https://news.mt.gov/Governors-Office/_documents/EO-5-2022-Establishing-Housing-Advisory-Council.pdf; see also MONTANA DEPARTMENT OF ENVIRONMENTAL QUALITY, GOVERNOR'S HOUSING TASK FORCE, https://deq.mt.gov/about/Housing-Task-Force#:~:text=Background,affordable%20and%20attainable%20for%20Montanans.

[44]   Montana Governor's Housing Task Force, RECOMMENDATIONS AND STRATEGIES TO INCREASE THE SUPPLY OF AFFORDABLE, ATTAINABLE WORKFORCE

rights in a manner that differs from an expectation established by zoning at the time their property was purchased."[45] But their recommendations nonetheless included ambitious pro-housing regulatory reforms.

The following year, the Republican-dominated Montana legislature put these recommendations into action by passing a flurry of ambitious zoning bills.[46] Most importantly, Senate Bill 382—the Montana Land Use Planning Act—requires cities of at least 5,000 people to adopt a land use plan after public review and comment. Once the plan is adopted, the local government must enact or amend zoning regulations to implement it. The Act requires local governments to include at least five of 14 specified pro-housing measures in their regulations, ranging from allowing duplexes, triplexes, or quad-plexes in any zone that permits single-family housing to eliminating or reducing required off-street parking, minimum lot sizes, setbacks, or impact fees.[47]

Once a jurisdiction adopts its plan and the zoning code and other regulations needed to implement the plan, it must permit a proposed development without further discretionary review or public hearing if the proposed development is in substantial compliance with the jurisdiction's regulations, and all impacts resulting from the development passed the public review process for the land use plan or implementing regulations.[48] As the City of Missoula put it, the Act "shifts the opportunities for public engagement ... to be during the planning

---

HOUSING, 5 (2022), https://deq.mt.gov/files/About/Housing/HTF_PhaseI_Final_10142022.pdf.

[45] *Id.* at 42.

[46] In addition to the Land Use Planning Act discussed in the text, the legislature passed (and governor signed): HB 211 (see Mont. Code Ann. §§ 76-3-615, 76-3-617, 76-3-623(2023)) and SB 170 (see Mont. Code Ann. § 76-3-609(2023)), to streamline the subdivision review process; SB 528, to require local governments to allow accessory dwelling units, see Mont. Code Ann. § 76-2-345 (2023); SB 245, which required localities to allow mixed-use and multiple-dwelling units in commercial areas, see Mont. Code Ann. § 76-2-304(4), (5) and (c), (d) (2023); SB 323, to require cities to allow duplexes, see Mont. Code Ann. §§ 76-2-304(3), (5), and 76-2–309 (2023); SB 406, prohibiting local building codes more stringent than the state code, see Mont. Code Ann. § 50-60-30; SB 407, eliminating local design review by volunteer boards, see Mont. Code Ann. § 76-2-302(2)(8)(2023); SB 131, to mandate that a locality review applications for subdivisions within 20 days, see Mont. Code Ann. § 76-3-201(5)(c), 76-3-207(4)(c); and SB 240, which exempts applications for smaller subdivisions from review by the Montana Department of Environmental Quality if those subdivisions meet certain requirements, see Mont. Code Ann. § 76-4-136.

[47] See Mont. Code Ann. § 76-25-302 (2023).

[48] See Mont. Code Ann. § 76-25-305(4) (2023).

and adoption of city land use plans and codes, rather than during [review of] site-specific development."[49]

Dubbed the "Montana Miracle," these measures fulfilled a litany of land use reform goals, going further than what many states with more left-leaning politics have achieved in their land use reforms.[50] The Montana Senate adopting the bills had 34 Republicans to 16 Democrats, and the House had 68 to 32, but support for the bills did not align with traditional partisan divides.[51] The sweeping Land Use Planning Act, for example, was passed unanimously in the Senate, and 95 to 5 in the House.[52] As the head of a right-leaning free-market think tank put it, "We were able to go to mostly Republicans and talk about free markets and the importance of property rights. They [progressives] were able to go to folks on the left and talk about climate and social impacts."[53] Montana libertarians wholeheartedly supported the charge on pro-housing reforms, characterizing reform as an effort to undo "excessive California-Style zoning" and arguing that the reforms makes "sure cities are planning for the future and providing landowners the freedom they need to build homes to accommodate Montana's population growth."[54]

C.   Utah

Like Arizona and Montana, Utah has experienced a marked increase in population in recent years—the state's population grew by more than 450,000 between 2015 and 2023.[55] One housing expert reported that "An income of $101,400 would be needed to finance the median-price home in 2021, compared with only $58,100 in 2015 ... Utah housing prices have been increasing

---

[49]   City of Missoula, Montana, *The New Montana Land Use Planning Act*, https:// www.engagemissoula.com/the-new-montana-land-use-planning-act-sb382#:~:text =The%20Montana%20Land%20Use%20Planning%20Act%20requires%20that %20cities%20in,the%20passage%20of%20the%20Act.

[50]   Kriston Capps, *How YIMBYs Won Montana*, BLOOMBERG (Apr. 28, 2023), https://www.bloomberg.com/news/articles/2023-04-28/montana-s-yimby-revolt -aims-to-head-off-a-housing-crisis.

[51]   See Roll Call: MT SB382, https://legiscan.com/MT/votes/SB382/2023.

[52]   *Id.*

[53]   Capps, *supra* n. 50.

[54]   *Frontier Institute Statement in Support of SB 382*, FRONTIER INSTITUTE (22 February 2023), https://frontierinstitute.org/frontier-institute-statement-in-support -of-sb-382/.

[55]   Emily Harris, *State and County Population Estimates for Utah*, KEM C. GARDNER POLICY INSTITUTE (Dec. 2023), https://d36oiwf74r1rap.cloudfront.net/ wp-content/uploads/UPC-Estimates-Dec2023.pdf?x71849.

twice as fast as household income."[56] State lawmakers have eschewed a common initial answer to complaints about housing affordability—increasing state funding for income-restricted housing—in favor of deregulation.[57] Utah Republican House Speaker Brad Wilson argued, for example: "[t]he biggest challenge in my opinion, still, is there are many cities that are blocking ... market-based solutions .... [t]here's demand for product, for types of housing in their cities, and the cities don't allow it to be built."[58] Legislators often invoked property rights in discussions about proposed reforms. Republican Senator Lincoln Fillmore, who sponsored one of the bills and served as co-chairman of the state's Commission on Housing Affordability, argued that his bill to streamline the subdivision approval process "strikes the right balance between protecting property rights and increasing housing supply and protecting the public's right to have input and a say."[59] Further, pro-property rights advocates such as the Property Rights Coalition and the libertarian-leaning Libertas Institute[60] strongly supported the reforms.[61]

---

[56]   James Wood, *Insight: Reflections on Affordability in Utah's Housing Market*, KEM C. GARDNER POLICY INSTITUTE (Aug. 3, 2022), https://gardner.utah.edu/blog/blog-reflections-on-affordability-in-utahs-housing-market/.

[57]   Brigham Tomco, *Lawmakers Tackle Housing Shortage Via Regulatory Reform, Not New Funding*, DESERET NEWS (Feb. 14, 2024), https://deseret.com/2024/2/14/24071783/utah-legislature-housing-shortage-regulatory-reform-no-new-funding-cox-budget-recommendation.

[58]   Katie McKellar, *Can a Freer Market Solve the Housing Crisis? Here's How Utah Lawmakers Want Cities to Get Out of Developers' Way*, DESERET NEWS (Jan. 11, 2023), https://www.deseret.com/utah/2023/1/11/23549456/housing-market-crisis-free-market-utah-legislature-developers.

[59]   Katie McKellar, *What Are Utah Lawmakers Doing to Address Utah's Housing Market Crisis?*, DESERET NEWS (Mar. 1, 2023), https://www.deseret.com/utah/2023/3/1/23617149/housing-market-crisis-utah-legislature-bills-affordable/.

[60]   See, for example, Lee Sands and Greg Brooks, *Make Zoning Make Sense: Three Tools for Clarity & Prosperity*, LIBERTAS INSTITUTE (Mar. 20, 2024), https://libertas.org/policy-papers/Make-Zoning-Make-Sense.pdf; see also Josh Daniels, *The Fundamental Right to Use One's Own Property*, LIBERTAS INSTITUTE (Dec. 16, 2015), https://libertas.org/policy-papers/property-rights.pdf.

[61]   Molly Davis, *Utah Needs More Affordable Housing, Less Zoning*, LIBERTAS INSTITUTE (Oct. 20, 2017), https://libertas.org/property-rights/utah-needs-more-affordable-housing-less-zoning/. See also, Katie McKellar, *What Are Utah Lawmakers Doing to Address Utah's Housing Market Crisis?* DESERET NEWS (Mar. 1, 2023), https://www.deseret.com/utah/2023/3/1/23617149/housing-market-crisis-utah-legislature-bills-affordable and Brigham Tomco, *Lawmakers Tackle Housing Shortage Via Regulatory Reform, Not New Funding*, DESERET NEWS (Feb. 14, 2024), https://deseret.com/2024/2/14/24071783/utah-legislature-housing-shortage-regulatory-reform-no-new-funding-cox-budget-recommendation.

Several recent bills illustrate the potency of property rights-based land use reform in Utah. First, in 2019, the state passed Senate Bill 34.[62] Among other requirements, the bill makes cities adopt at least three policies from a menu of options to encourage affordable housing—including allowing ADUs, permitting greater density or moderate-income housing in commercial zones, and eliminating or reducing minimum parking requirements near transit or in senior-living facilities.[63] Cities that do not comply will miss out on hundreds of millions in state transportation investment funds.[64] The bill's sponsor—a self-styled "conservative, borderline Libertarian Republican"[65]—prioritized property rights arguments in his pitch to voters.[66] As Bloomberg's CityLab wrote, "the bill's appeal to deregulation and property rights likely carried more water than its potential to address spatial inequality and access to public transit."[67] Republicans embraced the bill for "trying to restore some free-market principles to local zoning" and stopping land use decisions based solely on "what we don't like."[68] The bill kept localities in charge of their own destiny by allowing them to choose among strategies, and arguments were phrased in terms of property rights, not just affordability. This approach helped it avoid the opposition by local governments that other states had encountered and win support from the Utah League of Cities and Towns, the Wasatch Front Regional Council, and the Salt Lake Chamber.[69]

Private property arguments led to additional pro-housing reforms in Utah. In 2023, for example, the state passed a law blocking voters from using a referendum to overturn a unanimous local land use decision.[70] The bill's author also centered property rights in his pitch to the public, saying, "[w]e have an

---

[62] S. 34, 2019 Leg., 63rd Sess. (Utah 2019), https://le.utah.gov/~2019/bills/static/SB0034.html.

[63] *Id.*

[64] *Id.*

[65] Brandon Fuller and Nolan Gray, *A Red-State Take on a YIMBY Housing Bill*, BLOOMBERG (Feb. 20, 2019), https://www.bloomberg.com/news/articles/2019-02-20/utah-pro-housing-bill-is-zoning-reform-red-state-style.

[66] *Id.*

[67] *Id.*

[68] Katie McKellar, *Utah Lawmaker Pushing Bill Requiring Cities to Zone Affordable Housing if They Want State Dollars*, DESERET NEWS (Feb. 1, 2019), https://www.deseret.com/2019/2/1/20664798/utah-lawmaker-pushing-bill-requiring-cities-to-zone-affordable-housing-if-they-want-state-dollars.

[69] *Id.*

[70] S. 199, 2023 Leg., 65th Sess. (Utah 2023), https://le.utah.gov/~2023/bills/static/SB0199.html.

affordable housing issue in this state, and it's going to be really difficult to address and tackle affordable housing if we don't respect the private property rights and those that choose to move forward with projects."[71] Some opponents pushed back on these arguments, claiming that the deference to property owners would "further restrict an already difficult [referendum] process and remove constitutional rights."[72] But, legislators ultimately favored the bill, agreeing that growth pressure had made it necessary to prioritize property owners' right to develop their own property over neighborhood concerns.[73] Similarly, private property arguments were instrumental in securing a set of state laws breaking down regulatory barriers for ADUs.[74]

II.   THE OTHER SIDE OF THE COIN: THE PERILS OF PROPERTY RIGHTS ARGUMENTS IN THE LAND USE REFORM DEBATES

While property rights arguments helped secure reform in the three states detailed above,[75] they are also beginning to be used to challenge land use reforms. Homeowners who purchased their homes under the more restrictive land use regimes are claiming that changing those regimes violates *their* rights. Montana's ambitious land use reforms, for example, have sparked litigation from homeowners who invoked property rights as fundamental to

---

[71]   Katie McKellar, *Have Referendums Been "Weaponized" Against Housing Projects? This Utah Lawmaker Thinks So,* Deseret News (Feb. 14, 2023), https://www.deseret.com/utah/2023/2/14/23599487/housing-market-crisis-referendum-weaponized-utah-bill/.

[72]   *Id.*

[73]   Katie McKellar et al., *What Happened During the 2023 Utah Legislature? What You Need to Know,* Deseret News (Mar. 3, 2023), https://www.deseret.com/utah/2023/3/3/23617130/utah-legislature-what-happened-end-session-need-to-know/.

[74]   H.B. 82, 2021 Leg., 64th Sess. (Utah 2021); Katie McKellar, *Utah Bill to Break Barriers for Basement Apartments Sparks Local Control Debate*, Deseret News (Feb. 1, 2021), https://www.deseret.com/utah/2021/2/1/22256723/2021-legislature-want-to-break-barriers-basement-mother-in-law-apartments-local-control. The ADU law was later strengthened with revisions in 2023. See S. 174, 2023 Leg., 65th Sess. (Utah 2023).

[75]   Support from both left-leaning pro-housing advocates and more libertarian groups may also have played a role in some of the land use reforms California has recently adopted. See Kenneth Stahl, *The Power of State Legislatures to Invalidate Private Deed Restrictions: Is It an Unconstitutional Taking?*, 50 Pepp. L. Rev 579, 604 (2023).

their grievances. In *Montanans Against Irresponsible Densification, LLC v. Montana*, a group of homeowners (known by their acronym, MAID) made three legal arguments.[76] First, they claimed that the laws violated Equal Protection and Due Process guarantees by drawing arbitrary distinctions between localities of different sizes and by requiring local governments to allow ADUs and duplexes only in areas not covered by restrictive private covenants. MAID argued this would create "two classifications ... unrelated to any legitimate government purpose" and place an "inordinate burden" on residents without restrictive covenants.[77] On that claim, they sought a declaratory judgment that the laws "may not be used by any person or governmental entity to invalidate or displace covenants that are more restrictive than those developed by Montana's municipal governments."[78] Second, MAID argued that the streamlined land use decision-making process in Senate Bill 382 violated Montana's constitutional right to public participation.[79] Finally, MAID argued that the laws unconstitutionally pre-empted local power.[80] Throughout, MAID couched their argument in the language of property rights. They asserted, for example, that "[i]n bringing this lawsuit, Plaintiffs now exercise their inalienable rights of protecting their property and their inalienable right to seek safety, health and happiness in lawful ways."[81] The plaintiffs characterized their

---

[76] First Amended Complaint at 1, *Montanans Against Irresponsible Densification, LLC v. Montana*, No. DV 23–1248 (Mont. 18 Dist. Dec. 19, 2023). MAID is a limited liability corporation composed of property owners in single-family neighborhoods in Whitefish, Bozeman, Billings, Missoula, Great Falls, Columbia Falls, and Kalispell.

[77] *Id.* at 36.

[78] *Id.* at 58.

[79] *Id.* at 42. This right-to-notice argument is reminiscent of a successful approach taken by Texan homeowners in a similar lawsuit against zoning reforms in Austin. See Audrey McGlinchy, 'Judge Orders Austin to Scrap Rules that Let Developers Build More in Exchange for Affordable Housing', KUT NEWS (Dec. 12, 2023), https://www.kut.org/austin/2023-12-12/judge-orders-austin-to-scrap-rules -that-let-developers-build-more-in-exchange-for-affordable-housing (explaining the judge's decision that the city failed to adequately notify property owners about the implications of the zoning changes); Press Release, Doug Becker, Attorney for *Acuna* Plaintiffs, Travis County District Court Slams City of Austin in December 8, 2023, Order: 2022 Austin City Council Violated the Prior Court Order and State Law on Zoning Notice and Protest Rights (Dec. 11, 2023), https://theaustin-bulldog.org/wp-content/uploads/2023/12/20231211-Release.pdf (using property rights language to express the hope that the city stops pursuing zoning reform and, "respects the interests and legal rights of Austin homeowners").

[80] First Amended Complaint, supra n. 76, at 29.

[81] *Id.* at 41.

lawsuit as a necessary defensive measure to protect the "single most important monetary investment in their lifetime" against "top-down 'densification.'"[82]

Just weeks after MAID's initial complaint, Gallatin County Judge Mike Salvagni issued an "eyebrow-raising" decision preliminarily enjoining two of the bills that had yet to be implemented.[83] Judge Salvagni argued that pausing the laws would prevent "little harm" to the state, while single-family home-owners would suffer an irreparable injury, with the "concern[] that ... they could wake up one morning to find that, without any notice at all, a new duplex or ADU ... is going up next door in their previously peaceful and well-main-tained single-family neighborhood."[84]

The decision drew broad criticism. Montana's Republican Senate President lamented the ruling's impact on the state's ability to address its housing afford-ability crisis.[85] Pro-housing advocates and libertarians both decried the impli-cations of the decision.[86] Property rights advocates voiced the most vociferous criticism. From their perspective, rather than protecting the plaintiff's prop-erty rights, the lawsuit and Judge Salvagni's ruling instead trampled on the "rights and freedoms [of] property owners to build affordable starter homes

---

[82] *Id.* at 3, 25.

[83] Christian Britschgi, *Court's Wild Zoning Decision Blocks "Montana Miracle,"* REASON (Jan. 2, 2024), https://reason.com/2024/01/02/courts-wild-zon-ing-decision-blocks-montana-miracle/. Senate Bill 323 (allowing duplexes) and Senate Bill 528 (allowing ADUs) were enjoined before they went into effect at the start of 2024. The two remaining bills had been in place since their passage and have longer-term deadlines for localities to comply, so they did not require immediate action. See Darrell Ehrlick, *Judge Issues Injunction Against Two "Affordable Housing" Bills Passed by Montana Legislature,* DAILY MONTANAN (Dec. 29, 2023), https://dailymontanan.com/2023/12/29/judge-issues-injunction -against-two-affordable-housing-bills-passed-by-montana-legislature/.

[84] TRO and Prelim. Inj. at 15, *Montanans Against Irresponsible Densification, LLC v. Montana,* No. DV 23–1248 (Mont. 18 Dist. Dec. 29, 2023).

[85] See Jason Ellsworth, *Guest View: Homelessness Rises as Courts Block Housing,* RAVALLI REPUBLIC (Feb. 10, 2024), https://ravallirepublic.com/opinion /column/guest-view-homelessness-rises-as-courts-block-housing/article_5a96ffda -c6a5-11ee-9adf-575e919582bb.html.

[86] See, for example, Charles Gardner (@oldurbanist), X (Dec. 31, 2023, 8:20pm), https://twitter.com/OldUrbanist/status/1741630442153935231 (arguing that the decision was rushed, lacked citations to case law, and was "highly vulner-able to being reversed on appeal") and Christian Britschgi, *Court's Wild Zoning Decision Blocks "Montana Miracle,"* REASON (Jan. 2, 2024), https://reason.com /2024/01/02/courts-wild-zoning-decision-blocks-montana-miracle/.

on their own property,"[87] gave wealthy single-family homeowners veto power over their neighbors' housing opportunities,[88] and sought to "tell[] people what they can and can't do with their private property."[89]

The Montana Supreme Court unanimously overturned the district court's grant of a preliminary injunction on September 3, 2024, finding that "[g]iven MAID's thin evidence of imminent harm, the District Court abused its discretion in finding that the balance of equities tipped in favor of preliminary relief".[90] MAID's attorney responded that the plaintiffs will now proceed to trial.[91] The battle between property owners who want to use their land for denser development and nearby owners who argue that they are exercising "inalienable rights of protecting their property" in seeking to prevent that development thus will continue––with implications for land use reform across the Big Sky state and the nation.[92]

III.   WHAT RIGHTS DO NEIGHBORS HAVE TO OBJECT TO CHANGES IN THE ZONING OF NEIGHBORING PROPERTIES?

Existing law generally rejects the notion that neighbors have a property right to protect the value of their homes against denser development. The courts have addressed such claims in a variety of circumstances—protest petitions, spot zoning, right-to-farm laws, and the invalidation of covenants—explored below. States and localities generally grant neighbors significant opportunities to be heard about zoning changes, even if their property itself is not directly subject to the change. Furthermore, legislatures and courts often grant

---

[87]   Josh Margolis, *Questions Linger After Judge Temporarily Blocks Housing Density Bills*, NBC Montana (Jan. 5, 2024), https://nbcmontana.com/news/local/questions-linger-after-judge-temporarily-blocks-housing-density-bills.

[88]   Daniel J. Brooks, *Housing Haves vs Housing Have-nots*, Billings Gazette (Jan. 7, 2024), https://billingsgazette.com/opinion/column/daniel-j-brooks-housing-haves-vs-housing-have-nots/article_3f3d3334-abe4-11ee-9912-1b7b1821dfff.html.

[89]   Jonathan Ambarian, *Judge Puts Hold on Montana Zoning-Related Laws*, Missoula Current (Jan. 3, 2024), https://missoulacurrent.com/montana-zoning-laws/.

[90]   *Montanans Against Irresponsible Densification, LLC v. State*, 2024 MT 200, 21 (Mont. 2024).

[91]   Eric Dietrich, *Supreme Court Lifts Lower Court Hold on Two Pro-construction Housing Laws*, Montana Free Press (Sept. 5, 2024), https://flatheadbeacon.com/2024/09/05/supreme-court-lifts-lower-court-hold-on-two-pro-construction-housing-laws/.

[92]   1st Amended Complaint, supra n. 76, at 41.

considerable weight to neighbors' interests when considering the validity of land use changes. But neighbors typically do not have a right to the continuation of any particular zoning restriction, which governments can change as the public interest requires.[93] Hints that some courts might be more solicitous of the interests of neighbors (as the trial court was in *Montanans Against Irresponsible Densification*), however, raise a concern that homeowners could successfully defeat land use reforms by wrapping themselves in the mantle of property rights.

A.   Protest Petitions: Neighbors Can Be Given Significant Power Over Changes in Zoning Restrictions

Zoning laws often give landowners a substantial say over neighboring land use in the form of protest petitions. Protest petition provisions in zoning ordinances require a supermajority of the jurisdiction's governing body to approve a rezoning application if a specific percentage of landowners within a certain distance of the rezoned land lodge a formal objection.[94] As of 2022, 20 states and many other local governments allow protest petitions,[95] which have been a feature of zoning processes since the nation adopted its first comprehensive zoning ordinance.[96]

Today, critics argue that protest petitions give small groups of neighbors the power to disrupt cities' efforts to promote additional housing options by allowing more density and a broader range of housing types.[97] As a result, some states have repealed or rolled back the availability of protest petitions.[98]

---

[93]   See Daniel R. Mandelker, *Spot Zoning: New Ideas for an Old Problem*, 48 URB. LAW. 737, 760–61 n.105 (2016) (listing relevant cases).

[94]   See Salim Furth and Kelcie McKinley, *Rezoning Protest Petitions Are Ripe for Reform*, MERCATUS CTR. GEORGE MASON UNIV., 4 (2022), https://www.mercatus.org/system/files/furth_and_mckinley_-_policy_brief_-_rezoning_protest _petitions_are_ripe_for_reform_-_v1.pdf. Note that local ordinances can also allow for protest petitions, but they generally cannot exceed the restrictions set by the state. See, for example, *City of Springfield v. Goff*, 918 S.W.2d 786 (Mo. 1996).

[95]   Furth and McKinley, *supra* n. 94, at 1.

[96]   See N.Y.C., N.Y., Board of Estimate & Apportionment, Building Zone Resolution (July 25, 1916) and David W. Owens, Protest Petitions, School of Government, University of North Carolina at Chapel Hill, April 2020, https:// www.sog.unc.edu/resources/legal-summaries/protest-petitions.

[97]   Furth and McKinley, *supra* n. 94, at 7.

[98]   See, for example, John Moritz, *NC Legislature Approves Bill to End Protest Petitions*, THE ASHEVILLE CITIZEN-TIMES, Jul. 15, 2015, https://www.citizen -times.com/story/news/2015/07/15/nc-legislature-approves-bill-end-protest-peti- tions/30200909/.

Courts, however, have generally upheld the constitutionality of protest provisions against arguments that they give legislative power to neighbors.[99] The Supreme Court of Massachusetts, for example, upheld its state's protest petition scheme, reasoning that it did not unconstitutionally delegate legislative power, violate equal protection, or unreasonably or arbitrarily grant neighbors too much power.[100] Courts have not held that neighbors have a property right to significant power over changes to the zoning of neighboring land, but have upheld the basic premise of protest provisions: that legislatures have flexibility to give neighbors significant input over changes in the rules governing adjacent land uses.

B. Spot Zoning: Neighbor's Interests Matter, But Aren't Determinative

The courts have crafted a number of protections for neighboring property owners under the rubric of "spot zoning" protections. The definition of spot zoning varies among the states, but generally refers to situations in which a small parcel of land is rezoned to impose less onerous density or use restrictions than the surrounding area, for the benefit of the developer-owner, to the detriment of neighboring properties, and without benefit to the public.[101] When

---

[99] See Michael Allen Wolf, 12 POWELL ON REAL PROPERTY § 79C.13 (2024) ("In general, the courts have sustained the constitutionality of protest provisions, rejecting arguments that they provide neighbors with a veto over governmental action or are an unlawful delegation of legislative authority").

[100] See *Trumper v. Quincy*, 358 Mass. 311, 313–14 (1970); see also *Farmer v. Meeker*, 63 N.J. Super. 56, 64 (Law Div. 1960) (upholding New Jersey's protest petition scheme on similar grounds); *Klein v. City of Shawnee*, 1998 U.S. Dist. LEXIS 6621 (D. Kan. 1998) (upholding Kansas's protest petition scheme against due process and equal protection challenges).

[101] See generally Robert Ellickson, Vicki Been, Roderick Hills and Christopher Serkin, LAND USE CONTROLS 361 (5th Ed. 2021) ("rezonings that single out particular landowners for purely private benefits to the detriment of the neighbors"); for a sampling of courts' definitions, *compare,* for example, *Griswold v. City of Homer*, 925 P.2d 1015 (Alaska 1996) ("The 'classic' definition of spot zoning is 'the process of singling out a small parcel of land for a use classification totally different from that of the surrounding area, for the benefit of the owner of such property and to the detriment of other owners. ....' [1 Robert M.] Anderson, [American Law of Zoning] §5.12, at 359 [(1986)]," with *Ani Creation, Inc. v. City of Myrtle Beach Bd. of Zoning Appeals*, 890 S.E.2d 748, 756 (S.C. 2023) ("There are two types of spot zoning. Traditional spot zoning occurs when a small parcel of land is singled out for a use classification different from that of the surrounding area, for the benefit of the parcel's owner(s) and to the detriment of others.... In

courts find that a rezoning is spot zoning, some invalidate the rezoning as a violation of substantive due process or equal protection or of the state zoning enabling law.[102] Others treat a finding of spot zoning as triggering more searching scrutiny of the rezoning, but will uphold the action if they find the rezoning justified after that scrutiny.[103] Many have criticized the spot zoning doctrine as a hodgepodge of different concerns that make it hard to predict how any particular case will be decided.[104]

Critically, "[s]ubstantive review of spot zoning starts with the rule that neighbors ... do not have a vested right in the continuation of existing zoning restrictions on neighboring property, which local governments are entitled to change."[105] In *Fallin v. Knox County Bd. of Comm'rs*, the Tennessee Supreme Court upheld a rezoning that would have allowed approximately 275 apartment units on land previously zoned for agricultural use. The neighbor claimed the rezoning would "change the existing character of the neighborhood" and "destroy the desirability and value of the property in the neighborhood,

---

contrast, reverse spot zoning occurs when a zoning ordinance restricts the use of a property when virtually all the property's adjoining neighbors are not subject to the use restriction"); see also *Konigsberg v. Board of Aldermen, 283 Conn.* 553, 591–92, 930 A.2d 1 (2007) ("'Spot zoning is the reclassification of a small area of land in such a manner as to disturb the tenor of the surrounding neighborhood' … [it] is often considered impermissible because it benefits an individual property owner at the expense of the community's interest in a harmonious, comprehensive zoning plan"). See also *Lime Lounge, LLC v. City of Des Moines*, 4 N.W.3d 642, 660 (Iowa 2024) (quoting *Jaffe v. City of Davenport*, 179 N.W.2d 554, 556 (Iowa 1970)) ("Spot zoning arises 'when a zoning ordinance creates a small island of property with restrictions on its use different from those imposed on the surrounding property'").

[102]   See, for example, *Rando v. Town of N. Attleborough*, 692 N.E.2d 544 (Mass. App. Ct. 1998).

[103]   See, example., *Save Sunset Beach Coal. v. City & County of Honolulu*, 78 P.3d 1, 9 (Haw. 2003) (upholding spot zoning in the absence of "[any] indication of arbitrariness or concern over whether rights have been properly safeguarded" and when "substantial public comment and deliberation took place").

[104]   See, for example, John Mixon and Kathleen McGlynn, *A New Zoning and Planning Metaphor: Chaos and Complexity Theory*, 42 HOUS. L. REV 1221, 1231 (2006) and Osborne M. Reynolds, Jr., *"Spot Zoning" — A Spot That Could Be Removed from the Law*, 48 WASH. U. J. URB. & CONTEMP. L. 117, 135–37 (1995).

[105]   Mandelker, *supra* n. 93, at 760; Kenneth Stahl, *Reliance in Land Use Law*, 2013 BRIGHAM YOUNG UNIV. L. REV 949, 960 and n. 25 (citing cases). See, for example., *Rodgers v. Vill. of Tarrytown*, 96 N.E.2d 731, 733 (N.Y. 1951) ("Changed or changing conditions call for changed plans, and persons who own property in a particular zone or use district enjoy no eternally vested right to that classification if the public interest demands otherwise").

including plaintiff's properties, for highly desirable single family residential purposes."[106] The court held, however, that evidence the community needed additional apartments, along with other factors, meant it could not conclude that the rezoning lacked a rational basis, and therefore could not be invalidated as spot zoning.[107] Even courts that employ a more searching standard than rational basis review when confronted with claims of spot zoning often find that a public purpose justifies a rezoning, even if neighboring property owners may suffer a reduction in the value of their land.[108]

In sum, the spot zoning doctrine considers harm to neighboring properties when determining whether a rezoning is spot zoning and in reviewing the validity of the rezoning. However, the courts do not view neighbors' interests in their property values as determinative.

C.   Neighbor's Takings Claims: Land Use Reforms that Reduce Constraints on Neighboring Land Uses Are Unlikely to be Considered a Taking Requiring Just Compensation

State overrides of local land use rules that protect the property values of single-family homeowners may be attacked as violating the rights of those homeowners by taking their property without paying just compensation. While courts are just beginning to grapple with such claims, they are likely to take several forms. First, homeowners may claim that by changing zoning regulations to allow uses that will decrease the value of their land and homes, the government is taking their property without paying just compensation.[109] Second, they may argue that the reforms take away their right to prevent nuisances—uses of neighboring lands that harm their use and enjoyment of their own land. Third,

---

[106]   656 S.W.2d 338, 340 (Tenn. 1983).

[107]   *Id.*

[108]   See, for example: *Smith v. City of Papillion*, 270 Neb. 607, 626 (2005) (evidence that neighbors might suffer a diminution in property values "does not establish that the rezoning is either illegal or arbitrary and capricious"); *Decuir v. Town of Marksville*, 426 So. 2d 766 (La. Ct. App. 3d Cir. 1983), writ denied, 430 So. 2d 83 (La. 1983) (need for apartments, among other factors, justifies the rezoning); and *City of Pharr v. Tippitt*, 616 S.W.2d 173 (Tex. 1981) (need for apartments and fact that areas zoned for multifamily use were already built up justified the rezoning of a 10-acre site).

[109]   Note that plaintiffs claiming that land use reforms constitute uncompensated takings may have some difficulty identifying whether the state or the local government is responsible for the taking, because many of the reforms involve states telling their localities to allow greater density or a wider range of uses, but giving the localities some discretion about exactly how to do that.

homeowners that hold covenants prohibiting other property owners from using their land for the purposes that the zoning reforms would now allow may claim that any zoning reform that invalidates, or prohibits enforcement of, their covenant constitutes a taking. Assessing the feasibility of these claims is difficult, given the "absolutely incoherent morass" of takings jurisprudence.[110]

1. Is a decrease in the value of neighbors' properties caused by land use reform a taking?

The first type of claim is unlikely to succeed. The first step in any takings analysis requires assessing whether the claimant is alleging the taking of a recognized property interest.[111] The owner of a home affected by a change in the jurisdiction's land use regime undoubtedly has a property interest in that home, and the land on which it sits.[112] But courts are skeptical about property owners' claims that they have a property interest in how a neighbor uses its property.[113]

Even assuming that a court were to find that a homeowner has an interest in preventing uses on another person's land that might affect the value of the homeowner's land and home, the effect that a change in the zoning of surrounding parcels may have on that interest would not qualify as a taking under any of the *per se* takings rules the United States Supreme Court has yet articulated. First, a zoning change involves no physical occupation of the neighboring land and therefore would not trigger the rule announced in *Loretto v. Teleprompter Manhattan CATV Corp.*[114] *Loretto* held that "permanent physical invasion" constitutes a taking "without regard to whether the action achieves an important public benefit or has only minimal economic impact on the owner."[115] Nor

---

[110]   Stahl, *Power of State Legislatures, supra* n. 75, at 609.

[111]   See, for example, *Air Pegasus of D.C., Inc. v. U.S.*, 424 F.3d 1206, 1212 (Fed. Cir. 2005) (quoting *Am. Pelagic Fishing Co. v. United States*, 379 F.3d 1363, 1372 (Fed. Cir. 2004), cert. denied, 545 U.S. 1139 (2005) ("First, as a threshold matter, the court must determine whether the claimant has established a property interest for purposes of the Fifth Amendment").

[112]   See, for example, John A. Humbach, *Law and a New Land Ethic*, 74 MINN. L. REV 339 (1989) and Mark W. Cordes, *Takings, Fairness, and Farmland Preservation*, 60 OHIO ST. L.J. 1033, 1069–70 (1999).

[113]   See, for example, *In re DJK, LLC WW & WS Permit*, 2024 VT 34, 41 (Vt. 2024) (neighbors contesting a wastewater system permit issued to a nearby landowner failed "to show that they were deprived of any cognizable property interest") and *Harms v. City of Sibley*, 702 N.W.2d 91, 101 (Iowa 2005) (rezoning that permitted the construction of a concrete plant near owners' property did not constitute a compensable governmental taking).

[114]   458 U.S. 419 (1982).

[115]   *Id.* at 434–35.

does a zoning change on neighboring land allow any "government-authorized invasions of property," such as the regulation allowing union organizers to enter an employer's property that the Court declared a *per se* taking of the owner's right to exclude in *Cedar Point Nursery v. Hassid*.[116]

The Supreme Court announced another *per se* rule in *Lucas v. South Carolina Coastal Commission*:[117] "when the owner of real property has been called upon to sacrifice all economically beneficial uses in the name of the common good, that is, to leave his property economically idle, he has suffered a taking."[118] As the Court recognized, the force of that rule depends in large part on how the property interest against which the loss of value is to be measured is defined.[119] *Lucas* involved two lots on which the owner hoped to build single-family houses. The Court noted:

> ... [W]e avoid this difficulty in the present case, since the "interest in land" that Lucas has pleaded (a fee simple interest) is an estate with a rich tradition of protection at common law, and since the [trial court] ... found that the Beachfront Management Act left each of Lucas's beachfront lots without economic value.[120]

The lots at issue were owned by Mr Lucas, and he was complaining about the effects land use restrictions had on the value of those lots. Even if a court were to extend the holding of *Lucas* to reach owners of already-built homes complaining about a diminution in the value of those homes allegedly caused by development on nearby properties, it is hard to imagine any case in which neighboring homes would be "render[ed] ... valueless" by development at greater density or with different kinds of homes following a zoning change.[121]

If neither the *Loretto* and *Cedar Point* physical invasion rules, nor the *Lucas* complete diminution in value rule, apply to the reduction in value that the claimant argues is a taking, the Court has said that the correct analysis involves the "ad hoc, factual inquiries" laid out in *Penn Central Transportation Co. v. New York City*.[122] There are three main factors in that inquiry: "The economic impact of the regulation on the claimant and, particularly, the extent to which the regulation has interfered with distinct investment-backed expectations are, of course, relevant considerations. So, too, is the character of the governmental

---

[116] 594 U.S. 139 (2021).
[117] 505 U.S. 1003 (1992).
[118] *Id.* at 1019.
[119] *Id.* at 1016 n. 7.
[120] *Id.*
[121] *Id.* at 1009 (quoting the trial court).
[122] *Penn Cent. Transp. Co. v. City of New York*, 438 U.S. 104 (1978).

action."[123] Professors Jim Krier and Stewart Sterk studied more than 2,000 cases decided under *Penn Central* between 1979 and the end of 2012 and determined that property owners are rarely successful in proving that a regulation has taken their property when the *Penn Central* factors are applied.[124] That record does not bode well for property owners demanding compensation for changes land use reforms render on neighboring properties, because their claims are particularly problematic under the *Penn Central* factors. And, as noted earlier, a court is unlikely to even reach the *Penn Central* analysis because takings cases generally concern a claimant's property interest based on restrictions placed on their own land, not on nearby land.

The minimal economic impact that land use reform might have on nearby properties is unlikely to justify a finding that the neighbor's property has been taken. While the case law is unclear about what kind or level of economic impact constitutes a taking,[125] courts have refused to find a taking for even

---

[123]   *Id.* at 124 (citations omitted). Penn Central's analytic framework, and the factors it considers most relevant, echo the approach the Court took in one of the earliest regulatory takings cases, *Pa. Coal Co. v. Mahon*, 260 U.S. 393, 415 (1922), in which Justice Holmes, writing for the majority, held that "The general rule at least is that while property may be regulated to a certain extent, if regulation goes too far it will be recognized as a taking." To determine whether the challenged regulation went too far, the Court considered such factors as "the extent of the diminution"; the nature and extent of the public interest; whether the regulation makes the use of the property "commercially impracticable," "abolishes" a property interest, or has "very nearly the same effect ... as appropriating or destroying it"; and whether the regulation secures "average reciprocity of advantage." *Id.* at 413–15.

[124]   James E. Krier and Stewart E. Sterk, *An Empirical Study of Implicit Takings*, 58 Wm. & Mary L. Rev 35 (2016). The difficulties the *Penn Central* ad hoc inquiry poses for property owners have generated enormous criticism. See, for example, Gideon Kanner, *Making Laws and Sausages: A Quarter-Century Retrospective on* Penn Central Transportation Co. v. City of New York, 13 Wm. & Mary Bill Rts. J. 653 (2005).

[125]   For discussions of the confusion courts have shown about the concept of economic impact and its relevance to the takings inquiry, see, for example: William W. Wade, *Theory and Misuse of Just Compensation for Income-Producing Property in Federal Courts: A View from Above the Forest*, 46 Tex. Envtl. L.J. 139, 140 (2016); Alan Romero, *Why is the Magnitude of a Regulation Relevant to Determining Whether it Takes Property?*, 30 J. Land Use & Envtl. L. 271; Steven J. Eagle, *Economic Impact in Regulatory Takings Law*, 19 Hastings W.-N.W. J. Envtl. L. & Pol'y 407 (2013); and William W. Wade, *Sources of Regulatory Takings Economic Confusion Subsequent to Penn Central*, 41 Envtl. L. Rep News & Analysis 10936, 10937 n. 11 (2011).

dramatic diminutions in value under *Penn Central*.[126] Empirical studies of the effect that multifamily housing has on the value of homes in surrounding single-family neighborhoods find relatively little, if any, impact.[127]

Nor is the interference with distinct investment-backed expectations prong of *Penn Central*[128] likely to help neighbors claiming that their property has been taken through state land use reforms that allow greater density or a wider range of uses on nearby land. It is certainly true, as Professor Stahl, among others, has noted, that "The idea that segregating single-family homes from other uses is necessary and desirable to protect single-family neighborhoods has been established since at least 1926 ...."[129] Further, single-family homeowners have exerted enormous political pressure to maintain their privileged position in the land use regime and have been remarkably successful at doing so at all levels of government.[130] Nevertheless, a long line of cases upholding zoning changes, such as the spot zoning cases discussed in part II.B, have made it clear that "[c]hanged or changing conditions call for changed plans, and persons who own

---

[126] See, for example, *Walcek v. U.S.*, 49 Fed. Cl. 248 (2001) (finding that a 60% diminution in value was not enough to consider a wetlands regulation to be a taking, and collecting cases considering the issue), aff'd, 303 F.3d 1349 (Fed. Cir., 2002).

[127] For recent studies exploring the effects additional new housing has on for-sale housing prices in the neighborhood, see: Santosh Anagol, Fernando V. Ferreira and Jonah M. Rexer, *Estimating the Economic Value of Zoning Reform: Evidence from Sao Paulo* (2024), conditional acceptance, AM. ECON. J.: ECON. (finding that a zoning reform in São Paulo resulted in a 0.5% reduction in neighborhood housing prices); and Christian A. Nygaard, George Galster and Stephen Glackin, *The Size and Spatial Extent of Neighborhood Price Impacts of Infill Development: Scale Matters?*, 69 J. REAL EST. FIN. & ECON. 277 (2024), https://doi.org/10.100//s11146 -022-09916-x (finding that new infill housing developments that generate a net increase of four or fewer dwellings typically result in an appreciation in the average sales prices of nearby dwellings, while moderate and large-scale developments generate negative price effects for apartments and townhouses, but not the dominant detached house submarket); and Mats Wilhelmsson, *Evaluating the Price Effects of Multifamily and Single-Family Housing Construction on Surrounding Single-Family Homes in Stockholm: A Difference-in-Difference Analysis*, 16 INT'L J. HOUSING MARKET & ANALYSIS 103 (2023) (finding that new multifamily construction in Stockholm had no effect on the prices of nearby single-family homes, while new single-family homes reduced the sales prices of surrounding homes).

[128] Then-Justice Rehnquist described the factor as interference with "reasonable investment-backed expectations" in *Kaiser Aetna v. United States*, 444 U.S. 164, 175 (1979), and that is the current formulation.

[129] Stahl, *Power of State Legislatures*, supra n. 75, at 617.

[130] Fischel, *supra* n. 14.

property in a particular zone or use district enjoy no eternally vested right to that classification if the public interest demands otherwise."[131] Homeowners buy into a system of intensive regulation that is subject to change.[132]

That said, it is conceivable that the Supreme Court could hold that homeowners in low-density neighborhoods have reasonable expectations against regulatory change. The Supreme Court has both bought into and fed the notion that zoning exists primarily to protect single-family residential uses. Its 1926 opinion upheld zoning after characterizing apartment houses as "mere parasite[s], constructed in order to take advantage of the open spaces and attractive surroundings created by the residential character of the district" that "come very near to being nuisances." [133] Further, less than fifty years ago, the Court upheld zoning meant to limit the occupancy of single-family homes to "traditional" families or not more than two unrelated individuals by noting that:

> A quiet place where yards are wide, people few, and motor vehicles restricted are legitimate guidelines in a land-use project addressed to family needs. ... The police power is not confined to elimination of filth, stench, and unhealthy places. It is

---

[131]   *Rodgers, supra* n. 105, at 733.

[132]   For attempts to provide guidance on when the courts will consider an expectation that things won't change to be reasonable, see, for example, J. David Breemer, *Playing the Expectations Game: When Are Investment-Backed Land Use Expectations (Un)reasonable in State Courts?*, 38 URB. LAW. 81, 110 (2006).

[133]   *Vill. of Euclid, Ohio v. Ambler Realty Co.*, 272 U.S. 365, 394–95 (1926) ("With particular reference to apartment houses, it is pointed out that the development of detached house sections is greatly retarded by the coming of apartment houses, which has sometimes resulted in destroying the entire section for private house purposes; that in such sections very often the apartment house is a mere parasite, constructed in order to take advantage of the open spaces and attractive surroundings created by the residential character of the district. Moreover, the coming of one apartment house is followed by others, interfering by their height and bulk with the free circulation of air and monopolizing the rays of the sun which otherwise would fall upon the smaller homes, and bringing, as their necessary accompaniments, the disturbing noises incident to increased traffic and business, and the occupation, by means of moving and parked automobiles, of larger portions of the streets, thus detracting from their safety and depriving children of the privilege of quiet and open spaces for play, enjoyed by those in more favored localities—until, finally, the residential character of the neighborhood and its desirability as a place of detached residences are utterly destroyed. Under these circumstances, apartment houses, which in a different environment would be not only entirely unobjectionable but highly desirable, come very near to being nuisances.")

ample to lay out zones where family values, youth values, and the blessings of quiet seclusion and clean air make the area a sanctuary for people.[134]

At the same time, however, the *Euclid* court noted that:

> Until recent years, urban life was comparatively simple; but, with the great increase and concentration of population, problems have developed, and constantly are developing, which require, and will continue to require, additional restrictions in respect of the use and occupation of private lands in urban communities. Regulations, the wisdom, necessity, and validity of which, as applied to existing conditions, are so apparent that they are now uniformly sustained, a century ago, or even half a century ago, probably would have been rejected as arbitrary and oppressive ... . And in this there is no inconsistency, for, while the meaning of constitutional guarantees never varies, the scope of their application must expand or contract to meet the new and different conditions which are constantly coming within the field of their operation. In a changing world it is impossible that it should be otherwise.[135]

Society's expectations about low-density zoning have evolved[136]— homes in sprawling, low-density subdivisions rife with manicured lawns have come under increasing scrutiny for their racially exclusionary origins and their continued effects.[137] Critics also point to impacts on greenhouse gas emissions, habitat, and biodiversity, as well as costs imposed on renters and prospective

---

[134]   *Vill. of Belle Terre v. Boraas*, 416 U.S. 1, 9 (1974).

[135]   Euclid, 272 U.S. at 386–87.

[136]   See Christopher Serkin, *What Property Does*, 75 VAND. L. REV. 891 (2022), for a discussion about how the notion of reasonable expectations does and should reflect that property is a nexus of competing and dynamic reliance interests that can change over time.

[137]   The Supreme Court has recognized the racial origins and implications of many of our land use regulations. See, for example, *Texas Dep't of Hous. & Cmty. Affs. v. Inclusive Communities Project, Inc.*, 576 U.S. 519, 528–30 (2015) ("*De jure* residential segregation by race was declared unconstitutional almost a century ago, but its vestiges remain today, intertwined with the country's economic and social life."). See also: Katherine Levine Einstein, *The Privileged Few: How Exclusionary Zoning Amplifies the Advantaged and Blocks New Housing—and What We Can Do About It*, 57 URB. AFFAIRS REV. 252 (2019); Michael Manville, Paavo Monkkonen and Michael Lewis, *It's Time to End Single-Family Zoning*, 86 J. OF THE AMER. PLANNING ASS'N 106, 107 (2022); Matthew Resseger, *The Impact of Land Use Regulation on Racial Segregation: Evidence from Massachusetts Zoning Borders,* Mercatus Research Paper (2022), https://ssrn.com/abstract=4244120; David Schleicher, *Exclusionary Zoning's Confused Defenders,* 2021 Wis. L. Rev 1315, 1323–33; Trounstine, *supra* n. 3; and Xi Yang, *Land Use Regulations and Urban Growth of African Americans*, 35 ECON. DEV. Q. 35 (2021).

homebuyers.[138] The prevalence of battles over proposals for new development illustrates that society has increasing doubts about the wisdom of the existing land use system and that those who have benefited from the existing system understand that the status quo is not guaranteed.[139]

Penn Central's third factor—the character of the government's action—is perhaps the most ambiguous of the three factors (which is a fairly high bar given the vagueness of the first two factors).[140] The original purpose of the factor was probably to address regulations that required actual physical occupancy of the property, but that concern has largely been supplanted by the Court's decisions in *Loretto* and *Cedar Point*. Other courts have used the factor to explore whether the regulation would be justified under nuisance law.[141] As noted above, apartment houses have not been considered nuisances, despite the *Euclid* court's statement that they could be "near nuisances." Still, other courts use the factor to consider the strength of the government's interest in the regulation.[142] Given the long history of deference to the goals state and local governments have advanced for zoning regulations, and the considerable body of evidence about the need for more housing in the United States, it is hard to imagine that the goal of allowing more housing to be built in neighborhoods already well served by infrastructure and amenities would count against the land use reforms being adopted across the country.

There is no getting around the fact that *Penn Central*'s three factors are ambiguous (at best), and it is unclear whether the overall inquiry is a balancing test, a "one strike, you're out" analysis, or just a requirement that courts take full measure of the equities. But claimants rarely win under *Penn Central*, even when they are asserting that a restriction on their own land reduced its value, much less when they are arguing that they have a property interest in

---

[138]   Yonah Freemark, *Zoning Change: Upzonings, Downzonings, and Their Impacts on Residential Construction, Housing Costs, and Neighborhood Demographics*, 38 J. of Plan. Lit. 548 (2023) (reviewing literature); Jaehee Song, *The Effects of Residential Zoning in U.S. Housing Markets* (2024), https://ssrn.com/abstract=3996483.

[139]   See Vicki Been, *City NIMBYs*, 33 J. LAND USE & ENVTL. L. 217 (2018).

[140]   See Thomas W. Merrill, *The Character of the Governmental Action*, 36 VT. L. REV. 649 (2012) and Mark Fenster, *The Stubborn Incoherence of Regulatory Takings*, 28 STAN. ENVTL. L.J. 525 (2009).

[141]   See, for example, Steven J. Eagle, *Character of the Governmental Action*, in Takings Law: Past, Present, and Future, SJ052 ALI-ABA 459 (2004).

[142]   See, for example., *Keystone Bituminous Coal Ass'n v. DeBenedictis*, 480 U.S. 470, 485 (1987) ("[T]he character of the governmental action involved here leans heavily against finding a taking; the Commonwealth of Pennsylvania has acted to arrest what it perceives to be a significant threat to the common welfare").

preventing regulation that would allow neighboring landowners to use their property in a way that the government can show serves the public interest. A hard look at the claimants' probable arguments suggests that existing home-owners are unlikely to win a claim that their property has been taken by land use regulations that allow denser development or a wider range of housing types nearby.

2. Have the neighbors' rights to prevent a nuisance been taken?

Neighboring property owners are also unlikely to succeed in arguing that their right to prevent a nuisance has been taken. Activity on neighboring property that interferes with an owner's use and enjoyment of a single-family home may give that owner a cause of action for nuisance.[143] But land use reforms that allow additional density or a wider range of uses near single-family homes do not abrogate that right. No one loses a right to sue for nuisance through the land use reforms being adopted around the country. The homeowner can still litigate and seek to prove that the neighboring land use, even though permitted by zoning, is a nuisance. Most such cases do not succeed because courts determine whether something is a nuisance by looking at the same costs and benefits of the activity, neighborhood context, and other factors, as zoning offi-cials typically consider in determining how neighboring properties should be zoned.[144] Further, as Jon Goldberg has pointed out, "activities whose only ill

---

[143] See, for exampleL: *Prah v. Maretti*, 321 N.W.2d 182 (Wisc. 1982); *Boomer v. Atlantic Cement Co.*, 257 N.E.2d 870 (N.Y. 1970); and *Campbell v. Seaman*, 63 N.Y. 568, 577 (1896).

[144] See Robert C. Ellickson, *Can an Apartment Building be a Nuisance?*, 10 PROP. RIGHTS J. 57, 59 nn. 14 & 15 (2021) (with only one exception, no courts in the United States have found the mere fact of an apartment building to constitute a nuisance). Indeed, Maureen Brady has shown that historically "although some tenements had faced judicial scrutiny for poor sanitation conditions that may well have led to nuisance-generating smells, sounds, or substances, claims that adjoin-ing well-built apartments constituted a nuisance because they would block light or airflow or cause some devaluation simply did not succeed." Maureen E. Brady, *Turning Neighbors into Nuisances*, 134 HARV. L. REV 1609, 1644 (2021) (citations omitted). Further, the courts were reluctant to interpret deed restrictions and "nui-sance covenants" that prohibited "injurious" or "offensive" uses to prohibit apart-ments. *Id.* at 1644–53. Brady argues that zoning regulation became the focus of efforts to separate single-family residential uses from other uses (and their users), in part to get around those roadblocks. *Id.* Putting land to uses sanctioned by zon-ing is also unlikely to be considered a nuisance because, as Christopher Essert has argued: "[T]o determine whether or not defendant is liable in nuisance is not sim-ply about comparing the costs or benefits of the two activities. Rather, it is a fun-damentally correlative inquiry into the question whether defendant, in performing

effects are to reduce the value or profitability of another's land are not private nuisances (even though lost value or profits often provides the main head of damages in a successful nuisance action)."[145]

Even where changes in the law have completely eliminated a right to sue for nuisance that landowners had enjoyed in the past, the courts have generally refused to find the loss of the nuisance cause of action to be a taking. The history of right-to-farm laws best illustrates how the courts have evaluated such claims. Right-to-farm laws, which exist in all 50 states, serve to protect agricultural interests against residential neighbors.[146] While these laws vary in important ways,[147] they usually block nuisance claims against farms for smells, noise, and unsightliness.[148] In many states, homeowners have alleged that these laws create an unconstitutional taking by foreclosing their right to bring a nuisance claim. The cases have largely been unsuccessful.[149]

In most states, right-to-farm laws are an attempt to codify the coming-to-the-nuisance doctrine by protecting existing farms against complaints

---

this activity with these effects on plaintiff's land, is unreasonably interfering with plaintiff's control over her own property. And in performing this inquiry into reasonableness, the court is also determining what it means to own property." Christopher Essert, *Nuisance and the Normative Boundaries of Ownership*, 52 TULSA L. REV 85, 107 (2016).

[145] John C.P. Goldberg, *On Being a Nuisance*, 99 N.Y.U. L. REV 864, 878 (2024); see also John Copeland Nagle, *Moral Nuisances*, 50 EMORY L.J. 265, 299 (2001) ("A loss of property value alone cannot justify a nuisance claim"); Michael D. Riseberg, *Exhuming the Funeral Home Cases: Proposing a Private Nuisance Action Based on the Mental Anguish Caused by Pollution*, 21 ENVTL. AFF. 557, 566 (1994) ("[T]he courts have long recognized that a depreciation in property value, without other harm, does not constitute an actionable interference with the use and enjoyment of property"); 1 Horace G. Wood, A PRACTICAL TREATISE ON THE LAW OF NUISANCES IN THEIR VARIOUS FORMS; INCLUDING REMEDIES THEREFOR AT LAW AND IN EQUITY 4–5 (3d ed. 1893).

[146] See Terence J. Centner, *Governments and Unconstitutional Takings: When Do Right-to-Farm Laws Go Too Far?*, 33 B.C. ENVTL. AFF. L. REV. 87, 87 (2006).

[147] See Jesse J. Richardson, Jr. and Theodore A. Feitshans, *Nuisance Revisited After Buchanan and Bormann*, 5 Drake J. AGRIC. L. 121, 128 (2000) (separating right-to-farm laws into six categories).

[148] See Adam Van Buskirk, Note, *Right-to-Farm Laws as "Takings" in Light of Bormann v. Board of Supervisors and Moon v. North Idaho Farmers Association*, II ALB. L. ENVTL. OUTLOOK 169, 170 (2006).

[149] See, for example, *Lindsey v. DeGroot*, 898 N.E.2d 1251, 1259 (Ind. Ct. App. 2009); *Moon v. North Idaho Farmers Ass'n*, 140 Idaho 536 (2004); *Barrera v. Hondo Creek Cattle Co.*, 132 S.W.3d 544 (Tex. App. 2004).

by newcomers.[150] In these states, courts are unconvinced by takings claims because the newcomers knew or should have known that they were buying next to an existing farm, and they still have recourse in case of new neighboring land uses.[151]

A few states' right-to-farm laws go further by protecting farms against nuisance suits even if their operations expand or change, so that there is no argument that the neighboring homeowner "came to the nuisance."[152] For example, Iowa "allows for protection of farming operations from nuisance suits, no matter the day the operation started, nor if such operations had expanded."[153] As a result, Iowa's Supreme Court sparked considerable debate when it struck down this right-to-farm law as a violation of the Takings Clause in the 1998 case of *Bormann v. Bd. of Supervisors*.[154] The court reasoned that the immunity the law extended gave a farm an easement against the neighboring homeowners' property, which the court held was a taking of the neighbors' property under either the USA or the Iowa constitutions.[155]

---

[150] Joseph Malanson, Note, *Returning Right-to-Farm Laws to Their Roots*, 97 WASH. U. L. REV 1577, 1581 (2020); see also *Riddle v. Lanser*, 421 P.3d 35, 46 (Alaska 2018) ("Right to Farm Acts address the problem caused by the urbanization of farming areas").

[151] See generally Jennifer L. Beidel, Comment, *Pennsylvania's Right-to-Farm Law: A Relief for Farmers or an Unconstitutional Taking?*, 110 PENN ST. L. REV 163 (2005) (discussing how the different structures of right-to-farm laws may impact their constitutionality). See also *Barrera*, 132 S.W.3d at 547 (rejecting a takings claim against a Texas law that bars nuisance suits against agricultural operations in existence for a year or more, so long as conditions there have been substantially unchanged); *Labrayere v. Bohr Farms, LLC*, 458 S.W.3d 319, 326 (Mo. 2015) (denying a takings claim against a Missouri law that limited nuisance liability for farmers) and *Overgaard v. Rock Cnty. Bd. of Comm'rs*, 2003 WL 21744235 (D. Minn. 2003) (ruling that imposing a 2-year window after which an agricultural operation cannot be sued for nuisance is not an unconstitutional taking).

[152] See, for example, Ind. Code Ann. § 32-30-6-9 (2024); see also *Lindsey*, 898 N.E.2d at 1257 (upholding an Indiana law that bars nuisance claims against existing agricultural operations, even when those operations make changes to the type of agriculture, ownership, size, technology, and more).

[153] Beau R. Morgan, Note, *Iowa and Right to Farm: An Analysis of the Constitutionality of Right to Farm Statutes Across the United States*, 53 CREIGHTON L. REV. 623, 637 (2020).

[154] 584 N.W.2d 309, 321 (Iowa 1998), cert. denied sub nom. *Girres v. Bormann*, 119 S. Ct. 1096 (1999).

[155] *Bormann v. Bd. of Supervisors*, 584 N.W.2d 309, 321 (Iowa 1998) (*en banc*), cert. denied sub nom. *Girres v. Bormann*, 119 S. Ct. 1096 (1999). See also *Gacke v. Pork Xtra, L.L.C.*, 684 N.W.2d 168 (Iowa 2004) (setting out a three-part test

The logic of *Bormann* should not apply to neighbors claiming that zoning changes eliminated their right to prevent a nuisance.[156] As noted earlier, these claimants still have the right to bring a nuisance action (which the right-to-farm laws explicitly deny). Further, if *Bormann's* logic were extended—if zoning were defined as creating an easement over neighboring property[157]—current property owners could claim a taking against virtually any governmental decision to change its zoning.[158]

Not surprisingly, however, property owners tried to argue that *Bormann* prevents zoning changes. But in *Harms v. City of Sibley*, the Iowa Supreme Court rejected that tactic.[159] Landowners Kenneth and Myrna Harms claimed that the local government had violated the Takings Clause by rezoning neighboring land to allow for a ready-mix plant, which caused a nuisance that decreased their property values.[160] The district court ruled for the plaintiffs under the logic of *Bormann*, but the Iowa Supreme Court reversed and went to great lengths to differentiate the cases.[161] It noted that in *Bormann*, the right-to-farm law represented direct government action against the plaintiffs' property right—the right to protect the use and enjoyment of their property through nuisance litigation.[162] However, the court reasoned, the construction of the ready-mix plant in *Harms* was not the *direct* consequence of government action. Instead, it was the plant owner who "decided, subject to the ordinance, where the plant was to be built and how it would be operated."[163] While some called the Iowa Supreme Court's reasoning "not entirely convincing," the decision recognized that removing a nuisance cause of action that property owners had enjoyed is different from allowing homeowners to claim a property inter-

---

to evaluate whether the right-to-farm statute constituted a taking); *Honomichl v. Valley View Swine, L.L.C.*, 914 N.W.2d 223 (Iowa 2018) (rejecting calls to modify *Gacke*); and *Garrison v. New Fashion Pork LLP*, 977 N.W.2d 67 (Iowa 2022) (modifying *Gacke*).
[156] See Jennifer L. Beidel, Comment, *Pennsylvania's Right-to-Farm Law: A Relief for Farmers or an Unconstitutional Taking?*, 110 PENN ST. L. REV 163, 178 (2005) (explaining the "slippery slope" that *Bormann* presents).
[157] *Cf. Fontainebleau Hotel Corp. v. Forty-Five Twenty-Five, Inc.*, 114 So.2d 357 (Fla. Dist. Ct. App. 1959); see also *Boardman v. Davis*, 3 N.W.2d 608, 610 (Iowa 1942) (holding that although a zoning ordinance can "lay an uncompensated burden" on property owners, it does not "constitute an easement upon the property").
[158] Beidel, *supra* n. 156.
[159] 702 N.W.2d 91, 95 (Iowa 2005).
[160] *Id.* at 93–95.
[161] *Id.* at 101.
[162] *Id.* at 102.
[163] *Id.* at 101.

est in being free from any effect that subsequent zoning decisions on nearby lands might have on the use and enjoyment of their land.[164]

It must also be emphasized that *Bormann* itself is an outlier among the states.[165] Subsequent cases in Iowa have cabined the holding somewhat, and indicated that *Bormann* may only apply to the Iowa takings clause and not the federal takings clause.[166] Furthermore, many other states have upheld the constitutionality of right-to-farm laws of various types.[167] Even the courts in some states with right-to-farm laws that exceed the coming-to-the-nuisance doctrine and impart additional protections for farms have upheld the laws against takings challenges.[168] For example, in a recent Indiana case, a rural farm switched from growing crops to raising hogs.[169] This caused neighbors' property values to drop by up to 60%.[170] Nonetheless, the court held that the Indiana right-to-farm law—which precludes a nuisance claim—was not a taking because "the Plaintiffs have not been deprived of all or substantially all economic or productive use of their properties."[171]

3. Have the neighbors' restrictive covenants been taken?

Led by California, states are passing laws, or being urged to do so, that override private covenants, conditions, and restrictions (CCRs) enforced by Homeowners Associations (HOAs).[172] Historically, state legislatures and courts have invalidated CCRs on particular issues that the state considered contrary to public policy.[173] For example, multiple states overrode private covenants

---

[164] Stahl, *Power of State Legislatures, supra* n. 75, at 607 n.164.

[165] See *Garrison v. New Fashion Pork LLP*, 977 N.W.2d 67, 78–79 (2022).

[166] See Terence J. Centner, *Governments and Unconstitutional Takings: When Do Right-to-Farm Laws Go Too Far?*, 33 B.C. ENVTL. AFF. L. REV 87, 119–20 (2006); *Garrison, supra* n. 165, at 81.

[167] See, for example, *Lindsey v. DeGroot*, 898 N.E.2d 1251, 1257–59 (Ind. Ct. App. 2009); *Moon v. N. Idaho Farmers Ass'n*, 96 P.3d 637, 642–46 (Idaho 2004); *Barrera v. Hondo Creek Cattle Co.*, 132 S.W.3d 544, 549 (Tex. App. 2004).

[168] See Ginger Pinkerton, Note, *Sanctioning Nuisance: How the Modern Right to Farm Impermissibly Burdens Neighbors*, 72 CASE W. RES. 141, 156 (2021); see also *Moon*, 96 P.3d, at 642–46 (upholding a law providing immunity from nuisance and trespass claims over crop residue burning because, despite the regulatory taking, owners had not been deprived of all economic use of their land).

[169] *Himsel v. Himsel*, 122 N.E.3d 935, 939 (Ind. Ct. App. 2019).

[170] *Id.* at 947.

[171] *Id.*

[172] See generally Stahl, *Power of State Legislatures, supra* n. 75.

[173] See Paul Boudreaux, *Homes, Rights, and Private Communities*, 20 U. FLA. J.L. & PUB. POL'Y 479, 482 (2009) (discussing "hit-and-miss regulation by subject matter" on topics such as pet prohibitions or lawn maintenance).

which prohibited property owners from drying laundry outside.[174] Others have
overridden private covenants that prohibit property from being used for group
homes.[175] The California legislature has authorized a wide variety of property uses, regardless of any private restrictions, including "small residential
care facilities for the elderly, small child day care facilities, employee housing
for six or fewer persons ... and employee housing for up to 36 beds in group
quarters or 12 units for single-family or households when located in an agricultural area".[176] At least one court has invalidated CCRs that prohibit political
signs,[177] and a number of legislatures have overridden CCRs prohibiting the
display of the American flag.[178] On the other hand, the California Supreme
Court refused to override covenants that prohibit homeowners from keeping
pets, reasoning that "courts must enforce the restriction unless the challenger
can show that the restriction is unreasonable because it is arbitrary, violates a
fundamental public policy, or imposes burdens on the use of the affected property that substantially outweigh the restriction's benefits."[179]

The case law is not well developed about when a legislature can invalidate,
or a court can refuse to enforce, covenants because they conflict with public
policy.[180] Accordingly, despite the urgency of the housing affordability crisis,

---

[174]   See Martha Neil, *19 "Right to Dry" States Outlaw Clothesline Bans; Is
Yours Among Them?*, ABA J., (Aug. 14, 2013) https://www.abajournal.com/news/
article/20_right_to_dry_states_outlaw_clothesline_bans_is_yours_among_them.
[175]   See Dirk Hubbard, *Group Homes and Restrictive Covenants*, 57 UMKC L.
REV 135, 140 (1988) (collecting cases).
[176]   Karl E. Geier, *Statutory Overrides of "Restrictive Covenants" and Other
Private Land Use Controls: The Accelerating Trend Towards Legislative
Overwriting of Contractual Controls of the Use and Development of Real Property*,
32 No. 4 Miller & Starr, REAL ESTATE NEWSALERT NL 1 (citations omitted).
[177]   See, for example, *Mazdabrook Commons Homeowners' Ass'n v. Khan*, 210
N.J. 482 (2012) (HOA's prohibition on all political signs violated the unit owner's
right to free speech under the state's expansive constitution). A number of courts,
however, have refused to hold that a court's enforcement of a CCR limiting free
speech would constitute state action and thereby implicate the First Amendment's
Free Speech Clause, see, for example, *Loren v. Sasser*, 309 F.3d 1296 (11th
Cir. 2002).
[178]   *Local Government Law — Homeowner Association Regulation — Illinois
Act Prevents Homeowner and Condominium Associations from Interfering with
Residents' Ability to Fly American and Military Flags. — Act of Aug. 8, 2003*, 117
HARV. L. REV. 2047 (2004).
[179]   *Nahrstedt v. Lakeside Vill. Condo. Assn.*, 878 P.2d 1275, 1292 (CA 1994).
[180]   See Nicole Stelle Garnett and Patrick E. Reidy, C.S.C., *Religious Covenants*,
74 FLA. L. REV. 821, 878 (2022) (observing that the scope of the "public policy"
limitation on the enforceability of covenants "does not appear to be capacious").

a court could decline to find that CCRs prohibiting denser housing development violate public policy. But many of the uses that legislatures have overridden or courts have refused to enforce, such as group homes, daycare facilities, and employee housing, posed challenges for communities quite similar to the problems stemming from the housing supply gap many areas of the country now face.

Assuming that a state has the power to override CCRs that are contrary to the public interest, it is unlikely that those overrides will be considered a taking requiring just compensation.[181] As noted above, courts are generally skeptical of takings claims that focus on regulations regarding the claimant's neighbors' land.[182] But most courts find that covenants themselves are a property right, separate and apart from the land and home the covenant protects.[183] The holder of a covenant could therefore claim, similar to the claims of neighbors deprived of their right to sue for nuisances caused by nearby farms, that the state override took the covenant.

In California, at least one appellate decision suggests that courts will reject takings claims arising from legislative overrides of covenants based on the same theory of state action that the Iowa Supreme Court applied in *Harms v. City of Sibley*, discussed above. Under that theory, courts would hold that the

---

[181] See: Gerald Korngold, *Repealing Single-Family Zoning Is Not Enough: A Proposal for Removing Existing Parallel Private Covenants for Violating Public Policy*, 89 Mo. L. Rev. 1 (2024), https://scholarship.law.missouri.edu/cgi/viewcontent.cgi?article=4650&context=mlr; Stahl, *Power of State Legislatures, supra* n. 75; Mark D. Savin and Kinnon W. Williams, *The Taking of Restrictive Covenants and Just Compensation*, CD002 ALI-CLE 953 (2022); Geier, *supra* n. 176, at 250; and Thomas F. Guernsey, *The Mentally Retarded and Private Restrictive Covenants*, 25 Wm. & Mary L. Rev 421, 442–61 (1983). A separate line of inquiry is whether state overrides of covenants could be considered a violation of the contracts clause. See, for example: Maureen E. Brady, *Covenants and the Contracts Clause*, VA Envt'l L.J. (forthcoming 2025); Korngold, *supra*; and Stahl, *Power of State Legislatures, supra* n. 75.

[182] Stahl, *Power of State Legislatures, supra* n. 75, at 607 (explaining that "[t]he idea that one could have a property right in how a neighbor uses their land, and therefore that your property could be 'taken' simply because your neighbor can use their property in a way you dislike, might seem absurd").

[183] See Korngold, *supra* n. 181, at 22–23 & nn. 113–14 (collecting cases and commentary); *Flynn v. New York, W. & B. Ry. Co.*, 218 N.Y. 140, 147 (1916) ("something in the nature of an easement of privacy over another's land may be acquired by covenant in order that one may live apart from the disagreeable sights and sounds of business if one desires, and if that right has a value and ... [the government violates it] by building on the restricted land, it is difficult to conceive why compensation should not follow").

government's override of the covenant is not the direct cause of any harm. In *Barrett v. Dawson*, a California appellate court upheld a state law that voided covenants restricting family daycare homes.[184] The court rejected the neighbors' taking claim, reasoning that there was no state action impacting their property directly.[185] Further, the court disagreed with the "proposition that the *absence* of the enforcement of a particular restrictive covenant against *another* owner's property amounts to a governmental expropriation of one's own property."[186] The court accordingly declined to assess the law under a regulatory takings analysis.[187]

Even if a court conducts a Takings Clause analysis, plaintiffs would face an uphill battle. An override allowing ADUs or denser housing types would not qualify as a physical invasion—nothing in the legislative override forces the covenant holder to suffer a physical intrusion on their own land, and the covenant itself is not capable of being physically occupied.[188] The override may

---

[184]   71 Cal. Rptr. 2d 899, 900 (Ct. App. 1998).

[185]   *Id.* at 902.

[186]   *Id.*

[187]   *Id.* at 900. *Barrett* proceeded to consider the plaintiffs' claim that the law violated the contracts clause. The court stated that, "the right of the neighbors to enforce a restrictive covenant limiting the use of neighboring property is clearly contractual." *Id.* at 902. Nonetheless, it rejected the contracts clause claim by declaring that ensuring adequate daycare is sufficient public policy to justify the override. See also *Hall v. Butte Home Health, Inc.*, 70 CAL. RPTR. 2d 246, 247 (Ct. App. 1997) (upholding a state law voiding covenants that restricted group homes for the disabled because there was "a compelling governmental interest in providing adequate housing for the disabled" that outweighed the plaintiffs' interests in "remaining free of insubstantial interferences with their property rights").

[188]   See *Loretto v. Teleprompter Manhattan CATV Corp.*, 458 U.S. 419 (1982); *Cedar Point Nursery v. Hassid*, 594 U.S. 139 (2021). Professor Korngold has raised the possibility that courts might find that a covenant has been physically invaded, even though it is a legal right, not a physical thing, and thus can't be physically "invaded," citing a decision of the Kansas Supreme Court, *Creegan v. State*, 391 P.3d 36 (Kan. 2017). *Creegan* reasoned that the government had "vaporized" the plaintiff's property right by continually violating the covenant, which was equivalent to a physical invasion. Korngold, *supra* n. 181, at 30–34. The *Creegan* court's reasoning is remarkably unhelpful in introducing yet another ambiguous term into the already muddy takings inquiry. See also *Forest View Company v. Town of Monument*, 464 P.3d 774, 779 (Colo. 2020) (a restrictive covenant can't be physically occupied). The government's continued violation of the covenant at issue in *Creegan* destroyed all its value, which (at most) is a *per se* taking under *Lucas*. That much more straightforward approach recognizes that *Lucas* contains an inherent limitation on title exception that a *Loretto* or *Cedar Point* analysis misses.

be found to destroy the entire value of the covenant, however, triggering the *Lucas* analysis.[189] As *Lucas* noted, however, that will depend upon what the court considers to be the boundaries of the property interest. Given that a covenant is inseparable from the land which it is meant to protect, it may be that courts will not consider each individual covenant, or even the entire package of covenants relevant to the land, to be the property against which diminution in value should be measured. Instead, the court may view the CCR as simply one stick in the bundle of rights that make up the homeowner's property, along with many others that give the homeowner rights to possess, use, and transfer the home and the land on which it sits.[190]

Further, *Lucas* held that even a complete destruction of a property interest does not constitute a taking if it simply codifies a limitation that "inhere[s] in the title itself, in the restrictions that background principles of the State's law of property and nuisance already place upon land ownership."[191] The case law provides little help in determining what kinds of limitations "inhere in the title itself." The history of the law's gradual recognition of covenants shows, however, that legislatures and judges have always understood that covenants pose a danger of becoming an obstacle to progress as times change, and have overridden covenants if they are contrary to public policy.[192] As Professor Stahl suggests, "a reasonable landowner would anticipate that if housing supply and affordability reached the crisis level they have in many states today, CCRs [covenants] limiting the residential use of nearby properties would have to yield to urgent public policy considerations."[193]

Lucas accordingly is likely inapplicable because an override of a covenant is not a complete diminution in the value of the property interest and because

---

[189]   See: *Lucas v. California Coastal Commission*, 505 U.S. 1003, 1016 n. 7 (1992); *Murr v. Wisconsin*, 582 U.S. 383 (2017); *Tahoe-Sierra Preservation Council, Inc. v. Tahoe Regional Planning Agency*, 535 U.S. 302 (2002); Lynda L. Butler, *Murr v. Wisconsin and the Inherent Limits of Regulatory Takings*, 47 FLA. STATE. UNIV. L. REV. 99 (2019); David Dana, *Why Do We Have the Parcel-as-a-Whole Rule?*, 39 VT. L. REV. 617 (2015); and Stewart E. Sterk, *Dueling Denominators and the Demise of* Lucas, 60 ARIZ. L. REV. 67 (2018).

[190]   See Korngold, *supra* n. 181.

[191]   *Lucas,* 505 U.S. at 1029.

[192]   For cases recognizing that homeowners' associations' covenants contrary to public policy can be voided, see *Mazdabrook Commons Homeowners' Ass'n v. Khan*, 210 N.J. 482 (2012) (covenant restricting political signs was void against public policy) and *Lake Naomi Club Inc. v. Rosado*, 285 A.3d 1 (Pa. Cmwlth. Ct. 2022) (covenant prohibiting registered sex offenders from living in the community violated public policy).

[193]   Stahl, *Power of State Legislatures, supra* n. 75, at 624.

a background principle of covenant law is that covenants may be invalidated or ignored when they infringe too significantly on public policy. The takings analysis would then turn to *Penn Central*. For the reasons explored above, *Penn Central* is unlikely to require the government to pay compensation for limiting the ability of private covenants to stymie states' efforts to address the housing affordability crisis. The economic impact of the government action is minimal (or may even be positive for many homeowners subject to covenants). The owners of covenants have no reasonable expectation of the status quo given how legislatures and courts have balanced the public interest against the benefits of allowing property owners to bind themselves and their successors in interest to restrictions on the use of the land. The absence of any physical invasion and the strength of the government's interest in allowing more housing to be built suggest that the character of the government action is such that the courts would not find a taking.

IV.   IMPLICATIONS AND CONCLUSION

The coalition between pro-housing progressive advocates and property rights advocates has helped secure extensive land use reforms in a number of states—most obviously in Arizona, Montana, and Utah. But those seeking reforms should be careful what they wish for. The language of property rights that has been used in the debates over reform thus far has focused on the rights of existing homeowners to build an ADU to house elderly parents, caretakers, adult children, or to bring in rental income to cover ever-escalating property taxes and maintenance. It also has focused on the property rights of developers who want to use land more intensively for the single-family starter homes and multifamily housing for which there is such a critical shortage. However, existing homeowners seeking to preserve the quality of life they've enjoyed in less dense neighborhoods also are beginning to invoke property rights to help them retain their current lifestyles and the wealth that has accrued in their homes as a result of the neighborhood's low density, amenities, and exclusivity.

This chapter demonstrates that those homeowners are unlikely to succeed under our land use laws and traditional takings analysis. But the Supreme Court has surprised us before with extraordinary solicitude for those fortunate enough to own homes in neighborhoods "where family values, youth values, and the blessings of quiet seclusion and clean air make the area a sanctuary."[194] State and local governments, accordingly, would be wise to try to limit the viability of any such claims. Those governments (and advocates for more pro-housing land use reforms) can take several steps to reduce the risk that such

---

[194]   *Vill. of Belle Terre v. Boraas*, 416 U.S. 1, 9 (1974).

claims succeed. First, they should build an evidentiary foundation in the legislative record and public debates that the expectations people can reasonably hold about maintaining the value of their homes have changed. Indeed, those expectations must evolve even further given the need to house a growing population affordably; to avoid, mitigate, and adapt to climate change and extreme weather events caused by that change; to prevent further environmental degradation and habitat loss; to reduce the racial wealth gap and other legacies of residential segregation; and to ensure the physical and social mobility that having a better match between job and housing opportunities would promote.

Second, when reforms can be structured around existing doctrines that have made it clear that neighbors have limited rights to affect zoning decisions or development choices on land they don't own, those established paths may be more defensible than newer, blunter measures. For example, Professor Korngold has argued that overriding covenants on traditional public policy grounds may be less risky than overriding the covenants in legislation authorizing specific land use reforms.[195] Those crafting legislative overrides should consider how best to fit the overrides into existing paradigms rather than using them in boilerplate fashion in every land use reform bill.

Third, but relatedly, advocates should be careful and strategic about the rhetoric used in their campaigns. Blunt arguments that the land use reforms will protect property rights should be more carefully honed to talk about people's reasonable expectations that they can use their own property to care for family members needing special attention, as families have done for centuries. Similarly, rather than invoking the property rights of landowners broadly, a more targeted message about the right to use one's land to help meet the need for more housing and promote more sustainable land use patterns may be preferable. Those urging land use reforms that may be threatening to existing homeowners should avoid incendiary and inaccurate rhetoric about "ending single-family zoning" and seek instead to focus on the need to adapt to evolving knowledge about how communities can be more sustainable so that the children of existing residents have a place to return to where they can raise their families. Language also can be crafted to bring others into the coalition by focusing on the need for housing to attract the residents communities need to provide health care, child care, education, and other essential services.

Finally, more research is required about how land use reforms actually work—how much housing results from different kinds of reforms, how the additional housing affects the growth in rents and prices in the community, how neighborhoods change in response to the reforms, and how existing

---

[195]   Korngold, *supra* n. 181, at 49–57.

homeowners in low-density neighborhoods are affected by the reforms.[196] That information can help policymakers both refine the reforms as needed and defend the reforms.

It would be ironic indeed if the monumental efforts that are going into designing and securing better land use regulatory systems lead to judicial decisions that give existing homeowners in low-density neighborhoods even greater rights to limit development around them. Careful attention to minimizing that risk is an imperative part of the work that must be done to recalibrate the regulation of land use to be both more efficient and fairer.

ACKNOWLEDGEMENTS

I would like to thank participants in the Private Property and the Police Power Conference held at the University of Denver Sturm College of Law in April 2024, and in the Land, Climate & Justice Conference hosted by the University of Virginia's Program on Law, Communities, and the Environment, the Karsh Institute for Democracy, the Local Equity and Democracy Working Group, and the Virginia Environmental Law Journal in March 2024, for helpful questions and comments. Will Gomberg and Elise Brown provided excellent research assistance and thoughtful comments, and Jessica Kwon was a careful and thoughtful copyeditor. I am grateful for the support provided for my research by the Filomen D'Agostino and Max E. Greenberg Research Account. Although I am a faculty director of the NYU Furman Center, which is affiliated with NYU's School of Law and Wagner Graduate School of Public Service, this work does not represent the institutional views (if any) of NYU or any of its schools.

---

[196] See *supra* n. 3.

PART B

Private property and the natural environment

7. Just add water: the muddy world of private property rights in a panarchal reality

Robin Craig

> But why is land—immovable, enduring land—the central symbol for property? Why not, say, water? Water, after all, is in fact the subject of important and valuable property rights, and indeed, concerns about water can substantially modify rules about land. If water were our chief symbol for property, we might think of property rights—and perhaps other rights—in quite a different way.[1]

INTRODUCTION

Private property is often the locus for negotiating social and legal priorities. In particular, the tensions between individual freedom and community well-being often manifest in legal conflicts over the use of real property. This chapter argues that the property law pendulum has swung too far in favor of liberal individualism and that the law needs to better account for the fact that real property, in particular, *always* participates in complex systems at multiple scales. Because real property always participates in multiple communities, those larger public interests should always factor into the scope of real property rights—particularly because the private property owner also benefits from preserving that connectivity.

This is not an argument for a radical change in real property law, but rather for a revolving back to certain views of property that were most obviously present during the Progressive Era. Two aspects of this argument are critical. First, there is no absolutely correct way to balance individual liberty as manifested in property rights and the needs of the several scales (local, state, regional, national) of societies that encompass parcels of real estate. Indeed, this chapter offers several examples of how the "proper" balance between privileging the

---

[1]   Carol Rose, *Property as the Keystone Right?*, 71 Notre Dame L. Rev 329, 351 (1996).

individual and privileging the community has shifted over time. Negotiating that tension has been a focus of US political philosophy and jurisprudence since the nation's founding, with particularly sharp reconceptualizations in the Progressive Era before World War I[2] and with the political rise of conservative-based individualism (neoliberalism), often associated with Ronald Reagan's election in 1980.[3] Progressives before World War I "challenged the idea of natural, prepolitical rights held by autonomous individuals in isolation from society, associated law and constitutions with this erroneous conception, and rejected the related position that a laissez-faire government should do little more than protect individual rights."[4] World War II, McCarthyism, and the Cold War represented the height of the USA's swing toward privileging the community (in context, meaning the nation) in law and politics, while at the same time revealing the potential dangers to individual liberty posed by the government.[5] The United States has been swinging back hard to privilege the individual ever since, most succinctly illustrated by the rise of neoliberalism.[6]

Closely tied to the debate over whether the individual or the society should be the primary focus of law and policy, although not precisely identical with it, are arguments over the "proper" role of government. Both 19th-century liberals and 21st-century neoliberals stress that government should be limited, emphasizing free markets and the pursuit of capitalism instead.[7] In contrast to both, Progressives viewed individuals as interdependent social beings whose own interests could be harmonized with broader community interests. They were confident that individuality could best be realized in a cooperative society sharing common values that transcended the materialism of capitalism. Instead of perceiving government as a threat to individuals, they believed that an active state could help create a consensual community by providing the

---

[2]   For example, David M. Rabban, *Free Speech in Progressive Social Thought*, 74 Tex. L. Rev 951, 956–62 (1996).

[3]   Like most broad-brush reviews of history, this association of neoliberalism with Ronald Reagan is an oversimplification. For example, Paul M. Renfro, *Pinning the Rise of Neoliberalism on Ronald Reagan Lets Democrats Off Easy*, Jacobin (June 25, 2023), https://jacobin.com/2023/06/righting-the-american-dream-diane -winston-book-review-neoliberalism-democrats-ronald-reagan. However, because my focus is general timing rather than causation, it will serve well enough.

[4]   Rabban, *supra* note 2, at 958.

[5]   *Id.*

[6]   Kevin Vallier, *Neoliberalism*, *in* Edward N. Zalta and Uri Nodelman (eds.), The Stanford Encyclopedia of Philosophy (Winter 2022), https://plato.stanford.edu/archives/win2022/entries/neoliberalism/.

[7]   *Id.*; Rabban, *supra* note 2, at 958–59.

resources needed for the actual exercise of positive and not merely formal rights.[8]

Notably—although not the focus of this chapter—the debate regarding the circumstances under which government action (or inaction) promotes or hinders individual liberty—and *whose* liberty, exactly—continues in many fields of law.[9] Instead, the second critical aspect of this chapter's argument is why the reinvigoration of the public aspects of property law are particularly important now: we have increased scientific understanding of real property's deep interconnectedness to larger systems in a world that is approaching tipping points, at least some of which pose existential threats to societies and perhaps humanity as a whole.[10] Property law in the United States, however, is evolving directly counter to the increasing on-the-ground need for a public, society-minded perspective on how land contributes to human survival not just in terms of food production and shelter but also in terms of preserving the society-supporting functionality of a variety of complex adaptive systems.[11] Specifically, at this point in the early 21st century, property law and property rights enthusiasts (including a majority of the US Supreme Court) tend to treat real property as if individual parcels of land are discrete things—not just as the legal metaphor of the individual bundle of sticks (my bundle is separate from your bundle) but also as an on-the ground reality—my land is physically distinct from your land. However, as with the increasing emphasis on individualism in other contexts,[12] the increasing emphasis on discreteness in property law elides the fact that individual properties, like individual human beings,

---

[8]   Rabban, *supra* note 2, at 958.

[9]   *Id.*

[10]   Tessa Möller et al., *Achieving Net Zero Greenhouse Gas Emissions Critical to Limit Climate Tipping Risks*, 15 NATURE COMMUNICATIONS art. 6192, at 1 (2024), https://doi.org/10.1038/s41467-024-49863-0 ("Consequences of climate tipping would be severe and potentially include a global sea level rise of several metres, ecosystem collapse, widespread biodiversity loss, and substantial shifts in global heat redistribution and precipitation patterns" (citation omitted)).

[11]   See, for example, Luca Salvati, Anastasios Mavrakis, Andrea Colantoni, Giuseppe Mancino, and Agostino Ferrara, *Complex Adaptive Systems, Soil Degradation and Land Sensitivity to Desertification: A Multivariate Assessment of Italian Agro-forest Landscape*, 521–22 SCI. TOTAL ENV'T 235, 241 (2015), https://doi.org/10.1016/j.scitotenv.2015.03.094 (using a complex systems approach to help explain the multivariate complexities of soil degradation but emphasizing human land use and water decisions as drivers of change).

[12]   Rabban, *supra* note 2, at 952–53 (noting that leftist Free Speech scholars increasingly "worry that the First Amendment, instead of protecting unpopular dissenters from a repressive state, is now being invoked by the economically and politically powerful to prevent regulation of campaign financing, the

interact at multiple scales and that one person's freedom to do what they want with their land can *always* affect society more broadly—even in the absence of those more immediate interferences that the law recognizes as trespass and nuisance and *even to the detriment of the acting landowner.*

This chapter seeks to highlight those larger connections between parcels of real property, the larger landscape, and society at large as a pathway toward reinvigorating governmental police powers to protect the public at large. Part I begins with an overview of some of the legal doctrines and political developments that have helped to solidify the view of real property as a series of discrete and generally privately owned parcels of land, free (or nearly free) of public rights. This survey highlights in particular the US Supreme Court's exaltation of the right to exclude, the development of its regulatory takings jurisprudence, and the reactions of the states and the public to the Court's 2005 decision in *Kelo v. City of New London*.[13] In contrast, Part II discusses the very different treatment in law of riparian properties—that is, parcels of land that intersect with water.[14] Unlike its treatment of land, the law pervasively acknowledges that water connects people and places in ways that often give both the water itself and the adjacent lands a public dimension, while at the same time enhancing the value of riparian property. This public dimension is particularly evident when the water in question is navigable, but even non-navigable waterbodies can change the normal rules that apply to real property, such as by giving the public a right to recreate above privately-owned submerged lands. Finally, Part III generalizes the publicly-minded insights of riparian law through the model of panarchy, illustrating some of the myriad ways that so-called "discrete" parcels of land interact with each other and with society more generally, even in the absence of surface water. In light of these connections, the chapter concludes by arguing that there would be many benefits to reinvigorating the "promoting public good" aspect of the police power as a legal force, especially in light of the fact that the private property owners themselves also usually benefit from publicly-minded regulation.

---

media, and harmful speech directed against minorities, women, and children" (citations omitted)).

[13]   545 U.S. 469 (2005).

[14]   Technically, riparian properties border a river or stream, while littoral properties border a lake or the ocean: Robin Kundis Craig, Robert W. Adler, and Noah D. Hall, Water Law: CONCEPTS AND INSIGHTS (2d ed.) 17 (2024). However, while there are a few technical legal differences between them, for the most part riparian and littoral law are the same. *Id.* Thus, this chapter uses "riparian law" to refer to both types of real estate.

I.   HOW THE LAW MAKES REAL PROPERTY DISCRETE

Dividing land into discrete legal parcels is a social choice; indeed, many indigenous conceptions of land and robust legal traditions of commons (and particularly the English enclosures of the commons) are vastly different. Even when land becomes atomized into parcels, moreover, society continues to make choices about the extent to which individual landowners must take account not just of their similarly situated neighbors—a concern policed in USA property law primarily through trespass and private nuisance doctrines—but also of public values.

Coincident with the Progressive Era, the appearance and rapid spread of zoning and land use planning at the beginning of the 20th century marked a pendulum swing in US property law away from individual rights and toward societal well-being and other public values, such as public health. Perhaps most famously, in 1926, in *Village of Euclid, Ohio v. Ambler Realty*, the Supreme Court declared zoning constitutional despite Ambler Realty's claims that its constitutionally protected private property rights were being violated.[15] The Court explicitly took the view that restrictions on private property owners could evolve over time to address the new societal problems that emerged from changing social conditions:

> Building zone laws are of modern origin. They began in this country about 25 years ago. Until recent years, urban life was comparatively simple; but, with the great increase and concentration of population, problems have developed, and constantly are developing, which require, and will continue to require, additional restrictions in respect of the use and occupation of private lands in urban communities. Regulations, the wisdom, necessity, and validity of which, as applied to existing conditions, are so apparent that they are now uniformly sustained, a century ago, or even half a century ago, probably would have been rejected as arbitrary and oppressive. Such regulations are sustained, under the complex conditions of our day, for reasons analogous to those which justify traffic regulations, which, before the advent of automobiles and rapid transit street railways, would have been condemned as fatally arbitrary and unreasonable. And in this there is no inconsistency, for, while the meaning of constitutional guaranties never varies, the scope of their application must expand or contract to meet the new and different conditions which are constantly coming within the field of their operation. In a changing world it is impossible that it should be otherwise.[16]

---

[15]   Village of Euclid, Ohio v. Ambler Realty, 272 U.S. 365, 386 (1926).
[16]   *Id.* at 386–87.

Moreover, the Court emphasized, zoning finds its legal justification in the police power and the protection of public welfare.[17]

Similarly, in the 1940s, the Court began to curb real property owners' liberty to discriminate against particular kinds of buyers and tenants, promoting public values of equality before the law. Thus, in 1948, in *Shelley v. Kraemer*, the Court declared state enforcement of racially restrictive covenants unconstitutional on Equal Protection grounds.[18] The case at its core pitted individual liberties against individual liberties—the white property owners' asserted rights to deal with their property as they wished versus the black couple's right to purchase and own real property. Given the Fourteenth Amendment's requirement for state action, however, the Court decided the case as a matter of which government's—state or federal—set of public values should prevail in the face of conflicting liberty demands, concluding "that the power of the State to create and enforce property interests must be exercised within the boundaries defined by the Fourteenth Amendment."[19]

These public incursions into property-based liberal individualism remain: the Supreme Court has not eliminated the police power authority of states and local governments to zone real property (although as-applied challenges by individual landowners remain potentially viable), and housing law has grown even more protective of individuals against whom landlords and real estate agents might discriminate. In many other respects, however, both the Supreme Court and many individual states have increasingly atomized real property, problematizing governments' exercises of their police and eminent domain powers. This part examines three of these atomizing threads: the elevation of the right to exclude and its impact on physical takings; regulatory takings' denigration of the police power; and states' reactions to the Supreme Court's decision in *Kelo v. City of New London*.

A.   Real Property as Fortress: The US Supreme Court's Elevation of the Right to Exclude

One of the most important ways in which the US Supreme Court promotes an individualistic and atomistic view of real property is through its elevation of the right to exclude. Notably, until the later 20th century, when neoliberalism gained a firm foothold in US politics and then law, most of the Court's property-related discussions regarding the right to exclude involved the rights

---

[17]   *Id.*

[18]   Shelley v. Kraemer, 334 U.S. 1, 22–23 (1948).

[19]   *Id.* at 22.

of patent holders,[20] not landowners. Those cases that *did* involve landowners' rights, in turn, reflected a Progressive balancing of public and private values. For example, in a 1956 case involving unions' rights to organize workers at their places of employment, the Court noted that the employers' right to exclude was flexible: "when the inaccessibility of employees makes ineffective the reasonable attempts by nonemployees [i.e., union organizers] to communicate with them through the usual channels, the right to exclude from property has been required to yield to the extent needed to permit communication of information on the right to organize."[21] Similarly,

> [t]he right of self-organization depends in some measure on the ability of employees to learn the advantages of self-organization from others. Consequently, if the location of a plant and the living quarters of the employees place the employees beyond the reach of reasonable union efforts to communicate with them, the employer must allow the union to approach his employees on his property.[22]

In the case before it, however, "no such conditions" existed to warrant overruling the employer's right to exclude.[23]

In contrast, the progression of the Supreme Court's Free Speech/shopping mall cases illuminate the evolution in the Court's views about the importance of the right to exclude. Initially, in the late 1960s, the Court deemed shopping centers to be public spaces for Free Speech purposes, effectively denying the shopping centers' private owners from excluding members of the public who

---

[20] For example: United Shoe Machinery Corp. v. U.S., 258 U.S. 451, 464–65 (1922) (discussing the patent right to exclude in the context of the Clayton Act); Crown Die & Tool Co. v. Nye Tool & Machine Works, 261 U.S. 24, 34–35 (1923) (discussing the implications of assigning a patent's right to exclude); Ethyl Gasoline Corp. v. U.S., 309 U.S. 436, 456 (1940) (discussing the limits of the patent right to exclude); Wilbur-Ellis Co. v. Kuther, 377 U.S. 422, 424–25 (1964) (discussing the relevance of the patent right to exclude in determining whether patent infringement had occurred); Parker v. Flook, 437 U.S. 584, 593 (1978) (under patent law, discovery of an existing phenomenon of nature creates no right to exclude.); and Dawson Chem. Co. v. Rohm & Hass Co., 448 U.S. 176, 201 (1980) (discussing contributory infringement).

[21] Natl. Labor Relations Bd. v. Babcock & Wilcox Co., 351 U.S. 105, 112 (1956).

[22] *Id.* at 113.

[23] *Id.* at 113–14. See also generally Central Hardware Co. v. Nat'l Labor Relations Bd., 407 U.S. 539 (1972) (remanding union case for further factual development on the issue of whether union organizers needed to be able to access the employer's parking lot to effectively communicate with employees).

wanted to picket and distribute handbills.[24] In less than a decade, however, the Court reversed that position, holding that property does not "lose its private character merely because the public is generally invited to use it for designated purposes," and that "[t]he essentially private character of a store and its privately owned abutting property does not change by virtue of being large or clustered with other stores in a modern shopping center."[25] By 1979, in *Kaiser Aetna v. United States*, the Court named the right to exclude as "one of the most essential sticks in the bundle of rights that are commonly characterized as property ... ."[26]

The elevation of the right to exclude also changed how the Court evaluates one group of constitutional takings claims. The Fifth and Fourteenth Amendments to the US Constitution prohibit the taking of private property for public use without compensation by, respectively, the federal and state or local governments.[27] Importantly,

[t]he U.S. Supreme Court recognizes three categories of taking. First, the government can physically take private property by taking title, by actually occupying that property, or by forcing the private landowner to endure some physical invasion by the government or by the general public. In a classic physical taking, for example, a government condemns private land for a public road or a government building. ... Until 1922, the prohibition on uncompensated governmental taking of private property was limited to physical taking. In 1922, however, in *Pennsylvania Coal Co. v. Mahon*, the U.S. Supreme Court recognized that a second category of unconstitutional taking exists—specifically, that federal, state, and local *regulation* might also amount to an unconstitutional taking of private property. ... Finally, in *Lucas v. South Carolina Coastal Council*, the U.S. Supreme Court recognized a small

---

24   See generally Amalgamated Food Emp. Union Local 590 v. Logan Valley Plaza, Inc., 391 U.S. 308 (1968) (deeming a shopping center to be open to the public for purposes of union picketing).
25   Lloyd Corp. v. Tanner, 407 U.S. 551, 569 (1972). See also Hudgens v. NLRB, 424 U.S. 507, 517–20 (1976) (overruling *Logan Valley Plaza*).
26   Kaiser Aetna v. U.S., 444 U.S. 164, 176 (1979).
27   The Fifth Amendment states that "[n]o person shall be ... deprived of life, liberty, or property, without due process of law; nor shall private property be taken for public use, without just compensation." U.S. Const., amend. V. In turn, under the Fourteenth Amendment, "[n]o State shall ... deprive any person of life, liberty, or property, without due process of law ... ." U.S. Const., amend. XIV, § 1. The Supreme Court has made it clear that the Fifth Amendment's substantive prohibition on takings of property without compensation also applies to the states as a matter of incorporation through the Fourteenth Amendment. Dolan v. City of Tigard, 512 U.S. 374, 383–84 (1994); Keystone Bituminous Coal Association v. DeBenedictis, 480 U.S. 470, 481 n.10 (1987).

set of *categorical takings.* In *Lucas*-type taking claims, a government regulation deprives the property owner of *all* economic use of the property.[28]

Choosing which of these three analyses applies often determines the result, because physical and categorical takings automatically require compensation, unless the government's action was within inherent limitations on property rights, such as abating a public nuisance or dealing with a public necessity.[29]

The right to exclude has become critical to the Court in categorizing government actions as physical takings. This, however, is a relatively recent development. For example, when California sought to expand Free Speech rights through its own constitution, the Supreme Court in 1980 upheld the resulting invasion of shopping center owners' private property rights.[30] Emphasizing that its prior decisions did not turn on state constitutional provisions or rights, the Court evaluated California's action as a *regulatory* taking, noting that it is "well established that a State in the exercise of its police power may adopt reasonable restrictions on private property so long as the restrictions do not amount to a taking without just compensation or contravene any other federal constitutional provision."[31] Moreover, the Court used the regulatory taking analysis *even though* "one of the essential sticks in the bundle of property rights is the right to exclude others"[32] and the appellants might have physically invaded the property.[33]

By 1982, however, any government-forced physical occupation of real property constituted an unconstitutional taking, and the right to exclude was elevated slightly to being "one of the most treasured strands in an owner's bundle of property rights."[34] As the Court later explained in *Lucas,* "Where 'permanent physical occupation' of land is concerned, we have refused to allow the

---

[28]   Craig, Adler, and Hall, *supra* note 14, at 306–307 (citing *Pennsylvania Coal,* 260 U.S. 393 (1922), and *Lucas,* 505 U.S. 1003, 1017, 1019 (1992)).

[29]   *Id.* at 318; *Lucas,* 505 U.S. at 1027–29 & 1029 n.16.

[30]   PruneYard Shopping Ctr. v. Robins, 477 U.S. 74 (1980).

[31]   *Id.* at 82; see also *id.* at 82–84 (applying the *Pennsylvania Coal* balancing test).

[32]   *Id.* at 82 (citing *Kaiser Aetna,* 444 U.S. at 176).

[33]   *Id.* at 84. See also Widmar v. Vincent, 454 U.S. 263, 277 (1981) (affirming that state universities have a "right to exclude even First Amendment activities that violate reasonable campus rules or substantially interfere with the opportunity of other students to obtain an education" but insisting that their exclusions be content neutral (citations omitted)).

[34]   *Loretto,* 458 U.S. at 435–46 (citing *Kaiser Aetna,* 444 U.S. at 179–80; RESTATEMENT OF PROPERTY § 7 (1936)).

government to decree it anew (without compensation), no matter how weighty the asserted 'public interests' involved."[35]

The Court thus eliminated the possibility that new public values and needs could infringe upon a property owner's *right to exclude* through the police power, even if governments continue to have the right to limit the uses to which the property may be put.[36] Moreover, in 1999, the Supreme Court declared that "[t]he hallmark of a protected property interest is the right to exclude others."[37] Thus, the very way that the Court now identifies a protected property right is by its discreteness, manifested in the ability of an owner to exclude everyone else from it. The Supreme Court emphasized this point by connecting the right to exclude others from private property to a legitimate expectation of privacy for Fourth Amendment purposes.[38]

The Court has continued to categorize the right to exclude as the "fundamental" and "essential" private property right, almost always citing—somewhat perversely, as the discussion in Part II will make clear—*Kaiser Aetna* as its authority.[39] Indeed, in 2005, the Court opined that the right to exclude was "perhaps *the most* fundamental of all property interests."[40]

Furthermore, making good its prior announcements, the Court most recently has eschewed any Progressive-like balancing of public interests against the right to exclude, declaring in 2021 that "[w]e cannot agree that the right to exclude is an empty formality, subject to modification at the government's pleasure. On the contrary, it is a "fundamental element of the property right," that cannot

---

[35] *Lucas*, 505 U.S. at 1028 (quoting *Loretto*, 458 U.S. at 426).

[36] *Id.* at 1028–29.

[37] College Savings Bank v. Florida Prepaid Postsecondary Educ. Expense Bd., 527 U.S. 666, 673 (1999). Compare this statement to a similar discussion by the Court in 1918: "An essential element of individual property is the legal right to exclude others from enjoying it. If the property is private, the right of exclusion may be absolute; *if the property is affected with a public interest, the right of exclusion is qualified.*" [emphasis added] International News Service v. Associated Press, 248 U.S. 215, 250 (1918).

[38] Byrd v. U.S., 584 U.S. 395, 405 (2018) (citing Rakas v. Illinois, 439 U.S. 128, 144 n.12 (1978)).

[39] Ruckelshaus v. Monsanto, 467 U.S. 986, 999, 1011 (1984); Hodel v. Irving, 481 U.S. 704, 716 (1987); Nollan v. California Coastal Comm'n, 483 U.S. 825, 831 (1987); Yee v. City of Escondido, Cal., 503 U.S. 519, 528 (1992); Dolan v. City of Tigard, 512 U.S. 374, 384, 393 (1994); U.S. v. Craft, 535 U.S. 274, 283 (2002); Lingle v. Chevron USA, Inc., 544 U.S. 528, 539 (2005); and Alabama Ass'n of Realtors v. Department of Health & Human Servs., 594 U.S. 758, 765 (2021).

[40] *Lingle*, 544 U.S. at 539 (emphasis added).

be balanced away.[41] As a result—at least for the current conservative Court majority—*any* intrusion on the right to exclude now qualifies as a *per se* physical taking of private property, requiring the regulating government either to compensate the property owner or to repeal the offending requirement.[42]

B.   Regulatory Takings and the Diminishment of the Police Power

As the previous section illustrated, the elevated right to exclude now leads the Court to determine that government actions to protect certain members of society (such as displaced workers during the pandemic[43] or itinerant farm workers[44]) constitute physical takings of the affected real properties. These recent cases effectively displace earlier jurisprudence in which the Court was willing to diminish the importance of the right to exclude when balancing it against either other private civil rights (such as California's broad state constitutional protections for free speech, evaluated under the regulatory takings test) or laws and regulations that promoted public values or protected public interests, such as the laws that protected workers' rights to unionize. In this sense, therefore, contemporary *physical* takings jurisprudence eliminates police power authority when governments exercising that power tamper with property owners' rights to exclude.

Although less decisive in its real-world impact on the public values inherent in private property, *regulatory* takings jurisprudence similarly exists to undermine the police power—that is, the power of governments to protect and promote public health, safety, and welfare. As noted, until 1922, the concept of a "regulatory taking" did not exist, and proper assertion of the police power

---

[41]   Cedar Point Nursery v. Hassid, 594 U.S. 139, 158 (2021) (quoting *Kaiser Aetna*, 444 U.S. at 179–80).

[42]   *Alabama Ass'n of Realtors*, 594 U.S. at 765–66 (invalidating the moratorium during the COVID-19 pandemic on landlords being able to evict non-paying tenants because that moratorium "intrudes on one of the most fundamental elements of property ownership—the right to exclude" (citing *Loretto*, 458 U.S. at 435)) and *Cedar Point Nursery*, 594 U.S. at 151–52 (holding that a California regulation that allowed labor organizers to access agricultural employer's properties constituted a per se physical taking requiring compensation and noting that "[g]iven the central importance to property ownership of the right to exclude, it comes as little surprise that the Court has long treated government-authorized physical invasions as takings requiring just compensation").

[43]   *Alabama Ass'n of Realtors*, 594 U.S. at 765–66.

[44]   *Cedar Point Nursery*, 594 U.S. at 151–52.

was a complete defense to a takings claim.[45] Indeed, in speaking of the police power in 1915, the Supreme Court emphasized that:

> It is to be remembered that we are dealing with one of the most essential powers of government—one that is the least limitable. It may, indeed, seem harsh in its exercise, usually is on some individual, but the imperative necessity for its existence precludes any limitation upon it when not exerted arbitrarily. A vested interest cannot be asserted against it because of conditions once obtaining. To so hold would preclude development and fix a city forever in its primitive conditions. There must be progress, and if in its march private interests are in the way, they must yield to the good of the community. The logical result of petitioner's contention would seem to be that a city could not be formed or enlarged against the resistance of an occupant of the ground, and that if it grows at all it can only grow as the environment of the occupations that are usually banished to the purlieus.[46]

Thus, as in the zoning cases, the Court was more interested in cities' and states' authority to adjust to changing conditions than in established businesses and property rights.

The Court's 1922 decision in *Pennsylvania Coal* changed that legal landscape. Justice Oliver Wendell Holmes articulated for the Court that "while property may be regulated to a certain extent, if regulation goes too far it will be recognized as a taking."[47] The "too far" language from *Pennsylvania Coal* means that most regulatory takings are evaluated through a balancing test—the three-factor balancing test that the Supreme Court established in *Penn Central Transportation Co. v. New York City*.[48] Under this test, courts analyzing regulatory takings under federal law examine: (1) "[t]he economic impact of the regulation on the claimant," (2) "the extent to which the regulation has interfered with distinct investment-backed expectations," and (3) "the character of the governmental action."[49]

The shift effected through the progression of decisions from *Hadacheck* in 1915 to *Penn Central* in 1978 is from the primacy of governmental police

---

[45]   For example, Northern Pac. Ry. Co. v. Puget Sound & W.H. Ry. Co., 250 U.S. 332, 335–36 (1919); Hadacheck v. Sebastian, 239 U.S. 394, 410–14 (1915). "Indeed, '[p]rior to Justice Holmes's exposition in *Pennsylvania Coal Co. v. Mahon*, 260 U.S. 393 ... (1922), it was generally thought that the Takings Clause reached only a direct appropriation of property, or the functional equivalent of a practical ouster of the owner's possession," like the permanent flooding of property. *Lucas v. South Carolina Coastal Council*, 505 U.S. 1003, 1014 ... (1992)."

[46]   *Hadacheck*, 239 U.S. at 410 (citing Chicago & A. R. Co. v. Tranbarger, 238 U.S. 67, 78 (1915)). *Murr*, 582 U.S. at 392.

[47]   *Pennsylvania Coal*, 239 U.S. at 415.

[48]   438 U.S. 104 (1978).

[49]   *Id*. at 124.

power authority and concern for the evolving welfare of society to individual rights in real property—from the societal need for a regulation to that regulation's particular impact on a specific property and the owner's plans for that property. As the Court explained in 2017, whereas prior to 1922 the police power was supreme, the contemporary regulatory takings analysis attempts to reconcile "two competing objectives."[50] "One is the individual's right to retain the interests and exercise the freedoms at the core of private property ownership," because "[p]roperty rights are necessary to preserve freedom, for property ownership empowers persons to shape and to plan their own destiny in a world where governments are always eager to do so for them."[51] "The other persisting interest is the government's well-established power to 'adjus[t] rights for the public good.'"[52]

As such, given the *Penn Central* test, regulatory takings evaluations reinforce an atomistic view of real property, dividing land into discrete parcels. Nowhere is this result more clear than in the regulatory takings "denominator problem."[53] Figuring out the impact of a new regulation on a specific property, particularly in terms of diminution in value or loss of use, requires defining what exactly the original property was—the denominator against which the change is measured.[54]

The Supreme Court's 2017 decision *Murr v. Wisconsin* provides a recent example of the denominator problem. The Murr siblings (two sisters and two brothers) received from their parents two lots along the St. Croix River in

---

[50]   Murr v. Wisconsin, 582 U.S. 383, 394 (2017).

[51]   *Id.*

[52]   *Id.* (quoting Andrus v. Allard, 444 U.S. 51, 65 (1979)).

[53]   For more extensive discussions of the denominator problem, see generally: Steward E. Sterk, *Dueling Denominators and the Demise of* Lucas, 60 ARIZ. L. REV. 67 (2018); W.C. Bunting, *What* Murr v. Wisconsin *Tells Us About Regulatory Takings Doctrine*, 47 REAL ESTATE L.J. 258 (2018); Benjamin Allee, Note, *Drawing the Line in Regulatory Takings Law: How a Benefits Fraction Supports the Fee Simple Approach to the Denominator Problem*, 70 FORDHAM L. REV. 1957 (2002); and Marc R. Lisker, *Regulatory Takings and the Denominator Problem*, 27 RUTGERS L.J. 663 (1996).

[54]   As the Supreme Court stated in 2017: "What is the proper unit of property against which to assess the effect of the challenged governmental action? Put another way, '[b]ecause our test for regulatory taking requires us to compare the value that has been taken from the property with the value that remains in the property, one of the critical questions is determining how to define the unit of property "whose value is to furnish the denominator of the fraction."'" *Murr v. Wisconsin*, 582 U.S. at 395 (quoting Keystone Bituminous Coal Assn. v. DeBenedictis, 480 U.S. 470, 497 (1987) (quoting Michelman, *Property, Utility, and Fairness*, 80 HARV. L. REV. 1165, 1992 (1967))).

Wisconsin, which was designated as a federal Wild and Scenic River in 1972.[55] The lots were adjacent and originally purchased separately, and they were conveyed to the children separately, on different dates.[56] One lot had a cabin that the parents built in 1960, and the children wanted to sell the other lot to pay for moving and upgrading that cabin.[57] However, to protect Wild and Scenic River values, "[f]or the area where petitioners' property is located, the Wisconsin rules prevent the use of lots as separate building sites unless they have at least one acre of land suitable for development."[58] As a result Wisconsin determined that the children could not sell the undeveloped lot separately from the lot with a cabin.

The children sued, arguing that the State of Wisconsin had effected a complete taking of the undeveloped lot. Wisconsin countered that, because of its Wild and Scenic River regulations, the two lots constituted a single parcel. The Court sided with Wisconsin, in effect analogizing the regulation to zoning and concluding that:

> The merger provision here is ... a legitimate exercise of government power, as reflected by its consistency with a long history of state and local merger regulations that originated nearly a century ago. Merger provisions often form part of a regulatory scheme that establishes a minimum lot size in order to preserve open space while still allowing orderly development. ... Petitioners' insistence that lot lines define the relevant parcel ignores the well-settled reliance on the merger provision as a common means of balancing the legitimate goals of regulation with the reasonable expectations of landowners. Petitioners' rule would frustrate municipalities' ability to implement minimum lot size regulations by casting doubt on the many merger provisions that exist nationwide today.[59]

As a result, "[c]onsidering petitioners' property as a whole, the state court was correct to conclude that petitioners cannot establish a compensable taking in these circumstances," especially because the larger parcel had lost less than 10 percent of its value.[60]

Murr is an important case for articulating the specific factors that help to define what a legal parcel of land is.[61] Notably, however, the context of the regulations disappears after the Court's brief introduction to the case; the facts that the property is riparian to a Wild and Scenic River and that the Wisconsin

---

[55]   *Id.* at 388–89 (citing 16 U.S.C. § 1274(a)(6), (9) and 41 Fed. Reg. 26,237 (1976)).

[56]   *Id.* at 390.

[57]   *Id.* at 389, 390.

[58]   *Id.* at 389 (citing Wis. Admin. Code §§ NR 118.04(4), 118.03(27), 118.06(1)(a)(2)(a), and 118.06(1)(b) (2017)).

[59]   *Id.* at 401–402.

[60]   *Id.* at 405.

[61]   *Id.* at 397–99, applied at 402–405.

Department of Natural Resources is attempting to "limit[] development in order to 'guarantee the protection of the wild, scenic and recreational qualities of the river for present and future generations'"[62]—a fact that should be relevant under the third *Penn Central* factor—simply vanish from the case because the impact on the parcel as finally defined was simply too small to worry about. Thus, while in the end the Court upheld Wisconsin's police power regulatory authority, the private property was what mattered, not the public values of the land or larger aquatic ecosystem.

C.   State Legislative Reactions to *Kelo v. City of New London*

In contrast to its takings jurisprudence, the Supreme Court has been much more supportive of governments in its eminent domain jurisprudence—that is, the rules that apply when governments consciously decide to take private property and pay for it. The critical constitutional issue in these cases is whether the government's *reason* for taking the property qualifies as a "public purpose" under the Fifth Amendment.

It is a bedrock principle of constitutional eminent domain that "[p]rivate property can be taken for a public purpose only, and not for private gain or benefit."[63] Thus, when governments began to use eminent domain for redevelopment purposes, the question arose whether the removal of blight or other land use problems constituted a legitimate public purpose. In 1954, in *Berman v. Parker*, the Supreme Court announced great deference to legislative bodies in addressing the District of Columbia's use of eminent domain to address substandard housing and urban blight.[64] Recognizing such projects as exercises of the police power, the Court concluded that, "[s]ubject to specific constitutional limitations, when the legislature has spoken, the public interest has been declared in terms well-nigh conclusive. In such cases the legislature, not the judiciary, is the main guardian of the public needs to be served by social legislation ... ."[65] Moreover, "[i]t is within the power of the legislature to determine that the community should be beautiful as well as healthy, spacious as well as clean, well-balanced as well as carefully patrolled."[66] Thus, using eminent domain to revitalize blighted urban neighborhoods was constitutional.[67]

---

[62]   *Id.* at 388 (citing Wis. Stat. § 30.27(1) (1973)).
[63]   Rine Grove Township v. Talcott, 86 U.S. 666, 676 (1873).
[64]   Berman v. Parker, 348 U.S. 26, 28–29 (1954).
[65]   *Id.* at 32.
[66]   *Id.* at 33.
[67]   *Id.* at 36.

Hawaii tested the Court once more, enacting state legislation to break up the pervasive land oligarchies in the islands:

> [T]he Hawaii Legislature discovered that, while the State and Federal Governments owned almost 49% of the State's land, another 47% was in the hands of only 72 private landowners. The legislature further found that 18 landholders, with tracts of 21,000 acres or more, owned more than 40% of this land and that on Oahu, the most urbanized of the islands, 22 landowners owned 72.5% of the fee simple titles. The legislature concluded that concentrated land ownership was responsible for skewing the State's residential fee simple market, inflating land prices, and injuring the public tranquility and welfare.[68]

The legislation allowed the Hawaii Housing Authority, at the request of lessees, to use eminent domain to acquire title to rented properties and then convey title to the lessees.[69] While the Court of Appeals held that this private-to-private conveyance violated the Constitution's "public use" requirement, the Supreme Court unanimously disagreed, holding that "[t]he 'public use' requirement is … coterminous with the scope of a sovereign's police powers."[70] More specifically, "where the exercise of the eminent domain power is rationally related to a conceivable public purpose, the Court has never held a compensated taking to be proscribed by the Public Use Clause."[71]

Given *Berman* and the equation of a constitutional "public use" to a police power "public purpose" in *Hawaii Housing Authority*, most property lawyers found the Supreme Court's 2005 decision in *Kelo v. City of New London*[72] doctrinally unsurprising, even though it split a new set of Justices 5–4. In this case, the City of New London used eminent domain to effectuate a redevelopment plan to address its economic blight.[73] In the majority's view, the redevelopment plan served a clear purpose: "Those who govern the City were not confronted with the need to remove blight in the Fort Trumbull area, but their determination that the area was sufficiently distressed to justify a program of economic rejuvenation is entitled to our deference."[74]

Nevertheless, the Court majority also emphasized that states remain free to restrict the use of eminent domain more narrowly than the Constitution would allow. That recognition, bolstered by bodies politic ready to act on the

---

[68]   Hawaii Housing Auth.v. Midkiff, 467 U.S. 229, 232 (1984).

[69]   *Id.* at 232–33.

[70]   *Id.* at 240.

[71]   *Id.* at 241.

[72]   545 U.S. 469 (2005).

[73]   *Id.* at 472, 474–75.

[74]   *Id.* at 483.

property rights sentiments expressed by the dissenting Justices,[75] turned the rather predictable Supreme Court *Kelo* decision into a cultural phenomenon. As one commentator noted, *Kelo* became

> the most universally despised Supreme Court decision in recent memory. Most people cannot believe that the Supreme Court would sign off on allowing the government to take your home, your small business, or your church and give it to Wal-Mart, or give it to a shopping mall, or give it to a builder of private condominiums.[76]

Susette Kelo and her little pink house became public symbols of the law's willingness to derogate private property rights. In 2008, the house itself "was disassembled and moved piece-by-piece over the past year to its new location" in downtown New London, where "it now serves not only as a monument to those who battle eminent domain abuse."[77] The iconization of the house—as the New London monument, in the book *Little Pink House*,[78] and most recently in the movie "Little Pink House"[79]—illuminates the contemporary tendency to atomize real property: what mattered to Kelo originally was as much the waterfront location as the house itself,[80] but the house makes a more concrete, individual, and discrete symbol of property rights violated.

The more important reaction legally came in state legislatures, where a strong majority of states amended their eminent domain statutes (and occasionally their constitutions) to better protect private property rights. According

---

[75] See, for example, *id.* at 505–506 (Thomas, J., dissenting) (extolling "the sacred and inviolable rights of private property").

[76] Douglas M. Kmiec, *2006 Templeton Lecture: Eminent Domain Post-*Kelo, 9 U. PENN. J. CONST. L. 501, 518 (2007).

[77] *Ain't That America? Little Pink House Rises Again*, INSTITUTE FOR JUSTICE (Aug. 1, 2008), https://ij.org/ll/ainacanact-that-america-little-pink-house -rises-again/. (For the record John Cougar Mellencamp's little pink house was in Indiana, and the song has nothing to do with the *Kelo* decision, having been released in 1983.)

[78] Jeff Benedict, LITTLE PINK HOUSE: A TRUE STORY OF DEFIANCE AND COURAGE (2009).

[79] "Little Pink House," Dada Films (2017).

[80] According to the Institute for Justice: "Susette Kelo dreamed of owning a home that looked out over the water. She purchased and lovingly restored her little pink house where the Thames River meets the Long Island Sound in 1997, and had enjoyed the great view from its windows. The richness and vibrancy of this neighborhood reflected the American ideal of community and the dream of homeownership." *Kelo Eminent Domain*, INSTITUTE FOR JUSTICE (viewed Aug. 15, 2024), https://ij.org/case/kelo/.

to property rights scholars and advocates, 45[81] to 47[82] states amended their eminent domain laws to limit state and local use of eminent domain, often by limiting or eliminating economic motivations as a source of eminent domain authority. How effective these changes might or might not have been is not the point here; rather, a strong majority of the American public, acting through their state legislatures, announced that individual property rights were more important than revitalizing (or at least attempting to revitalize[83]) an entire community.

II.   JUST ADD WATER: HOW RIPARIAN AND LITTORAL LAW REVEAL CONNECTIVITY

Interestingly, all the threads discussed in Part I have riparian properties in key legal positions: Kelo wanted waterfront property, the Murrs owned property on a Wild and Scenic River, and the *Kaiser Aetna* case that so forcefully elevated the private right to exclude over public values was a wrongly decided navigable water case (more on that below). These three riparian[84] properties became poster properties for the individualistic and atomistic view of real property only because the Court submerged their riparian character. Normally, the reverse is true: the presence of water tempers individual private property rights in favor of government oversight and the public interest.

To start with the obvious, water is a flow resource that connects people and places. Even the real estate parcels surrounding a terminal lake cannot deny that they are all affected by the lake's level at any given moment and the uses that they and members of the public make of the lake. Until roads, automobiles, and trucks became common, rivers, streams, and lakes were the main arteries of commerce that connected the various parts of the United States

---

[81]   ILYA SOMIN, THE GRASPING HAND: "KELO V. CITY OF NEW LONDON" AND THE LIMITS OF EMINENT DOMAIN (2016).

[82]   *Eminent Domain*, INSTITUTE FOR JUSTICE (viewed Aug. 15, 2024), https://ij .org/issues/private-property/eminent-domain/.

[83]   The ultimate tragedy of both *Kelo* and *Hawaii Housing Authority* is that neither legislative scheme actually worked. Regarding the failure of the redistribution scheme at issue in *Hawaii Housing Authority*, see Gideon Kanner, Kelo v. New London: *Bad Law, Bad Policy, and Bad Judgment*, 38 URBAN LAWYER 201, 212–14 (2006). In New London, Pfizer pulled out of the proposed development in 2009, and the condemned properties remained undeveloped. Patrick McGeehan, *Pfizer to Leave City that Won Land-Use Case*, THE NEW YORK TIMES (Nov. 12, 2009), https://www.nytimes.com/2009/11/13/nyregion/13pfizer.html.

[84]   Again, this chapter uses "riparian" as the catch-all term. The property in *Kaiser Aetna* was littoral to the Pacific Ocean.

through navigation, travel, trade, and naval operations. Indeed, the importance of rivers and other waterways to sovereignty, to society, and to public values became enshrined American law from the earliest days of the Republic. As the US Supreme Court has recognized both explicitly and implicitly throughout its history, "[n]avigable waters uniquely implicate sovereign interests."[85]

These connective, society- and nation-building, and public aspects of water are particularly strong when riparian and littoral properties abut *navigable* waters. "Navigability" and "navigable waters" are two of the most complex terms of art in American law. Nevertheless, to call a stream or lake "navigable" automatically imbues it with public rights and acknowledges that both the relevant state and the federal government have authority to regulate the activities that occur on, in, and under that waterbody.

This part explores how riparian law complicates the atomistic approach to real property rights. It begins with a short summary of the benefits of owning riparian land as a legal matter. Then, because the public facet of riparian properties is particularly strong when the waterbody is navigable water, it moves to navigable waters and their legal implications for riparian landowners, before concluding with non-navigable waters.

A.   The Benefits to Landowners of Being Close to Water

Despite very real risks of flooding in most parts of the USA, people want to own properties near water, invading floodplains, hurricane zones, and coasts vulnerable to sea level rise to fulfill that desire. Riparian law, similarly, gifts riparian landowners with additional rights that are generally inapplicable to non-riparian properties. "Moreover, while the western states have adopted prior appropriation to replace riparianism with respect to rights to withdraw and consume surface water, most western states continue to apply ... those rights directly related to riparian land ownership."[86]

The rights are numerous. First, riparian land ownership extends to the beds and banks (submerged lands) of non-navigable waterbodies[87]—and sometimes of artificial waterbodies, as well.[88] Second, "[r]iparian property ownership includes the right to build piers and wharf out to deeper water, subject to the authority of regulatory agencies and the reasonable use doctrine."[89] Third, riparian landowners have the right to access the water for a variety of purposes, potentially including—according to the relevant state's law—navigation, rec-

---

85   Idaho v. Couer d'Alene Tribe of Idaho, 521 U.S. 261, 284 (1997).
86   CRAIG, ADLER, AND HALL, *supra* note 14, at 17.
87   *Id.* at 19–22.
88   *Id.* at 18–19.
89   *Id.* at 33.

reation, hunting, and fishing.[90] If the waterway is not navigable, moreover, it may be *only* riparian landowners who have these rights; in contrast, if the waterway is navigable, the riparian landowner shares these use rights with the general public as a member of the general public, as subpart B will explain. Fourth, with access and use rights, in most states the landowner also acquires the right to use the entire surface of the waterbody, not just the waters above the landowner's submerged lands.[91] Thus, ownership of one parcel along a river or lake generally comes with rights to use the entire waterbody.

Fifth, unlike most real estate, the riparian landowner's property changes with the gradual changes in the waterway through the doctrines of accretion, erosion, and reliction.[92] As the waterway gradually adds material such as sand and silt, or as the water gradually erodes the shoreline, the landowner's parcel of real estate grows or shrinks simultaneously; in other words, the water boundary that makes land riparian is ambulatory. However, if the waterway experiences a sudden or avulsive change—perhaps because of an earthquake, flood, or severe storm—the property lines stay where they were.[93] Courts generally disfavor categorizing changes as "avulsive," however, because some properties will lose their water connection.

Finally, in some states, riparian rights also include the right to an unobstructed view, which acknowledges the real economic value that attaches to the aesthetics of waterfront property, and a right to water of a certain quality.[94] States vary considerably in their willingness to recognize these two rights, however. Moreover, the right to water of a certain quality has, as a practical matter, often been supplanted by the federal Clean Water Act.[95]

B.   Navigable Waters

In the context of riparian real estate, navigable waters represent the quintessential intersection of public rights and interests with private land ownership. To call a waterway "navigable" is, almost by definition, to acknowledge that both the general public and federal and state governments have interests in and rights to that waterway, limiting riparian landowners' rights to exclude and control.

---

[90]   *Id.* at 34.
[91]   *Id.* at 35–36.
[92]   *Id.* at 36–38.
[93]   *Id.* at 36–37.
[94]   *Id.* at 38.
[95]   33 U.S.C. §§ 1251–388.

1.   Traditional navigable waters under federal law

Under English common law, surface waters were considered "navigable" if they were influenced by the ebb and flow of the tide,[96] and the United States adheres to that rule.[97] Tidal navigability remains important along the coasts of the United States and for some rivers that empty into the ocean or that are tributaries of rivers that connect to the ocean. For example, in 1968 the US Geological Survey noted that "[t]ides from the Pacific Ocean affect flow in the Columbia River inland for 146 river miles [to the Bonneville Dam] and cause the main part of the Willamette River … to be tide affected to Willamette Falls, which is nearly 15 miles upstream from the center of Portland."[98] Similarly, on the East Coast, "[t]he Delaware River is tidally influenced for over 130 miles from the Atlantic Ocean to Trenton, N.J. This section of the river, which includes the cities of Wilmington, Del., Camden, N.J. and Philadelphia, Pa., is known as the Delaware Estuary."[99]

Since at least the middle of the 19th century, the US Supreme Court has declared that:

> It is the settled law of this country that the ownership of and dominion and sovereignty over lands covered by tide waters, within the limits of the several states, belong to the respective states within which they are found, with the consequent right to use or dispose of any portion thereof, when that can be done without substantial impairment of the interest of the public in the waters, and subject always to the paramount right of congress to control their navigation so far as may be necessary for the regulation of commerce with foreign nations and among the states.[100]

Moreover, in 1988 the Court reaffirmed the continuing vitality of the tidal test for navigability. Specifically, in *Phillips Petroleum Co. v. Mississippi*,[101] the Court addressed the issue of whether the State of Mississippi or private riparian landowners had title to the submerged lands below waters that *were*

---

[96]   *Illinois Central R.R. Co.*, 146 U.S. at 435.

[97]   Phillips Petroleum Co. v. Mississippi, 484 U.S. 469 (1988).

[98]   GEORGE R. DEMPSTER AND GALE A. LUTZ, WATER-DISCHARGE DETERMINATIONS FOR THE TIDAL REACH OF THE WILLAMETTE RIVER FROM ROSS ISLAND BRIDGE TO MILE 10.3, PORTLAND, OREGON, at H4 (1968), https://pubs.usgs.gov/wsp/1586h/report.pdf.

[99]   *DRB Info for Students & Teachers: Fun Facts about the DRB*, DELAWARE RIVER BASIN COMMISSION (modified June 12, 2023), https://www.nj.gov/drbc/public/outreach/fun-facts.html#:~:text=The%20Delaware%20River%20is%20tidally,known%20as%20the%20Delaware%20Estuary.

[100]   *PPL Montana*, 132 S. Ct. at 1227. See also Pollard's Lessee v. Hagan, 44 U.S. 212, 223 (1845).

[101]   Phillips Petroleum Co. v. Mississippi, 484 U.S. 469 (1988).

subject to the ebb and flow of the tide but were *not* navigable in fact. The Court resolved the issue in the state's favor, emphasizing once again that tidally influenced waters are public.[102]

Nevertheless, tidal influence does not come close to defining actual navigability in the United States' large interior, and reliance solely on the English tidal test would have left the Great Lakes, the Missouri River, much of the Mississippi River, and many other critically important rivers and lakes legally non-navigable and hence subject to private control. As a result, relatively early in its history the US Supreme Court adopted a "navigable in fact" test to render public the large inland waters important to the developing nation. Under the classic test of navigability from *The Daniel Ball*, waters are navigable in fact

> when they are used, or are susceptible of being used, in their ordinary condition, as highways for commerce, over which trade and travel are or may be conducted in the customary modes of trade and travel on water. And they constitute navigable waters of the United States within the meaning of the acts of Congress, in contradistinction from the navigable waters of the states, when they form in their ordinary condition by themselves, or by uniting with other waters, a continued highway over which commerce is or may be carried on with other states or foreign countries in the customary modes in which such commerce is conducted by water.[103]

Once the Supreme Court allowed internal waters to be considered public through "navigable in fact" status, much of the ensuing litigation focused on application of the "navigable in fact" test to waters such as the Red River in Oklahoma[104] and the Green River in Utah.[105] This intensive focus on "navigable in fact" waters helps to explain what went wrong in *Kaiser Aetna*.[106] The case involved the Hawaii Kai Marine in Hawai'i, a former Hawaiian fish pond made navigable in fact by engineering permitted by the US Army Corps of Engineers, and the Court had to decide whether that engineered navigability opened the marina to the public.[107] The majority evaluated the case solely through the navigable-in-fact test and, as noted, ended up favoring the private right to exclude.[108] Dissenting Justices Blackmun, Brennan, and Marshall,

---

[102] *Id.* at 476–81.
[103] The Daniel Ball, 77 U.S. (10 Wall.) 557, 563 (1870). See also Utah v. United States, 403 U.S. 9, 10–11 (1971) (citing *The Daniel Ball* as the first important test of navigability for state title purposes and stating that that test applies to all waters, not just rivers).
[104] Oklahoma v. Texas, 254 U.S. 574, 587–89 (1922).
[105] United States v. Utah, 283 U.S. 64, 75–78 (1931).
[106] Kaiser Aetna v. U.S., 444 U.S. 164, 176 (1979).
[107] *Id.* at 166–68.
[108] *Id.* at 172–80.

however, criticized the majority for ignoring the tidal navigability test, even though the United States actively argued for it.[109] They concluded that, under the tidal test of navigability, "Kuapa Pond, which is contiguous to Maunalua Bay, and which in its natural state must be regarded as an arm of the sea, subject to its tides and currents as much as the Bay itself," was a navigable water that had *always* been open to the public.[110] In light of *Phillips Petroleum*,[111] which the Supreme Court decided less than a decade after *Kaiser Aetna*, the dissent's view was the correct one: the fish pond itself was navigable and public long before people developed it into a marina.

2.   Federal law consequences of calling a waterway "navigable"

Four important consequences flow from a waterway meeting the federal law definitions of navigability, three of which subject private property rights in riparian properties to publicly-minded limitations.[112] First, if the waterway was navigable at the time of statehood, the relevant state—not private riparian landowners—owns the bed and banks (submerged lands) of that waterway.[113] The rule displaces the normal rules for riparian properties, under which the private landowners divide the submerged lands as part of their real estate titles.[114] State ownership of the submerged lands underscores the waterway's public character and also gives the state authority to regulate activities such as sand and gravel mining.

Notably, moreover, the states themselves have long been aware of the importance of keeping navigable waters public. For example, In 1856, before the US Supreme Court decided *The Daniel Ball*, the Iowa Supreme Court rejected a claim that the non-tidal internal stretches of the Mississippi River were privately owned and controllable. Its outrage at the very thought of privatizing

---

[109]   *Id.* at 182–84 (Blackmun, J., dissenting).

[110]   *Id.* at 183 (Blackmun, J., dissenting).

[111]   *Phillips Petroleum Co.*, 484 U.S. at 476–81.

[112]   While "navigable water" is a legal term of art in most contexts, it has *multiple* precise technical meanings depending on the exact context in which it is being used: Robin Kundis Craig, *Navigability and Its Consequences: State Tile, Mineral Rights, and the Public Trust Doctrine*, 60 RMMLF-INST 7-1, at §§ 7.01, 7.02 (2014). For this discussion, however, *The Daniel Ball* navigable-in-fact test and the ebb-and-flow tidal test are sufficient to identify the navigable waters with a federal law public character.

[113]   Phillips Petroleum Co. v. Mississippi, 484 U.S. 469, 476–81 (1988) (tidally influenced waters) and *Illinois Central Railroad Co.*, 146 U.S. at 435–37 (navigable in fact waters).

[114]   CRAIG, ADLER AND HALL, *supra* note 14, at 19–22 (illustrating the various rules for dividing private ownership or submerged lands).

the Mississippi into the hands of the riparian landowners along its shore is palpable:

> Are we to be told that the Mississippi river is not a navigable stream, and its bed private property? The father of the floods, private property! The great river, to see which the conqueror of Florida periled the lives of his followers, to find for himself a grave in its waters, instead of gold in its sands, belongs to every petty owner who pays a dime for the land on its banks! The river, which carries to the sea the products of millions of people, the boundary of states without number; which carries to a single port commerce numbered by hundreds of millions of dollars, and numbers the ships which float on its waters by thousands, cannot be private property. We know that men, with the wealth of Crœsus, and the genius of Archimedes, have spanned its waters with a bridge. So has science bridged and tunneled the Thames, at London, and the thundering car has swept across the straits of Menai, and Niagara at the falls; but they are navigable streams, and the father of waters has yielded to the genius of progress, not to diminish, but increase, the trade and intercourse on this great highway of the republics which have grown, and will continue to grow, on its borders.[115]

Thus, in the mid-19th century, the federal government and the states were in agreement that the nation's arteries of commerce, travel, and discovery needed to remain public.

Second, navigable waters are subject to the federal government's navigation servitude. This servitude insulates the federal government from Fifth Amendment takings liability when the federal government acts to maintain navigation. Specifically, the federal government owes private property owners no compensation when it damages or destroys private property (for example, docks, shellfish beds, water power) below the high water line in a navigable water, so long as it acts in aid of navigation.[116] As such, the navigation servitude is an inherent limitation on private riparian rights and applies even if the state has granted the riparian landowner private title to submerged lands below the high water mark.[117]

The navigation servitude thus is another legal doctrine that elevates the public values of navigable waters over private property rights, as the Supreme Court made clear in 1945. Noting that "[t]he doctrine of riparian rights attained its maximum authority on non-navigable streams," where "[n]o overriding public interest chilled the contest between owners to get the utmost in benefits from flowing streams,"[118] the Court emphasized that:

---

[115] McManus v. Carmichael, 3 Iowa 1, 6 (1856).
[116] United States v. Commodore Park, 324 U.S. 386, 390–92 (1945) and United States v. Chicago, M., St. P. & P.R. Co., 312 U.S. 592, 596–98 (1941).
[117] *Commodore Park*, 324 U.S. at 390.
[118] United States v. Willow River Power Co., 324 U.S. 499, 505 (1945).

On navigable streams a different right intervenes. While riparian owners on navigable streams usually were held to have the same rights to be free from interferences of other riparian owners as on non-navigable streams, it was recognized from the beginning that all riparian interests were subject to a dominant public interest in navigation. ...

Without detailing the long struggle between such conflicting interests on navigable streams, it may be pointed out that by 1909 the lines had become sharply drawn and were then summarized by a leading author:

"The older authorities hold that such an owner has no private rights in the stream or body of water which are appurtenant to his land, and, in short, no rights beyond that of any other member of the public, and that the only difference is that he is more conveniently situated to enjoy the privileges which all the public have in common, and that he has access to the waters over his own land, which the public do not."[119]

Furthermore, "[a]ccess to and use of the stream by the riparian owner is regarded merely as permissive on the part of the public and liable to be cut off absolutely if the public sees fit to do so."

Thus, all property rights in the navigable waters and the lands submerged beneath them—whether owned by states or private citizens—are subject to the federal government's paramount right to maintain and improve navigation.[120]

Third, calling a water "navigable" under federal law means that Congress can automatically regulate activities in that waterway pursuant to its Commerce Clause authority. The Commerce Clause of the US Constitution gives Congress authority "[t]o regulate Commerce with foreign Nations, and among the several States, and with the Indian Tribes."[121] As discussed, especially in the United States' early years, navigability had a clear connection to interstate and foreign commerce, and the US Supreme Court in cases like *The Daniel Ball* fairly quickly extended Congress's Commerce Clause authority to all "navigable in fact" waters; *The Daniel Ball* test is a commerce-based test.[122]

Like the navigation servitude, Commerce Clause authority allows the federal government to maintain the navigable waters' public values. Nevertheless, Congress has used its general authority over "navigable waters" to regulate in a variety of different ways. The Rivers and Harbors Act of 1899, for example, requires either a permit from the Army Corps of Engineers or congressional permission before anyone can build within or obstruct the navigable waters[123]—unless what the person or entity is building is a hydroelectric

---

[119] *Id.* at 507 (quoting 1 LEWIS ON EMINENT DOMAIN (3rd Ed.) 116, 119 (1909) and WOOD ON NUISANCES (1st Ed.) 592).
[120] United States v. Kansas City Life Ins. Co., 339 U.S. 799, 808 (1950).
[121] U.S. Const., art. I, § 8, cl.3.
[122] *The Daniel Ball*, 77 U.S. (10 Wall.) at 563.
[123] 33 U.S.C. §§ 402, 403.

dam, in which case, under the contemporary version of the Federal Power Act of 1935, the Federal Energy Regulatory Commission (FERC) is in charge.[124] Thus, these two statutes prevent private riparian landowners from clogging the navigable waters with dams, bridges, marinas, and docks without the federal government's permission, ensuring that the public values of these waterways remain.

Perhaps the most frustrating use—on all sides—of Congress's Commerce Clause authority over "navigable waters" was Congress's decision to tie federal water quality regulation under the 1972 Clean Water Act to a statutorily defined set of "navigable waters,"[125] but then to define "navigable waters" as "the waters of the United States, including the territorial seas."[126] Unfortunately, this single definition applies to both of the Act's permitting programs, which intersect with private real property rights in very different ways:

> [T]he Act's two permit programs—the section 402 National Pollutant Discharge Elimination System (NPDES) program and the section 404 "dredge and fill" program—resonate in different legal webs. Specifically, regardless of where a discharge occurs, the NPDES permit program resonates with public nuisance by protecting human health and the public welfare from water pollution, including toxic pollution. In contrast, as the section 404 permit requirement moves away from the larger navigable-in-fact waters to higher ground, it increasingly interferes with private property use, development, and landowner profit, resonating with land use planning limitations and constitutional takings concerns. While the environmental impacts of development in and near smaller waters and wetlands are both real and substantial, the U.S. Supreme Court has made clear that it views section 404 permitting less as preventing nuisance and far more as meddling in the affairs of states, municipalities, and private landowners. As a result, no single geography of "waters of the United States" can possibly accomplish the nuisance-preventing functions of section 402 while simultaneously avoiding the interference with land development that the Court has found suspect since 2001.[127]

As a result, Congress's decision to broaden the Clean Water Act's scope from the traditional navigable waters has so far generated four US Supreme Court decisions interpreting "waters of the United States"—all of which have arisen in the context of Section 404 and restrictions on the development of private property.[128] While these cases can be complicated illustrations of federal stat-

---

[124] 16 U.S.C. § 797(e).

[125] 33 U.S.C. § 1311(a).

[126] *Id.* § 1362(7).

[127] Robin Kundis Craig, *There Is More to the Clean Water Act Than Waters of the United States: A Holistic Jurisdictional Approach to the Section 402 and Section 404 Permit Programs*, 73 CASE WESTERN RESERVE L. REV. 349, 352–53 (2022).

[128] United States v. Riverside Bayview Homes, Inc., 474 U.S. 121, 131–34 (1985) (unanimously upholding jurisdiction over wetlands adjacent to traditional

utory interpretation, in the context of this chapter they embody an ongoing effort—by both the federal agencies involved and the courts—to find the "proper" balance between the private interest in real estate development and the public interest in water quality and aquatic ecosystem integrity when real property encompasses water resources.

Finally, navigability also influences relationships between the states and the federal government. Specifically, incidents involving ships and their crews on the navigable waters are subject to federal admiralty jurisdiction, not state tort law. Article III of the US Constitution gives the federal courts jurisdiction to hear "all Cases of admiralty and maritime jurisdiction."[129] Classically, waters subject to admiralty jurisdiction included the high seas and the tidewaters—that is, waters subject to the ebb and flow of the tide.[130] However, in 1852, in *The Genesee Chief v. Fitzhugh*, the US Supreme Court extended admiralty jurisdiction to all "navigable in fact" waters, including lakes and streams.[131]

Admiralty jurisdiction serves primarily to divest state courts of jurisdiction in admiralty cases. Federal courts use a "locality test" to determine whether federal admiralty jurisdiction applies, and as such "[e]very species of tort, however occurring, and whether on board a vessel or not, if upon the high seas or navigable waters, is of admiralty cognizance."[132] Congress accepted but also expanded upon this locality test in 1948 when it enacted the Extension of Admiralty Jurisdiction Act, providing that "[t]he admiralty and maritime jurisdiction of the United States shall extend to and include all cases of damage or injury, to person or property, caused by a vessel on navigable water, notwithstanding that such damage or injury be done or consummated on land."[133]

---

navigable waters); Solid Waste Agency of Northern Cook County v. U.S. Army Corps of Engineers, 531 U.S. 159, 162–65, 172–74 (2001) (denying, by a 5–4 majority, jurisdiction over "isolated" waters solely on the basis that migratory birds used them); Rapanos v. United States, 547 U.S. 715, 741–45 (Scalia, J., for the majority), 779–80 (Kennedy, J., concurring), 810 (Stevens, J., dissenting (2006) (creating three different tests for "waters of the United States"); and Sackett v. Envtl. Protection Agency, 598 U.S. 651, 671 (2023) (unanimously adopting Justice Scalia's surface water connection test from *Rapanos*).

[129]   U.S. Const., art. III, § 2; see also 28 U.S.C. § 1331(1) (including admiralty jurisdiction as one aspect of the federal courts' federal question jurisdiction).

[130]   Executive Jet Aviation, Inc. v. City of Cleveland, OH, 409 U.S. 249, 253 (1972) (quoting Thomas v. Lane, 23 Fed. Cas. 957, 960 (C.C. Me 1813)).

[131]   *Id.* and The Genesee Chief v. Fitzhugh, 53 U.S. 443, 453–58 (1852).

[132]   The Plymouth, 70 U.S. 20, 36 (1865) and Sisson v. Ruby, 497 U.S. 358, 360–61 (1990) (quoting The Plymouth, 70 U.S. at 36).

[133]   46 U.S.C. App. § 740.

3.   State law consequences of calling a waterway "navigable" under federal law

Because the states get title to the submerged lands beneath navigable waters, classifying a waterway as "navigable" has implications for state as well as federal law. Most important for preserving the public interest in those waters are the states' public trust doctrines. These public trust doctrines both give the public rights in the waters to which the doctrine applies and, in most states, limit the state's authority to cede navigable waters to private ownership and control.

As scholars have discussed at length, the public trust doctrine has an extensive history dating back to Roman law.[134] The principle that navigable waters should remain public also has a long history in English common law;[135] for example, "[t]he Magna Carta provided that the Crown would remove 'all fishweirs ... from the Thames and the Medway and throughout all England, except

---

[134]   For example, the U.S. Supreme Court has traced the protections for public rights in water to the Institutes of Justinian, which stated that "'[r]ivers and ports are public; hence the right of fishing in a port, or in rivers are in common ....'" Idaho v. Coeur d'Alene Tribe of Idaho, 521 U.S. 261, 284 (1997). For more extensive discussions of the public trust doctrine's history, see: J.B. Ruhl and Thomas A.J. McGinn, *The Roman Public Trust Doctrine: What Was It, and Does It Support an Atmospheric Trust?*, 47 ECOLOGY L.Q. 117, 134–71 (2020); Barton H. Thompson, *The Public Trust Doctrine: A Conservative Reconstruction and Defense*, 15 SOUTHEASTERN ENVTL. L.J. 47, 50–54 (Fall 2006); Eric Nelson, *The Public Trust Doctrine and the Great Lakes*, 11 ALB. L. ENVTL. OUTLOOK J. 131, 136–40 (2006); George D. Smith II and Michael W. Sweeney, *The Public Trust Doctrine and Natural Law: Emanations within a Penumbra*, 33 BOSTON C. ENVTL. AFF. L. REV. 307, 310–14 (2006); Jeffrey W. Henquinet and Tracy Dobson, *The Public Trust Doctrine and Sustainable Ecosystems: A Great Lakes Fisheries Case Study*, 14 N.Y.U. ENVTL. L.J. 322, 324–30 (2006); Allan Kanner, *The Public Trust Doctrine, Parens Patriae, and the Attorney General as the Guardian of the State's Natural Resources*, 16 DUKE ENVTL. L. & POL'Y F. 57, 61–86 (Fall 2005); Richard J. Lazarus, *Changing Conceptions of Property and Sovereignty in Natural Resources: Questioning the Public Trust Doctrine*, 71 IOWA L. REV. 631, 633–36 (1985); and Joseph L. Sax, *The Public Trust Doctrine in Natural Resources Law: Effective Judicial Intervention*, 68 MICH. L. REV. 471 (1970).

[135]   "The special treatment of navigable waters in English law was recognized in Bracton's time. He stated that '[a]ll rivers and ports are public, so that the right to fish therein is common to all persons. The use of river banks, as of the river itself, is also public.'" *Id.* (quoting 2 H. BRACTON, DE LEGIBUS ET CONSUETUDINIBUS ANGLIAE 40 (S. Thorne transl. 1968)).

on the sea coast,'"[136] keeping the internal rivers clear for navigation. Bringing this tradition to the United States, the US Supreme Court declared in 1842 that "when the [American] revolution took place, the people of each state became themselves sovereign; and in that character hold the absolute right to all their navigable waters, and the soils under them, for their own common use, subject only to the rights since surrendered by the constitution to the general government."[137]

The historical persistence of a public trust concept reflects a pragmatic recognition, as the Iowa Supreme Court amply demonstrated regarding the Mississippi River, that relinquishing public ownership and control of waters—especially navigable waters—in favor of private control and profit is likely to undermine the overall well-being of a nation or state. The US Supreme Court most explicitly recognized the existence of the public trust doctrine in the 1892 case of *Illinois Central Railroad Co. v. Illinois*,[138] which remains the "lodestar" Supreme Court case in this area.[139] This opinion underscored the public character of navigable waters, with the Court adopting the New York courts' view that:

> The title to lands under tide waters, within the realm of England, were by the common law deemed to be vested in the king as a public trust, to subserve and protect the public right to use them as common highways for commerce, trade, and intercourse. The king, by virtue of his proprietary interest, could grant the soil so that it should become private property, but his grant was subject to the paramount right of public use of navigable waters, which he could neither destroy nor abridge ....
>
> The principle of the common law to which we have adverted is founded upon the most obvious principles of public policy. *The sea and navigable rivers are natural highways, and any obstruction to the common right, or exclusive appropriation of their use, is injurious to commerce, and, if permitted at the will of the sovereign, would be very likely to end in materially crippling, if not destroying, it.* The laws of most nations have sedulously guarded the public use of navigable waters within their limits against infringement, subjecting it only to such regulation by the state,

---

[136]   *Id.* (quoting M. Evans and R. Jack, SOURCES OF ENGLISH LEGAL AND CONSTITUTIONAL HISTORY 53 (1984) and citing Martin v. Waddell's Lessee, 41 U.S. 367, 410–13 (1842) ("tracing tidelands trusteeship back to Magna Carta")).

[137]   Martin v. Waddell's Lessee, 41 U.S. 367, 410 (1842).

[138]   146 U.S. 387 (1892). For discussions of the history of this case and its relationship to state public trust doctrines, see generally: Joseph D. Kearney and Thomas W. Merrill, *The Origins of the American Public Trust Doctrine: What Really Happened in* Illinois Central, 71 U. CHI. L. REV. 799 (Summer 2004); Douglas L. Grant, *Underpinnings of the Public Trust Doctrine: Lessons from* Illinois Central Railroad, 33 ARIZ. ST. L.J. 849 (Fall 2001); and Eric Pearson, Illinois Central *and the Public Trust Doctrine in State Law*, 15 VA. ENVTL. L.J. 713 (Summer 1996).

[139]   Lazarus, *supra* note 134, at 640.

in the interest of the public, as is deemed consistent with the preservation of the public right.[140]

In so doing, the Court, like the New York courts before it, connected the overall protection of public rights in navigable waters to the protection and promotion of commerce and economic growth as a matter of overriding public policy.

The public character of the navigable waters limits what states can do with their submerged lands, as well. According to the *Illinois Central* Court, while the state does hold title to submerged lands:

> it is a title different in character from that which the state holds in lands intended for sale. It is different from the title which the United States hold in the public lands which are open to pre-emption and sale. It is a title held in trust for the people of the state, that they may enjoy the navigation of the waters, carry on commerce over them, and have liberty of fishing therein, freed from the obstruction or interference of private parties.[141]

Thus, the three public uses of waters that the classic public trust doctrine protects are navigation, commerce, and fishing.[142]

---

[140]   Illinois Central Railroad Co. v. Illinois, 146 U.S. 387, 458 (1892) (emphasis added; quoting People v. New York & S.I. Ferry Co., 1877 WL 11834, at *3 (N.Y. 1877)). See also Shively v. Bowlby, 152 U.S. 1, 11 (1894) ("By the common law, both the title and the dominion of the sea, and of rivers and arms of the sea, where the tide ebbs and flows, and of all the lands below high-water mark, within the jurisdiction of the crown of England, are in the king. Such waters, and the lands which they cover, either at all times, or at least when the tide is in, are incapable of ordinary and private occupation, cultivation, and improvement; and their natural and primary uses are public in their nature, for highways of navigation and commerce, domestic and foreign, and for the purpose of fishing by all the king's subjects. Therefore the title, jus privatum, in such lands, as of waste and unoccupied lands, belongs to the king, as the sovereign; and the dominion thereof, jus publicum, is vested in him, as the representative of the nation and for the public benefit."). But see FLORIDA CONST., art. 10, § 11 ("The title to lands under navigable waters, within the boundaries of the state, *which have not been alienated* ... is held by the state, by virtue of its sovereignty, in trust for all the people. *Sale of such lands may be authorized by law, but only when in the public interest*" [emphasis added]).

[141]   *Illinois Central R.R.*, 146 U.S. at 452.

[142]   *Id.* See also Shively v. Bowlby, 152 U.S. 1, 13 (1894) (emphasizing the public rights of fishing and navigation).

In addition, according to the *Illinois Central* Court, the doctrine acts as a restraint on the state's ability to alienate the beds and banks of navigable waters or to abdicate regulatory control over those waters:

> The interest of the people in the navigation of the waters and in commerce over them may be improved in many instances by the erection of wharves, docks, and piers therein, for which purpose the state may grant parcels of the submerged lands; and, so long as their disposition is made for such purpose, no valid objections can be made to the grants. ... But that is a very different doctrine from the one which would sanction the abdication of the general control of the state over lands under the navigable waters of an entire harbor or bay, or of a sea or lake. Such abdication is not consistent with the exercise of that trust which requires the government of the state to preserve such waters for the use of the public. The trust devolving upon the state for the public, and which can only be discharged by the management and control of property in which the public has an interest, cannot be relinquished by a transfer of the property. The control of the state for the purposes of the trust can never be lost, except as to such parcels as are used in promoting the interests of the public therein, or can be disposed of without any substantial impairment of the public interest in the lands and waters remaining.[143]

This restraint on alienation – and its perception as a federal law requirement – has been important in several states, notably Arizona.[144]

Since *Illinois Central*, however, the Supreme Court has made clear that the public trust doctrine is a matter of *state* law,[145] despite the fact that it is rooted in state title to submerged lands, a federal law test.[146] As a result, even within the federally navigable waters, states have been free to expand the public uses protected by their public trust doctrines. For example, "about half the states have expanded their public trust doctrines to protect public recreation on the navigable rivers."[147]

Other states have left open the future scope of their public trust doctrines through broad but enigmatic statements of the uses that the doctrine protects. The Florida courts, for example, have indicated that "[t]he public has the right

---

[143]   Illinois Central Railroad Co. v. Illinois, 146 U.S. 387, 452–53 (1892).

[144]   See, for example, Defenders of Wildlife v. Hull, 18 P.3d 722, 726–28 (Ariz. App. 2001) (relying on *Illinois Central Railroad* to conclude that the restraint on alienation of submerged lands is a common-law rule grounded in the Constitution that invalidates the Arizona legislature's attempts to disclaim or restrict state ownership of those lands).

[145]   Appleby v. City of New York, 271 U.S. 364, 395–99 (1926); Idaho v. Coeur d'Alene Tribe of Idaho, 521 U.S. 261, 284–86 (1997); and PPL Montana, LLC v. Montana, 565 U.S. 576, 603–604 (2012).

[146]   *Utah v. United States*, 403 U.S. 9, 10 (1971) (quoting *The Daniel Ball*. 77 U.S. (10 Wall.) 557, 563 (1870)).

[147]   CRAIG, ADLER, AND HALL, *supra* note 14, at 134.

to use navigable waters for navigation, commerce, fishing, and bathing and 'other easements allowed by law.'"[148] Louisiana's statutes declare that the public rights in navigable waters include navigation, fishing, recreation, "and other interests."[149] The Massachusetts public trust doctrine "includes all necessary and proper uses, in the interest of the public,"[150] while New Hampshire holds the public trust waters for the benefit of the people "for all useful purposes"[151] and Ohio's public trust doctrine extends to all "the public uses to which it might be adapted."[152] Finally, pursuant to Wisconsin's public trust doctrine, the public can use the public trust waters for navigation, hunting, fishing, recreation, "or any other lawful purpose."[153] In 1974, the California Supreme Court announced in *Marks v. Whitney* that the public trust uses of the state's tidewaters were inherently flexible.[154]

Probably most famously, while California's public trust doctrine remains tethered to the traditionally navigable waters, the California Supreme Court has expanded the doctrine within the state to protect ecological and scientific values and to limit private water rights when necessary.[155] However, "Hawaii's ecological public trust doctrine is even broader, affecting not only water rights but also environmental permits and extending to both surface water and groundwater."[156] About 13 states have in some way extended their public trust doctrines to environmental values, decreasing riparian landowners' ability to use their properties in ways that cause ecological harm.

In addition, many states that have allowed private ownership in navigable waters to extend lower than the mean high water line or mean high tide line nevertheless still allow public use to the water and submerged lands between the low- and high-water lines, essentially adopting the same rule as the federal government does for the navigation servitude. Massachusetts, for example, originally recognized that state ownership in tidal waters extended to the mean high tide line. However, through the Colonial Ordinance of 1641–1647,

---

[148]   Brannon v. Boldt, 958 So.2d 367, 373 (Fla. Ct. App. 2007) (quoting Broward v. Mabry, 50 So. 826, 830 (Fla. 1909)).

[149]   LA. REV. STAT. ANN. § 14:1701.

[150]   Home for Aged Woman v. Commonwealth, 89 N.E.124, 129 (Mass. 1909).

[151]   Opinion of the Justices, 649 A.2d 604, 609 (N.H. 1994).

[152]   Beach Cliff Board of Trustess v. Ferchill, 2003 WL 21027604, at *2 (Ohio Ct. App. 2003).

[153]   Meunch v. Public Service Commission, 53 N.W.2d 514, 519 (Wis. 1952).

[154]   491 P.2d 374, 380 (Cal. 1974).

[155]   National Audubon Society v. Superior Court of Alpine County, 658 P.2d 709, 712–29 (Cal. 1983).

[156]   CRAIG, ADLER, AND HALL, *supra* note 14, at 138 (citing In re Water Use Permit Applications, 9 P.3d 409, 441–43 (Haw. 2000)).

its colonial government conveyed title to private landowners to the low-tide line in order to encourage private construction of wharves, piers, and other aids to navigation.[157] Nevertheless, public rights continue to extend to the high tide line.[158] Similar rules apply in Delaware,[159] Illinois,[160] Kentucky,[161] Louisiana,[162] Maine,[163] Massachusetts,[164] Minnesota,[165] Mississippi,[166] New York,[167] Ohio,[168] Pennsylvania,[169] and West Virginia.[170] In each of these states, therefore, the public retains the right to use a waterway even though the riparian landowner owns part or all of the submerged lands.

C.   Non-Navigable Waters

In contrast to federal navigable waters, which are by definition public, non-navigable waters are presumptively private. This reality is most clearly evident in the fact that, as discussed, riparian title to lands abutting or encompassing a non-navigable water includes the submerged lands beneath that water.

Even so, many states have used state public trust doctrines and state water law to recognize public rights in even these ostensibly private waterways. They do so primarily by adopting more expansive state-law definitions of navigability and (mostly in the West) expanding the implications of state/public ownership of the water itself.

---

[157]   Boston Waterfront Development Corp. v. Commonwealth, 393 N.E.2d 356, 359–60 (Mass. 1979).
[158]   *Id.*
[159]   Groves v. Secretary, Department of Natural Resources & Environmental Control, 1994 WL 89804, at *6 (Del. Super. Ct. 1994).
[160]   Schulte v. Warren, 75 N.E. 783, 785 (Ill. 1905).
[161]   Pierson v. Coffey, 706 S.W.2d 409, 411 (Ky. Ct. App. 1985).
[162]   LA. CIV. CODE ANN., art 456.
[163]   Stanton v. Treasurers of St. Joseph's College, 233 A.2d 718, 721–22 (Me. 1967).
[164]   Brosnan v. Gage, 133 N.E. 622, 624 (Mass. 1921).
[165]   Mitchell v. City of St. Paul, 31 N.W.2d 46, 49 (Minn. 1948).
[166]   Ryals v. Pigott, 580 So.2d 1140, 1149 n.19, 1171 (Miss. 1990).
[167]   Adirondack League Club, Inc. v. Sierra Club, 615 N.Y.S.2d 788, 790 (N.Y. App. Div. 1994).
[168]   State ex rel. Brown v. Newport Concrete Co., 336 N.E.2d 453, 455 (Ohio Ct. App. 1975).
[169]   Fulmer v. Williams, 15 A. 726, 727 (Pa. 1888).
[170]   Gaston v. Mace, 10 S.E. 60, 63 (W. Va. 1889).

1.   Expanded state definitions of "navigable" waters

As noted, the early federal law tests for navigability focus on tidal influence and commercial navigability—i.e., navigability by bigger vessels. Nevertheless, as recreational water sports like kayaking and rafting have become more pervasive and economically important, many states have adopted state-law definitions of "navigable waters" that open "private" waters to public recreation, even though riparian landowners own the submerged lands. For example, Arkansas adhered to the federal commerce test for both submerged land title and public trust purposes until 1980. However, in 1980, the Arkansas Supreme Court decided to follow broader public trust doctrines decisions in Massachusetts, Ohio, Michigan, California, Minnesota, and Oregon and extended public rights to waters that are useful only for recreational purposes.[171] As a result, private riparian landowners could not prevent kayakers, canoeists, and rafters from using the waterways in front of their upland properties. Ohio, similarly, began with the federal "navigable-in-fact" test, but by 1955 the Ohio Supreme Court acknowledged a "gradually changing concept of navigability" and considered any water that supports recreational uses to be "navigable" for public trust purposes.[172]

Some states' definition of navigable waters also reflect important industries in that state that rely on waters that do not necessarily meet the federal navigability tests. For example, Michigan,[173] Missouri,[174] and Oregon[175] all adopted log floatation tests for navigability, opening ostensibly private waters to timber transportation. By statute, South Carolina uses a "valuable floatage" test,[176] which its courts have interpreted "to include any 'legitimate and beneficial public use.'"[177] Most idiosyncratic is Alaska, which by statute, and for purposes of establishing public rights in waters, defined a "navigable water" to be:

> any water of the state forming a river, stream, lake, pond, slough, creek, bay, sound, estuary, inlet, strait, passage, canal, sea or ocean, or any other body of water or waterway within the territorial limits of the state or subject to its jurisdiction, that is navigable in fact for any useful public purpose, *including but not limited to water*

---

[171]   State v. McIlroy, 595 S.W.2d 659, 665 (Ark. 1980).

[172]   Coleman v. Schaeffer, 126 N.E.2d 444, 445–47 (Ohio 1955).

[173]   Michigan Citizens for Water Conservation v. Nestle Waters North America, Inc., 709 N.W.2d 174, 218 (Mich. Ct. App. 2005), unrelated MEPA claims rev'd on standing grounds, – N.W.2d —, 2007 WL 2126497 (Mich. July 25, 2007).

[174]   Hobart-Lee Tie Co. v. Grabner, 219 S.W. 975, 976 (Mo. Ct. App. 1920).

[175]   Felger v. Robinson, 3 Or. 455, 458 (1869).

[176]   S.C. CODE ANN. § 49-1-10.

[177]   White's Mill Colony, Inc. v. Williams, 609 S.E.2d 811, 815 (S.C. Ct. App. 2005) (quoting State ex rel. Medlock v. South Carolina Coastal Comm'n, 346 S.E.2d 716, 719 (S.C. 1986)).

suitable for commercial navigation, floating of logs, landing and takeoff of air-craft, and public boating, trapping, hunting waterfowl and aquatic animals, fishing, or other public recreational purposes ... .[178]

In addition, the public has rights in "public waters," which by statute include not only navigable waters but also "all other water, whether inland or coastal, fresh or salt, that is reasonably suitable for public use and utility, habitat for fish and wildlife in which there is a public interest, or migration and spawning of fish in which there is a public interest ...."[179] While Alaska is the only state that explicitly identifies use of waters by seaplanes as an important public use, it shares its concern for supporting the sustainability of critical aquatic foods with Oregon[180] and Washington,[181] both of which have adopted public trust doctrines that reflect the importance of salmon and shellfish, respectively, to their citizens.

State navigability tests for public uses are thus highly variable. However, they share one thing in common: a state decision to open to public use waters that might not be public under the federal law navigability tests. These state-law tests thus represent re-balancings of private riparian property rights in favor of the public interest, reflecting public needs and values as more locally defined.

---

[178]   ALAS. STAT. ANN. § 38.05.965(13) (emphasis added).

[179]   ALAS. STAT. ANN. § 38.05.965(18).

[180]   For example, in Oregon, the state's public trust responsibilities have been applied to fishing regulation. As a result, statutes purporting to convey exclusive rights to fish in navigable waters violated the Privileges and Immunities Clause in the Oregon Constitution. Hume v. Rogue River Packing Co., 92 P. 1065, 1072–73 (Or. 1907); see also Johnson v. Hoy, 47 P.2d 252, 252 (Or. 1935) (holding that the Legislature cannot grant an exclusive right to fish for salmon). Nevertheless, because the state has jurisdiction over navigable waters, it can regulate fishing. Oregon v. Nielsen, 95 P. 720, 722 (Or. 1908) and Antony v. Veatch, 220 P.2d 493, 498–99 (Or. 1950). Specifically, fishing methods can be enjoined if they interfere with the public's common right of fishing. Radich v. Frederckson, 10 P.2d 352, 355 (Or. 1932) and Johnson v. Hoy, 47 P.2d 252, 252 (Or. 1935).

[181]   "[I]n Washington, the public trust doctrine does not encompass the right to gather clams on private property" because shellfish rights follow title to the submerged lands. Washington v. Longshore, 982 P.2d 1191, 1195–96 (Wash. App. 1999), *affirmed*, Washington v. Longshore, 5 P.3d 1256, 1259–63 (Wash. 2000) (*en banc*); see also Washington State Geoduck Harvest Ass'n v. Washington State Department of Natural Resources, 101 P.3d 891, 895 (Wash. App. 2004) (noting that shellfish are not typical wildlife in Washington because they are considered part of the land). However, state regulation of geoducks does not violate the public trust doctrine. Washington State Geoduck Harvest Ass'n v. Washington State Department of Natural Resources, 101 P.3d 891, 895, 896–97 (Wash. App. 2004).

2.   State ownership of the water

A similar re-balancing of private riparian rights and public values occurs in many western states, albeit through a different legal mechanism. While most eastern states still follow some version of riparian law to define rights to withdraw and use the water itself—i.e., deriving the right to use water from riparian property ownership[182]—most western states have adopted prior appropriation ("first in time, first in right") as their water rights doctrine, splitting off rights to use the water from the riparian land ownership bundle of sticks.[183] As part of prior appropriation, moreover, western states generally declare that the water itself belongs to either the state or the public—and this public ownership of water becomes a means of establishing public rights to use non-navigable waters.

For example, according to the Montana Supreme Court, "*[a]ll* waters are owned by the State for the use of its people."[184] As a result, "the public has the right to use the water for recreational purposes and minimal use of underlying and adjoining real estate essential to enjoyment of its ownership in water," even if the bed and banks are privately owned.[185] Similarly, in 1947 the New Mexico Supreme Court declared that all waters are public waters until beneficially appropriated, and hence that the public can use all waters in the state for recreation, sports, and fishing.[186] Wyoming also has extended public use rights to all waters based on its ownership of the water itself.[187]

Under Utah's statutes, waters are owned by the public.[188] As a result,

---

[182]   Craig, Adler, and Hall, *supra* note 14, at 17.

[183]   *Id.* at 39–48.

[184]   Galt v. Montana by and through Department of Fish, Wildlife, & Parks, 731 P.2d 912, 915 (Mont. 1987) (emphasis added).

[185]   *Id.* and Montana Coalition for Stream Access, Inc. v. Hildreth, 684 P.2d 1088, 1092 (Mont. 1984) (noting that underlying ownership of the bed does not matter for the public's recreational use right); Montana Coalition for Stream Access, Inc. v. Curran, 682 P.2d 163, 171 (Mont. 1984) (holding that "under the public trust doctrine and the 1972 Montana Constitution, any surface waters that are capable of recreational use may be so used by the public without regard to streambed ownership or navigability for nonrecreational purposes").

[186]   New Mexico ex rel. State Game Commission v. Red River Valley Co., 182 P.2d 421, 429–32 (N.M. 1947).

[187]   Day v. Armstrong, 362 P.2d 137, 143–45 (Wyo. 1961).

[188]   UTAH CODE ANNOTATED § 73-1-1.

[u]nder this "doctrine of public ownership," the public owns state waters and has *"an easement over the water regardless of who owns the water bed beneath."* In granting this public this easement, "state policy recognizes an interest of the public in the use of state waters for recreational purposes." This court has enumerated the specific recreational rights that are within the easement's scope. They include *"the right to float leisure craft, hunt, fish, and participate in any lawful activity when utilizing that water."*[189]

Thus, bed ownership is irrelevant to the public's rights to use waters in the state.[190] Moreover, "the scope of the public's easement in state waters provides the public the right to engage in all recreational activities that *utilize* the water and does not limit the public to activities that can be performed *upon* the water."[191] As a result, "the public has the right to touch privately owned beds of state waters in ways incidental to all recreational rights provided for in the easement."[192]

South Dakota went one step further. When increased precipitation created brand new lakes over private property, the South Dakota Supreme Court declared that "the State of South Dakota retains the right to use, control, and develop the water in these lakes as a separate asset in trust for the public," because the state's public trust doctrine applies independently of bed ownership.[193] As such, "all waters within South Dakota, not just those waters considered navigable under the federal test, are held in trust by the State for the public.[194]

D.   The Benefits to Riparian Landowners of Public Rights in Waterways

As the above discussions illustrate, "navigable" (however defined) surface waters are shared spaces where state and federal sovereign interests overlap with both public and private rights. If a water was navigable at the time of statehood, private landowners probably do not own the submerged lands— even those beneath a river running through the middle of the property or a lake that the property entirely surrounds. As a result, the landowner has no right to exclude members of the public who want to use the federally navigable waters for navigation, commerce, fishing, and usually recreation. Moreover,

---

[189]   Conater v. Johnson, 194 P.3d 897, 899–900 (Utah 2008) (quoting JJNP Co. v. Utah, 655 P.2d 1133, 1137 (Utah 1982) (emphasis added)).
[190]   *Id.*
[191]   *Id.* at 901.
[192]   *Id.* at 901–902 (limiting criminal trespass liability for water users).
[193]   Parks v. Cooper, 676 N.W.2d 823, 838 (S.D. 2004).
[194]   *Id.* at 838–39.

any activities that the riparian landowner wants to undertake in the navigable waters—including exercise of the panoply of riparian property rights—require at least a permit from the Army Corps or FERC and perhaps permission from Congress.

Even if the landowner *does* own the submerged lands, the public often still has rights to use the water, particularly for recreation and particularly in the West. Again, therefore, riparian law limits the right to exclude. Moreover, building in, mining, disturbing, or polluting non-navigable waterways is also often subject to regulation, although the regulator may more often be the state.[195]

To be a riparian landowner, in other words, is to be constantly reminded that your land affects the community and public interests operating at multiple scales, from accommodating the neighbors' docks to maintaining nationally important navigation. The presence of water thus makes legally cognizant the property's connections to the larger societies within which it sits.

It does not follow, however, that the life of a riparian landowner is unmitigated sacrifice to the public good. As a basic matter, lakefront, riverfront, and oceanfront properties remain some of the most valuable real estate in the United States, generally reflecting the added value that buyers ascribe to the aesthetics of and recreational opportunities available with waterfront homes.[196] Moreover, riparian landowners are also members of the general public and hence also benefit from any rights accorded to the public as a whole. Thus, for example, riparian landowners as well as the general public benefit (in the form of lower prices for goods) from river commerce that does not require businesses and shipping companies to pay tolls to every riparian landowner along

---

[195] For example, "each state has its own set of regulations governing dock construction and permitting." *Navigating Dock Permits: A Must-Read Guide on Boat Dock Rules and Regulations*, POLYDUCK PRODUCTS (Apr. 25, 2024), https://www.polydockproducts.com/resources/news-plus-events/content-container/navigating-dock-permits-a-must-read-guide-on-boat-dock-rules-and-regulations/.

[196] *What Is Waterfront Worth?*, ZILLOW (Sept. 11, 2014), https://www.zillow.com/research/what-is-waterfront-worth-7540/ ("Nationally, waterfront homes are worth more than double of the value of homes overall").

the route,[197] much as frequent flyers benefit from not having to pay airspace tolls for every property line they cross in flight.[198]

Similarly, when states choose to open presumed private waters to public use, riparian landowners are no longer able to exclude the public from floating past the property—but they and future landowners simultaneously also acquire the right to use more than just the water in front of them, particularly with respect to rivers. This expansion of rights is clearest in states that limit riparian use of a non-navigable waterway to the water over the submerged lands that the riparian actually owns.[199] If the waterway is subject to public use, however, the riparian—like the general public—acquires the right to use the entire waterway.

A right to use the entire waterway is valuable. Indeed, for lakes, the majority of states give the relevant riparian landowners the right to use the *entire* surface of a non-navigable lake,[200] acknowledging that full use is what most riparians want. In contrast, riparian landowners along non-navigable rivers generally feel free to block others' passage or fishing as a trespass[201] and states

---

[197]   While river commerce has declined over time, it is still significant. For example, the Mississippi River alone "supports more than $1 trillion worth of economic activity annually, with over 40% of U.S. exports passing through its ports." *The Role of Rivers in Trade and Commerce*, MEDIUM (Apr. 30, 2023), https://medium .com/@seedbaba/the-role-of-rivers-in-trade-and-commerce-bd3f0dbbc124#:~ :text=Today%2C%20the%20river%20supports%20more,exports%20passing %20through%20its%20ports.

[198]   See United States v. Causby, 328 U.S. 256, 260–61 (1946) (limiting real property owners' rights to airspace). According to the *Causby* Court: "It is ancient doctrine that at common law ownership of the land extended to the periphery of the universe—*cujus est solum ejus est usque ad coelum*. But that doctrine has no place in the modern world. The air is a public highway, as Congress has declared. Were that not true, every transcontinental flight would subject the operator to countless trespass suits. Common sense revolts at the idea. To recognize such private claims to the airspace would clog these highways, seriously interfere with their control and development in the public interest, and transfer into private ownership that to which only the public has a just claim." *Id.* (citation omitted). Thus, as in the navigable waters context, once the invention of the airplane and World War II made airspace invaluable for commerce and transportation, both Congress and the Court acted to keep that space public.

[199]   Craig, Adler, and Hall, *supra* note 14, at 36.

[200]   For example: Holton v. Ward, 847 N.W.2d 1, 6–7 (Mich. App. 2014) (citation omitted); Johnson v. Seifert, 100 N.W.2d 689, 695–96 (Minn. 1960); and Snively v. Jaber, 296 P.2d 1015, 1019 (Wash. 1956) (*en banc*).

[201]   For example, People v. Emmert, 597 P.2d 1025, 1026–27 (Colo 1979) (*en banc*); Haines v. Hall, 20 P. 831, 832–33 (Or. 1888).

tend to limit these landowners' riparian rights to their section of the river.[202] For example, the Illinois Supreme Court affirmed in 2022 that even upstream *riparian* landowners do not have the right to kayak the entire length of a non-navigable stream, past other riparian private properties.[203] Again, therefore, opening these non-navigable waters to public use simultaneously increases the riparian landowners' own rights to use the waterbody.

Given that the recreational amenities of waterfront property often comprise a substantial portion of buyers' willingness to pay more to own these properties, it may well be that broad state-law definitions of "navigable waters" actually increase the market value of riparian properties in many cases, particularly along rivers. This added value undoubtedly varies by specific property and general location. The larger point, however, is that recognizing the value of connectivity and increasing *public* rights can simultaneously increase the riparian landowner's own rights and the overall value of the property.

III.   REAL PROPERTY AND PANARCHY

While water enjoys significant legal cognizance, it is not the only example of how legally discrete parcels of real estate participate in larger systems that are important to the public good. Wider deployment of systems thinking reveals that *all* real estate can both affect the wide societies in which it is located *and* be affected by them, as this part explores in more detail.

A.   Systems Thinking and Complexity

Scientists have increasingly recognized that both natural systems and human societies are *complex systems*—that is, systems where seemingly simple

---

[202]   For example, *Emmert*, 597 P.2d at 1027 (noting that "the ownership of the bed of a non-navigable stream vests in the owner the exclusive right of control of everything above the stream bed, subject only to constitutional and statutory limitations, restrictions and regulations. Thus, … ownership of the stream bed was held to include the exclusive right of fishery in the waters flowing over it. It follows that whoever 'breaks the close' intrudes upon the space above the surface of the land without the permission of the owner, whether it be for fishing or for other recreational purposes, such as floating, as in this case, commits a trespass.") and Spivey v. Barwick, 122 S.E. 594, 594 (Ga. 1924) ("The owner of land adjoining a nonnavigable stream is the owner of the soil to the center of the thread of the stream, and of the fishing rights to the center of the thread on his side of the stream. If one proprietor owns the land on both sides of the stream, he has the exclusive right of fishing therein").

[203]   Holm v. Kodat, 211 N.E.3d 310, 318 (Ill. 2022).

entities or components self-organize into intricate and interrelated networks of functions, products, and responses.[204] Thus, "[i]n complex systems, many simple parts are irreducibly entwined, and the field of complexity is itself an entwining of many different fields."[205] Examples of complex systems include insect colonies, immune systems, brains, and economies[206]—and, some would argue, law.[207]

1.   Complex versus complicated

Complexity scientists generally distinguish *complex* systems from *complicated* systems.[208] As John Miller and Scott Page have explained:

> In a complicated world, the various schemes that make up the system maintain a degree of independence from one another. Thus, removing one such element (which reduces the level of complication) does not fundamentally alter the system's behavior apart from that which directly resulted from the piece that was removed. Complexity arises when the dependence among the elements become important. In such a system, removing one such element destroys system behavior to an extent that goes well beyond what is embodied by the particular element that is removed.[209]

To dramatize the point: "A complex system dies when an element is removed, but complicated ones live on, albeit slightly compromised."[210]

In contrast to these developments, however, law has long treated real property as, at best, a *complicated* system capable of being managed for individual components, when in fact real property has always been part of complex adaptive systems. The mismatch of legal component-based thinking and ecological

---

[204]   MELANIE MITCHELL, COMPLEXITY: A GUIDED TOUR 4 (2009).
[205]   *Id.*
[206]   *Id.* at 4–12.
[207]   Gregory Todd Jones, *Dynamical Jurisprudence: Law as a Complex System*, 24 GA. STATE U. L. REV. 873 (Summer 2008); J.B. Ruhl, *Law's Complexity: A Primer*, 24 GA. STATE U. L. REV. 885 (Summer 2008); Eric Kades, *The Laws of Complexity and the Complexity of Laws: The Implications of Computational Complexity Theory for the Law*, 49 RUTGERS L. REV. 403 (Winter 1997); J.B. Ruhl, *The Fitness of Law: Using Complexity Theory to Describe the Evolution of Law and Society and Its Practical Meaning for Society*, 49 VANDERBILT L. REV. 1407 (Nov. 1996); and J.B. Ruhl, *Complexity Theory as a Paradigm for the Dynamical Law-and-Society System: A Wake-Up Call for Legal Reductionism and the Modern Administrative State*, 45 DUKE L.J. 849 (March 1996).
[208]   John H. Miller and Scott E. Page, COMPLEX ADAPTIVE SYSTEMS: AN INTRODUCTION TO COMPUTATIONAL MODELS OF SOCIAL LIFE 4 (2007).
[209]   *Id.* at 9.
[210]   *Id.*

complexity is the most important basis for resisting an overly individualistic and atomistic approach to property rights.

2.   Features of complex systems

Complex systems have several distinguishing properties. First, they exhibit complex collective behavior—that is, individual components, following readily discernible rules of behavior, act collectively in vast numbers to "give rise to the complex, hard-to-predict, and changing patterns of behavior that fascinate us."[211] In other terminology, complex systems are *self-organizing*, and the difficult-to-predict results of that self-organization are *emergent* behaviors or properties.[212]

Second, complex systems "produce and use information and signals from both their internal and external environments."[213] As Neil Johnson has emphasized, the behavior of objects in a complex system "is affected by memory or 'feedback,'" meaning "that something from the past affects something in the present, or that something going on at one location affects what is happening at another ...."[214] Moreover, "the nature of this feedback can change with time."[215] In other words, how components of the system respond to each other and to outside stimuli is also subject to evolution and change.

Finally, complex systems "adapt—that is, change their behavior to improve their chances of survival or success—through learning or evolutionary processes."[216] These "complex adaptive systems"[217] are thus dynamic systems because "they change over time in some way."[218]

The combination of these properties allows complex adaptive systems to cope with change. Thus, "[w]hile complex systems can be fragile, they can

---

[211]   Mitchell, *supra* note 204, at 12. See also NEIL JOHNSON, TWO'S COMPANY, THREE IS COMPLEXITY 13, 15 (2007) (noting that a complex system "contains a collection of many interacting objects or 'agents,'" that it "exhibits emergent phenomena which are generally surprising, and may be extreme," and that "the emergent phenomena typically arise in the absence of any sort of 'invisible hand' or central controller").

[212]   Mitchell, *supra* note 204, at 13 (2009). See also MILLER AND PAGE, supra note 208, at 9 ("The behavior of many complex systems emerges from the activities of lower-level components") and JOHNSON, *supra* note 211, at 5–9 (discussing emergent behavior and giving examples from a number of areas).

[213]   Mitchell, *supra* note 204, at 13.

[214]   Johnson, *supra* note 211, at 14.

[215]   *Id.*

[216]   Mitchell, *supra* note 204, at 13. See also JOHNSON, *supra* note 211, at 14 ("The objects can adapt their strategies according to their history").

[217]   Mitchell, *supra* note 204, at 13.

[218]   *Id.* at 15.

also exhibit an unusual degree of robustness to less radical changes in their component parts."[219] Indeed, these systems' emergent properties are typically "the result of a very powerful organizing force that can overcome a variety of changes to the lower-level components."[220]

3.   Implications of complexity theory for real property law in the 21st century

One of the important lessons for law from complexity science is that uncertainty and unpredictability are inherent limitations on the legal system's ability to perfectly control and regulate its subjects. As John Miller and Scott Page have emphasized, "At the most basic level, the field of complex systems challenges the notion that by perfectly understanding the behavior of each component part of a system we will then understand the system as a whole."[221] Or, in Neil Johnson's more colorful appraisal, complexity theory "represents a slap in the face for traditional reductionist approaches to understanding the world."[222]

This is the challenge that systems theory and complexity science pose for the future of property law: how do we rebalance individualistic property rights to acknowledge that land is part of scaled complex adaptive systems and the complex ways in which any individual property owner manipulating a single parcel of real property can affect much larger communities? The concepts of panarchy[223] and social-ecological resilience[224] can help to illuminate why a more systems-grounded approach to property law is imperative.

---

[219]   MILLER AND PAGE, *supra* note 208, at 9.

[220]   *Id.*

[221]   Miller and Page, *supra* note 208, at 3.

[222]   JOHNSON, *supra* note 211, at 17.

[223]   See, for example, Ahjond S. Garmestani, Craig R. Allen, & Heriberto Cabezas, *Panarchy, Adaptive Management and Governance: Policy Options for Building Resilience*, 87 NEB. L. REV 1036 (2009) and C.S. Holling, Lance H. Gunerson, and Garry D. Peterson, *Sustainability and Panarchies, in* Lance H. Gunderson and C.S. Holling, PANARCHY: UNDERSTANDING TRANSFORMATIONS IN HUMAN AND NATURAL SYSTEMS 63–102 (2002) (describing the importance of panarchy theory's nested hierarchies of resilience loops).

[224]   See, for example: C.S. Holling and Lance H. Gunderson, *Resilience and Adaptive Cycles*, in Lance H. Gunderson and C.S. Holling, PANARCHY: UNDERSTANDING TRANSFORMATIONS IN HUMAN AND NATURAL SYSTEMS 25–62 (2002) (describing the four-stage looped model of resilience); Brian Walker and David Salt, RESILIENCE THINKING: SUSTAINING ECOSYSTEMS AND PEOPLE IN A CHANGING WORLD (2006); Barbara Cosens, *Resolving Conflict in Non-Ideal, Complex Systems: Solutions for the Law-Science Breakdown in Environmental and Natural Resource Law*, 48 NAT. RESOURCES J. 257 (2008); Barbara Cosens, *Transboundary River Governance in the Face of Uncertainty: Resilience Theory*

B.   The Panarchy Model

Even the brief review above of complex systems theory makes it clear that we cannot think about complex systems (such as land) and their components (such as real property parcels) in isolation or at single scales. Instead, the panarchy model helps to show how land can participate in multiple scales of dynamism simultaneously.

1.   Ecological resilience

Ecological resilience is one way to describe the adaptive responsiveness of complex systems and is the key to the panarchy model. "Resilience" usually invokes what theorists call *engineering resilience*—that is, the ability of a person, thing, or system to *resist* a shock or disturbance in the first place or to *bounce back* to its former state.[225] This definition "focuses on efficiency, constancy, and predictability—all attributes at the core of engineers' desires for fail-safe design."[226] Engineering resilience also supports a view that systems have (or should have) a preferred equilibrium state to which the system tends to return, supporting legal goals of sustainability, preservation, and restoration.[227]

In contrast, *ecological resilience* captures the ability of complex adaptive systems to cope—to absorb change, become altered in small ways, but still maintain core identity. As defined by one of resilience theory's founders, the late C.S. "Buzz" Holling, ecological "resilience determines the persistence of relationships within a system and is a measure of the ability of these systems to absorb changes of state variables, driving variables, and parameters, and still

---

and the Columbia River Treaty, 30 J. Land, Resources & Envtl. L. 229, 231–42 (2010); Robin Kundis Craig, *"Stationarity Is Dead"—Long Live Transformation: Five Principles for Climate Change Adaptation Law*, 34 Harv. Envtl. L. Rev 9, 39–40 (2010); Lance H. Gunderson, Craig R. Allen, and C.S. Holling, Foundations of Ecological Resilience (2010); Robin Kundis Craig, *Legal Remedies for Deep Marine Oil Spills and Long-Term Ecological Resilience: A Match Made in Hell*, 2011 B.Y.U. L. Rev 1863, 1886–96; and Brian Walker and David Salt, Resilience Practice: Building Capacity to Absorb Disturbance and Maintain Function (2012).

[225]   C.S. Holling, "Engineering Resilience versus Ecological Resilience," *in* National Academy of Engineering, Engineering Within Ecological Constraints 31, 33 (The National Academies Press 1996), https://doi.org/10.17226/4919, *available at* https://www.nap.edu/read/4919/chapter/4#33.

[226]   *Id.*

[227]   Melinda Harm Benson and Robin Kundis Craig, The End of Sustainability: Resilience and the Future of Environmental Governance in the Anthropocene 30 (2017).

persist."[228] Ecological resilience describes the amount of change the system can absorb and still retain the same functions and core structure[229] without transforming into a qualitatively different state controlled by a different set of processes.[230] This ability reflects the system's adaptive capacity—that is, the "capacity of actors, both individuals and groups, to respond to, create and shape variability and change in the state of the system."[231] Adaptive capacity reflects a system's flexibility and often reflects both functional diversity and redundancies within a system.[232]

However, ecological resilience also acknowledges that complex systems can and do transform, known as a regime shifts.[233] A common regime shift in fresh water occurs when nutrient pollution transforms a clear, cold, trout-supporting aquatic ecosystem into a warm, algae-dominated eutrophied system.[234] Moreover, in this and many other regime shifts, or the crossing of "tipping points," returning the system to its original state is often extremely difficult, even if the driver of the change (for example, the nutrient pollution) is removed.

2.   Panarchy: interactive scales of complex systemic change

One way of describing the dynamism of complex adaptive systems is through the four-phase adaptive cycle, which Gunderson and Holling first described in 2002.[235] In this model, ecosystems (later extended to social-ecological

---

[228]   C.S. Holling, ADAPTIVE ENVIRONMENTAL ASSESSMENT AND MANAGEMENT 17 (1978).

[229]   Benson and Craig, *supra* note 227, at 57.

[230]   Stephen B. Carpenter, Brian Walker, J. Marty Anderies and Nick Abel, *From Metaphor to Measurement: Resilience of What to What?* 4 ECOSYSTEMS 765, 766 (2001).

[231]   F. Stuart Chapin, Carl Folke and Gary P. Kofinas, *A Framework for Understanding Change, in* PRINCIPLES OF ECOSYSTEM STEWARDSHIP 23, 26 (Stuart Chapin, Gary P. Kofinas and Carl Folke, eds., 2009).

[232]   Carl Folke, Johan Colding and Fikret Berkes, *Synthesis: Building Resilience for Adaptive Capacity in Social-Ecological Systems, in* NAVIGATING SOCIAL-ECOLOGICAL SYSTEMS: BUILDING RESILIENCE FOR COMPLEXITY AND CHANGE 352, 354 (2002).

[233]   Holling, *supra* note 225, at 31.

[234]   Motomi Genkai-Katoi and Stephen R. Carpenter, *Eutrophication Due to Phosphorous Recycling in Relation to Lake Morphology, Temperature and Macrophytes,* 86 ECOLOGY 210, 210 (2005).

[235]   Walker and Salt, *supra* note 224, at 75–78; GUNDERSON AND HOLLING, PANARCHY, *supra* note 224, at 33–35.

systems) cycle through an infinity-loop of change[236] in phases of rapid growth, conservation, release, and reorganization.[237]

A forest can provide a good example. A young forest proceeds through rapid growth to a mature conservation phase, when large trees tie up nutrients and limit further growth in the understory. A forest fire triggers the release phase, destroying structure and releasing nutrients, and the area will reorganize and begin to grow again. All else being equal, the area is likely to regenerate a new forest that looked a lot like the last one—but maybe not.[238] As one specific example, if the wildfire burns the forest down after significant climate change, a different forest—or a different ecosystem altogether—may emerge in the rapid growth phase.[239]

Thus, within a single scale, the release and reorganization phases can explain and model the sometimes unpredictable responses of complex adaptive systems to shocks and ongoing stresses. Gunderson and Holling's panarchy model, however, goes further by capturing the interactions of adaptive cycles operating at different geographic and temporal scales (Figure 7.1).[240]

Climate change provides a perfect example of panarchy at work. Climate is a large, slow system, near the top of any panarchy scale. So long as the planet's climate remained stably within the conservation phase, as it did through most of the Holocene when human civilization developed, that large-scale stability operated to dampen transformations at smaller scales—for example, forests growing back in the same climatic conditions tended to produce the same kinds of forests. This stability is the "remember" function in Figure 7.1. Nevertheless, changes at smaller scales can, either cumulatively or when timed well (or poorly), push larger-scale adaptive cycles out of the conservation phase and into release and reorganization. Since the Industrial Revolution, the accumulation of greenhouse gases in the atmosphere as a result of the increased burning of fossil fuels—increases resulting from decisions at lower scales, from a household's decision to install electricity to regional- and national-scale decisions to invest in coal-fired power plants—reached the point where it could (and has) nudged the climate cycle toward, if not into, a release phase, an example of the "revolt" function in Figure 7.1. The resulting instability at

---

[236]   *Id.*

[237]   Gunderson and Holling, *supra* note 224, at 33–35.

[238]   Robin Kundis Craig, *Resilience Theory and Wicked Problems*, 73 VAND. L. REV 1733, 1760 (2020).

[239]   Jonathan D. Coop et al., *Wildfire-Driven Forest Conversion in Western North American Landscapes*, 70 BioScience 659, 664, 666 (2020), doi:10.1093/biosci/biaa061.

[240]   *Id.* at 72–76.

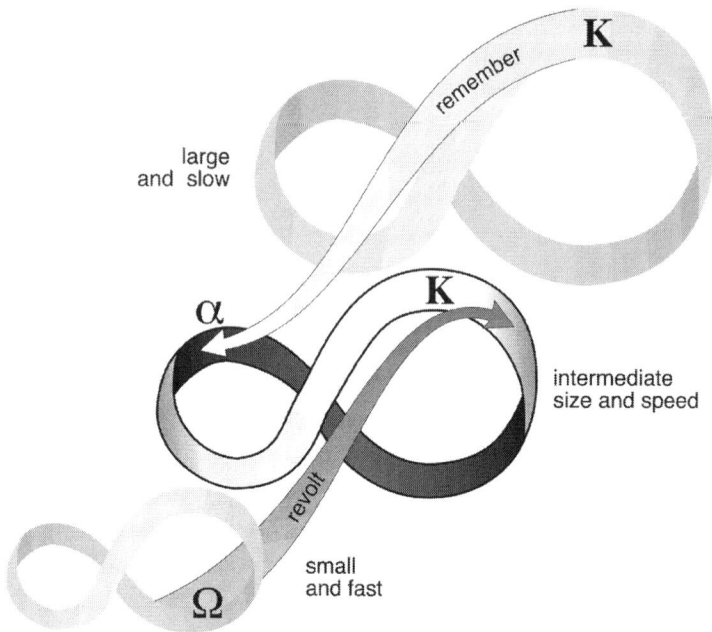

large
and slow

K

remember

α

K

intermediate
size and speed

revolt

small
and fast

Ω

Figure 7.1   *Gunderson and Holling's panarchy model (adapted from
Panarchy, edited by Lance H. Gunderson and C.S. Holling.*

the climate scale is simultaneously destabilizing adaptive cycles operating at
lower scales.

The forest example is just one illustration of how land participates in adaptive cycles and panarchic interactions. Three further examples make clear that
the same is true for the parcels of land we call real property.

C.   Non-Water Examples of Real Estate Panarchy

Surface water is perhaps the most obvious and widespread—as well as most
legally enshrined—example of how individual parcels of real estate participate in larger societal processes and public welfare. However, real property
is always part of multiscale complex adaptive systems that can affect society more generally, although the law takes cognizance of very few of these
other panarchal aspects of real estate—particularly not in terms of collective
and cumulative impacts to the public good or systemic risk. These failures of

property law are particularly dangerous for continued societal well-being in the Anthropocene,[241] especially as climate change perturbs adaptive cycles at all levels.[242]

This Section presents three additional examples, ranging from the well recognized to emerging science, of how individual parcels of real property remain part of complex landscapes and adaptive cycles, with panarchic capacities to impact and disrupt society at larger scales. Importantly, while climate change will certainly intensify real property owners' abilities to induce these disruptions, climate change did not create that capability. Moreover, climate change revealed, rather than caused, the holes in tort and property law that allow panarchic capacities to remain legally uncognizable. Instead, the harm principle and its legal corollary of *de minimis non curat lex*[243] have been responsible for much of the legal veiling. Specifically, the common law tort system's insistence that plaintiffs be able to prove real and individualized harm caused by specific defendants before they can either enjoin certain uses of real property or collect damages from particular landowners means that dangers that manifest only through collective action, as accumulations of individual minor impacts, or in the form of systemic risk generally slide under the law's radar—even, sometimes, when the harm to society as a whole becomes obvious.[244]

1. Externalities and environmental law

To be fair, property law has always acknowledged through the doctrine of public nuisance that, at least to some extent, the exercise of individual property rights could affect the public at large. Public nuisance law, however, is notoriously difficult to apply and tends to address problems only after they have manifested and caused harm. Nor is public nuisance law generally cognizant of complexity or adept at dealing with cumulative impacts or collective

---

[241] See generally J.B. Ruhl and Robin Kundis Craig, *4°C*, 106 MINN. L. REV 191 (2021) (graphically describing the impacts of climate change on the United States).

[242] Benson and Craig, *supra* note 227, 149–57.

[243] "The law is not concerned with trifles."

[244] Notably, real property law is not the only genre where courts and policymakers struggle with the harm principle's limits. Much of toxic tort law, for example, can be categorized either as litigants finding ways to satisfy the common-law harm principle under difficult circumstances (for example, proof of causation based on epidemiology) or as courts and legislatures deciding that the principle needs to be modified in certain ways (for example, the invention of market share liability).

action, as the public nuisance litigation to address greenhouse gas emissions has been demonstrating.[245]

Environmental law, especially pollution control laws, came about in part because of these common-law failings. Pollution control laws also, in the eyes of many, represent a first cut at managing the complexity of social-ecological systems. Removing pollutants, especially toxics, eliminates an important driver of some kinds of system change; conversely, as nutrient pollution amply demonstrates, failure to remove some kinds of pollutants promotes regime shifts to unproductive and unhealthy states. As Yale law professor Donald Elliott once wrote, "[e]nvironmental law represents the state-of-the-art in using legal institutions and techniques to manage complex systems to achieve social goals."[246]

Before complexity theory had gained prominence, however, law-and-economics scholars long used different terminology both to acknowledge that individual property use can affect the greater society and to explain why law must grapple with the fact that real property is panarchical: externalities.[247] As with individual decisions to use coal (directly as fuel or indirectly through electricity use), individual decisions by landowners regarding how they use their properties can impose costs on the public as a whole. Pollution control laws are, therefore, an ongoing recognition that individual properties participate in the more general society at multiple scales.

Moreover, it is the problems that the major federal pollution control statutes fail to effectively address that most graphically illustrate how externality issues remain real and important. Nutrient pollution of water remains a pervasive and persistent example. The federal Clean Water Act largely exempts both nonpoint source pollution like farm runoff and farming activities in general from its regulatory scheme.[248] As a result, thousands of farmers making individual decisions to fertilize crops in the Mississippi River watershed have collectively created an extensive "dead zone" (hypoxic zone") in the Gulf of Mexico, inflicting wildly disproportionate harm on Mississippi, Louisiana,

---

[245]   See, for example, Kate Markey, Note, *Air Pollution as Public Nuisance: Comparing Modern Day Greenhouse Gas Abatement with Nineteenth-Century Smoke Abatement*, 120 MICH. L. REV 1535, 1541–52, 1560–69 (2022).

[246]   E. Donald Elliott, *Environmental Law at a Crossroad*, 20 N. KENTUCKY L. REV 1, 2 (1992).

[247]   See generally Bruce Yandle, *Property Rights or Externalities?*, in Terry L. Anderson and Fred S. McChesny, eds., PROPERTY RIGHTS: COOPERATION, CONFLICT, AND LAW 227–54 (Princeton University Press 2003).

[248]   Robin Kundis Craig, *The Clean Water Act and the Ocean: An Unfulfilled Promise*, 14 KY. J. EQUINE, AGRIC. & NATURAL RESOURCES L. 309, 320–25 (2021–2022).

and fleets of Gulf fishers.[249] Nutrient runoff from agriculture and other activities similarly creates significant problems for the Chesapeake Bay.[250]

Thus, as Don Elliott and Dan Esty recently reviewed, the US pollution control laws of the 1970s both recognized the externality problem and compromised with landowners and businesses by incorporating technological and economic feasibility into their regulatory requirements[251] as well as protecting politically sensitive land uses like farming from regulation. Nevertheless, they acknowledge that this "approach delivered the low-hanging fruit, and environmental conditions across America are much better today as a result."[252] However, for the next generation Elliott and Esty would up-end entirely our current assumptions regarding who holds which rights in favor of giving the public the right to a healthy environment. Under this new approach, property owners and industries who impose externalities on others would have to pay full compensation for the harms they cause.[253] While unlikely to be adopted anytime soon, this proposal makes clear—as the evolution away from strict public nuisance remedies did before it[254]—that in recognizing that many land uses impose costs on the general public, the issue of which side to compromise—public welfare or private property—is a law and policy *choice*, not a property rights given.

---

[249]   *Dead Zone in the Gulf of Mexico*, Nat'l Oceanic & Atmos. Admin Ocean Today (viewed Aug. 17, 2024), https://oceantoday.noaa.gov/deadzonegulf/.

[250]   *Nutrient Runoff*, Chesapeake Bay Program (viewed Aug. 17, 2024), https://www.chesapeakebay.net/issues/threats-to-the-bay/nutrient-runoffmode _comment.

[251]   E. Donald Elliott and Daniel C. Esty, *The End Environmental Externalities Manifesto: A Rights-Based Foundation for Environmental Law*, 29 N.Y.U. Envtl. L.J. 505, 514–15 (2021) ("Policy decisions to tolerate certain levels of pollution are not the main reasons why we as a country have, to date, been unable to eliminate all harmful environmental externalities and have come instead to accept significant levels of ongoing emissions. We believe the primary culprit has been the emergence of a dominant vision of environmental policy based on benefit-cost analysis rather than the right to a healthy environment. This alternative vision limits our environmental aspirations by holding that government should only regulate if it is prepared to prove that a regulatory measure is scientifically justified and would produce net benefits to society" (citations omitted)).

[252]   *Id.* at 506–507.

[253]   *Id.* at 509–11.

[254]   See, for example Boomer v. Atlantic Cement Co., 257 N.E.2d 870 (N.Y. Ct. App. 1970) (overriding the traditional injunctive remedy of shutting down a public nuisance in favor of a permanent damages approach).

2.   Wildfire and the wildland-urban interface

The intersection of land as individual real estate parcels and land as a complex adaptive system is particularly obvious at the wildland-urban interface (WUI). The federal government defines the WUI as places "where humans and their development meet or intermix with wildland fuel."[255] Development in the WUI, especially for residential housing, has been increasing significantly since the 1990s.[256] However, these developments "create[] risks for both the humans moving in and the species and ecosystems already there," especially from wildfire.[257]

Because, "in most WUI communities, including in the USA, there is no clear line of WUI demarcation, and wildland fuels are continuous outside of and within developed areas," the WUI "is an intertwined social-ecological system (SES)"—that is, a complex adaptive system.[258] Moreover, "the feedback mechanisms and emergent properties characteristic of complex adaptive systems are the source of both system resilience and *systemic risk*."[259]

Craig and Ruhl argued in 2020 that these realities demanded a different approach to WUI management than just the suppression of wildfire.[260] The point for this chapter is far more basic: development at the WUI is itself a cause of increased fire risk because that development "often significantly impairs the ecosystem processes that previously prevented large and uncontrolled wildfires from occurring."[261] Moreover, wildfire can, perversely, help to make development at the WUI self-perpetuating: "there is evidence that federal investment in firefighting at the WUI has only intensified encroachment, as it subsidizes the built environment."[262]

Thus, through their degradation of certain ecosystem processes, private property owners in the WUI collectively perturb the complex SES that they

---

[255]   United States Forest Service (USFS), Urban Wildland Interface Communities Within the Vicinity of Federal Lands That Are at High Risk From Wildfire, 66 Fed. Reg. 751, 753 (2001).

[256]   V.C. Radeloff et al., *Rapid Growth at the US Wildland-Urban Iinterface Raises Wildfire Risk*, 115 PROCEEDINGS OF THE NATIONAL ACADEMY OF SCIENCES (PNAS) 3314, 3316 (2018).

[257]   Robin Kundis Craig and J.B. Ruhl, *Adaptive Management for Ecosystem Services Across the Wildland-Urban Interface*, 14 INT'L J. COMMONS 611, 612 (2020) (citations omitted).

[258]   *Id.* at 613–14.

[259]   *Id.* at 614 (original emphasis).

[260]   *Id.* at 614–15, 621–23 (citations omitted).

[261]   *Id.* at 613, 622 (citing Radeloff et al., *supra* note 256).

[262]   *Id.* at 621 (citing Patrick Baylis and Judson Boomhower, *Moral Hazard, Wildfires, and the Economic Incidence of Natural Disasters*, NAT'L BUREAU ECON. RESEARCH (2019), doi: 10.3386/w26550).

are part of toward catastrophic failure. These failures most frequently (so far) manifest in the form of wildfire—a catastrophic failure that often threatens not just those property owners that helped to cause it, but also communities far distant, including through pervasive human health impacts resulting from smoke inhalation.[263] Thus, the increase of individual property ownership in the WUI graphically demonstrates the panarchic risks to society that these private homes impose.

3.   Nutrient sharing and plant communication

Other evidence of real property interconnectedness is far more subtle than wildfire at the WUI. It turns out, for example, that plants and fungi communicate—and they do so without respect for property lines, allowing events on one parcel to affect the health and well-being of the landscape more generally.

To begin, plants emit volatile organic compounds (VOCs) for a variety of communicative purposes.[264] "Notably, flowers use VOCs to attract pollinators and ensure reproduction." Most interestingly, plants exposed to stressors such as extreme heat or cold, disease, or damage emit VOCs to communicate with other plants.[265] "The airborne signals are diffused to reach undamaged plants nearby, giving them the chance to strengthen their defense systems."[266] However, herbivores have also evolved the abilities to detect these chemical "SOS" signals, helping them to find the damaged plant.[267] Perhaps most impressively, "[b]y changing the volatile compounds and their blend ratios, plants can create specific messages for communication."[268]

Such communication among plants may be increasingly important to plants' capacities to adapt to changing conditions. "Two studies published in 1983 demonstrated that willow trees, poplars and sugar maples can warn each other about insect attacks: Intact, undamaged trees near ones that are infested with hungry bugs begin pumping out bug-repelling chemicals to ward off attack."[269]

---

[263]   For a recent summary of wildfire impacts in Washington, Oregon, and California, including statistics about the WUI in each state, see generally Savannah M. D'Evelyn et al., *Wildfire, Smoke Exposure, Human Health, and Environmental Justice Need to be Integrated into Forest Restoration and Management*, 9 CURR. ENVT'L HEALTH RPT. 366 (2022), https://doi.org/10.1007/s40572-022-00355-7.

[264]   Hirokazu Ueda, Yukio Kikuta and Kazuhiko Matsuda, *Plant Communication: Mediated by Individual or Blended VOCs?*, 7 PLANT SIGNALING & BEHAV. 222, 222 (2012).

[265]   *Id.*

[266]   *Id.*

[267]   *Id.*

[268]   *Id.*

[269]   Kay McGowan, *The Secret Language of Plants*, QUANTA MAGAZINE (Dec. 16, 2013), https://www.quantamagazine.org/the-secret-language-of-plants

While these original studies generated considerable scientific controversy regarding their validity, more rigorous controlled experiments have reached the same conclusions. "It's now well established that when bugs chew leaves, plants respond by releasing volatile organic compounds into the air," and multiple studies also "confirm that other plants detect these airborne signals and ramp up their production of chemical weapons or other defense mechanisms in response."[270]

Even less obvious are the massive networks of multispecies communication in the soil. "A mycorrhiza is typically a mutualistic symbiosis between a fungus and a plant root, where fungal-foraged soil nutrients are exchanged for plant-derived photosynthate."[271] Mycorrhiza form complex adaptive systems within the soil in the form of mycorrhizal networks:

> The extent of fungal mycelium in the soil is vast and the mutualisms between the fungal species and host plants are usually diffuse, enabling the formation of mycorrhizal networks (MNs). These MNs are composed of continuous fungal mycelia linking two or more plants of the same or different species. The MN can thus integrate multiple plant species and multiple fungal species that interact, provide feedbacks and adapt, which comprise a complex adaptive social network. The MN is considered ecologically and evolutionarily significant because of its positive effects on the fitness of the member plants and fungi.[272]

MNs in the soil act as neural networks that facilitate communication and nutrient exchange among trees.[273] Moreover, interactions between soil fungi and trees help to regulate the dispersion and demographics of trees in forests.[274] "MNs can influence plant establishment, survival, physiology, growth and defence chemistry."[275] Most importantly, the soil MNs connect

---

-20131216/.

[270] *Id.*

[271] Monika A. Gorzelak, Amanda K. Asay, Brian J. Pickles, and Suzanne W. Simard, *Inter-plant Communication through Mycorrhizal Networks Mediates Complex Adaptive Behaviour in Plant Communities*, 7 AoB PLANTS plv50, at 1 (2015) (citation omitted), https://doi.org/10.1093/aobpla/plv050.

[272] *Id.*

[273] Suzanne W. Simard, *Mycorrhizal Networks Facilitate Tree Communication, Learning, and Memory*, *in* Frantisek Baluska, Monica Gagliano, and Guenther Witzany (eds.), MEMORY AND LEARNING IN PLANTS: SIGNALING AND COMMUNICATION IN PLANTS 191, 191–213 (Springer 2018), https://doi.org/10.1007/978-3-319-75596-0_10.

[274] Minxia Liang et al., *Soil Fungal Networks Maintain Local Dominance of Ectomycorrhizal Trees*, 11 NATURE COMMUNICATIONS art. 2636 (2020), https://doi.org/10.1038/s41467-020-16507-y.

[275] Gorzelak et al., *supra* note 271, at 3 (citations omitted).

directly to larger ecosystem function: "Underground 'tree talk' is a foundational process in the complex adaptive nature of forest ecosystems. Since plants form the basis of terrestrial ecosystems, their behavioural interactions, feedbacks and influences are important in generating the emergent properties of ecosystems."[276] Thus, MNs increasingly demonstrate that individual parcels of real estate participate in and influence much larger complex adaptive systems.

Property lawyers do not have to think very hard to imagine the plant-communication-based lawsuits of the future. Is the landowner whose poplars warned neighboring sugar maple farmers' trees of a coming insect attack entitled to a share of the maple syrup profits that the successfully forewarned maple trees produce?[277] Does it matter whether all the chemical activity changed the syrup's flavor, or allowed the sap only to be used for maple candy? And perhaps most importantly, what if one or two landowners destroy the portions of a vast MN underlying their properties, to the detriment of the properties, communities, and social-ecological systems of which that MN remains a part—are they liable in nuisance, either public or private? *Should* they be?

Again, however, the larger point here is that these interconnections cut both ways. Legal respect for the interactions of plants, trees, and fungi across property lines may require limiting some actions that individual property owners might take that would destroy these communications. Simultaneously, however, those property owners also benefit from keeping these functions intact. The value of these functions will, of course, vary according to the uses being made of the properties—maple sugar farmers, orchardists, and homeowners who love their mature trees may well place a higher value on them than landowners who aspire to build high-rise apartment buildings. Nevertheless, the benefits do exist and should be cognized in property law.

CONCLUSION: RECOGNIZING CONNECTIVITY AND BENEFIT IN REAL PROPERTY LAW

As the above discussions make clear, riparian and littoral properties make particularly visible the fact that *all* real property involves ongoing negotiations between private rights and public welfare, the individual and the community, the real estate plot and the multiple complex adaptive systems in which that

---

[276]   *Id.* at 9.

[277]   The forewarning would be an ecosystem service. For more on ecosystem services and the property rights and valuation issues they raise, see J.B. Ruhl and James Salzman, *Who Owns Ecosystem Services?*, in this volume.

land participates. This more fluid panarchy model of dynamic and interacting scales better suits the on-the-ground realities of real property, particularly in an era of climate change, than the recent legal emphasis on discrete and atomistic parcels controlled by individual land owners. It also better explains the need for law and government to mediate in a more nuanced way the cross-scalar influences and potentially conflicting interests at stake any time a real estate owner modifies land, whether that land abuts a navigable water or supports part of an MN that keeps healthy the surrounding plant community and the social-ecological system that it supports.

The Progressives of the early 20th century acknowledged that knowledge is "contingent, provisional, and subject to the unending tests of new inquiry," and emphasized "uncertainty, experimentation, and change …."[278] This view informed their willingness to subrogate private rights and interests, including private property rights, to public welfare and changing public values.

The first quarter of the 21st century is another moment where our understandings of how complex adaptive social-ecological systems function, as well as what exactly those functions are, are changing. We know more, both about the interactions among parcels of real estate and about systemic changes occurring at multiple scales as a result of climate change and other stressors like pollution—particularly as multiple stressors act in concert to induce undesirable regime shifts. Moreover, we know that many of these changes threaten property values, human health, system function, and, perhaps, societal stability.

From this perspective, it is a small thing to ask property law to be a little less concerned with protecting individualistic bundles of rights and a little more concerned about the myriad ways in which property owners can negatively impact the public interest. In particular, property law needs to be more cognizant of the *benefits* that public rebalancings and the police power accord private landowners, particularly in light of the connectedness of all real property.

Takings law and eminent domain, both of which emphasize real property valuation, are good places for courts to start—as, indeed, some of them are already beginning to do. For example, the Borough of Harvey Cedars in New Jersey used its eminent domain authority to build up sand dunes on the ocean side of Long Island Beach. Because it was eminent domain, the Karans, as oceanfront landowners, were clearly entitled to compensation; the fight was over how to value the damage. As the Court of Appeals described, "The formerly-spectacular ocean view from defendants' house is now partially blocked by the twenty-two-foot high dune, which occupies one-third of their land.

---

278   Rabban, *supra* note 2, at 959.

However, their house is now safer from storm damage because the dune was constructed."[279] The issue was whether the jury had to consider the benefit conferred to the home as well as the damage done because of the loss of view. The trial judge ruled that the benefit was irrelevant to the valuation context, refusing to acknowledge that public benefit can also be private benefit. Specifically, he concluded "that construction of the dune did not confer a special benefit on the property. Instead, he found that the only benefit conferred was the general benefit for which the dune was constructed, i.e., to protect the island and its inhabitants from the destructive impact of hurricanes and nor'easters."[280] On this basis, the jury concluded that the Borough owed the Karans $375,000 for the partial taking, and in March 2012, the Court of Appeals affirmed.[281]

The Borough appealed to the New Jersey Supreme Court. Before that court could decide the case, however, Superstorm Sandy ravaged the East Coast, reaching New Jersey on October 29, 2012.[282] The storm damaged or destroyed 364,000 homes along the New Jersey coast[283]—but not the Karans'. Perhaps not coincidentally, when the New Jersey Supreme Court decided the case in July 2013, it reversed, ruling that the trial court erred in not allowing the Borough to present evidence of the benefits of the dune project to the Karans. Specifically, the court concluded:

> that when a public project requires the partial taking of property, "just compensation" to the owner must be based on a consideration of all relevant, reasonably calculable, and non-conjectural factors that either decrease or increase the value of the remaining property. In a partial-takings case, homeowners are entitled to the fair market value of their loss, not to a windfall, not to a pay out that disregards the home's enhanced value resulting from a public project. To calculate that loss, we must look to the difference between the fair market value of the property before the partial taking and after the taking. In determining damages, the trial court did not permit the jury to consider that the dune would likely spare the Karans' home from total destruction in certain fierce storms and from other damage in lesser storms. A formula—as used by the trial court and Appellate Division—that does not permit consideration of the quantifiable benefits of a public project that increase the value of the remaining property in a partial-takings case will lead to a compensation

[279]   Borough of Harvey Cedars v. Karan, 40 A.3d 75, 77 (N.J. Super App. Div. 2012), rev'd, 70 A.3d 524 (N.J. 2013).
[280]   Id.
[281]   Id. at 77–78.
[282]   Remembering Superstorm Sandy, N.J. DEP'T OF ENVTL. PROTECTION (Oct. 26, 2022), https://dep.nj.gov/sandy-10/.
[283]   Id.

award that does not reflect the owner's true loss. Compensation in a partial-takings case must be "just" to both the landowner and the public.[284]

After this decision, a jury awarded similarly situated property owners a mere $300.00 under the new formula for calculating fair market value, while the Karans settled their case for $1.00.[285]

Borough of Harvey Cedars is a "givings" case. At the turn of this century, Abraham Bell and Gideon Parchomovsky created a taxonomy of "givings," arguing that "[l]ike a reflection in a mirror, the massive universe of takings is everywhere accompanied by givings. For every type of taking, there exists a corresponding type of giving."[286] Understandably, however, in their massive undertaking, they stuck to conventional conceptions of real property. This chapter in effect goes one or two steps further, concluding that any conception of givings must also embrace the reality that parcels of real property always connect, whether water is involved or not. Land is always part of multiple complex adaptive systems operating at multiple scales. The police power cannot do its jobs of either preventing public harms or affirmatively protecting the public good unless the law takes cognizance of this real property panarchy.

ACKNOWLEDGEMENTS

My thanks to Professor Jan Laitos for inviting me to participate in this book project and the 2024 University of Denver Sturm College of Law Symposium, "Private Property and the Police Power," sponsored by the Juhan Program for Private Property Rights.

---

[284] Borough of Harvey Cedars v. Karan, 70 A.3d 524, 526–27 (N.J. 2013). For more discussions of the decision, see generally Bianca Iozzia, Case Note, *Putting a Price Tag on an Ocean View: The Impact of* Borough of Harvey Cedars v. Karan *on Partial-Taking Valuations,* 25 VILL. ENVTL. L.J. 501 (2014); Brittany Harrison, *The Compensation Conundrum in Partial Takings Cases and the Consequences of* Borough of Harvey Cedars, 2015 CARDOZO L. REV DE NOVO 31.

[285] Kirk Moore, *Harvey Cedars, NJ win second beach easement case,* APP.COM (us updated July 10, 2014), https://www.app.com/story/news/local/southern-ocean -county/2014/06/30/dune-easment-harvey-cedars-ocean-county/11814891/.

[286] Abraham Bell and Gideon Parchomovsky, *Givings,* 111 YALE L.J. 547, 550 (2001).

8. Who owns ecosystem services?

J.B. Ruhl and James Salzman

INTRODUCTION

When Justice Scalia famously distinguished regulatory takings from the "restrictions that background principles of the State's law of property and nuisance already place upon land ownership,"[1] he also acknowledged that "changed circumstances or new knowledge may make what was previously permissible no longer so."[2] Background principles of property and nuisance must evolve as conditions and understandings change.

At one time, for example, wetlands were deemed nuisances, derided as desolate bogs and swamps. A landowner claiming that public draining of wetlands constituted a taking of property would have had no success.[3] Decade after decade, the nation continued to lose wetlands to agricultural and urban development.[4] Over time, however, knowledge grew regarding the ecological importance of wetlands in providing wildlife habitat, buffering floods, and filtering water.[5] Courts eventually turned 180 degrees, finding the draining of wetlands to constitute a public nuisance and upholding regulation of development in wetlands against claims of takings.[6] Legal scholars have traced similar trends in the evolution of other background property doctrines.[7]

---

[1] Lucas v. South Carolina Coastal Council, 505 U.S. 1003, 1029 (1992).

[2] *Id.* at 1030.

[3] For this history see John Copeland Nagle, *From Swamp Drainage to Wetlands Regulation to Ecological Nuisances to Environmental Ethics*, 58 CASE W. RES. L. REV 787, 790–92 (2008).

[4] See *id.*

[5] See James Salzman and J.B. Ruhl, *The Law and Policy Beginnings of Ecosystem Services*, 22 J. LAND USE & ENVTL. L. 157 (2007).

[6] Palazzolo v. State, 2005 WL 1645974 at *5 (R.I. Super. Ct. July 5, 2005).

[7] For a survey, see Michael C. Blumm and J.B. Ruhl, *Background Principles, Takings, and Libertarian Property*, 37 ECOLOGY L.Q. 805 (2010).

Overall, property doctrine has been clumsy at best in acknowledging the value of ecosystem services that private landowners deliver to the public and other private landowners. Ecosystem services such as pollination and groundwater recharge often originate from resources owned by one set of property owners and are delivered as benefits to other property owners, yet property law has not defined ownership interests in these ecosystem services, if any, largely ignoring the question. Core doctrines such as *sic utere* and *ad coelum* can be leveraged for guidance on how to treat ecosystem services but, as explored further below, don't provide an exact fit. Indeed, there is no existing "off the shelf" doctrine that can readily map directly onto the property relations dynamic of ecosystem services supplied by one property owner to another.

Given the immense economic value that ecosystem services provide, it is surprising that private property rights in ecosystem services have received so little attention in legal scholarship.[8] In this chapter, we argue this needs to change. New scientific knowledge regarding the provision and value of ecosystem services—the benefits ecosystems deliver to human communities—and radically changed circumstances brought on by harms from climate change converge to make private property law ripe for re-examination.

Our call for action could not be better timed. As we were writing this chapter, the February 18, 2024, edition of the *New York Times* featured a front-page story titled, "Nature Has Value. Could We Literally Invest in It?"[9] The article described efforts (fruitless so far) to launch "natural asset companies" whose value lies in their provision of ecosystem services. The article is a good read, but it fails to consider the basic question of how we should even think about ownership of ecosystem services, an essential issue before any decisions are taken about investing in them. Similarly, only a week later, the White House Office of Management and Budget issued its final "Guidance for Assessing Changes in Environmental and Ecosystem Services in Benefit-Cost Analysis," explaining to federal agencies how to account for the impacts of their regula-

---

[8]   J.B. Ruhl suggested over a decade ago that nuisance doctrine may offer a useful model for defining the relationship between the supplying and beneficiary property owners. See J.B. Ruhl, *Making Nuisance Ecological*, 58 CASE W. RES. L. REV 753 (2008). Kalyani Robbins later explored the broad question of property and ecosystem services (see Kalyani Robbins, *Allocating Property Interests in Ecosystem Services: From Chaos to Flowing Rivers*, 42 HARV. ENVTL. L. REV 197 (2018)) and then proposed that the usufructuary rights approach of water rights law could be mapped onto ecosystem services. See Kalyani Robbins, *Uncharted Waters: Can Water Rights Principles Stem the Tide of Ecosystem Services Losses?*, 31 N.Y.U. ENVT'L L. REV. 155 (2023). We expand on these themes *infra*.

[9]   Available at https://www.nytimes.com/2024/02/18/business/economy/natural-assets.html.

tory initiatives on the distribution of ecosystem services.[10] The guidance is built on the new understanding that ecosystem services are of vast value, but it offers no insight into the fundamental question of who owns them.

We focus on that question in this chapter, unpacking it into two components: *(1)* the allocation question, *Who should own ecosystem services?*; and *(2)* the design question, *How should ecosystem services be owned?* We open in Part I with the background on ecosystem services and climate change necessary to explore these property doctrine questions from the "changed circumstances or new knowledge" perspective. Part II then steps back to reframe the biophysical and economic features of ecosystem services in terms relevant to property doctrine. Using that foundation, in Part III we work through different doctrinal design options, identifying gaps in existing doctrine and focusing on nuisance law as a model for doctrinal evolution.

Ownership of ecosystem services is a complex problem with no perfect solution. This chapter sets out the specific challenges in developing a more effective private property regime for these services and the specific design choices that will need to be made.

I. THE VALUES OF ECOSYSTEM SERVICES

Largely taken for granted, the natural capital in ecosystems provides a variety of critical goods and services that support life itself.[11] Created by the interactions of living organisms with their environment, it is no exaggeration to state that the suite of "ecosystem services"—purifying air and water, detoxifying and decomposing waste, renewing soil fertility, regulating climate, mitigating droughts and floods, controlling pests, and pollinating vegetation—quite literally underpins human society. One cannot begin to understand flood control, for example, without realizing the impact that widespread wetland destruction has had on the ecosystem service of water retention; nor can one understand water quality without recognizing how development in forested watersheds has degraded the service of water purification.

Over the past 25 years, there has been an explosion of interest in natural capital and ecosystem services from scientists, economists, government officials,

---

[10] Office of Management & Budget, *Guidance for Assessing Changes in Environmental and Ecosystem Services in Benefit-Cost Analysis* (Feb. 28, 2024), https://bidenwhitehouse.archives.gov/wp-content/uploads/2024/02/ESGuidance .pdf.

[11] This section is adapted from Salzman and Ruhl (2007), *supra* note 5, and James Salzman, *Valuing Ecosystem Services*, 24 ECOLOGY L.Q. 887 (1997).

entrepreneurs, and the media.[12] Yet the importance of nature's services to human welfare is neither a novel nor a recent idea in Western thought. One can trace references to ecosystem services as far back as Plato and, more recently, through the writings of George Perkins Marsh, the father of modern-day ecology, as well as the observations of famed environmental writer, Aldo Leopold, among others.

Unlike the musings of Plato and Marsh, modern ecosystem services theory is a rigorous scientific discipline merging ecology, economics, and geography to go beyond simply observing the importance to humans of healthy ecosystems, to actually measuring those values, their ecological sources, and their human beneficiaries.

As set out in the foundational report, the Millennium Ecosystem Assessment,[13] the benefits from ecosystem services flow to human populations through four streams: (1) provisioning services include commodities such as food, wood, fiber, and water; (2) regulating services moderate or control environmental conditions, such as flood control by wetlands, water purification by aquifers, and carbon sequestration by forests; (3) cultural services include recreation, education, and aesthetics; and (4) supporting services, such as nutrient cycling, soil formation, and primary production, make the previous three service streams possible.

To make this concrete in property terms, imagine Ann's Parcel A and Bob's adjacent Parcel B, both of which abut a free-flowing river. Parcel A is undeveloped. On it, we find a riparian forest area that captures sediment and other pollutants and slows stormwater runoff flow into the river. A wetland area elsewhere on the parcel provides those services and also recharges a groundwater aquifer. Between these two habitats is a wide expanse of open field that supports various pollinator species.

From an ecological perspective, Ann's Parcel A performs various ecosystem functions—capturing pollutants, recharging groundwater, and supporting pollinators. On Parcel B, downstream of Parcel A, Bob operates a farm where he and his family live. The farm draws water from the river and aquifer to irrigate the crops; pollinators originating on Ann's parcel pollinate Bob's crops; Parcel B is protected from runoff flooding by Ann's wetland and riparian habitat. What Ann sees as ecosystem *functions* leaving her property, Bob sees as valuable ecosystem *services* flowing into his. In other words, the water purification and other ecosystem functions provided by Parcel A only become valuable

---

[12]   For a graph showing the growth from a handful of journal articles discussing payments for ecosystem services in 1996 to over 1,400 in 2014, see James Salzman et al., *Payments for Ecosystem Services: Past, Present and Future*, 6 TEX. A&M L. REV. 199, 202 (2018).

[13]   MILLENNIUM ECOSYSTEM ASSESSMENT (2004).

services because they provide benefits to Parcel B. Parcel A provides the "natural capital" from which ecosystem services flow to the benefit of Parcel B.

The concepts of natural capital and ecosystem services have quickly (and not without some controversy) become a dominant framework for science and policy. Law and policy efforts have largely focused on regulating and supporting services because, unlike provisioning services, they behave like nonmarket public goods and are therefore underprovided. A forest owner's timber has a market value that is easily measured and monitored. By contrast, it is difficult for the forest owner to charge for the water purification or flood control services enjoyed by the properties downstream.

More generally, landowners and urban dwellers enjoying services flowing from other parcels see them as "free" and thus have little incentive to invest in the resources providing them. Landowners have incentives to optimize their provisioning and cultural services, but little incentive to provide regulating and supporting services that benefit people in other places. As a result, these services are taken for granted, until the damage from their loss strikes home. How do you make trees worth more standing than cut down?[14]

Ann would find it difficult to persuade Bob to pay her for the ecosystem service benefits he has always enjoyed for free from Ann's parcel, most likely never even thinking about it. Why should he? But when Ann decides to pave paradise, so to speak, he will most certainly suffer the loss.[15]

Climate change is only intensifying the damages from the loss of ecosystem services. Sea-level rise threatens coastal dunes providing inland protection from storm surge; drought threatens pollinator habitats and water resources; the list goes on. In effect, the value of ecosystem services will continue to rise as climate change threatens people and property, meaning more eyes will be on the natural capital supplying them. And much of that natural capital is found on private property.

Despite the importance of ecosystem services, they have been largely overlooked in both property doctrine and regulatory statutes. Our major environmental laws were passed in the 1970s, well before the rise of significant research on ecosystem services by scientists and economists. There are some scattered statutory provisions that incidentally conserve some ecosystem services, but you have to look to find them, and their policy focus is primarily on conserving natural resources, not on ensuring the flow of services from those resources to people. Only in the past decade or so have regulatory agencies

---

[14] Borrowed from remarks delivered by Michael Jenkins, Forest Trends workshop on payments for ecosystem services, Washington, D.C., May 3rd, 2010.
[15] Courtesy of Joni Mitchell, *Big Yellow Taxi* (1970).

focused on adding management of ecosystem services to the policy goals.[16] Private property doctrine, our focus in this chapter, remains even less attentive to the ecosystem services dynamic.

II.   ECOSYSTEM SERVICES AS A PROPERTY RELATIONSHIP

In the previous section, we described the ecological and economic features of ecosystem services. We now turn to an exploration of how property doctrine does and could treat ecosystem services.

Returning to our simple two-parcel scenario, we find the natural capital on Ann's parcel supplying a flow of benefits to Bob's parcel: the wetlands recharge the groundwater supply Bob uses; the pollinator habitat supports species that pollinate Bob's crops; the riparian habitat captures sediment, helping to keep the river flowing by the parcels clean; and both the wetlands and the riparian habitat reduce flooding on Bob's parcel. Ann now proposes to pave over her parcel to open an outdoor movie venue (they are back in vogue), which would terminate all of the ecosystem services benefits Bob has been enjoying (at no cost) from Ann's natural capital.

The current doctrinal state of play is straightforward. In most cases, the default rule is that the owner of natural capital has no obligation to provide ecosystem services to beneficiaries on other properties. The doctrines of *ad coelum* and accession provide that Ann owns the natural capital on Parcel A, free to do with as she wishes (subject to harms she causes resulting in nuisance or violation of the *sic utere* principle), and if it so happens that neighbors benefit from flows of ecosystem services off her property, all the better for them as accessioners.[17] The honeybee hive owner owns the bees; the neighbors don't have a property interest requiring the bees to pollinate their crops, but if their crops are pollinated, they are entitled to the benefits.

But this could change. We could allocate entitlements such that property owners have an obligation to maintain a baseline flow of particular services that does not harm beneficiaries. This is easier said than done. How should we even begin to think about determining the baseline, identifying the services, and the trigger limits of harm, much less the appropriate relief?

This section takes on these challenging questions, considering five aspects of such a doctrinal shift: (1) characterization of the externalities;

---

[16]   For a history of this policy uptake, see J.B. Ruhl and James Salzman, *No Net Loss? The Past, Present, and Future of Wetlands Mitigation Banking*, 73 CASE W. RES. L. REV. 411 (2022).

[17]   For a summary of the doctrine of accession, see CHRISTOPHER SERKIN, THE LAW OF PROPERTY 35–36 (2nd ed. 2016).

(2) characterization of Ann's actions; (3) the types of injuries Bob suffers; (4) time; and (5) scale.

A.   Externalities—Positive or Negative?

A large part of traditional nuisance doctrine—substantial and unreasonable interference with the use and enjoyment of property—focuses on problems of negative externalities, such as when one property owner bothers another through introducing noise, smell, lights, etc.[18] In these instances and other cases of negative externalities, the job of nuisance law is to sort out when the state should impose a remedy through judicial intervention. At what point should "live and let live" give way to state restriction of private activity? The common law over time has developed significant guidance for judges to determine what should count as unreasonable. Does the value of the offending action, for example, outweigh the cost of the interference?[19] Did the offending action, as a further consideration, predate the presence of the offended property owner who "came to the nuisance"?[20]

But what about when the harm comes not from the negative externalities created by neighboring properties but, rather, from losing access to a positive externality? In other words, rather than the typical situation of a property owner angered over harms imposed on her by the noxious smells or loud sounds from a neighbor, what about when the property owner no longer enjoys a prior benefit? The classic case of *Fontainebleau Hotel Corp. v. Forty-Five Twenty-Five, Inc.* provides a useful analysis.[21]

The iconic hotels, the Eden Roc and the Fontainebleau, have long stood alongside one another on Miami Beach. When the Fontainebleau began building a 14-story addition, the Eden Roc owners quickly realized this would block the sunlight over much of their sunbathing area. The question for the court was whether the Eden Roc could halt the Fontainebleau construction—whether the Eden Roc had a right to the unobstructed flow of sunlight.

The court held in favor of the Fontainebleau. Unlike the English doctrine of "ancient lights" that guarantees homeowners unobstructed light to their windows,[22] Florida landowners cannot enjoin neighboring development that

---

[18] For a summary of the doctrine of nuisance, see SERKIN, THE LAW OF PROPERTY, *id.*, at 203–15.

[19] *Id.* at 202–203.

[20] *Id.* at 209.

[21] 114 So. 2d 357, 1959 Fla. App.

[22] Adopted in 1633, the doctrine safeguards windows used for light by an owner for 20 years or more from obstruction by actions of an adjacent landowner. See SERKIN, THE LAW OF PROPERTY, *supra* note 17, at 175–76.

stops the flow of sunlight. The classic explanation is that such a restriction would lock in structures and impede development.

On its face, the similarities between *Fontainebleau* and ecosystem services are suggestive. One could credibly argue that the higher building has reduced the benefit of "sunlight provision." Through this framing, why should property law treat the loss of ecosystem services any differently from the loss of other positive externalities? In fact, traditional property law disfavors such negative easements. The beneficiary of the service has no right to restrict the behavior of the provider, even when it results in a reduction of the service.

At the same time, tort common law has long recognized the right of lateral and subjacent support.[23] Landowners may prevent actions by their neighbors that undermine the soil in its natural condition. If excavation by a neighbor causes subsidence, the neighbor is liable for the loss of lateral support. This looks like the imposition of a negative externality—subsidence resulting from excavation. But can this situation equally be framed as the law ensuring the continued provision of a positive externality—the service by neighbors of lateral support?

The first framing question for the natural capital/ecosystem services relationship thus is how to view the externalities Ann is "causing" through her paving over the parcel—is she causing negative externalities that harm Bob (more like a classic nuisance), or is she reducing positive externalities that Bob was enjoying at no cost and has no right to expect as a property interest (more like *Fontainebleau*)? Put another way, is there a meaningful distinction between the reduction of a positive externality and the imposition of a negative externality?

Consider a scenario in which Ann's parcel was an open pasture with none of the natural capital providing Bob's benefits. Surely Bob could not reasonably demand that Ann somehow *create* the wetlands, pollinator habitat, and riparian habitat so Bob can enjoy the benefits at no cost. But if Ann, with an interest in natural resources conservation, did so of her own volition, Bob's benefits spigot would turn on. This could only be described as Ann providing positive externalities for the benefit of Bob.

If Ann later asks Bob to contribute to some of the expenses of maintaining the natural capital and Bob refuses, what if Ann then moves to her outdoor movie venue proposal? The effect would be to withdraw the positive externalities she provided through her conservation project. Having refused to contribute to the maintenance of Ann's parcel when her positive externalities benefits spigot was turned on, it would seem unreasonable for Bob to now demand that

---

[23]   For a summary of the doctrine of support, see JOSEPH WILLIAM SINGER, PROPERTY 134–37 (3rd ed. 2010).

Ann must keep the spigot on. How, then, is it different if the natural capital was always on the parcel, since well before Ann came into its ownership, and Bob's parcel was enjoying the benefits all along, at no cost?

Consider Ann's outdoor movie venue plan. The impervious cover of the parking lot could lead to increased stormwater runoff onto Bob's parcel. And the bright lights late at night could disturb Bob's sleep. These effects are classic negative externalities, the fodder of private and public nuisance doctrine (and of public regulation). The convenience of having those existing property doctrines at hand, however, does not alone justify describing the natural capital/ecosystem services dynamic between Ann and Bob as a negative externalities story. As we noted, property doctrine has been built largely around the problem of introduced negative externalities. The problem of reduced positive externalities, if that is how we frame the effect of Ann's actions, remains a relatively uncharted frontier in property doctrine.

Justice Scalia may well have scoffed at attempting to make this distinction, arguing as he did in *Lucas* that identifying a land use regulation as preventing harms or conferring benefits is a fool's errand.[24] The answer depends on your perspective—are you an Ann or a Bob?[25] Fearful that legislatures would pick whichever side of the harms/benefits coin best suits their needs when characterizing their legislative purpose, Scalia turned to the background principles of nuisance and property law to be the referee. These judicially time-tested doctrines, presumably, would clarify when an action has been deemed a harm and thus open for legislative restriction without exposure to a regulatory takings claim. As we show in Part III, though, this is not so obvious when it comes to ecosystem services.

B.   Actions—Commission or Omission?

The externalities analysis begs the related question of how to characterize Ann's actions, as commission or omission. To be sure, filling in the wetlands, razing the pollinator and riparian habitats, and replacing them with pavement are all affirmative actions. The effects, however, are qualitatively different. The pavement newly introduces the negative externality of increased flooding. The habitat losses do not. For example, what if, instead of paving the parcel, Ann converts it into a soybean crop field with no runoff effect on Bob's parcel? In this case, as discussed above, Ann arguably is not introducing a negative externality but rather is reducing a pre-existing benefit. At the other extreme,

---

[24]   *Lucas, supra* note 1, 505 U.S. at 1024–25.

[25]   For an accessible analysis of how externalities vary between positive or negative depending on the framing, see Lisa Grow Sun and Brigham Daniels, *Mirrored Externalities,* 90 NOTRE DAME L. REV. 135 (2014).

consider a scenario in which, if Ann simply did nothing at all, the natural succession of vegetation on the parcel would convert the pollinator habitat into some other form of cover, and the wetlands would eventually fill up and dry up. Indeed, climate change very likely could trigger these effects. Bob would feel the same losses in that scenario as he would if Ann, by filling the wetland and converting the pollinator habitat, were the change agent.

In the case of the pavement and its effects on Bob's parcel, Ann clearly would be deemed to have induced the effects through commission, one that would be ripe for a claim of private nuisance. In the case of the natural loss of the habitat, the effects on Bob's parcel would be the result of Ann's omission—she did nothing to cause or to prevent the habitat transitions. Property doctrine does not generally impose a duty to take action to prevent such natural reductions in positive externalities. The specialized doctrine of permissive waste, for example, could require a life estate holder to maintain structures for the benefit of the future interest holders,[26] but we know of no doctrine that would require Ann to intervene in the natural habitat transition process so that Bob maintains his ecosystem service benefits at no cost to him.[27]

The case of Ann converting the parcel into a soybean crop field is thus is a bit of neither fish nor fowl. Like the pavement, Ann's removal of the habitat causes effects on Bob's parcel; like the natural habitat transition, the effects are a reduction in benefits, not the introduction of a new negative effect. As we show in Part III, that is a rare bird in property doctrine.

Kalyani Robbins has argued that when owners of natural capital destroy the resources, the benefit-reducing effects on other property owners should be seen as negative externalities because the pre-existing baseline has been altered.[28] She analogizes this to when a parcel owner introduces a new land use (such as Ann's pavement) that introduces a new negative effect on the adjacent parcels (flooding), which would be described as a negative externality. Because the owner of pre-existing natural capital did not "create" the flow of ecosystem services, she argues, the benefits should not be described as positive externalities. Rather, it is only when the natural capital owner destroys the natural capital—i.e., changes the "baseline" conditions—that the externalities question should be asked, and they are all negative. In other words,

---

[26] For a summary of the doctrine of waste, see SERKIN, THE LAW OF PROPERTY, *supra* note 17, at 77–79.

[27] The closest example may be found in water law and the No Injury rule. The junior appropriator can sue to block a change in a senior appropriator's water right if the junior may be injured by a reduced flow of water resulting from the proposed changes in use.

[28] See Robbins, *Allocating Property Interests, supra* note 8, at 223–29.

maintaining the parcel as is, and thus the benefits that flow to others, isn't "causing" those benefits.

Consider, however, another scenario in which the effects of changing base-line conditions are difficult to fit into the negative externalities framing with-out placing unusual burdens on Ann. Instead of reducing Bob's pollination and groundwater recharge service benefits by destroying the natural capital on her parcel, Ann does so by capturing them before they leave her prop-erty. She plants crops on her property, the effect of which is to divert pollina-tors to her crops instead of Bob's, and she starts pumping groundwater, the effect of which is to capture the benefits of the recharge services her wetlands provided to the aquifer. Ann clearly took actions that change the pre-existing baseline and reduce Bob's pollination and groundwater benefits, which could be costly to him.

If we view the effects of Ann's actions as negative externalities that Ann should be expected to internalize, she might need to remove her crops and stop the pumping. In other words, once produced on Ann's parcel from her natural capital, Ann has lost any claim to the services, even to use them for her own benefit—she must let them go wherever they flow. Alternatively, if the baseline is that she has been allowing the benefits to escape onto Bob's property as posi-tive externalities, when she later decides to use them for her benefit, that is best viewed as a reduction in positive externalities, not the introduction of a new negative externality. Likewise, therefore, when she destroys the natural capital, which functionally produces the same effects on Bob as does her capturing the services *in situ*, that too can be framed as an action that reduces positive externalities. Why should it matter, in other words, whether she deprives Bob of the services by capturing them on her property after they are produced (on her property) versus preventing them from being produced at all?

To some extent, the focus on the *benefits* flowing from natural capital clouds this analysis. For example, wetlands also impose negative effects on adjoining parcels, such as foul odors and providing habitat for vermin and mosquitoes—the dismal image of swamps and bogs from centuries past. The adjacent land-owners might very well consider the wetlands' owner to be "causing" those effects, even though they arguably are inherent in the pre-existing baseline. Are those negative externalities, or should we defer the externalities question to when the wetlands' owner, presumably by filling the wetlands, changes the pre-existing state and thus causes positive externalities?

While this appears to be a two sides of the same coin puzzle, it is relevant to the property doctrine design for ecosystem services. We cannot think of any property doctrine that assigns *ownership* in one person of a positive externality produced by another person.[29] As discussed above, moreover, property doctrine has focused largely on managing the commission of negative externalities. Allowing Bob to claim ownership rights in the ecosystem services Ann's natural capital produces the moment they are produced on her property thus would require some innovation in property doctrine.

As noted above, the doctrine of support presents the same conundrum on a micro scale by imposing liability on a property owner if excavation causes the collapse of the adjacent parcel. If one conceptualizes the support service soil provides between parcels as a positive externality, the act of excavation reduces that positive externality, but the doctrine assigns liability nonetheless. We consider in Part III how the doctrine of support could assist in doctrine design for ecosystem services more broadly.

C.   Effects—Physical or Economic?

As the example of support shows, the reduction of positive externalities can lead to substantial impacts. Similarly, in Bob's case, Ann's depletion of the riparian habitat removes sediment filtration and flood control services, which could lead to increased downstream pollution and flooding on Bob's parcel. These are physical impacts that degrade Bob's parcel. Filling the wetland reduces groundwater recharge, meaning Bob may have less access to groundwater for irrigating his crops.

But not all changes in natural capital result in physical damage to the beneficiary parcel. Some are economic in nature. Razing the pollinator habitat has no physical impact on Bob's parcel, resulting only in the decline of natural pollination on his parcel. Bob could either endure the decline in crop yield or pay for commercial bee pollination services. In short, Bob's "injuries" range from physical impacts on his parcel to purely economic business losses. How does that matter?

One could point to nuisance law as providing a remedy for economic losses such as crop yield decline, as was the case in *Georgia v. Tennessee Copper*.[30] But there the crop losses were caused by pollution from copper smelting—i.e., the commission of introduced negative externalities. By contrast, economic impacts were deemed not to be a basis for claiming nuisance in *Fountainebleau Hotel* when those impacts resulted from interrupting the flow of light across the defendant's parcel to the plaintiff's hotel pool and beach. Some of Bob's

---

[29]   For an interesting discussion of why free-riding is socially beneficial and why we should avoid trying to capture the positive externalities of intellectual property, see Mark A. Lemley, *Property, Intellectual Property, and Free Riding*, 83 Tex. L. Rev. 1031 (2005).

[30]   206 U.S. 230 (1907).

injuries seem closer to *Tennessee Copper*, and some to *Fountainebleau Hotel,* the point being that property doctrine design for ecosystem services may need to account for this range of impact types.

D.   Time—Latent, Present, or Future?

In our original scenario, we find Bob and Ann in their relationship without respect to past or future, as if the conditions have been and always will be the same unless Bob or Ann change their land uses. Putting time into the dynamics complicates matters in ways that should be relevant to doctrine design.

For example, change the scenario so that Bob's family historically had left the parcel as a fallow field. The natural habitat on Ann's parcel was performing the relevant ecosystem *functions*, but none were being used on Bob's parcel as ecosystem *services*. There were no crops to pollinate and irrigate, neither was there a home to protect from flooding, nor any use of the river. At most, the functions could be described as providing latent ecosystem services—benefits that could provide value in the future if crops and homes show up. When Bob, in fact does start using the parcel for his home and farm, he has then tapped into the service values. Does he somehow at that point have a vested right of some kind in their continued flow from Ann's parcel? By analogy, nuisance doctrine's rule of "coming to the nuisance," which strictly applied barred an action for nuisance if the defendant's uses were there first, is usually treated as one of many factors, and would suggest Bob's claim is on tenuous ground.[31]

Similarly, go back to the original scenario in which there has been a long-standing flow of services to Bob's parcel. That is the present condition, and those services can be assigned economic value. Bob then decides to form a communal community on the parcel and to convert his crops to an expensive type of herb (like saffron). The flow of services from Ann's parcel remains constant, but the addition of people, structures, and a high-dollar crop makes them more valuable if the measure of value is the economic activity they support or the losses when the services are terminated. Doctrines such as the reasonable use rule applied to express appurtenant easements anticipate and allow for this kind of effect to some extent, but typically one pays for such an easement in the first place.[32] In Ann's case, she is watching her parcel provide increasing value to Bob's parcel, receiving nothing in return, not even some services flowing back in her direction.

---

[31]   For a summary of this doctrine, see SERKIN, THE LAW OF PROPERTY, *supra* note 17, at 209.

[32]   For a summary of the scope of express appurtenant easements, see SINGER, PROPERTY, *supra* note 23, at 212–14.

Timing also matters regarding the nature of the harm. Filling a wetland overnight such that a neighboring property is flooded a day later from a storm seems different to the slow filling of the wetland over years, though with the same flooding result when it no longer provides the service of flood buffering.

There are many other scenarios we could design using time to manipulate the relationship between Bob and Ann. Property law has developed specialized doctrines to account for time effects, suggesting the same could be done in doctrine design for ecosystem services.

E.   Scale—How Many Bobs and Anns?

We've used the two-parcel scenario as a platform for unpacking different factors we believe should be considered when designing property doctrine for ecosystem services, but it is largely unrealistic in terms of the level of services Ann's parcel provides to Bob and the distribution of those services. For example, it may be that hundreds of parcels in the region house wetlands providing groundwater recharge to the aquifer Bob draws from, and that many parcels near Bob's house provide pollination services to his parcel. If property doctrine assigns Bob some form of right to require Ann's continued delivery of services, he presumably would have the same right over all those other parcels. On its face, this appears unworkable.

Flipping the perspective, it is also likely that many parcels other than Bob's benefit from Ann's natural capital. Bob is not the exclusive withdrawer from the aquifer, and there are other parcels downstream of his benefiting from the sediment capture and flood control services Ann provides. If property doctrine assigns Bob some form of right to require continued delivery of services from Ann's parcel (and from the other parcels providing those services to him), all the other benefited parcels would have the same right over Ann (and over all those other parcels). This seems similarly problematic.

In short, while it is possible in some cases to isolate and quantify service flow in a two-parcel or small-scale context, such as through soil support, many ecosystem services flow from and to large numbers of potentially widely distributed parcels. At the extreme, every parcel in the world on which carbon is sequestered through vegetation growth is providing that service to every parcel on the planet. Just as the development of public nuisance doctrine can manage some degree of scale effects—for example, the smelters in Tennessee damaging crops on parcels in Georgia—property doctrine design for ecosystem services will surely need to take scale into account. One way to account for this may be focusing on vectors—the direction and size of flows. Uni-directional large flows are easier to manage than multi-directional small flows. Parcel A pollinating Parcel B is easier to manage through property (and contractual) arrangements than Parcel A pollinating Parcels B through Z.

Moreover, not all ecosystem services are the same. Perhaps it makes sense to treat different services differently under the law. Just as the flow of wind and passage of light are quite different from the flow of water (and treated differently under common law), so, too, might we want to treat diffuse services such as pollination and recharge differently from flood control or sediment retention. Arden Rowell's work on the psychology of ecosystem management suggests that ecosystem services that are particularly diffuse, complex, or nonhuman, and thus especially subject to psychological undervaluation, are the ones that most need legal management rather than being left to private ordering.[33]

III.   PROPERTY DOCTRINE DESIGN FOR ECOSYSTEM SERVICES

Part II described the significant factors in thinking about property doctrine, natural capital, and ecosystem services. We now move on to the doctrine design analysis. Going back to the original scenario, both Ann and Bob own their respective parcels in fee simple absolute—they have the complete "bundle of sticks." But how should the sticks be distributed when it comes to Ann's natural capital and Bob's claim to ecosystem service benefits flowing from them?

Ann's proposal to convert her parcel's land use requires that she exercise the right to destroy the natural capital on her property that supplies Bob's ecosystem services. Bob's ongoing farm and residential uses of his property suggest he has the right to capture and use the ecosystem services.

Assigning Ann an absolute right to destroy the natural capital means she can completely cut off Bob's capture and use of the ecosystem services with no liability to Bob. Doctrines like support have developed to moderate that risk in specific contexts. Without such a doctrinal adjustment in the ecosystem services context, Ann would be free to destroy the natural capital without regard to the harm it causes Bob and others. Given their nature as public goods, however, Ann has no practical way to charge Bob for the continued delivery of the benefits, short of threatening to destroy the natural capital.

The effect of assigning Bob an absolute right to capture and use the ecosystem services on his property depends on how we describe the status of the ecosystem services. Are they like wild animals, unowned until captured and constructively possessed by the landowner of the parcel on which they are

---

[33]   Arden Rowell, *Quantitative Valuation in Environmental Law*, 96 NOTRE DAME L. REV. 1539 (2021).

found?[34] That would mean Bob has no right to capture them until they enter his parcel, which leaves Ann still able to destroy the natural capital without liability to Bob. Yet, if she does not destroy the natural capital, once the services enter Bob's property, they are his to capture and use. In the end, this leaves Ann and Bob in essentially the same position as assigning Ann the absolute right to destroy.

Or are the ecosystem services produced from the natural capital the property of the supplier, Ann? This would favor characterizing the benefits as positive externalities Ann supplies but is unable to internalize through a market transaction, and her destruction of the natural capital as a reduction of those benefits through omission. The end result remains the same as above—Ann can destroy the natural capital without liability to Bob, but as positive externalities, Ann has no practical way to charge Bob for them short of threatening to cut them off by destroying the natural capital.

Or, in the version most favorable to Bob (he's out of luck in all the others), are the ecosystem services entitlements appurtenant to his parcel—do they inherently come along with ownership of the benefitted parcel? In this case, Bob would effectively own a negative easement over Ann's parcel such that she cannot destroy the natural capital without liability to Bob for the injury it causes him. This characterizes Ann as causing a negative externality that Bob can seek to enjoin or recover compensatory damages for. Ann is no longer freely able to threaten to destroy the natural capital and wreak harm on Bob without recourse.

Coase casts an obvious shadow over this issue,[35] as we could choose any of the above approaches and let Ann and Bob bargain for a different outcome through covenants and easements. Whether Ann controls the natural capital or Bob holds rights to the flow of services, the Anns and Bobs of the world can attempt to negotiate a resolution for their specific relationship. This could have happened in *Fontainebleau Hotel,* with Eden Roc paying its neighbor not to build the added stories. In some cases of small-scale, unidirectional, and easily traced services, perhaps this could work. But this does not describe much of the landscape.

As discussed above, the real world is more complex in spatial and temporal scales and is mired in transaction costs. Natural capital and ecosystem services take many forms and are blanketed over the landscape, with flows of services in all directions. It thus seems undesirable to adopt any of the doctrinal

---

[34]   For a summary of the law of wild animals and the doctrine of capture, see SERKIN, THE LAW OF PROPERTY, *supra* note 17, at 28–34.

[35]   For a summary of the operation of the Coase theorem in property doctrine, see SERKIN, THE LAW OF PROPERTY, *supra* note 17, at 206–207.

designs described above as a general rule and assume contracting will lead to efficient results.

Giving natural capital owners total control over the supply of ecosystem services can lead to substantial private and public harms. Giving beneficiaries total control over the supply of ecosystem services locks in land uses through negative easements blanketed across the landscape. Given the ubiquity of natural capital and the multi-directional flow of ecosystem services, relying on private bargaining to moderate these effects at scale would be frustrated by high transaction costs.

As an opposite to the Coasean private ordering approach, we could envision ecosystem services as publicly owned, to be managed under some kind of a sovereign public trust responsibility.[36] This would be a rather unusual form of public ownership, however, given that the source of the ecosystem services benefits (for our purposes) is privately owned natural capital. The traditional public trust doctrine, for example, is associated with *publicly* owned submerged lands and requires sovereign management for the benefit of the public (for example, providing access for fishing, swimming, and other uses).[37] That is far different from asserting public ownership in and public trust status over, say, the pollination services pollinators from Ann's privately owned parcel provide to Bob's crops, or the sediment capture services Ann's privately owned riparian habitat provides to downstream property owners. That would be a wholly new kind of public ownership and public trust regime. This is not to say that the public has no interest in ecosystem services falling within the scope of sovereign police powers, more on which later. Nor do we dismiss the idea of public ownership of ecosystem services as not worth consideration. For our purposes, however, the ownership question of interest is a matter of private property doctrine—i.e., allocating the "sticks" between the Anns and Bobs of our private property landscape.

To be sure, this is not the first time private property doctrine has had to balance multiple and conflicting public and private interests by designing doctrinal compromises rather than choosing between conflicting absolute rules. As we have suggested above several times, however, we can identify no such existing doctrine that maps directly onto the natural capital-ecosystem services

---

[36] For a summary of the doctrine of nuisance, see SERKIN, THE LAW OF PROPERTY, *supra* note 17, at 280–82.

[37] As we have argued in previous work, it is a small step in public trust doctrine to include the ecosystem services such publicly owned lands provide as falling within the scope of the sovereign's public trust responsibilities regarding access and alienation. See J.B. Ruhl and James Salzman, *Ecosystem Services and the Public Trust Doctrine: Working Change from Within*, 15 SE. ENVTL. L.J. 223 (2006).

dynamic. Some form of doctrinal innovation is needed, whether it bends an existing doctrine, picks and chooses features from several, or forges entirely new territory. In the sections that follow, we first establish the lack of any existing doctrine to apply "off the shelf" and propose a solution through the extension of nuisance doctrine to an ecosystem services framework. We then assess this new doctrinal innovation from several perspectives.

A.   Doctrinal Gaps—No Existing Doctrine Fits

The property doctrine toolkit is brimming with doctrines designed to solve puzzles like the natural capital-ecosystem services dynamic, but none easily applies in this context. Take the doctrine of support, which we have raised several times. While it can be translated into the ecosystem services context as requiring natural capital owners to maintain the flow of soil support benefits above a certain level to avoid collapse of the adjacent property, the flow of benefits is reciprocal between the two properties. Both properties are equally constrained and benefited. That is not the case between Ann and Bob, with Ann's natural capital supplying Bob's benefits and no reciprocal benefits flowing back to Ann. In the scaled-up landscape-level context, it is more likely that services flow in multiple directions and many property owners both supply and receive benefits. Yet that context stretches support doctrine even further beyond its highly localized reciprocal relationship in the same service benefits.

Implied easement and adverse possession doctrines also may seem to have some potential small-scale applications, but they too fail to map neatly onto ecosystem services given their technicalities.[38] Ann's destruction of the natural capital does not landlock Bob's parcel (easement by necessity), nor was Ann the prior user of the ecosystem services across a larger parcel and later severed her parcel to create Bob's (easement by prior use). Ann, who plausibly does not even know what benefits she is providing Bob, has not granted Bob a permissive license to the services upon her land she arguably should be estopped from rescinding (easement by estoppel). Bob has not in open and hostile manner exercised access to Ann's natural capital (prescriptive easement) or in any way asserted possession of it (adverse possession). These doctrines follow technical details for their formation for good reason—they lead to an involuntary servitude. Moreover, the resulting servitude is an affirmative easement, not a negative easement.

Surface water rights doctrines, as well as the various approaches to groundwater rights, are designed to manage larger-scale contexts within which

---

[38]   For a summary of implied easements and adverse possession, see SERKIN, THE LAW OF PROPERTY, *supra* note 17, at 57–66, 156–68.

multiple interests share in a common resource, water, akin to the flow of eco-system services.[39] The No Injury Rule in prior appropriation jurisdictions pro-tects the interests of junior appropriators from changes in use by seniors.[40] But this and other water rights doctrines define rights as between multiple *users* of the water competing for access, not between the users of the water and the owners of land distant from the river or aquifer in the respective watershed *supplying* the water. A riparian rights owner, for example, has no say in how a property owner in the watershed 10 miles inland from the river manages a wetland or forested area which might play some role in the supply of water to the river system. Likewise, the ecosystem services question is about the rela-tionship between the resource supplier (Ann) and the resource user (Bob)—not between competing resource users (multiple Bobs)—and thus is not a good fit for applying traditional water rights doctrine.

We could go on, but having cycled through every property doctrine we could think of (and being appreciative of the many suggestions we received from col-leagues along the way), we could not identify any doctrine to drop directly onto the ecosystem services context to solve the puzzle of how the "sticks" are allocated between the natural capital owner and the service flow beneficiary. Doctrinal innovation is needed.

B. Doctrinal Innovation—A Proposed Ecosystem Services Nuisance Doctrine

Taking a Goldilocks approach, one design strategy would be to start with either of the extreme absolute rules and develop and test doctrinal innovations that moderate the effects imposed by either assigning total control to the natural capital owner or to the ecosystem services beneficiary. Kalyani Robbins takes this approach in her work, starting from the position that beneficiaries have total control.[41] She uses the usufructuary rights doctrines of water law as her moderation model,[42] but, as discussed above, our view is that water rights law is a clumsy fit. By contrast, we propose an option starting from the position that natural capital owners have total control of the ecosystem services spigot, using nuisance doctrine as our moderation model.

Property doctrines defining the relationship between parcel owners do not aim to internalize *all* negative externalities. The doctrine of support, for exam-ple, addresses the substantial effect of subsidence but does not provide one

---

[39] See Robbins, *Uncharted Waters*, *supra* note 8.

[40] National Research Council, WATER TRANSFERS IN THE WEST: EFFICIENCY, EQUITY, AND THE ENVIRONMENT 81 (1992).

[41] See Robbins, *Allocating Property Interests*, *supra* note 8.

[42] See Robbins, *Uncharted Waters*, *supra* note 8.

property owner total control over the adjacent property owner's excavations. More to the point of the natural capital/ecosystem services dynamic, private nuisance doctrine assigns liability to a property owner who unreasonably and substantially interferes with another property owner's use and enjoyment of their property. Public nuisance doctrine also steps in when "live and let live" is inadequate—when the effect is significant interference with the public interest.

As such, nuisance doctrine balances competing uses of properties but does not attempt to assign ownership rights beyond use and enjoyment of property. For example, establishing that one property owner has caused a private nuisance resulting from excessive noise does not mean that the injured property owner owns "quiet," but rather that they are entitled to use and enjoyment without unreasonable and significant interference. Nor does nuisance regulate all noise at any level.

This relationship-based approach could be mapped onto the natural capital/ecosystem services dynamic in a similar way. Owners of natural capital supplying benefits to other parcels may develop the natural capital resources, and thus decrease ecosystem service flows, but only up to a point. The other parcel owners do not "own" the ecosystem services, but rather may protest if the effects of the loss of natural capital—i.e., the diminished ecosystem service benefits—unreasonably and significantly interfere with their use and enjoyment of their property. The defining feature is that a flow of positive externality benefits from the natural capital is diminished. This moves beyond traditional nuisance doctrine, in which the usual context is the introduction of a new flow of some injurious condition, such as increased light, noise, or odors imposing negative externalities from the offending land use. The ecosystem services nuisance doctrine thus extends nuisance into the realm of positive externalities by limiting their reduction.

Of course, like traditional nuisance doctrine, the hard question is what constitutes unreasonable and significant interference with use and enjoyment. Like nuisance doctrine, this form of ecosystem services claim would depend on the nature of the land use destroying the natural capital and the type and magnitude of the resulting injury. Qualitatively, for example, Ann's reduction of pollination services for Bob's farm due to there being fewer pollinators is different from the flooding and pollutants that may occur more often on Bob's property when Ann destroys the riparian and wetland habitats. The former imposes economic injury to Bob's crop business; the latter alters the physical conditions on the parcel itself. Quantitatively, however, the loss of pollination may be more costly to Bob than the increased flooding and pollution.

The more modest doctrinal change would restrict *private* ecosystem services claims to cases of *physical* effects imposing substantial losses. This keeps the claim closer to traditional nuisance law but would open up new territory for managing property owner relations involving one's actions having negative effects on another's use and enjoyment.

Moreover, just as public nuisance doctrine facilitates scaling up when the negative impacts of a land use threaten many private and public interests, so too could the ecosystem services nuisance doctrine where there are (potentially) many natural capital owners changing their land uses and many injured interests. Indeed, this is the approach the Rhode Island state court took in *Palazzolo* on remand from the Supreme Court, finding that filling wetlands would cause a public nuisance by reducing pollutant filtration services benefiting the local community. In retrospect, this could also have justified the South Carolina state courts, on remand from the Supreme Court's *Lucas* decision, finding destruction of the dunes would cause a public nuisance as a result of reduced storm surge protection (rather than finding no nuisance effect).

The key point to keep in mind is that entitlements do shift over time as values and conditions change and can certainly do so for ecosystem services. In the era of renewable energy, for example, the law is re-thinking whether neighbors can interrupt the flow of light and wind. In the 1982 Wisconsin case *Prah v. Moretti*, for example, the court changed how the nuisance law doctrine of reasonable use should be interpreted regarding the obstruction of access to light (in that case shading of solar panels).[43] In a reverse of the Eden Roc case, the court held for the solar panel owners who objected to neighbors shading their panels. The Court described, "Courts should not implement obsolete policies that have lost their vigor over the course of the years. The law of private nuisance is better suited to resolve landowners' disputes about property development in the 1980's than is a rigid rule which does not recognize a landowner's interest in access to sunlight. As we said in *Ballstadt v. Pagel,* 'What is regarded in law as constituting a nuisance in modern times would no doubt have been tolerated without question in former times.'"[44]

Such shifts are part and parcel of property law. Almost two centuries ago, water law doctrine made a similar transition. The natural flow doctrine from English riparian law had carried over to the new colonies, providing that a riparian landowner cannot interfere with the natural flow of a river. This worked fine in Colonial America but proved problematic with the rise of water power and the need for mill ponds. In short time, the natural flow doctrine was replaced by the "American Rule" of reasonable use, providing that the natural flow may be disrupted for reasonable purposes.[45] While the 21st century is witnessing a move *against* interference with the flows of light and air, the

---

[43] Prah v. Maretti 108 Wis. 2d 223 (1982).
[44] *Id.*
[45] Barton H. Thompson, Jr., et al., Legal Control of Water Resources 54 (6th ed. 2018).

19th century saw the opposite—a move *encouraging* interference with the flow of water.[46]

It is not hard to see the parallels to interfering with or encouraging flows of ecosystem services. The owners of natural capital control the "spigot" of ecosystem functions the resources produce. Through scientific advancements over the past several decades, we now appreciate the vast economic values those functions provide in the form of ecosystem service benefits and the extensive private and public injury that could ensue if the spigots are turned off completely. Climate change will only intensify those conditions. Traditional nuisance doctrine is about restricting how far open the negative externality spigot can be turned; the ecosystem services nuisance doctrine we propose is simply the flip side, restricting how far the positive externality spigot can be closed. Both have the same reference point—the reasonableness and substantiality of the injury.

C.   Innovation Assessment—Will It Work?

We now step back to assess the proposed ecosystem service nuisance from several perspectives we believe should matter most in property doctrinal innovations motivated by "changed circumstances or new knowledge."

First, how radical is the innovation in terms of departure from existing property doctrine? Radical doctrinal shifts in the allocation or restriction of property rights raise numerous concerns, including disrupting settled expectations and perhaps, as some Supreme Court Justices have suggested, scrutiny as a possible judicial taking.[47] With that concern in mind, we believe the proposed ecosystem services nuisance is a modest move in the background principles of property and nuisance law. Indeed, by recognizing that there is also a positive externalities "spigot" and placing a limit on how far landowners can close it, we see the proposed innovation as bringing the nuisance doctrine round full circle. If the concern is unreasonable and a significant interference

---

[46]   Interestingly the *Prah* court made a similar point in citing *State v. Deetz*, which rejected the common enemy rule for surface water in place of the reasonable use rule, where the landowner is subject to liability only if her interference with the flow of surface waters unreasonably invades a neighbor's interest in the use and enjoyment of land. As the *Deetz* court described, the common enemy rule may have served society "well in the days of burgeoning national expansion of the mid-nineteenth and early-twentieth centuries," but it was no longer "in harmony with the realities of our society." 66 Wis. 2d 1, 224 N.W.2d 407 (1974).

[47]   See Stop the Beach Renourishment v. Florida Department of Environmental Protection, 560 U.S. 702 (2010).

with use and enjoyment, why should it matter whether the defendant's new land use increases a negative or reduces a positive?

Once the positive externalities spigot is brought into the nuisance doctrine framework, it broadly leverages existing doctrine, requiring no further changes to nuisance doctrine. That is, the same tests and standards for intent, reasonableness, and assessment of utility and injury applied in traditional nuisance doctrine, with its focus on turning the negative externalities spigot on too far, apply in mirror fashion to the ecosystem services nuisance claim. For example, a public ecosystem nuisance claim can step in when the effects are dispersed across parcels and distant from the natural capital parcel(s). And remedies remain the same as well: injured landowners can seek compensatory damages and could seek to enjoin proposed natural capital destruction through an anticipatory nuisance claim. In short, the entire body of case law giving life to traditional nuisance doctrine maps surprisingly easily onto the ecosystem services nuisance claim.

Second, how clear is the innovation in terms of defining the respective private property interests? Nuisance doctrine, to say the least, lacks bright-line rules and has been critiqued for being a muddle. Our proposed ecosystem services nuisance doctrine inherits that baggage. But nuisance doctrine's flexibility to context, and its durable capacity to evolve with changed conditions and understandings, are features rather than bugs in this realm of complex landowner relationships. Absolute rules assigning controlling interests to either natural capital owners or ecosystem services beneficiaries, while offering clarity, simply don't work as a practical matter.

The upshot of this approach, moreover, is not as murky as might be claimed. There is some advantage to focusing on the natural capital ownership question and what flows from its resolution rather than shifting attention to the ecosystem service flows. On that score, our proposal is crystal clear: the owners of natural capital retain complete ownership of those resources—they own the spigot. From there, it is about what they do with the spigot. Our proposal takes away only the option of turning it off so much as to unreasonably cause substantial private or public harm. Short of that, Coase steps back into the picture, in that private beneficiaries or the public could pay the landowner either to keep service flows above the minimum level set by the nuisance threshold or even to enhance them. Indeed, that is the underlying basis for carbon offset programs (for example, preserve forest sequestration capacity) and restoration-based payment for ecosystem services programs (for example, payments to restore wetlands).

Third, how does the innovation intersect with the police power and takings doctrine? Regulation of land use impacts on natural resources is already firmly established within the scope of police power authority.[48] If anything, new knowledge about ecosystem services and their value in a climate change future only reinforces the justification for regulating natural resources to protect the public interest. Our proposed refinement of property doctrine aligns the private law and public law spheres of ecosystem services conservation without radical reform of either.

As to the regulatory takings aspect, our proposed doctrinal innovation once again mirrors the outcome for traditional nuisance doctrine—i.e., the permissible scope of public regulation unquestionably extends to outlawing and otherwise managing private and public nuisances, and so too would it extend to ecosystem services nuisances. The upshot is that Justice Scalia's conclusion in *Lucas*—that public land use regulations duplicating the prohibitions of nuisance doctrine, even if the end result is a total economic wipeout, are not open to challenge as regulatory takings—would fully apply to public regulation of land uses degrading or destroying natural capital and closing the services spigot to the degree that it would constitute public or private ecosystem services nuisances.

CONCLUSION

Ecosystem services sustain human flourishing, and yet the property law of wild animals and footpaths is far more developed than is the case for ecosystem services. Why is that? As we have shown, the fit between ecosystem services and property doctrine has been complicated by the nature of ecosystem services as positive externalities flowing from one private parcel to another. Managing property relations in positive externalities has not been the traditional domain of property doctrine—it is much more about managing negative externalities. As a consequence, there is no ready-made existing property doctrine to simply map onto ecosystem services. Nuisance law, however, offers a platform for relatively modest doctrinal reform that balances the interests of owners of the natural capital generating ecosystem services and owners of parcels benefiting from them. More radical doctrinal reform, such as placing total ownership interests over the flow of ecosystem services in the owner of the natural capital or the owner of the beneficiary parcel, risks either serious harm to the public interest under the former or extreme restrictions on the use of private property under the latter. Our proposed ecosystem services nuisance doctrine moderates both effects, aligns with trends in public law regarding natural resources, and fits neatly into existing regulatory takings theory and doctrine.

---

[48]   Whether and to what extent it should be are different questions altogether.

Index

riparian *see* riparian land
state ownership of water and 289–290
takings for 44, 80–81, 267–268, 277,
 308–310
use rights for 73, 272–293
welfare rights 10

wetlands 311, 313–314, 316, 318,
 320–321, 324–325, 331
wildfires 299, 304–305
wildland-urban interface 304–305

zoning *see* land use regulations